An O.S.S. Secret Agent
Behind Enemy Lines

First Lieutenant Leif Bangsboll, 82nd Airborne Division, 1946.
(*Photo courtesy of the United States Army*)

An O.S.S. Secret Agent Behind Enemy Lines

The Second World War Exploits of Lieutenant Leif Bangsbøll

Brook G. Bangsbøll

Frontline Books

First published in Great Britain in 2024 by
Frontline Books
An imprint of Pen & Sword Books Limited
Yorkshire – Philadelphia

Copyright © Brook G. Bangsbøll 2024

ISBN 978 1 03611 942 3

The right of Brook G. Bangsbøll to be identified as Author of this Work has been asserted by him in accordance with the Copyright, Designs and Patents Act 1988.

A CIP catalogue record for this book is available from the British Library.

All rights reserved. No part of this book may be reproduced or transmitted in any form or by any means, electronic or mechanical including photocopying, recording or by any information storage and retrieval system, without permission from the Publisher in writing.

Typeset by Mac Style
Printed in the UK by CPI Group (UK) Ltd, Croydon, CR0 4YY.

MIX
Paper | Supporting responsible forestry
FSC® C013604

Pen & Sword Books Limited incorporates the imprints of After the Battle, Atlas, Archaeology, Aviation, Discovery, Family History, Fiction, History, Maritime, Military, Military Classics, Politics, Select, Transport, True Crime, Air World, Frontline Publishing, Leo Cooper, Remember When, Seaforth Publishing, The Praetorian Press, Wharncliffe Local History, Wharncliffe Transport, Wharncliffe True Crime and White Owl.

For a complete list of Pen & Sword titles please contact

PEN & SWORD BOOKS LIMITED
47 Church Street, Barnsley, South Yorkshire, S70 2AS, England
E-mail: enquiries@pen-and-sword.co.uk
Website: www.pen-and-sword.co.uk
or
PEN AND SWORD BOOKS
1950 Lawrence Road, Havertown, PA 19083, USA
E-mail: uspen-and-sword@casematepublishers.com
Website: www.penandswordbooks.com

An O.S.S. Secret Agent Behind Enemy Lines *is dedicated to my sisters, Leslie and Wendy, who left us far too soon. And to my two brothers, Chris and Mark, whom I have always admired and looked up to and who set the standard for me to follow. Their help and assistance in the research and confirming names, dates and locations of the various events described in this book was invaluable.*

This book is dedicated to the four of you in the memory of our father, Leif Bangsbøll.

He was a sailor, aviator, soldier and secret agent. But he was also a son, brother, husband, father and grandfather.

In your eyes, I hope these pages do justice to his life and legacy.

Testimonial

"When our nation must turn to war, we turn to warriors like Leif Bangsboll to carry the fight to our enemy. Consistent with his Viking ancestry, in this detailed recounting we see the warrior's journey through the adventures and tragedies that war throws at those in the brawl. Read *An OSS Secret Agent Behind Enemy Lines* and its sequel: *U.S. Special Forces Commando* and remember those we have a duty to never forget."

General Jim Mattis, U.S. Marines (ret.)
and 26th Secretary of Defense

Contents

Foreword ix
Invictus xi
Acknowledgements xii
Abbreviations xiii
Introduction xv
Prologue: Where Valor Rests xvi

Chapter 1	Forty-Two Godfathers	1
Chapter 2	Headstones by the Sea	16
Chapter 3	An Apprenticeship at Sea	33
Chapter 4	Friends at Last…	61
Chapter 5	In the Shadow of Brandenburg Gate	68
Chapter 6	Blitzkrieg	75
Chapter 7	Finding the *Folkstone*	85
Chapter 8	The Ensign	92
Chapter 9	Sailing Over the Horizon	102
Chapter 10	A Transformations Begins	108
Chapter 11	Preparing for War in the Shadows	120
Chapter 12	Camp X	127
Chapter 13	A Chance Encounter	138
Chapter 14	A Reason to Return	146
Chapter 15	Veritas	151
Chapter 16	Escape and Evasion	170

Chapter 17	Agent Alexander Hudson	181
Chapter 18	Operation Carpetbagger	187
Chapter 19	The Network	197
Chapter 20	Miss Sophie	209
Chapter 21	Desperate Times, Deliberate Measures	219
Chapter 22	Christmas on the Run	232
Chapter 23	The Reckoning	244
Chapter 24	Do What Must Be Done	257
Chapter 25	The World is a Stage	270
Chapter 26	The Road Ends	282
Chapter 27	Just One More Mission…	296

Epilogue 304
Appendix: Introduction to U.S. Special Forces Commando 305
Bibliography 307

Foreword

Many sons have written books about their fathers, but few have had such a richness of substance or strength of impact to convey as Brook Bangsboll.

Brook's father, Army Lieutenant Colonel Leif Bangsboll, himself the son of a Danish Navy Admiral, was an accomplished man who lived a fascinating life. The result is two historical novels: *An OSS Secret Agent Behind Enemy Lines* and its sequel: *U.S. Special Forces Commando*. Leif Bangsboll was born in Denmark, served in the Danish Navy, the Norwegian Air Force, the Office of Strategic Services and the United States Army. His story is one of heroic actions in two wars and important service as an original member of the Army's Green Berets.

Brook was too young to understand his father's impact until after all of this had occurred. But as he got older, he realized that Leif's life as a sailor, soldier and spy was worthy of his fullest admiration and respect. He learned that at one point, Leif had started to write his autobiography but didn't get very far. By writing these books, Brook is telling the full story that he wished his father had written.

Leif Bangsboll's story gets better with each chapter, and Brook has done a masterful job in creating this narrative. Written more than 20 years after his father's death in 2001, Brook has crafted these books in which the main story line and all major events are true and verified, but many of the details are constructed from the recollections of himself and others, augmented by written accounts in various forms. – both factual and inspired by grand memories. Both books are well-researched, informative and entertaining.

I never knew Leif Bangsboll but as a former Navy SEAL officer and descendant of Norsemen, I felt a special link to him. I dove into this book and read it with ever-growing awe. It is, simply, a son's wonderful account of his legendary father, told with both loving care and attention to its historical significance. Brook also connects the reader to his father's Viking ancestry, sure that retired Lieutenant Colonel Leif Bangsboll resides in the Halls of Valhalla, where the most courageous of Vikings live forever as celebrated heroes.

In life, Leif Bangsboll was awarded the Army's Distinguished Service Cross and Silver Star Medal, his adopted nation's second and third highest awards for valor against the enemy. In death, he has been acclaimed with awards and distinctions by both the Army's Special Forces and the United States Special Operations Command – two organizations that trace their roots directly back to the secretive Office of Strategic Services in which Leif Bangsboll served so heroically. And now he is honored by his son, Brook Bangsboll, in a two-volume opus that merits all of our careful attention. I salute both the father and the son.

Admiral Eric Thor Olson,
United States Navy (Retired) -
Former Commander of the United States
Special Operations Command (USSOCOM)

Invictus

(Unconquered)

Out of the night that covers me,
Black as the pit from pole to pole,
I thank whatever gods may be
For my unconquerable soul.

In the fell clutch of circumstance
I have not winced nor cried aloud.
Under the bludgeoning of chance
My head is bloody, but unbowed.

Beyond this place of wrath and tears
Looms but the horror of the shade,
And yet the menace of the years
Finds and shall always find me unafraid.

It matters not how strait the gate,
How charged with punishment the scroll,
I am the master of my fate.
I am the captain of my soul.

William Ernest Henley, 1888

Acknowledgements

Like most major literary endeavors, the creation of *An OSS Secret Agent Behind Enemy Lines* took the dedicated efforts of many people – family members, friends and professional colleagues, all contributed to bring this story to life. To my two big brothers, Chris and Mark, your knowledge of our family history, and in particular Dad's extensive military career was invaluable and aided me to focus on the key elements of each story within each chapter – adding details, such as dates and locations to many of the stories Dad recounted. Our Danish cousin Jeanette Dunn has been instrumental in providing not only the record of the Bangsboll family lineage, but access to the Danish archives and the Danish Resistance Museum along with many old family photos which were crucial to telling the full story. Creative advice and encouragement from my sister-in-law Nancy and my nephew Bradley Bangsboll were inspiring and kept me slogging through the tough times and focused during the successes. Likewise, I cannot understate the value of those who I call my *beta readers* – Brian Wrong, Neil Bolt, and my nephew Bryce Morawiec, who read the rough drafts and first cuts of each chapter and provided insightful feedback on what worked and what didn't.

To the wonderfully talented, Jennifer Yates, my first editor, who's passion for the literary word was inspiring. Jennifer's editing skills and enthusiasm for the original Onward to Valhalla project was crucial to the eventual success of *An OSS Secret Agent Behind Enemy Lines* and *US Special Forces Commando* – keeping track of our edits during the COVID-19 pandemic was a herculean task! Likewise, my dear friend and colleague, Cathy Priestman, and her technical guru Daniel whose limitless energy and creative ideas brought the story on-line through our webpage, and managed the book's inventory of photographs..

Finally, to the three most important people in my life – my wife Jan, son Garrett and daughter Emily – thank you from the bottom of my heart for your continuous support over the 15 years it took me to research, write and complete this family record. Without your love, support and encouragement, I don't think I could have reached the finish line.

Abbreviations

AOO	Area of Operation
BCATP	British Commonwealth Air Training Plan
BEF	British Expeditionary Force
BSC	British Security Coordination
CIA	Central Intelligence Agency
CO	Commanding Officer
COI	Coordinator of Information
COS	Chief of Staff
DC	District of Columbia
DNA	A Person's Genetic Code
DSC	Distinguished Service Cross
DSM	Distinguished Service Medal
FCSB	Frederik Christian Sørensen Bangsbøll
FDR	President Franklin D. Roosevelt
HDMS	His Danish Majesty's Ship
Hrs	Hours
KGB	Committee for State Security – Soviet Union's Security Service
MI5	Military Intelligence 5 – British Security Service (domestic)
MI6	Military Intelligence 6 – British Security Service (overseas)
MIA	Missing in Action
MP	Military Police
NATO	North Atlantic Treaty Organization
NCO	Non-Commissioned Officer
OCS	Officer Candidate School
OSS	Office of Strategic Services
OUT	Operational Training Unit
PoW	Prisoner of War
PT	Personal Training
RAF	Royal Air Force
RCAF	Royal Canadian Air Force
RCMP	Royal Canadian Mounted Police
RTU	Replacement Training Unit

SI	Secret Intelligence
SOE	Strategic Office Executive
SS	Nazi Schutzstaffel (the paramilitary arm of the German government)
SS	Steamship
US	United States
USA	United States of America
USAAC	United States Army Air Corps
USAAF	United States Army Air Force
USO	United Services Organization
USS	United States Ships
WAAF	Women's Auxiliary Air Force

Introduction

An *O.S.S. Secret Agent Behind Enemy Lines*, book one of two, is the true account of my father's incredible life and military career, up to the end of the Second World War. Other than the prologue, each story in every chapter of this book is based upon oral recollections conveyed by my father to me, my siblings and family friends, many times over – recollections that were, at times, very emotionally difficult to articulate, despite the long passage of time. All the central events described in the book are in some way corroborated by extracts from military records or other documented media or reference materials, including medal citations, letters and photographs with handwritten notes on the back.

Throughout this book and its sequel, *U.S. Special Forces Commando*, I have taken literary license to generate much of the dialogue between the characters, but the entire storyline of events is firmly based on historical facts and colorfully augmented by the detailed description of events recounted by my father, and in some cases, by his friends and military colleagues during his lifetime.

Prologue

Where Valor Rests

'He is a soldier fit to stand by Caesar.'
William Shakespeare,
Othello, 1603

According to ancient Viking lore, a warrior has two deaths. The first, to which all Vikings aspire is to meet death in battle, culminating in the slain warrior being chosen by the Valkyries – the Norse god Odin's twelve handmaidens – as worthy of earning a place in Valhalla, the Viking afterlife. Where, upon ascension, the fallen warrior is taken to sit and feast with Odin in the great hall of their Viking ancestors. Sadly, the second and final death occurs when a Viking warrior's name is spoken on earth for the last time. Thus, the fervid importance of the oral tradition and clan stories passed down through the generations, which create, in essence, Viking immortality.

On 20 November 2001, my father, Lieutenant Colonel (Retired) Leif Bangsbøll, the Danish descendant of Vikings and the patriarch of the Sørensen-Bangsbøll clan, died – his first Viking death. Though not in battle as all Vikings dream of, my father had seen his share of combat – some on the field of battle, many in the shadows of the field of battle and some within his very soul. In my heart, on that November day, I knew the Valkyries had come and my father was in Valhalla.

A month later, on 18 December 2001, after complex arrangements to transfer his body from London, Ontario, Canada to Arlington, Virginia, my father was laid to rest at Arlington National Cemetery.

Arlington National Cemetery is a spectacularly beautiful piece of real estate, sprawling across manicured acres upon a ridge on the western shore of the Potomac River, adjacent to The Pentagon and across the river from the Lincoln Memorial and Washington DC. The vast number and symmetry of the headstones is mesmerizing and evocative. The view from the crest of the ridge is breathtaking, yet so very somber. The military precision and grace of the Honor Guard that lay my father to rest was deeply moving. Kind words were spoken about my father, words that paid homage to a life well lived, a life of service, a life of duty, and a life of courage and sacrifice. Thankfully, with such

Pershing's Own Military Marching Band, Arlington National Cemetery, 18 December 2001. Lieutenant-Colonel Leif Bangsbolls' internment ceremony. (*Photo courtesy of the author's family collection*)

accolades, my father's second Viking death appeared to be a very long way off. As expected, the funeral service was a solemn military occasion. Unexpected, was what I came to realize during that service…

As black as night and impeccably groomed, the six horses were led by their grooms into the courtyard adjacent to their stable. Their coats gleamed in the morning sun, their hot breath condensing in the cool December air, creating gentle wafts of mist from their flaring nostrils. The impatient horses pranced upon the cobbled stones, and the distinctive clatter of hooves on stone echoed amongst the adjacent buildings then ebbed across the open expanses of the cemetery. The stunning chargers were held firmly by their leather reins, yet with a gentle, caring touch of their three soldier grooms. The horses' ears were cocked forward, eyes wide open, glancing excitedly around the courtyard in anticipation of their coming work. They were not nervous; they trusted and knew what to expect from their handlers and the routine of their daily work. They were eager to commence their daily mission, a mission bringing men and beasts together in a time honored ritual of silent precision, coordinated grace and deliberate, methodical and somber execution of their duties.

Adjacent to the courtyard, in their ready room, soldiers of the 3rd United States Infantry Regiment had assembled. Known as The Old Guard, the regiment was one of the United States Army's oldest units. Established in 1784, the 3rd Infantry Regiment was America's military Honor Guard. The platoon of soldiers assigned to the day's duties were attending to the last minute details of their preparations. They wore dark blue uniforms accented with contrasting gold braid running the outside seams of their trousers and on the sleeves of their tunics. With their white gloves donned, they adjusted their service caps and inspected each other to ensure correctness and uniformity of the team. As the Honor Guard made their final preparations, the growing sound of musical instruments being tested and tuned emanated from the building across the courtyard. The army band, known as Pershing's Own, was preparing to go to work as well. Through the doorway of the ready room walked their platoon leader, 26-year-old First Lieutenant Jonathan Taylor. The room was immediately called to attention by the platoon sergeant, Sergeant First Class Ambrose Sánchez, the most senior non-commissioned officer in the platoon. Immediately the room fell silent and the men stood to attention. Taylor kept his eyes fixed forward and moved through the room with purpose and grace, giving only the hint of acknowledgement to the troops by a slight nod of the head or glance of an eye as he traversed to the center of the room. He stopped, scanned the room silently and called the men to ease, and announced in a clear and direct manner, 'Assembly point in five minutes, gentlemen. There is important work to be done.' He then continued towards the far door, which led to the stables. The soldiers, with quick glances at one another, immediately stepped up their preparations. The previous, collegial atmosphere – similar to a pre-game locker room with friendly banter amongst the players in their coach's absence – did not resume. The Honor Guard was all business now that their officer had arrived. With their weapons cleaned and oiled, shoes shone and uniforms immaculate, the Honor Guard was almost ready.

Taylor left the Honor Guard in the ready room and moved through the stable towards the assembly point and the task that awaited him in the courtyard, knowing Sánchez would see to the troops' final preparations. No indiscretion or sub-standard condition would pass this man's attention. Sánchez was a career soldier known as a lifer in the army. The army had transformed him. He had once been an active gang member from the mean streets of east Los Angeles where drugs, violence and crime were part of his everyday life. But a senseless, tragic event had changed his life forever. It had been just over fifteen years since his younger brother, a fledgling street gang member had been gunned down during a drug deal gone wrong. That personal tragedy had been Sánchez's tipping point and his inspiration to escape the dangerous, anti-social, dead-end path he was on. The day after he helped his mother bury his little brother, Sánchez had walked through the door of the local army recruiting office and

Honor Guard, U.S. Army's 3rd Army (Old Guard) escorting caisson with flag-draped casket of LTC (Retired) Leif Bangsboll. (*Photo courtesy of the author's family collection*)

signed his name on the army's service contract. Sánchez was strong and tough and learned the skills of a soldier quickly. He excelled at his chosen military profession and had served with distinction during combat tours in Iraq and Afghanistan. Sánchez, a high school dropout, was smart and tough and loyal to a fault. He was Taylor's command team partner. Upon arrival at his new unit in Washington DC, Sánchez had not particularly embraced this non-operational assignment. However, he quickly realized that this assignment was far better than some desk job or training billet he could have been given. Like his new boss and platoon leader, Taylor, a West Point graduate, Sánchez knew that this unique task carried with it a sacred duty, a duty like no other in the military and certainly not on civvy street. Over the past year, their work together at Arlington National Cemetery had proven deeply rewarding and made both Taylor and Sánchez immensely proud. It was their mutual responsibility to ensure that The Old Guard bestowed honor, respect and gratitude at every burial ceremony at Arlington. In the face of the unfathomable grief being endured by the family and friends of the fallen, Taylor and Sánchez, along with their platoon of thirty soldiers, would provide an honorable farewell, a positive and lasting memory for the grieving family to cherish. The Honor Guard would ensure that each family knew that their lost loved one had been a brave defender of a proud and grateful nation and that they would rest honorably amongst other heroes previously interred on the hallowed grounds of Arlington.

Sánchez watched Taylor exit the ready room and enter the stables on his way to the courtyard beyond. He knew what would come next; the precise routine was essential. Uniformity and the slow, deliberate and solemn protocol of movements were the key elements of success, and he knew that Taylor would insist on perfection. Taylor entered the courtyard to inspect the grooms and their six immaculate horses now harnessed to the caisson, loaded with its precious cargo. As he crossed the courtyard, Taylor focused on the three soldiers attending to the equine team. Though already standing at attention, the soldiers braced themselves another degree, an adjustment imperceptible to the untrained eye, but Taylor noticed it and was pleased. The distinct click of the metal cleats on the soles of his patent leather shoes striking the cobblestone surface of the courtyard produced a clear and methodical cadence as he crossed the space between him and the awaiting caisson. His stare remained focused straight ahead at the team of horses and the caisson harnessed to them. The gleaming coats of the jet-black horses, their immaculate tack and bridles, and the polished leather of the saddles, reigns and harnesses never failed to impress him. Taylor continued, click, click, click – the steel cleats kept cadence – as he passed by each of the soldiers in turn, coming within inches of each of their left shoulders. Once he had passed the third soldier who was holding the last two horses steady by their reigns, Taylor halted abruptly and executed a sharp 90° turn to face the caisson to begin his inspection. He took in the caisson carrying the flag-draped coffin and scanned the entire carriage in sequence to ensure its security, readiness and appearance. The brilliance and contrast of the colors was breathtaking. The red and white stripes of the flag next to the glistening dark wood and polished brass hardware of the caisson were stunning.

Taylor had been raised in a patriotic family in rural Iowa. The 4 July, Memorial Day and Veterans' Day, holidays were always honored with special family events. As a result, he could not recall a time when he did not feel emotionally moved by the sight of the stars and stripes waving majestically upon a flagpole. However, the presence of a casket draped in the national flag had taken on a new and powerful meaning for the officer. The stirring pride remained, yet with a painful realization that beneath this flag, under his watch, lay the nation's most recently fallen son. Taylor slowly reached out toward the flag-draped casket with his white-gloved hands and, with the palms of his hands, gently straightened a small crease in the flag – a tactile connection with his precious cargo had been made. Satisfied, Taylor carried on with his inspection. As he moved back towards the horses and the three troopers, he stopped once more and made two crisp 90° turns in order to face the first soldier. As he inspected each of the troopers, he ensured their medals were positioned correctly, and their brass buttons were shone and properly fitted. He removed a minute speck of lint from one of the

Honor Guard flag folding ceremony. (*Photo courtesy of the author's family collection*)

soldier's uniforms. The practiced routine kept him focused on every detail. But all the same, his mind was partially distracted, as he mentally reviewed the details of the biographies of the two soldiers he would plant in the national garden that December morning.

The previous night, while seated at his kitchen table with a can of beer at hand in his small apartment in Old Town, Alexandria – just south of Crystal City, The Pentagon and Arlington National Cemetery, and across the Potomac River from Washington DC – Taylor had read the folder on his laptop entitled 'Burials, December 18, 2001.' After almost a year as an Honor Guard commander, Taylor had established a routine for preparing for every interment he was responsible for at Arlington. Each new casket lowered into the ground and each new headstone erected in this garden had a story – a name, a face, a history – and he prided himself on knowing the essential details of their life prior to each ceremony, and particularly their military career. That evening, 17 December 2001, Taylor reviewed two files pertaining to the next morning's tasks. The first burial, scheduled for 0900 hours, was foremost on his mind. This burial was of a young second lieutenant infantry officer who had been killed in a non-combat related training accident. The report indicated that the second lieutenant's armored fighting vehicle, known as a *Striker*, had rolled over during a NATO exercise in Germany the previous week. The accident had killed the second lieutenant and injured several of his crew. A regrettable event, but a routine death attributed to training. 'Just another occupational hazard of our chosen profession', thought Taylor.

Juxtaposed to the first burial file, the file he had created for the second interment service, scheduled for 1130 hours the next morning, for an old, long-retired veteran named Lieutenant Colonel (Retired) Leif Bangsbøll. 'What kind of name is Bangsbøll anyway?' Taylor thought. Is that like Leif Erickson, the Viking explorer we learned about in school? he mused. Taylor read on and reviewed the information from the retiree's service biography:

> Born in Denmark in 1918 … spent time in the [Royal] Danish Navy and the [Royal] Norwegian Air Force … enrolled in the United States Army in 1942 … served with the Office of Strategic Services [OSS] in World War II, working with the Danish Resistance … fought in Korea … had been with the 82nd Airborne, [United States Army] Special Forces and was one of the very first special forces personnel designated as a Green Beret.

'Impressive', thought Taylor. But what really captured his interest was the biographical reference to the awarding of the DSC by order of none other than General Dwight D. Eisenhower, the Supreme Allied commander, presented for 'outstanding courage, high leadership and supreme daring in combat actions in 1944–1945.' The citation had gone on to describe Bangsbøll's night parachute mission behind enemy lines in the European theater of war as an agent in the OSS, which at the time was a recently formed, ultra-secret defense agency and the precursor of the CIA. The burial detail leader reflected upon the facts: A Danish-born sailor becomes a pilot in the Royal Norwegian Air Force, then becomes a United States Army officer who subsequently becomes a secret agent and is recognized by the Supreme Allied commander for 'supreme daring' in the face of the enemy. Those were credentials you didn't hear every day. Satisfied that he knew the key details of Bangsbøll's career and impressed with what he had read, Taylor logged-off his computer, finished his beer and went to bed.

The following morning, the interment of the young second lieutenant who had died during the NATO exercise was well attended. The ceremony went smoothly, having been completed with an air of solemn respect and sharp military precision. Both Taylor and Sánchez were pleased with the performance of their soldiers during the day's first internment. By 1030 hours, following that service, the Honor Guard had marched back to The Old Guards' stables at Fort Myer, Virginia, adjacent to Arlington National Cemetery where they had only a few minutes to rest and collect themselves before commencing with their second burial of the day.

As the Honor Guard approached the gravesite, all eyes of the mourners turned towards the military procession. Taylor gave the order to 'halt'.

Leif Bangsbøll, the man in the casket with the American flag draped over it was my father. At the time of his death, I thought I knew him. However, the things I learned about this man after his death made his life story more of an enigma to me. I could attest that I knew Leif Bangsbøll as a parent, but I never knew him as a man, a sailor, an aviator, a soldier or a spy. That bond, that link between us, would change forever in the years following his death, culminating in this book.

* * *

I do not have any personal memories of my father in his former life, as a special agent or Green Beret. By the time I was born, he was just a few years from leaving the service, and shortly after I started walking and talking, he had stowed away his military uniforms in a barrack box, and was on the road to interviewing for new, non-military employment, which he found with the Pinkerton Security Company, serving as regional operations officer in Toronto, Canada. According to my mother and older siblings, although my father reluctantly adjusted to 'civilian' life, he never saw himself as 'one of us', the non-military. My father found the stress levels of corporate culture to be ridiculous considering the low stakes involved. In all fairness, who could blame him? It's hard to get worked-up over payroll receipts and security guard work schedules when you've faced down Nazis, fought back hordes of North Korean and Chinese combat troops, and stared down Cold War communist agents. But it was more than that.

Life after the military seemed to be absent passion, as if a piece of my father's soul had been hollowed out when he retired. To his credit, unlike other retired officers, he didn't attempt to impose his military ethos or iron will on other employees, attempting to recreate a military hierarchy; my father performed his supervisory and managerial duties with competency and accepted his salary to care for his family and suffered silently, trying to discover new passions to compensate for the loss of his grand love and finding them all wanting – save for classical and jazz music, and cooking.

Less than a decade into his new, and still passionless career with Pinkerton Security Company, he badly injured his knees on duty, and his working days came to an abrupt end. He was retired now from both the military and the civilian workforce. The doctors said that his years as an infantry officer – especially his many parachute jumps – had taken a toll on his knees, and this normally routine injury completed the damage already well in progress. At that time, 1973, there wasn't much medical technology to reconstruct his knees, so he was provided with a cane and regular supply of painkillers.

Transitioning to a largely sedentary life meant several epochal changes for my father. The literally near crippling reality that his soldiering days were done, and his legacy of daring deeds had come to cash their first check on his aging body. Second, that he would have to suffer the ignominious fate of being a former Green Beret cashing disability cheques. And third, that he would be spending a significant amount of time at home and assuming the status of a normal 'dad'. And If I'm honest, Leif Bangsbøll – a trained warrior and spy who had confronted and subverted Nazis, North Koreans, Chinese and Soviets – was only able to achieve partial success in that role.

Years of 'being in command' had left their mark, war and espionage were permanent aspects of his personality that domesticity could not entirely dislodge, to the point that all my childhood friends were a bit wary of, if not unnerved by my father. He was the parent other children were glad they didn't have as their own. Calling him strict would be an understatement; calling him prying or overbearing would be kind.

When my friends came by our home in Willowdale, a suburb of Toronto, Canada they would have to run the proverbial gauntlet to earn his approval. He'd bombard them with questions about their interests, what their parents did for a living, what sports and clubs they participated in, and he would generally finish by asking what they planned to do with their lives. Mind you, many of them were just young teenagers – they had no life plans past the upcoming weekend! Arguably, my sisters had it far worse. My father routinely put prospective suitors on the spot to prove their intentions were honorable and that they were worthy to date his daughters. In theory, this might sound chivalrous, but in practice one must imagine these questions applied with the aptitude of a professional spy and combat-hardened soldier – not at all pleasant for the recipient.

When it came to his family, my father was very protective and objectively sterner. At an early stage, my siblings and I had to learn proper social protocols – to always respect our elders; to nod our heads politely when you met an adult; to consistently address adults with 'sir' or 'ma'am'. If we dared to breach a social or ethical norm – showing sub-standard respect, skip class, miss football practice in order to hang out with a girlfriend, or bring home a less than impressive report card – we could expect a stern rebuke, lengthy lecture, or new repercussions formulated on the spot. My father believed that if one's behavior was consistently moral and purposeful during routine times that in times of stress and emergency, those ingrained attributes and mental processes would prevail, override fear and allow you to make appropriate decisions under the most stressful conditions: 'If you consistently take care of the small stuff, the big stuff will also fall into place.' Matters of safety and security were always paramount. 'One must always be prepared for the unexpected', he would say. I'm not exactly sure what potentially fatal situation was going to befall us in tranquil Willowdale in the 1970s, but I didn't ask – better not to risk the lecture.

As a teenager, I didn't have what I'd call a 'close' relationship with my father, but I didn't actively rebel or question his authority much either – I was a good 'rule follower'. I was the youngest of five children – three sons and two daughters – and the roles had already been cast by the time I came of age. The role of semi-professional challenger of our father's authority fell to my sister, Leslie, and brothers, Chris and Mark. Leslie, the oldest of my siblings was, to her chagrin, very much like our father in temperament: stubbornness. Leslie was fiercely independent and over-protective of her siblings. Chris, Wendy, Mark and yours truly, had a much different relationship with our father. Chris, whose full name is Leif Christian Bangsbøll, is the oldest male child in the family and was not nearly so affronted by our father's overbearing ways. Chris respected and tolerated our father's approach. Chris became a sailor/naval officer in the Royal Canadian Navy. Apparently, Chris had inherited the love of the sea – through a deep ancestral connection to our grandfather, Frederik Christian Sørensen Bangsbøll, and to our father's great-great-grandfather, Frantz Peter 'Revolver' Sørensen, and their Viking forebearers. Wendy, the carefree, horse-loving, oh-so-naïve young girl was the only child our father and mother, Dorothy, ever really worried about. Probably undiagnosed with dyslexia, Wendy struggled in school and seemed, according to our father, destine to be a spinster, unless he stepped-in to help. Playing matchmaker, our father introduced Wendy to Bill McGarvey, a major in the United States Army. Within a year Wendy and Bill were married and soon had a noisy household of five little boys – a bit of a mad house, but Wendy was a wonderfully nurturing mother and always an optimist. Mark, the brother I shared a bedroom with for years growing up (and I have the scares to prove it), loved the military but seemed to be a polar opposite to our father in many of his views – fire and water – always on a collision course for confrontation. This was likely because, deep down, they were pretty much the same person. When Mark entered military service, he grudgingly realized the validity of our father's wisdom and lessons, and that following them allowed him to be highly respected as an officer and to rise quickly through the ranks. Their relationship would end up being very close in our father's latter years. As for me, being the youngest of the five, my experience with my parents was far different than that of my older siblings. I did not experience my father the army officer, and my mother the consummate officer's wife. I learned all about their exciting military life, and the many postings they had had through stories told and retold at the dinner table by my parents and siblings.

At times growing up, I felt that I was the only 'civilian' in the family. But to my advantage, when my father left Pinkerton Security Company on workman's compensation in the early 1970s, while I was still a teenager, I had the good fortune of spending more time with him – the domestic dad and chief cook of the household. I am sure that was not the role he would have chosen for himself, but he accepted his medical conditions – broken knees and angina – and embraced being the 'house frau'. For a few years, it was just me, my mother and father at home and I enjoyed it. Bending rules and breaking curfew was easier for me, because my siblings had already run the gauntlet and paved the way for me. My father's edges had softened over time and I benefited from that erosion.

If I had to define my relationship with my father in a single word, I might choose 'compliant'. I respected him and admired his military career accomplishments. He treated me like a son and as long as I was respectful, kept good grades, thought about the future and associated myself with 'nice kids' and stayed out of trouble it was smooth sailing. We seldom fought. But we didn't connect on many levels. Honestly, I sometimes wonder if it was because I was the youngest, and he'd expended all his energy on his other four children. I loved him. I know he loved me. But if you pinned either of us down as to why this love was reciprocal, we probably couldn't provide much of an introspective answer beyond 'he's my dad and he's my son'. In all fairness to him, in his twilight years he became much more effusive with his love and generosity. His deep pride in his children and grandchildren was always evident and much appreciated.

There was only one time before 18 December 2001, the day of my father's burial, that my father truly surprised me; that he had somehow colored outside the lines and broke his self-imposed ridged structure. And strangely, that event was over the theme of a song. My father loved music, classical as well as jazz and, of course, military marching band music and the bagpipes. On Saturday mornings, if you slept in too long, you could expect to be rudely awakened by military marching band music blasting from our giant oak stereo console in the living room. My father would be sitting in his comfy chair in the living room and grin as me and my siblings emerged from our beds in protest.

One day, curious at what his teenage son was listening to on his portable cassette player, he asked me to introduce him to a band outside his preferred genre of music: Chopin, Mozart, Rachmaninoff, Tchaikovsky, Wagner or Glenn Miller. I gave him the cassette player with earphones and a cassette: Pink Floyd's *The Wall*. Over the next ninety minutes he listened to the double album set and politely acknowledged 'the experience'. I considered that conversation closed, a two-syllable footnote in our relationship.

However, several days later, while driving together, my father said to me,

> That fellow, Pink Floyd, his songs had a connection to the British wartime experience. The song entitled *Vera* was clearly a reference to the famous singer Vera Lynn.

Like so many of my father's era, Vera Lynn was one of his favorite Second World War entertainers. Under his breath, my father lamented… "Vera, what has become of you?…" He went on to say there was a resonance in that song and others on *The Wall* that that spoke to the heart-wrenching aspects of the Second World War, to the pain, suffering and stoic resolve that the British so admirably displayed during their darkest hour – things he had experienced during the war too. He said that 'Pink's' lyrics were meaningful and profound.

I was suddenly uncomfortable. I thought Pink Floyd's lyrics were deeply meaningful as well. But I couldn't bear to admit that I shared similar tastes with my old warhorse of a father who somehow between grabbing the keys and our latest round of errands, became an aesthetic philosopher. Sometimes I do wish I had told him that I shared his sentiments on *The Wall*, but I tend to think he wouldn't have known what to do either if we shared something in common. Pink Floyd had made my father vulnerable, ripped him back to his past life. He could quietly, begrudgingly accept it from that 'Pink fellow', but not from his youngest son.

* * *

The next and final time my father would surprise me came on the day of his burial at Arlington. As expected, on that day, he was honored and consecrated in fine military fashion, with the time honored, solemn procession of horse-drawn caisson and Honor Guard troops slow-marching their way down from The Old Guards' stables at Fort Myer, then entering the cemetery through the black wrought iron gates at the top of the ridge. The methodic clatter of six sets of horses' hooves upon a cobbled stone road conveying my father's flag-draped coffin echoed across the cemetery. The thirty-man Honor Guard would travel through American history, past the time-worn headstones of Union soldiers from the Civil War, the aligned rows of fallen heroes from the First World War – the war to end all wars – then past the greatest generation who fought in the wars with my father. Next, my father and his Honor Guard would cross paths with the white headstones memorializing America's most controversial war: the Vietnam War, followed by the Gulf War and to the moment that the procession crested the Arlington ridge, set back from the stunning Tomb of the Unknown Soldier, to my father's final resting place. There, in plot-section 23, overlooking the sloping cemetery and the Potomac River, where my father could peer into the future, at the space reserved for the fallen who would answer the call of the 9/11 attacks and America's War on Terror.

At precisely 1130 hours on 18 December 2001, Taylor, standing in the lead position of the Honor Guard, which had positioned itself 30 yards from the Bangsbøll gravesite, gave a nod to Sánchez and then gave the order for the Honor Guard to advance.

Lieutenant Colonel (Retired) Leif Bangsbøll's ceremony was attended by his five children, his fourteen grandchildren and extended family, together with serving members from several of my father's former units with the United States Army Special Forces' Green Berets, including current members of the 82nd and 101st Airborne divisions and their sub-units, my father's wartime *alma maters* – the 187th and the 504th Airborne regiments. Also in attendance was the Danish ambassador to the United States, escorted by the military attachés of Denmark and Norway. During the service, the Danish ambassador said moving words about their 'son of Denmark', returning home as an American hero to help liberate his ancestral homeland. Also in attendance was the deputy director of the CIA who delivered an eloquent speech about honor and service and the need to remember those who lead the way in times of great darkness and peril; his words concluded by saying that my father was one of those who truly represented 'the tip of the spear', a phrase associated with and an unofficial motto of OSS and adopted by United States Army Special Forces to which my father had been an integral part in its early development.

Where Valor Rests xxix

Lone piper standing watch over Lieutenant-Colonel Leif Bangsboll, Arlington National Cemetery – RIP. (*Photo courtesy of the author's family collection*)

Our family was moved and collectively surprised, but very grateful by the size and star-studded nature of the turnout and the words of praise heaped on their fallen comrade and our family patriarch. It had been almost forty years since my father had retired from the United States Army, forty-eight years since his last combat during the Korean War; it was fifty-six years since the end of the Second World War. All his former units were represented at the graveside that December morning. My father had often spoken of friendships forged in combat, of the similar look veterans share, a gaze that crosses generations. You can go years without seeing a comrade-in-arms, but that intimacy is always there, shining, spread across their faces upon their reunion. It's a powerful, unbreakable bond, one which I have been both blessed and cursed with personally experiencing during my military career.

That cold December morning, I found myself overwhelmed, both from the loss of my father, but also – and I realized this only unconsciously at that moment – from the loss of never being able to know the version of Leif Bangsbøll, the warrior, that they did. The version of the man that made him unforgettable after decades of peaceful retirement. I only had the memories of Leif Bangsbøll: my father, the retired soldier.

* * *

Following the graveside service, family and friends caravanned across the Potomac River, over the Theodore Roosevelt Bridge to the University Club in Washington DC. There, in the opulent atmosphere, family stories of military postings were recounted and where my parents' life together was celebrated and toasted, and more tears shed as the reality of the loss of the old Viking warrior and his bride became unavoidable. Finally, the night was finished off in the club's library with nightcaps where more of my father's war stories were retold. The room was dimly lit, populated with high-back leather chairs and a fire crackling in a screened-in hearth made of stone. The floor-to-ceiling shelves were lined with old bound books, which I began inspecting, while nursing a cocktail and lost in thought.

As I stood listening to near-by conversations and scanning the spines of the impressive collection of books, Colonel David 'Dave' Meredith III, my godfather, appeared at my side, seemingly from out of nowhere. He was my father's closest and oldest friend – a friendship bound in honor and shaped in experience of combat. And knowing Dave, 'Uncle Dave', the way I did, I fully expected him to harangue me in his southern drawl and cigarette-scorched rasp with one of his favorite stories about my father; probably the one in which my father had miraculously returned to camp two days after being declared MIA during the Korean War.

To my surprise, Dave had a different tale to share. Perhaps it was the solemnity of the occasion, the hallowed nature of the setting, the searching and lost look on my face, or the several drinks we'd both had, but Dave broke the mold that night. He spoke about my father in ways I had never heard before. Of a man with doubts and reservations. My father, the man I knew, was always self-assured and you never wondered where he stood on a situation or topic – always right of center. Dave spoke of a time in early spring 1968, when he was recovering from war wounds suffered during a north Vietnamese/Vietcong surprise attack, known as the Tet Offensive, during the Vietnam War. Dave had been repatriated to the United States due to his wounds and my father had dropped everything and driven ten hours straight from Toronto to Washington DC to visit his one true buddy at Walter Reed Army Hospital. Dave said that they spoke for hours about many things: family, retired colleagues, lost colleagues, the frustration they both felt over the current war in Vietnam, and then he said that my father had broached a topic that he'd never touch before. 'Your father said to me "I'm not sure if I was a good enough officer".' Dave spoke in hushed tones, as if he didn't want anyone in our immediate earshot overhearing. I'm not certain whether it was seeing a man he trained wounded, or that my father was five years out of his military service and beginning to reflect on his military career, his life and his legacy but he had clearly moved into an introspective state of mind. 'I seem to have had a good effect on my soldiers', Dave continued, invoking my father's words by his bedside,

> He said that he tried to provide strong, consistent leadership. That he had made them train long and hard, probably longer and harder than most. He knew that sometimes his soldiers resented him for his harsh, demanding ways. But he knew in his heart that this training would give them a better chance of survival and a greater likelihood of success.

Dave took a deep breath and said,

> Your father just hoped to give them what they needed to fight and survive – to give them the best chance of making it through the meat-grinder so they could return home to their families in one piece.

Dave continued,

> Your father had a rare leadership quality about him and his men knew it. He could be friendly with his soldiers without losing his authority. When

you were around Leif Bangsbøll, the soldier and leader, you knew who was in charge.

Among most combat veterans, there is a reluctance, sometimes an absolute reticence to speak about their wartime experiences – and rightly so. If my father ever shared a story, it would usually be in association with delivering a life lesson, never a glorification of war, never about self-glorification, or triumph over the enemy. Hearing the graveside memorials about my father's unique and tremendously challenging military career made me proud beyond words. However, if Dave had chosen to share one of those tales or had unearthed one of the jeweled secrets of my father's still largely classified adventures with the OSS and CIA, or even expanded on his work with the United States Army Special Forces, this book would likely never have been written.

The sentiment Dave chose to share had stunned me, had demonstrably shown that my father was human, he was a regular person with doubts and fears, including those about his own abilities. All my life, I had never seen him evince a moment's indecision or doubt, nor a second of hesitation, on any topic, judgment or action. But after Dave's story – incidentally the shortest one he'd ever shared – a newfound desire had been implanted in me. I wanted to know my father, know him in a way he could never have shared with me in life, in a way I'd have to understand myself, and that would bring us closer together than we'd ever imagined. I had to meet the man Dave had just introduced me to. I wanted to honor that man. I wanted to ensure that version of Leif Bangsbøll, the one at Dave's bedside at Walter Reed Army Hospital, the man who would never suffer the dreaded Viking's second death. A warrior is fearful and fascinating; but a warrior who has faced his country's enemies countless times, led men into mortal peril and who down plays his valor and even minimizes the value of his contribution is the type of warrior based upon legends, epic poems, a man for the ages, worthy of Valhalla.

* * *

After the initial stir, I wavered for several weeks, unable to decide how to tell my father's story, literally and literarily. Where would I even begin excavating all the disparate facts and events that composed his life-long journey? And even armed with the essential details, where would be the perfect place to begin? Little did I know my father was about to begin a dialogue with me, as if he would steer this book from the beyond. What I now understood, from a eloquent passage I had once read and which was so eloquently stated by its anonymous author:

For those destined to outlive the war and die abed as old men half a century hence, the din of battle grows fainter without ever fading entirely.

Two weeks after my father's funeral service, my brother, Chris, who had been cleaning out our father's apartment in his London, Ontario home called me to say that among our father's papers, he had found what appeared to be an initial draft – only a dozen pages, of an autobiography of our father. Typed on now yellowed paper, it dated back to spring 1963. The date resonated with me. Our father had begun putting his thoughts on paper on the eve of his retirement from the army. He knew he was about to part ways with the United States Army; an army that had defended the nation and the free world. An army and a nation that had adopted him while his native country was under Nazi siege; an army and a nation he had dearly loved.

Despite so many of our family friends who had, on so many occasions emphatically stated, 'Someone has to write down these stories of your father's life.' I hadn't shared with anyone in my family that I was seriously considering taking on that task. My siblings treated this welcome, yet untimely, discovery of a draft biography as one of our father's many clandestine quirks – another secret that our father kept concealed to the end. But I understood perfectly. My father and I both knew that it had to be me, that I was the one who had to complete the task he had started. I was the youngest, the child who had the least time with him, the child with the most questions, the one who needed closure beyond death – to put my father's legacy on paper for all to read and enjoy. The document my brother found, albeit brief, would provide the direct inspiration, or at least my direct inspiration to write this book.

My father wanted his story to be about far more than his individual narrative, he wanted the world to know that he had been caught up in the larger winds of fate, that his battle against fascism, against totalitarianism, against a world that had seemingly lost its bearings and conscience, is the same war we face today, the same war we seem to have to perpetually fight. And I suppose I wanted the world to know that some generations had Leif Bangsbøll to fight their battles, and some generations have his son to tell the warrior's tale.

The following is how my father had planned to open the first chapter of his autobiography. It is my privilege to share his words with you and my honor to use it to guide my opening of his story:

I have finally decided to write my life's story; if not for the public, then for my children, who one day can get a full and better picture of a time so deadly serious to the world. A story written with the hope that my young children, together with all young and old people in the world, may believe in peace and learn to live and build a free, happy world together.

We are sitting some 10,000 feet up on the slopes of Jungfrau Mountain near Interlaken, Switzerland, nestled in the Bernese Alps. My wife Dorothy-Jean and I are enjoying a few days' rest from our home and work in Oberammergau, Germany. It is a beautiful day. The sun is warm, and the air is cool and clear. We lay on the mountainside in the sun and make small talk while taking in the vista of the magnificent Eiger and Mount Moench. There is eternal snow surrounding us - blanketing the peaks, high up in the mountains above us. Besides our two voices, only the sound of the alpine breeze can be heard.

Dorothy-Jean turns to me and says, 'Leif, isn't this wonderful here? It's so quiet and peaceful. It gives you the feeling somehow you could reach out to heaven and thank God for its creation.'

'Yes, Dorothy, I was thinking that too.' I pause and reflect for a moment. 'I remember my father saying that he had that same sense of being close to God whenever he stood on the deck of a ship and looked out upon the great expanse of the ocean.'

Dorothy pauses and then says to me, 'Leif, I am sorry I only met your father once and our children will never know him - he was a wonderful man.'

I smile and acknowledge Dorothy's regret, and I ask myself: 'Who was my father? What type of man was he?'

The answer to that question was clear but very complex. Frederik Christian Sørensen Bangsbøll was a man of the sea, from an era of wooden ships and iron men.

I lean towards my bride and say, 'Let me tell you a story about my father…'

Leif Bangsbøll,
March 1963

Chapter 1

Forty-Two Godfathers

'The gods favor the bold.'

Old Danish proverb

The military telegram, hand delivered the day before by a young sailor, lay on the bedside table. Rigmor Karla Martha Bangsbøll's eyes had been drawn to it countless times since its arrival, desperate to tease out its ambiguities, a hallmark of her husband's communiques.

> Rigmor, come to the naval yard, pier No. 6 at 0630 hours this Sunday. Bring little Jocom. It is time for him to be formally introduced to God.

To the untrained eye, it seemed clear. Lieutenant Commander Frederik Bangsbøll, Royal Danish Navy, was coming home for his son's christening. But it couldn't be that simple? Could it?

Her husband held a largely classified position during wartime and his messages bore out that level of secrecy. He could not tell his wife much of what his job entailed. She understood the need, but it did not make her feel any less alone. They hadn't been married long enough, hadn't been a couple long enough for her to understand everything about him, let alone how to read between the lines of the first telegram he'd sent since he left five weeks ago.

It had been 7 August 1918, when Rigmor waved goodbye to her husband, Frederik, from Pier No. 1 at Copenhagen's Holmen Naval Base. There, holding their 2-week-old son, Leif, Rigmor watched her husband's ship, HDMS *Grønsund*, sail out of the harbor and out of her life.

Lieutenant Fredrik Christian Sorensen- Bangsboll, Royal Danish Navy, Copenhagen, 1916. (*Photo courtesy of the author's family collection*)

At the time, she looked down and wondered if the little boy she held would one day follow in his father's peripatetic footsteps. The thought made her stomach tighten and hold her son closer. The baby, affectionately called Jocom by his father, reacted to the impromptu hug by cooing. She adjusted the blanket around his small face and whispered, 'Don't you worry, Leif, my love, we're going to be okay. Your father will be back soon.'

'And I'm going to make sure', she thought, 'that I raise you to never, ever do this to your own wife.' She smiled. 'You are going to have a quiet job and a quiet life. You can build ships, Leif, but you can never sail off in one during a war.'

* * *

Rigmor hadn't married Frederik unaware of his nature, they ran straight through his bloodline, a quasi-metaphysical attachment to the sea and the accompanying martial values. The entire Bangsbøll family still embraced the Viking spirit and sense of warrior honor, the foundations of the ideals on which the clan stood strong, united and proud. They were men of action who, by act and deed, controlled their own destiny. They had made that patently clear the first time she went to Frederik's house for dinner. Frankly, she was so infatuated with him that she had chosen to overlook the signs of her future, to store them in the back of her mind and reflect on them if that day should arrive.

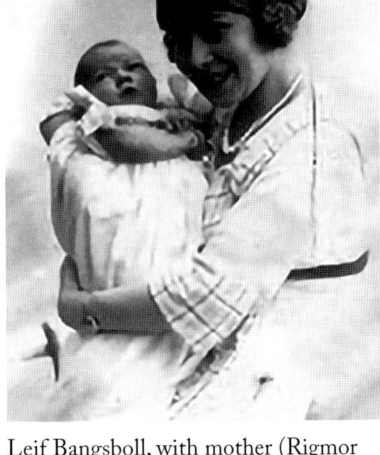

Leif Bangsboll, with mother (Rigmor Bangsboll), Copenhagen, September 1918. (*Photo courtesy of the author's family collection*)

It should have arrived the moment that Frederik suggested they name their son after Frederik Leif Julius Sørensen, a Danish army officer and ancestor of the Sørensen-Bangsbøll clan from the early 1800s, all of whom had Viking blood in their veins that they could date back as early as AD 935, back to the Danish Viking King Harald Blåtand Gormsson – known as 'Bluetooth', son of King Gorm the Old. The name Leif is of Scandinavian origins derived from the Old Norse name Leifr meaning 'heir' or 'descendant'.

Rigmor knew all the theories of how King Harald had obtained the moniker of Bluetooth. The first was based upon the unique sword he wielded. Forged from blue-tinted steel, the weapon had jagged edges, more like teeth, than the usual straight blade most warriors of the era used in combat. Rigmor's father-in-law, generally the one spinning these tales, suggested that Bluetooth's name may have come from the sword's distinctive design. Another possibility was that the king had been referred to by the English as 'Thane the Dark'. In ancient Danish dialect, thane meant chief and dark equated to blue, thus his name could be translated as the 'dark' or 'blue' chieftain. Finally, the simplest and least interesting theory – which Rigor's father-in-law scornfully discounted as being far too basic for the origins of a hallowed name – was that King Harald had a conspicuous dead tooth that appeared blue.

Bluetooth's reign could charitably be called contradictory, a unification project driven by his own warrior persona. Through sheer will and determination, he had united the other Viking clans into his own kingdom, which grew to include Denmark, most of present-day Jutland and a large region of southern Norway. He had also ordered a massive undertaking, his equivalent to pharaoh's pyramids, with a series of fortifications across Denmark and the portion of southern Norway that he controlled. These ring-shaped fortresses called Trelleborg provided safe havens for the king's warriors and fellow clans people, solidifying his authority over the region.

However, in Rigmor's opinion, the most significant change in Denmark under Bluetooth's reign occurred in AD 968. It was ten years into the king's reign, when a courageous German Christian missionary led a group of the faithful to spread the good word amongst the Danes. Upon arrival in Jutland, the missionaries were confronted by an angry mob of pagans, who challenged the missionary's faith and belief in an afterlife, by subjecting him to a gruesome ordeal by fire. Against all odds, the missionary was able to hold a piece of smoldering iron in both hands, longer than the pagans. Bluetooth was so impressed by the missionary's courage and unyielding faith in the face of such pain, that he converted to Christianity. This conversion of faith caused great turmoil within his realm for decades to come.

Rigmor could not help but reflect on how the adoption of Christianity hadn't been able to fully temper the Viking blood running through the Bangsbøll clan from Bluetooth down to Frederik's grandfather, Frantz 'Revolver' Sørensen, a merchant sea captain who had earned his nickname in the late 1800s by putting down a mutiny at sea, shooting several crew members who attempted to usurp his command.

* * *

Rigmor finished wrapping Leif in a soft blanket so he would not catch a cold waiting for Frederik at the pier, when she heard a knock at her front door. She pulled aside the bedroom curtain, and saw the black naval staff car outside, with the engine still running. The clock read '5.58 am'.

The driver was early. Rigmor shook her head, disappointed at herself for not anticipating the early call. Being the wife of a naval officer, she was familiar with the precise nature of military protocols, including fastidious punctuality. She realized then how nervous and excited she was to see her husband, and how exhausted she was having taken care of Leif by herself almost from the moment he was born.

She rushed to the front door, and standing there was a young sailor, she assumed no more than 18 years of age. Able Seaman Henrik Berg.' he offered by way of introduction, then snapped to attention, and moved quickly back to the vehicle to open the door for the mother and child.

Rigmor negotiated the walk down the drive before entering the car and said, 'Has there been any word from my husband's ship? Has the *Grønsund*, entered port yet?'

'I don't know madam.' Berg said, ushering her inside the vehicle. 'But I promise we'll be on time.' He shut the door, made his way to the driver's side, and upon sliding into the seat and continued. 'Other than churchgoers, these roads on Sunday mornings are very quiet.'

Ship's crew, Coastal Defence vessel HDMS *Hejmdal*, Holmen Naval Yard, Copenhagen 1915. Lieutenant Frederik Bangsboll fourth from the left. (*Photo courtesy of the author's family collection*)

'Do you know my husband, Mr Berg?' she asked. 'Do you know if he's coming home to stay?'

'I'm sorry, Frau Bangsbøll', he said, starting the car, 'I only know I'm supposed to pick you up and have you at Pier No. 6 by 0630 hours.'

Fifteen minutes later the staff car drove through the main gate of Holmen Naval Base. Berg had been right: the roads were almost empty. Upon arriving at the port of Copenhagen and entering the naval base, Rigmor realized she had never seen this pier before. The previous times she had visited the base to see her husband off or greet his return, his ship had always been moored at one of the main piers. It unnerved her. Clearly something had gone wrong, Berg had got the instructions wrong. She pulled the telegram from her purse, concerned she might be late or at the wrong location, and read it again: 'Rigmor, come to the naval yard, pier No. 6 at 0630 hours this Sunday. Bring little Jocom.'

'Mr Berg', she asked, 'can you please confirm where you were supposed to take me?'

'Pier No. 6 ma'am.' he said, not taking his eyes off the road. 'It's the last one on the quay, not used as often as the others.'

As they passed the piers with numerous, gray naval ships moored alongside, Rigmor's heart began to beat faster with anticipation, mentally willing the vehicle to move faster, to get her to Pier No. 6, to reunite her with Frederik, who had already spent large segments of their still young marriage at sea, and whom she was desperate to throw her arms around and become a family again.

Her face sank when they reached Pier No. 6, which was empty and silent, except for the wailing of seagulls as they sailed above and around the quay. 'Where is his ship, Mr Berg?'

Berg pulled the car to a stop, looked back at Rigmor, and saw his nervous passenger clutching her baby. 'We're still a few minutes early Frau Bangsbøll.'

The next few minutes were spent in silence. Berg did not feel comfortable making conversation with an officer's wife. Rigmor did not want to raise her voice to the young man who was just doing his job. However, she lost her patience again: 'Where is my husband's ship?'

Berg stared ahead. 'My orders were only to pick up Frau Bangsbøll and child from 32 Hausergade Street at 0600 hours and transport them to Pier No. 6.' He turned back and pointed to the face of his watch. 'By 0630 hours and await further instructions.' He smiled nervously and then added, 'It's 0624, your husband will be here soon, I'm sure ma'am.'

Rigmor tried to smile to reflect her understanding. 'Fine, Mr Berg. We'll wait.' Leif began to fuss in her lap. 'But can you please turn on the motor? It's getting cold in here for the baby.'

While reaching down into her bag for a bottle, Rigmor saw an officer emerge from a red bricked building running adjacent to the quay who began to walk briskly towards the staff car. His face was hidden by his up-turned collar and white scarf around his neck and chin. His eyes were shaded by the black brim of his naval forage cap. She could tell that it was not her husband by the rank on his shoulder boards.

Before Rigmor could say anything to Berg, who was fixated on the harbor's channel entrance, expecting to see the pointed gray bow of the *Grønsund*, appear any second, the officer knocked on the rear passenger door's window adjacent to Rigmor. The officer opened the car door and said, 'Good morning Frau Bangsbøll. My apologies for being late.' He smiled. 'May I join you please?'

Rigmor slid over to make room for the young officer and motioned him to enter. The officer entered the car and immediately noted the bundle that Rigmor was holding gently in her arms. 'Ah', the officer said, 'this must be little Leif.' He pulled back the corner of the blanket to reveal the baby enjoying his fresh bottle. 'If he's anything like his father, soon enough that milk will be replaced by good Danish Akvavit.' He looked up from under the brim of his cap and saw Rigmor staring back, still baffled by his presence.

> I beg your pardon Frau Bangsbøll. Allow me to introduce myself. I am Lieutenant Carl Winther. I'm the pastor assigned to the Flotilla *Norske* – your husband's squadron.

'Yes', Rigmor said, somewhat relieved, 'I believe we meet last spring at the squadron dinner.'

'I'm flattered you remember me, Frau Bangsbøll.' Winther said. Then he fell silent, not offering more.

There was an awkward silence as Rigmor thought 'Don't all these military men realize I haven't seen my husband in five weeks and I'm not interested in following military protocol at this moment'. She didn't care what couldn't be said, what was classified, she merely wanted answers. Obviously, she was going to initiate the conversation herself: 'Are you here to meet the *Grønsund*, as well Lieutenant Winther?'

'I'm here at the request of your husband, madam.'

'Why would he send you?' Her hopes were fading fast. 'Has he been injured? What has happened to my husband and his ship?'

Rigmor didn't get to finish her question because Able Seaman Berg let out an audible gasp from the front seat. Rigmor was about to admonish the driver for interrupting her, but her eyes suddenly affixed on the dream-like image appearing before them. Like a great, glistening sea monster, a column of cold, black steel began to rise from the harbor. Sheets of white, frothing water spewed over and down its growing mass. The glistening-black entity breached the surface of the steel-blue water and rose from the depths of the quiet Danish harbor.

'Good Christ!' Berg said. Then quickly realized his outburst may have offended Rigmor and the pastor.

'I've heard far worse at less impressive spectacles', Winther replied. Rigmor was too busy staring in wonder at the aquatic aberration to register the blasphemy or the pastor's comment.

The superstructure of the submarine's coning tower now loomed 12 feet above the surface of the water, as the hull of the *Havmaden*, began to find its buoyant equilibrium on the surface of the water.

At the outbreak of the First World War, the Royal Danish Navy was a modern, modest sized fleet equipped primarily with armored steam ships and a few wooden and steel sailing ships. Designed for national security and coastal defense only, neither Denmark's navy nor its government had the Vikings' expansionist ambition from years past, nor any desire to form political or military alliances. With the armistice looming and the end of the First World War in sight, Denmark intended to remain neutral. These were the circumstances in summer 1918, when Frederik led his small flotilla out into the Atlantic to protect Denmark's sovereignty and declared neutrality.

As Rigmor and Berg continued to stare at the submarine, Winther said, full of compassion and kindness, 'Frau Bangsbøll, your husband asked me to assist

Danish submarine, designated H1 – The *Havmaden*, arriving on station in North Sea to rendezvous with HMDS *Gronsund*, September 1918. (*Photo courtesy of the author's family collection*)

you and your son.' Then he addressed Berg, his tone severely shifting, 'Your duties are completed. Return the staff car to the motor garage. And do not discuss your morning duties with anyone. Is that clear?'

Berg nodded in understanding.

'If you hurry driver', Winther said, 'you can still make it to Pastor Sondergaard's early mass.' Then he turned to Rigmor and offered his hand. 'Allow me to help, Frau Bangsbøll.'

As they exited the car, an officer emerged from the submarine, and began assessing the positioning and distance between his boat and the pier. Satisfied, he spoke into the communications tube in front of him, giving orders to the crew below deck. The sound of the main forward hatch of the *Havmaden* opening with a distinctive, metal-on-metal 'clang', and came to rest on the exposed steel deck of the submarine's hull.

Rigmor approached the edge of the pier, nearing the craft. 'I don't understand, lieutenant. Where is my husband's ship? He said he would be here this morning at Pier No. 6, with the *Grønsund*.'

'Do not fret, Frau Bangsbøll.' Winther said. 'Your husband is known throughout the Royal Danish Navy as a man who knows what must be done and how to do it.'

'What must be done?' Rigmor asked. 'Is my husband on this submarine?'

'No, and your husband is not coming to Copenhagen. He sent the *Havmaden* to bring us to him on the *Grønsund*.' Winther waited until Rigmor had fully absorbed the reality and then explained,

> The *Grønsund* is on station in the North Sea supporting two other submarines approximately 55 miles north-east of our naval station at Frederikshavn – about a four-hour voyage from here. If all goes as planned, you will see your husband today, your child will be christened, and both you and Leif will be back home this evening.

'If all goes as planned? What's the plan?'

'I just told you, madam, your husband has made arrangements to bring you and your son to him.' Winther said, then gestured with his gloved hand toward the descending gangway and the waiting craft below.

Two sailors approached Rigmor at the end of the pier, holding a large, white life jacket. Winther took Leif from her arms to allow her to put on the safety device. It was far too big for her. 'I look ridiculous!' she thought. Then as soon as Winther returned Leif to her, the reason for the large life jacket became clear: there was room for both her and the baby to fit comfortably within its confines.

Standing on the deck of the submarine, Rigmor prepared herself for the awkwardness of negotiating the hatch and steel ladder, then descending into the bowels of the submarine while wearing a fine linen dress and bulky winter coat and her Sunday-best high-heeled shoes. The smell hit her immediately. The odor inside a submarine at sea is a foul, wretched thing. The mixture of diesel fumes and stale sweat can, for the uninitiated, be a demonic assault on the senses. Fortunately for Rigmor, the crew, embarrassed by having a woman breathing their fetid air, quickly whisked her to the galley where she would spend the remainder of her journey. The aroma of food being prepared was only marginally effective in masking the stale, foul air of the boat.

Four and a half hours later, after several cups of terrible tea and a grayish-brown stew with stale rye bread for lunch that she politely consumed, Rigmor heard the diesel engine distinctly change pitch, then felt the submarine slowing down. They had arrived at the rendezvous point with the *Grønsund*.

Once again, Rigmor had to don the oversized life jacket, shelter Leif against her bosom, pass through the eye-watering stench of the belly of the submarine, ascend the claustrophobic steep steel ladder, until she was close to the top, where the deck hatch was now open, allowing a rush of cold, fresh air to rush into the vessel. On the deck stood two of the submarine's sailors who simultaneously reached down to assist her and the baby onto the deck. As Rigmor rose, the more she was blinded by the brightness of the cloudless sky and the reflection of the sun off the ocean's surface. Her eyes adjusting slowly, she could barely make out the faces of the two sailors assisting her.

Once she cleared the hatch, and her eyes had fully adjusted, she was stunned by the ocean. It was everywhere, surrounding her, almost ready to devour her whole. She had never been this far from land. The horizon was composed of a perfect parallel of dark blue water and light blue sky. She began to understand why her husband had given his life, his eternal devotion to two wives: her and the sea. Although she could never embrace the pull of nature's vastness. It reminded her too much of her own insignificance once faced with the enormity of creation.

Leif remained blissfully unaware of the activities around him. He slept soundly, lulled by the vessel's vibrations and metronomic engine, cocooned by the blanket and his mother's breast. Mother and child were carefully assisted into a lifeboat sent over by the *Grønsund*. The four oarsmen began paddling to return to their ship. Rigmor scanned the deck of the massive gray ship searching for any sign of her husband. Even in a crowd of hundreds she would be able to pick him out. And although she saw dozens of uniformed sailors standing at the rails observing the lifeboat's approach, she could not see the man for whom she searched.

But he was there. Frederik watched the transfer from the bridge of the ship, his face betraying nothing. However, his heart could finally beat normally. He was relieved. The operation, bearing the most precious cargo in his life, had proceeded with military precision. Now he just had to figure out what to say. He hadn't seen Rigmor in five weeks, he couldn't just appear, he needed to find the right words to express how much he'd missed her, how much she meant to him. He narrowed his glance to see Rigmor and his son escorted below to his private quarters. Suddenly, one of his junior officers responsible for transferring Frederik's family from the *Havmaden*, appeared at his side holding a leather pouch containing dispatches from the Admiralty given to him from the submarine's commander. Frederik scanned the contents of the message, then turned to the officer and said,

> I'm leaving you in control of the vessel. We are still on schedule to rendezvous with the *Thetis* at 1500 hours this afternoon, 25 nautical miles south-west from our current position. Estimated sailing time is ninety minutes.

His face held back a smile. 'Prepare to get underway immediately following the deck ceremony.' He glanced at his watch. 'I need to check on my family.'

Frederik moved towards his quarters, took a few deep breaths to calm himself, then opened the door, saw Rigmor, and immediately moved over to her, ready to take her in his arms. However, he was blocked by her extended arm, and a scowl on her face. 'Frederik Bangsbøll', she said,

> do you have any idea how many military regulations you've broken today. Transporting civilians aboard Royal Danish naval vessels without permission. Sending a submarine to secretly come into port, during wartime, without orders from the Admiralty. I'm sure that you're going to be brought up on charges.

He raised an eyebrow and couldn't hold back a smile. 'Spoken like a true naval officer's wife.'

It was true. Even though Frederik's career could drive her mad with worry and she swore an oath to herself to never let her first born son follow in the Bangsbøll tradition, she also realized that the man she loved had been formed directly because of the military. 'A potentially ex-officer's wife!' she snapped back.

He shook his head, laughing. 'Please. We both know the Crown Prince would make the charges go away.'

Rigmor wouldn't give an inch. 'I doubt even he has that kind of power.'

'He's sorry he couldn't be here today.' Frederik said, referring to the monarch, his best friend since they attended Jomsberg School together. Then he looked at his wife. 'Do you have any plans to properly greet your husband with a kiss?'

'That depends', she said, 'do you plan on keeping that beard once the war ends?'

Frederik stood before her, took her in his arms, and began kissing her face and forehead. 'I can't believe you're standing here.'

'I can't either.'

'I trust the crew of the Havmaden has treated you well.'

Rigmor's demeanor began to soften and she said with a wry smile,

Yes, the captain and crew of the submarine were most accommodating, but my God, the odors in that ship was ghastly! I don't know how they can stand it day after day.

She continued, 'Although it pains me that our son seems to have his father's love of the sea. He was either sleeping or smiling contently the entire time.' Rigmor set her eyes upon Frederik. 'However, that is not what I wish for him.' Her face exploded in a smile. 'Or his poor wife.'

'Then you know?' said Frederik.

'That you're not coming back to Copenhagen today…', Rigmor said,

that Denmark still hasn't found its place in this god-awful war. That your country needs you more than Leif and I do. That you took these incredible risks today to have our son christened, because you didn't know when you'd be back home.

'I couldn't have said that better myself.' Frederik said with a wry smile.

'I know.' Rigmor replied.

That's why I said it for you. It makes me feel better the way I put it. You would have given me some speech about honor and duty and the needs of the Admiralty.

Frederik laughed. 'It's like we've never been apart.' Then he walked over to his desk, picked up a small parcel wrapped with a bow and handed the gift to Rigmor. 'We've got less than an hour for the ceremony.'

Rigmor opened the package. Inside was a gleaming white christening gown for Leif.

'I'm sorry', Frederik said,

I couldn't be clearer in my message and tell you to bring the outfit you made for Leif. They read all the communiques and I couldn't let them know what I had planned.

'It's beautiful.' Rigmor said, admiring the outfit. 'How did you get it?'

'I had the pastor pick it up from the shop in Copenhagen earlier this week and bring it with him this morning.'

Rigmor walked over to Leif, laying on his father's bed, and began to change his outfit. 'I'll just save the one I made for our next child.'

Frederik smiled again. 'Happy to oblige. Once the war's over.'

'You can divert a submarine on a secret mission to pick up our baby to be christened', Rigmor said, 'but you can't do the same to make a baby?'

He walked to the bed, placed his hands on her shoulders, rested his head next to her neck, and beamed with pride, while watching Rigmor dress their child in his christening whites.

Lieutenant Winther announced to the family and crew assembled on deck of the *Grønsund*, as it gently swayed to the undulating sea, 'Then the eleven disciples went away into Galilee, into a mountain where Jesus had appointed them.' The pastor intoned, as he sprinkled holy water on Leif's head.

And when they saw him, they worshiped him: but some doubted. And Jesus came and spake [spoke] unto them, saying, 'All power is given unto me in heaven and in earth. Go ye therefore, and teach all nations, baptizing them in the name of the Father, and of the Son, and of the Holy Ghost …' ['Matthew 28:16–20', *Bible*].

Beaming with pride, Frederik and Rigmor stood beside each other on the open deck of the *Grønsund*, with their fingers intertwined, and surrounded by the entire crew, their heads bowed in solemnity as their hearts soared.

Winther returned Leif to his mother's embrace, then looked into the crowd of sailors, and said 'Teach all the nations and baptize them. A valuable lesson to remember while conducting this ceremony, aboard a war ship in a time of world conflict.' A war that none present knew would be soon referred to as the war to end all wars.

A war to ensure that any child of Leif's age will never be called on to make such sacrifices. Winther continued,

Look on Leif now as your own godchild, and pledge to him that he will grow up in a better world, a world that will never lead its citizens into destruction and perdition.

Winther smiled at Leif and said,

> You have forty-two godfathers my young friend: the entire complement of this ship. And we are all forever linked, bonded with the promise that you will never walk alone, that we will never leave your side, that we will be better leaders, better men than the generation that has come before. Today, Leif, after your baptism at sea, you will go forth in God's care with the help of the crew of the *Grønsund* and thanks to the crew of the *Havmaden*.

Winther raised his hands to bring the crew to attention, then smiled at both proud parents, and concluded the ceremony by saying,

> Repeat after me everyone. 'Leif, you are forever bonded to all of us, and you my son, shall never walk alone. We will always be there with you, if not in body – in spirit.'

Rigmor held her child tight, and whispered into his ear, 'Leif, my love, you will never walk alone. I will never leave your side.'

The entire story and the events of that day in September 1918 were never completely made available to, nor fully understood by the Danish Admiralty. Ultimately, Frederik was required to testify and explain to the Naval Board of Inquiry concerning his rationale for particular orders given to the Flotilla *Norske* on that day and to clarify certain entries into the operation logbooks of the *Grønsund* and *Havmaden*. Explanations provided by Frederik would later be described by those senior naval officers on the Naval Board of Inquiry as a mélange of beautifully crafted fiction with just enough strands of truth and verifiable facts to leave the board at an impasse on their findings.

In addition, each and every member of the crews of the *Havmaden* and *Grønsund* who were questioned as part of the inquiry seemed to revere Frederik in their positive and, at times, effusive testimonies submitted on his behalf. The crews of both ships subsequently corroborated all the 'facts' presented surrounding the operational necessity of the *Havmaden*'s two sojourns into the port in one day, supported by the emphatic testimony of the Flotilla *Norske*'s pastor, Lieutenant Winther, regarding the routine religious service given to the *Grønsund*'s crew. There was not a single mention of a mother and her baby being transported on either the *Havmaden* or *Grønsund*, nor was any word spoken about a christening by any of the witnesses called to testify before the inquiry. The witnesses testified that Winther had provided a welcome, respectful religious service aboard the *Grønsund*. These facts left the Admiralty with no other option than to close the inquiry as 'Unfounded allegations of misconduct or inappropriate use of His Majesty's warships.'

Able Seaman Henrik Berg, the staff car driver was never questioned about his role in the incident and remained completely oblivious to his potential involvement in any naval inquiry. He and his girlfriend were married the following summer. Rigmor had heard about the upcoming Berg wedding through Lieutenant Winther and, though not officially invited to the wedding herself, she attended the small church service and sat quietly at the back of the church to watch the ceremony. Rigmor shed a few tears of joy for the young couple and left quietly and unobserved at the end of the ceremony, leaving a small, anonymous gift for the newlyweds in the office of the rectory.

Lieutenant Commander Sondergaard, the fleet pastor, was initially incensed at what he perceived as provocative actions by his subordinate, Lieutenant Winther. However, given the findings of the Naval Board of Inquiry, which acknowledged the keen initiative of Winther to arrange to go out to the flotilla on a resupply run and provide religious services to the crews of the *Grønsund* and *Havmaden* while on station at sea made a reprimand impossible. The fact that Rigmor was now completely content to rely on Winther for ministering her and her young son, left Sondergaard with no other options than to accept the events at face value and move on.

* * *

Though Frederik had been in the presence of the king's company numerous times before and since the 'The Christening Affair' aboard the *Grønsund*, the two had never spoken of the unusual events involving the *Norske* squadron on that September day in 1918. In fact, it was not until three years later that King Christian X, accompanied by his son Crown Prince Frederik, who was Frederik Bangsbøll's close friend and classmate from the Royal Danish Naval Academy, would congratulate Frederik during the naval officer's promotion ceremony to naval commander.

There, at the officers' club, the king quietly pulled Frederik Bangsbøll aside and said,

> Frederik, it appears that your keen personal initiative and your superior, clandestine execution of your son's high seas christening ceremony some years ago have finally been properly recognized by the Admiralty. I think it is finally the appropriate time to congratulate you on that extraordinary mission and now for your promotion to commander within my Royal Navy.

With that said and with the formalities of the promotion done, Crown Prince Frederik came over, slapped his old friend on the back and guided him towards the long, oak bar in the officers' wardroom. After a round of Akvavit was consumed with their fellow officers along with a toast to the navy's newest commander, the king walked out to the patio for a cigarette and motioned for his son and Frederik to join him.

The large patio with its low stone wall ran the full length of the officers' mess and overlooked Holmen harbor. As the king surveyed the port activities, he pulled from his jacket's chest pocket a silver cigarette case with the Royal Danish coat of arms adorning it. The case snapped open and the king offered his son and Frederik a cigarette. The king, his son and Frederik enjoyed a moment of quiet reflection together, smoking and speaking of nothing of consequence. A few minutes later the king dropped his cigarette onto stone balcony and with the sole of his royal shoe, ground the cigarette out. 'My physician says I must quit smoking, or it will be the end of me.'

Frederik looked back at his sovereign, smiled and took another deep inhale on his own cigarette and replied, 'I've been given the same advice sire.' At that, the king announced, 'The prince and I must get back to the palace.' He put out his hand to bid farewell and congratulate Frederik once more on his promotion. As their hands grasped, the king reached into his breast pocket with his free hand and withdrew the silver cigarette case and presented it to Frederik. 'For you, my loyal subject and faithful friend to my son. Maybe without this case, I'll smoke less.' The king smiled, gave a friendly wink, turned and walked back into the officers' mess. Crown Prince Frederik shook hands with his old friend, congratulated him again and followed the king.

Chapter 2

Headstones by the Sea

> 'They shall not grow old, as we that are
> left grow old. Age shall not weary them
> nor will the years condemn.'
>
> Laurence Binyon,
> 1914

Frederik Bangsbøll was not a man who strolled casually, unless accompanied by his wife. On this morning, dressed in a dark suit and wearing a fedora hat, Frederik walked with purpose and long, even strides. His son, Leif, now 13 years old, tried to match the measured military gait of his father, doing his best to keep up. Though they walked side-by-side, they were mentally worlds apart. Frederik's thoughts were far away, concentrating on the future and what lay ahead for himself and his young son. They were the thoughts of an adult, a parent, processing factors well beyond the boy's comprehension. Options needed to be considered, consequences needed to be weighed and difficult decisions needed to be made. To the contrary, Leif's thoughts were a torrent of anguished, unanswerable questions of a child in the here and now: Why was my mother taken away? Why my sisters, too? What will happen to me now?

The boy loved his father dearly and idolized the brave sea captain. But without his mother's comforting presence, the hard, stoic nature of his father made the boy apprehensive. For the first thirteen years of his life, Leif's mother had been there to nurture him and protect him from the gruff nature of the seafaring man who commanded merchant and naval vessels, challenging the dangerous Baltic Sea and the unforgiving North Atlantic Ocean time and time again. Throughout his naval career, Frederik had planned missions, executed assignments and given orders that put men's lives in harm's way – responsibilities not compatible with a nurturing style of child rearing. No, this man, a father, a naval officer, a Dane descended from ancient Viking kings, from a lineage of fearless explorers, a tanned-faced captain and a leather-handed sailor was always expected to be strong and firm in his teachings of the lessons of the sea, lessons of life. The same lessons he would teach the boy, lessons about the realities of life and death and how to survive in a dangerous world. This child, the student,

Headstones by the Sea   17

Rigmor with son Leif (7) and daughter Jytte (3), on the isle of Bornholm, 1925. (*Photo courtesy of the author's family collection*)

the son of a sailor, had his whole life ahead of him. Frederik's duty was clear: to ensure this child was well educated, challenged and grew into adulthood in order to lead the way into the future.

But those plans would have to wait. On that day, there were other, more pressing matters to attend to, here, on the island of Bornholm: a Danish jewel in the middle of the Baltic Sea, where the family's summer home sat, where Frederik had been born. Father and son were there to pay their respects and bid farewell to Rigmor, Leif's mother and Frederik's wife. Rigmor had died while Frederik was at sea.

The doctor had called it tuberculosis, a disease complicated by a case of pneumonia. All Leif knew was that his mother had been fine, then suddenly sick and now she was gone. It had all happened over a fortnight. 'Why had this happened? Why?' thought Leif. The unsettling realization struck him that his father, who once had all the answers, could not answer this question. Nor could his father answer, to his son's satisfaction, the question 'Why were you gone when this happened?'

With the warm Scandinavian summer sun on their backs and the cool, blustery ocean wind on their faces, they walked from their summer home towards the small seaside church in the village of Svaneke, on the southern coast of Bornholm. They walked amidst the calls of the seagulls as the birds drifted above them on invisible currents of air and swooped past the edge of the cliffs overlooking the sea. They walked along a path of slate gray stones worn smooth from the passage of time, the treading of countless footsteps and exposure to the harsh Baltic weather, stones laid hundreds of years ago when Vikings still ruled these lands. And each step they took brought them ever closer to the stark reality of their situation. Father and son walked in silence, Leif having already asked all the questions he could, with few satisfying answers. His mother had been ripped from their lives forever and he would never know why. But now, as the path led them along the side and back of the church to a secluded corner of the cemetery overlooking the sea, Leif, carrying a bouquet of wildflowers he had picked from their garden, began to feel anxious and reached for his father's hand. 'Is mother in heaven papa?' he asked, his blond hair blowing wildly in the wind.

Frederik stopped and looked into his son's blue eyes. 'Yes, Leif, your mother is surely in heaven. She was an angel to us here on earth and now she's an angel watching over us from above.'

Leif looked up at his father's tanned, weathered face, noting the wrinkles around his glistening eyes. Far too many wrinkles for a man of only 36 years old. Frederik seemed to have aged many years overnight.

'Are my sisters with mama now?'

Headstones by the Sea 19

Rigmor Bangsboll, sailing with husband Frederik, 1924. (*Photo courtesy of the author's family collection*)

It was almost too much for the hard-as-iron sea captain to withstand. He took a deep breath of the cool sea air and replied, not looking at his son, but gazing out over the blue expanse of the sea. 'Yes son, both little Inga and Jytte are in heaven with your mother. That I am sure, just as sure as I stand before you now, Leif.'

* * *

Death had visited the Bangsbøll family too often during Leif's young life. On 18 February 1923, when Leif was not quite 4 years old, his younger sister, Inga Gyda Bangsbøll, died of meningitis at their family home in Copenhagen. Inga was just 2 years old. Just a month prior to Inga's death, Jytte Gunvar Bangsbøll had been born. Jytte's welcome birth had served as new hope to the Bangsbøll family. Sadly, that hope and optimism would last less than three years. On 28

February 1926, Jytte, just 3 years old, also died of meningitis. A once happy family, the Bangsbølls had been decimated by a series of unforeseeable maladies.

The loss of his second daughter had been particularly hard on Frederik, who, immediately following her death, began to withdraw from his remaining family members and immersed himself more and more into his career, volunteering for more frequent and longer sea duty assignments. Like his forefathers, the sea had always been his refuge and now, more than ever, Frederik would rely on the sea's healing powers. Surely his ship and the sea would occupy his body and mind so that he would not go mad from the grief that had grown inside him.

Fredrik Sorensen-Bangsboll, sailing with his wife Rigmor, 1924. (*Photo courtesy of the author's family collection*)

As for Rigmor, the tragic loss of her two baby girls in the span of three years, though devastating to her very soul, had one redeeming effect. It allowed her to focus all her maternal love and attention on her son, Leif. With her husband away at sea more often, her time was devoted to her son's upbringing. But now, five years later, 13-year-old Leif was a boy without a mother.

* * *

From the Svaneke cemetery, where generations of the Sørensen-Bangsbøll clan had been buried, the view of the shimmering expanse of the Baltic Sea was breathtaking. The two mourners arrived at the family gravesite and gazed upon the three white marble gravestones. The headstones stood straight and aligned, gleaming in the summer sun; they were not dull gray and weather worn like most of the headstones that surrounded them in the ancient churchyard. The grass had grown over both Inga's and Jytte's graves over the years, but the soil was still freshly turned on top of Rigmor's final resting place. As Frederik had prearranged, fresh flowers lay at the base of the headstones of Rigmor and their daughters.

Father and son stood hand in hand by the graveside, silent in their grief. After a moment, and with a slight squeeze of his hand a nod of his head, Frederik indicated to his son that he should place his flowers on his mother's grave. Leif released his father's hand, knelt and gently place the sun-coloured flowers against the white marble headstone.

Overwhelmed by his grief and at a loss of what to say or do, Leif's thoughts were drawn back to the events of the summer and his last happy moments with his mother. Just weeks before her death, Rigmor had arranged with her parents – who were looking after Leif in Copenhagen – to bring him to her so they could spend the remainder of summer at their seaside cottage on Bornholm together. When Leif arrived in Bornholm, Rigmor had been so pleased to see her son happy and healthy. But when Leif arrived with his grandfather and grandmother, Bjerreby, he was shocked and frightened to see how weak and pale his mother had become. Wanting to cheer her up, Leif regaled his mother with stories of his recent Boy Scout trip to Germany while sitting by her bedside. His Scout troop had spent the entire month of June hiking from Luebeck, Germany to the Hars Mountains and back, a hike of over 300 miles. Leif was proud of this accomplishment and was pleased to see his mother smile as he recounted his summer adventure to her.

During the last few weeks of her life, Rigmor continued to convey great optimism about her medical condition. 'Don't you worry Leif, mummy will be better soon, and we will have a big party when your father returns from Greenland with Uncle Knud.' Rigmor had hoped that the warm summer sun and the cool moist air of the Baltic Sea would benefit her condition. It had not. Mercifully, the last days of her life were spent in the place she loved the most: quiet, beautiful Bornholm with her adoring son close by.

Still kneeling at his mother's graveside, with tears welling in his eyes, and unable to clearly see either the flowers or the headstone, Leif mustered the strength and whispered the only words he could: 'Bye-bye, mama.' Leif stood up and immediately turned to his father and leaned heavily into his torso and wept like he never had before.

* * *

Weeks before Rigmor's illness had become a concern, Leif's father had departed Copenhagen, destined for Greenland and assigned as the ship's captain and navigator of HDMS *Dagmar*, a rugged, 42-foot, 10-ton, motorized ocean-going vessel. The *Dagmar* was a sturdy vessel, and its relatively small size and shallow draft allowed the boat to navigate far into the many fjords and inlets that lined the east coast of Greenland. The Danish government sponsored expedition was tasked to conduct mapping, research terrestrial magnetism, and collect zoological, botanical and archaeological specimens. Frederik's task was to provide navigation and logistical support to Danish-Greenlander explorer and family friend, Knud Rasmussen, making his sixth government sponsored exploration of Greenland.

This expedition would focus upon the southeastern region from Cape Farewell, the southernmost tip of Greenland up to Angmagssalik.

Knud Rasmussen, known to Leif as 'Uncle Knud', had inspired the young man with his adventurous spirit and his fascination with the natural world. Uncle Knud was a hero within the Arctic's Danish-Greenland exploration community and would be immortalized as the first white man to navigate the Arctic Circle from Baffin Island to Alaska with sled dogs, using only traditional technologies to travel and survive. In the years to come, the name Rasmussen would become legendary within Denmark and Greenland amongst the annals of the *National Geographic*'s arctic exploration history.

At the time of his departure with the Sixth Thule Greenland Expedition, Frederik knew his wife was ill, but did not comprehend the severity nor did he anticipate the worsening of her condition. The *Dagmar* had been sailing off the southeastern coast of Greenland on the final stage of the expedition when Frederik received the wireless radio message from the Danish Admiralty informing him of his wife's death. Devastated at the news, Frederik had not realized that the April morning of his departure on this voyage would be the last time he would see his lovely wife alive – waiving farewell – with their son standing beside her on the Holmen pier in Copenhagen.

* * *

It had been almost two months since Rigmor had died, when Frederik, now a widower, finally arrived on the island of Bornholm. Rigmor's parents had been at their daughter's side until the end and had cared for Leif while his father made his way back to Denmark from Greenland. Frederik took the first ferry available from Copenhagen to Ronne, on the island of Bornholm. Once reunited, Leif and his father had been occupied with visits from friends and family who wished to pass on their condolences and offer support. Appreciative of these kind gestures, Frederik soon turned his attention toward addressing estate matters. He also knew he had to make arrangements for a suitable boarding school in Copenhagen for his son. Unaccustomed as he was to the day-to-day needs of a child, the stoic sea captain declined offers of family members on Bornholm and in Copenhagen to billet and care for Leif. They all knew, including Frederik himself, that Frederik's obligation to the navy would not be compatible with raising a 13-year-old boy. Though appreciative of the offers, Frederik had other plans for young Leif.

It was now late in the morning and time for Frederik and Leif to bid farewell to a faithful wife and beloved mother. Their departure from the family plot brought a new wave of tears and grief to Leif. As they walked away from the gravesite, Leif kept looking back at the three white headstones, hoping beyond hope that he was dreaming. Too soon, the markers disappeared from his sight. He turned away one last time, and together, Frederik and Leif slowly retraced their steps through the Svaneke churchyard and silently walked towards home. They would take the ferry back to Copenhagen that night, but for now, Frederik had an idea that he thought might help his son feel better.

On their way back to the house, they stopped at a small general store, where Frederik bid good morning to the shop owner, whom he recognised from previous shopping excursions with Rigmor. The proprietor recognised them both as well and conveyed his condolences at their recent loss. Leif stood silently looking out the shop window watching pedestrians, local villagers going about their business, while his father purchased a few items including a loaf of rye bread, cheese, two apples, a chocolate bar, a bottle of milk and bottle of beer.

Once home with their provisions, they collected their already packed belongings from the entry of their summer house and loaded their rental car. Frederik and Leif got in, but before putting the car in gear, Frederik turned to his son and said, 'Leif, I have an idea, a surprise for you. Shall we go on a picnic before we go to the ferry crossing?' Without looking at his father, with cheeks still salty and wet from his tears, Leif nodded his head slowly. His father smiled, put the car in gear and they drove off, not in the direction of Ronne, the port with the ferry landing, but in the opposite direction, north along a narrow road that hugged the coast of Bornholm. After a few minutes, the road began to rise higher and higher above looming cliffs, providing a spectacular view for Leif to survey the beach and the waves breaking on the shore far below. Leif recognised this place. He suddenly knew where they were going – the Castle Hammershaus!

As Frederik navigated the final turn, Castle Hammershaus, the largest medieval fortification in northern Europe came into view, filling the windscreen of the car. Perched upon a cliff, many of its massive walls remained standing as did the main central structure of the castle and its lookout towers. Leif was excited; he and his father had visited this spectacular thirteenth-century castle each summer they had visited Bornholm for as long as Leif could remember. Each time they came, father and son had pretended to be fierce Viking warriors or gallant crusading knights in mock battle amongst the massive ruins. Today, more than anything, Frederik wanted to distract his son from his grief and, hopefully, begin the gentle rekindling of their father-son relationship that had so recently been shattered.

As soon as the car stopped, Leif jumped out and ran across the stone bridge separating the roadway from the castle grounds. Onward and upward the young boy ran, following the winding cobblestone path that led to the massive gateway to his childhood playground.

Walking behind his son, Frederik carried the bag with their lunch inside, recalling how they had played out this annual excursion each summer. As he entered the large central courtyard through the main castle gate, he watched his son climb upon the battlements. Frederik scanned the massive interior of the castle – they appeared to be the only visitors at the moment. Frederik was thankful that the castle's remote location (on the northernmost tip of their small island in the middle of Baltic Sea) had prevented its turning into a busy tourist attraction.

Leif was content to play and explore the castle on his own. And Frederik was content to watch. After an hour, Frederik called to Leif and moments later, as his words echoed amongst the ruins, his son came running back to him. Breathing heavily, hair matted to his brow from sweat, and with bright red cheeks, Leif said, 'I'm famished papa'. He smiled and came and sat beside his father. Seated upon the massive stone base of one of the castle walls that had crumbled to the ground many years before, father and son looked out over the Baltic towards the distant shores of Sweden and consumed their meal, finishing with one of Leif's favorite treats: a chocolate bar.

The overnight ferry voyage from Ronne, the island's main port back to Copenhagen was spent in quiet reflection by both father and son. Despite the wonderful afternoon spent together at the Castle Hammershaus, Leif still felt anger and grief over the loss of his mother and laid much of the blame on his father. They both had so many unanswered questions about what had happened and what the future had in store for them.

* * *

Since his mother's death, Leif had felt betrayed by the fact that his father had been away when she died – and he made sure his father knew this. Frederik understood the cause of his son's bitter sadness and resentment: the boy had lost his loving mother, and his callus father seemed too focused on his naval duties to realize that Leif's mother was dying. This knowledge was a burden to Frederik, and one he would carry for the rest of his life. For now, it was a chasm between him and his son, one that he would have to try to bridge over time.

Copenhagen's Sølvgades school – Denmark' oldest school – was built in 1847 and had a very strong reputation. Academic achievement and discipline of character were paramount at Sølvgades school, and Frederik thought that it was just what his son needed. Sølvgades school had very good credentials – strong academics, an active sports curriculum, and a reputation for a strong disciplined faculty and students alike. The school was located just minutes away from Copenhagen's Holmen Naval Base, not far from the Bangsbølls' former home on Hausergade Street, but almost 6 miles from their new home in Nærum, a suburb of Copenhagen. Frederik had decided that Leif would board at the school. When Frederik was in port, the school would be close by to visit and when on extended stay ashore, the location of the new family home would offer son and father time to enjoy each other's company on the occasional weekend and holidays. Sølvgades school would provide Leif with everything that Frederik felt was required: dedicated teachers, coaches and dormitory mothers, classmates and friends. Leif would have a regimented daily routine and, above all, stability and structure in his life.

Leif entered Sølvgades school as a boarding student in September 1931. Leif was 13 years old. The first semester was a turbulent experience for all concerned: Leif, his teachers, the school's administrators and for Frederik as well. Whether it was just his adolescent age or his continuing anger and frustration at the loss of his mother, Leif's personal challenges were many. Unwilling to focus on his academics, Leif's first semester was a series of failed or unfinished assignments, multiple truancy violations and several brutal school yard fights.

Leif missed his mother terribly and was angry at everyone and everything.

Sølvgades school did have one redeeming feature for Leif, however: the chance to rekindle a friendship with his childhood friend, Jørgen Vejlby Bech, a boy Leif had known in elementary school, and although he was a year older than Leif, they had shared a close connection. The two boys renewed their friendship and became very close during their days together at Sølvgades school.

Jørgen was not academically strong relative to his classmates and he was often ridiculed by the more well-off, well-performing students. His academic frustrations manifested themselves in an overall negative attitude towards school, which fueled Leif's own troubled soul and led them both to frequent visits to the dean's and headmaster's offices for academic shortcomings and misbehavior.

By the end of Leif's second semester, letters from the headmaster to Frederik had become increasingly troubling for the naval officer and single father. Accustomed to dealing with disciplinary issues in a prompt and effective military manner, Frederik could not understand why the school was unable to bring Leif around to perform better academically and stay out of trouble. In mid-December, at the end of the first semester, Leif returned home with a dismal report card and a letter addressed to his father stating that his son was expelled and should not return to Sølvgades school following the Christmas break. Leif's brief tenure at Sølvgades school was at an end.

 Both surviving Bangsbøll men were at a crossroads. Leif had proven quite vividly his steadfast refusal to accept his new fate and his new school and accompanying home, and Frederik was going to have to accept the job he'd been avoiding since Rigmor's death: he would have to be the father Leif desperately needed. And in that role, there was only one solution in Frederik's arsenal that had met with proven success: Frederik was going to take Leif to sea.

* * *

Early in the New Year, Frederik's commander, aware of the family challenges facing his favorite subordinate, offered Frederik a rare opportunity that Frederik and Leif would never forget. Frederik was offered the opportunity to sail one of the Royal Danish Navy's few remaining schooners, HDMS *Svanen* – a classic, sleek, two-mast, wooden sailing vessel used primarily as a cadet training vessel – on a special diplomatic mission. Frederik thought that maybe, some time together at sea might be what he and his son needed to begin to mend their broken bonds.

The intended journey of the *Svanen*, and its twelve sea cadets, was from Copenhagen, Denmark to Bergen, Norway to participate in Norway's National Day celebrations. His colleagues at the Admiralty knew that Frederik was most comfortable at sea and thought he would benefit from a less operational voyage and some quality time with his son. Working with the other young naval cadets would help him heal some of the grief from the loss of his wife. Together, away from Copenhagen and the reminders of their loss, Leif and his father enjoyed a few days of welcome distraction.

They sailed the *Svanen* north through the Kattegat Straight and westward into the Skagerrak Straight and the North Sea. From there, it was due north up the western coast of Norway. Upon their arrival four days later in Bergen, they attended several Norwegian celebrations, formal dinners and tours of historic sites in and around the old port city. It was a long overdue time for father and son to bond. Little did they know, however, that the real adventure was about to unfold during their return voyage to Denmark, when their lives would be endangered as their small ship became disabled in the North Sea. The *Svanen* departed Bergen, Norway under gray, threatening clouds. Intending to navigate southward towards Denmark, parallel to the western coast of Norway, Frederik could not anticipate the magnitude of the gale storm that would confront them. On the first night of the storm, lightning struck and split the main mast halfway to the deck. After a second day and night of heavy rains, gale force winds and 10- to 15-foot waves, the *Svanen* had been severely battered and blown off course. As a result, the main sails could not be used, and the vessel's rudder and steering mechanism were disabled. The following day, the sea was still rough, but was becoming calmer, and Frederik turned his attentions to the cause of the problem to the navigation system. Despite his efforts he was unable to determine why he could not steer the vessel. But he knew what next action he had to take.

Not wanting to endanger one of the other cadets unnecessarily, Frederik asked his son to prepare to assist him with the inspection of the ship's rudder. Frightened at the prospects of diving into the dark, churning ocean, Leif nonetheless obediently prepared himself for the unwelcome task. A few minutes later, Frederik and his son jumped into the frigid, gray North Atlantic water with underwater goggles and flashlights to inspect the damage. After several dives to inspect the rudder and with labored breaths, Frederik declared that the schooner's steering mechanism was bent and jammed and could not be repaired at sea. As a result, the *Svanen* could not be steered, and its small crew would remain at the mercy of the ocean currents and winds of the North Atlantic.

Leif marveled at his father's calm assessment of the situation and his unwavering reassurance that all would be fine in due course. His father, confident in his abilities, knew he had to keep the young crew calm and focused on their duties until a rescue opportunity arose. His clear guidance on how to manage the crippled vessel kept both Leif, the youngest member of the crew at the age of 14, along with the seven other cadets who were between the ages of 15 and 17, reassured of their safety and eventual rescue.

To keep his young crew busy so that they would not dwell on their situation, Frederik used every waking hour to conduct hands-on training, including lessons on celestial navigation, the proper rigging and derigging of sails, and the repetitive tying of naval knots. In those days, all sailors were still required to be proficient in tying a multitude of knots, and Frederik kept the young cadets occupied with tying and untying half hitches and locking knots, bowlines, reverse-baker bowline knots and adjusting the sails' rigging until their hands became red and blistered. Leif lamented, 'By the end of this voyage, I'll be able to tie and untie those knots in my sleep.'

Frederik ensured that the ship's work was divided equally and equitably. He even took time to teach the boys some valuable food preparation lessons in the galley. This was done not only educate them, but also to get them to learn to fend for themselves to quell the almost insatiable appetites of the teenage boys.

* * *

Frederik also used their voyage adrift to share a plethora of maritime tales to help pass the time and steer the boys' attention away from their tenuous situation. It was during one of these evenings, as the *Svanen* drifted calmly under a star-filled sky in the North Atlantic, that Leif and the other cadets learned the story of Frantz 'Revolver' Sørensen and how the Bangsbøll family name came to be.

Leif's great-grandfather, Captain Frantz Peter Sørensen, had been a modestly successful Danish merchant sea captain, conducting trade between Scandinavia and Africa during the mid-1800s. During a particularly long and challenging voyage in the 1870s, there had been an attempted mutiny on board Captain Sørensen's ship as they sailed along the south-west coast of Africa. Although the exact cause of the mutiny was never revealed, according to legal records of testimonies at the maritime trial conducted in London, England several months after the incident, five mutineers had been shot, four were wounded and one killed by Captain Sørensen during the uprising. Five sailors were eventually found guilty of mutiny and Captain Sørensen was subsequently exonerated for his actions, and charges against him for murder and attempted murder charges were dropped. However, Captain Sørensen's reputation as a captain who was quite willing to shoot members of his crew had generated the nickname 'Revolver' Sørensen amongst the regional maritime community. Up until then, the meaning of the name Sørensen had been 'crowned with laurels', which, arguably, is much more regal. Though this new moniker of 'Revolver' Sørensen might have had some panache to it, the reality at the time was that Frantz 'Revolver' Sørensen's reputation as a strict and possibly dangerous captain had a significantly negative impact on his subsequent attempts to hire crews for his modest merchant enterprise. As a result, two years after the failed mutiny incident, Frantz Sørensen legally changed his family name to Sørensen-Bangsbøll. The origin of the name Bangsbøll, Frederik explained to the captivated cadets, was thought to be a combination of ancestral family names including 'Bangs' and 'Bøll'. With the birth of Frederik, the singular use of Bangsbøll became the legal name for this line of the Sørensen clan.

Though the story of 'Revolver' Sørensen intrigued the young castaway cadets, the tale they most enjoyed was one their captain final tale of the night, the tale of the Bangsbøll clan's ancestral connections to King Harald Blåtand Gormsson 'Bluetooth', the first Viking king of Denmark and Norway. In dramatic fashion, Frederik explained how Bluetooth was most famous for uniting the Viking clans of Jutland with southern Norway and for introducing Christianity to his kingdom.

Sitting at the head of the galley table, Frederik began by looking directly at Leif and emphasizing the first word of his statement:

OUR great ancestor, King Harald Blåtand Gormsson 'Bluetooth', ruled over the land and seas of Denmark and Norway for twenty-seven turbulent and productive years. Bluetooth brought Christianity to his pagan people; fought off enemy invaders from Sweden in the north and Germany from the south. But it was the enemy within that took his crown!

Frederik continued,

> In the year of our Lord AD 985, King Harald "Bluetooth" was overthrown on the field of battle by his once loyal, then treacherous, son Sweyn Haraldsson.

The boys sat around the galley table, memorized – even Leif, who had heard his father recite this family lore countless times, felt himself drawn into his father's performance. Frederik's gaze became fixed as if in a trance as he continued with the tale verbatim:

> Covered in sweat and mud and bleeding from mortal wounds, King Harald Bluetooth lay upon the battlefield amongst hundreds of his fellow clansmen and Viking warriors – both the dead and the dying. Bluetooth, the once noble Viking King had been overthrown, his reign usurped by his once loyal, now ambitious and victorious son Sweyn 'Forkbeard' Haraldsson. Gravely injured, Bluetooth was carried from the field of battle by a small band of loyal followers to the relative safety of Jomsberg Germany, a village just south of the Danish-German border. There, King Harald 'Bluetooth', the great communicator who united Denmark and Norway and brought Christianity to the Danes, unceremoniously died.

Frederik went on to explain how Forkbeard aggressively expanded Denmark's regional power during his reign through a series of hostile invasions in Norway, Sweden and eventually the British Isles. Though less well known than his father, Bluetooth, Forkbeard accomplished great things. At the turn of the tenth century, and over a decade of time, Forkbeard led a series of successful seaborne raids into northeastern England, Northumbria, plundering great riches and eventually establishing a permanent Viking fortification at the town of Gainsborough on the River Trent. From there, Forkbeard's Viking army made numerous attacks on the city of London. Though Forkbeard was unsuccessful in capturing the city, the British ruler at the time, King Æthelred, was believed to have paid a large ransom to the Vikings to cease their attacks. Then, inexplicably, on 25 December 1013, the *Anglo-Saxon Chronicle* announced that King Æthelred had fled to Normandy. With Æthelred's abdication, Forkbeard succeeded in extending the Danish kingdom to become the first Viking king of England. However, Forkbeard's reign would not last long. Less than two months into his rule over the English, Forkbeard died in his bed chambers – possibly murdered. Forkbeard had claimed the English thrown by right of conquest but was never crowned. With the death of Forkbeard, the Viking hold on the British Isles would would be tenuous until the rise to power of Forkbeard's son Cnut.

Until then, the reign of Forkbeard, the First Viking King of England would relegated to a mere anecdote in the long history of England and its ambitious Scandinavian neigbors.

Frederik paused for dramatic effect, then ended the story by winking at his attentive, young audience of cadets and observing:

> Clearly our more recent family ancestors have not done so well, because the current branch of the Sørensen-Bangsbøll family tree no longer has thrones to sit upon – just this splinter-ridden bench on this broken-down schooner in the middle of the North Sea!

At that, the boys burst out with laughter and applause, to which the skipper stood up and slowly folded one arm in front of himself and the other behind his back and bowed slowly and deeply towards his delighted audience. This gesture brought more cheers and laughter from the crew.

Those few harrowing days 'shipwrecked and lost at sea' would help redefine Frederik and Leif's father-son relationship. Despite the inherent danger of their situation, they grew closer together. And the young crew of sea cadets would forever remember their experience aboard the stricken schooner *Svanen* and their captain, Commander Frederik Bangsbøll, brave sailor, and teller of Viking lore and maritime tales!

* * *

Happily, early on the fifth day adrift, the crew of the *Svanen* who had been reported overdue, were located and rescued by a Norwegian Coast Guard ship 100 miles off the western coast of Norway. The *Svanen* had been slowly drifting towards Iceland. Now, the disabled vessel was towed to Stavanger for repairs.

Upon returning to Copenhagen, and before setting sail on his next assignment on the coastal defence vessel, HDMS *Hekla*, as the new commander of the *Hekla*, Frederik, and Leif moved into their new home on Hegnsvej Street, located north-west of the naval port of Holmen and close to the wide inlet leading to the mouth of Copenhagen harbor. Nærum was a quiet community; a place with expanses of trees, fields and paths that ran along the shore, overlooking the harbor. It was a peaceful place. And though both Frederik and Leif were very fond of their home on Hausergade Street, it held too many memories of lost loved ones. They needed a new start, and a new house would be a good first step.

The greatest regret of Frederik's life was that he was not at his wife's side when she died at the young age of 30 from tuberculosis. Had he realized the extent of her illness, he most assuredly would not have accepted the assignment as captain of the *Dagmar* and the Sixth Thule Greenland Expedition of 1930. However, the offer to be captain and navigator on such an exploration was too intriguing to turn down. The objective of the voyage was to explore the rugged east coast of Greenland during which the *Dagmar* and crew, along with its expedition leader Knud Rasmussen traversed over 700 nautical miles of dramatically rugged shores and glacier-filled fjords of the Greenland coast. However, Frederik would take some small degree of solace in his loss when Rasmussen published the following in report for the Danish government, which stated, amongst other achievements:

Lieutenant-Commander Frederik Bangsboll, 1930. (*Photo courtesy of the author's family collection*)

> After facing weeks of heavy seas and screeching gales, dangerous ice flows, hidden and uncharted reefs and all manners of hardship during the ten weeks of exploration, I and the crew realized what the expedition owed to her navigator and commander – Frederik Bangsbøll. I may have led this expedition, but it was he who was the author of its success.

Leif Bangsboll (7), Copenhagen 1925. (*Photo courtesy of the author's family collection*)

As a man of the sea, Frederik did what he was called on to do: go to sea. He would accept equally both praise for his success of the mission and criticism for his decision to go in the first place. Ultimately, it was only his son's opinion on this subject that mattered. In Leif's view, his father had chosen the sea over his mother.

Though it came as a small consolation to Frederik, up the coast from Cape Farewell, on the southeastern shores of Greenland is a bay (61° 48′N, 42° 02′W), which lies directly below the 2,300-foot cliffs of Cape Adelaer. This bay (or *Havn* in Danish) is named after Frederik Bangsbøll, captain of the *Dagmar*. According to Kund Rasmussen's records from the Sixth Thule Expedition, Bangsbøll *Havn* served as an emergency harbor when a sudden and violent storm endangered the crew of the *Dagmar* and commemorates Frederik's heroic efforts during the expedition of Greenland.

Chapter 3

An Apprenticeship at Sea

> 'Human beings come in three kinds: the Living, the dead, and those who go to sea.'
>
> Aristotle

Despite the resentment Leif felt towards his father and his chosen career, the voyage on the *Svanen* had opened Leif's eyes to the excitement, albeit inherently dangerous life at sea. Leif could not deny the powerful draw of the sea now ran through his veins. His father sensed this changing perspective in his son too.

With the spring and summer months stretching ahead of his son and no school to attend, Leif's father knew he needed to find something to keep the young lad busy and out of trouble. For Frederik, life aboard a ship, sailing the sea, had always been his best teacher. Maybe Leif could benefit from that experience too, he thought. It might distract him from the grief of his mother's death and turn his focus to other matters.

After a few telephone calls within the Admiralty, Frederik was given the authority to have Leif serve with the Royal Danish Naval Reserve Fleet. In May 1932, Junior Naval Apprentice Leif Bangsbøll was assigned to the submarine tender, *Hekla*, a 1,200-ton, former light cruiser, coastal defense vessel. The *Hekla* was a fine old ship built in 1891 and repurposed in 1915 as a submarine tender/logistical support vessel – the largest in the Danish fleet, crewed by seventy-five sailors and officers. Leif's role aboard the *Hekla* was to be cabin boy to the ship's captain, his father, Commander Frederik Bangsbøll.

Artist rendition of King Harald Bluetooth Gormsson, the Great Communicator and Danish King who brought Christianity to the Danes, reigned over Denmark and parts of Norway 958–985 AD. (*Photo courtesy of online source "The Collector"*)

Ancient Nordic initials of King Harald "Bluetooth" Gormsson which make up the modern day symbol of Bluetooth technologies. (*Photo courtesy of online source*)

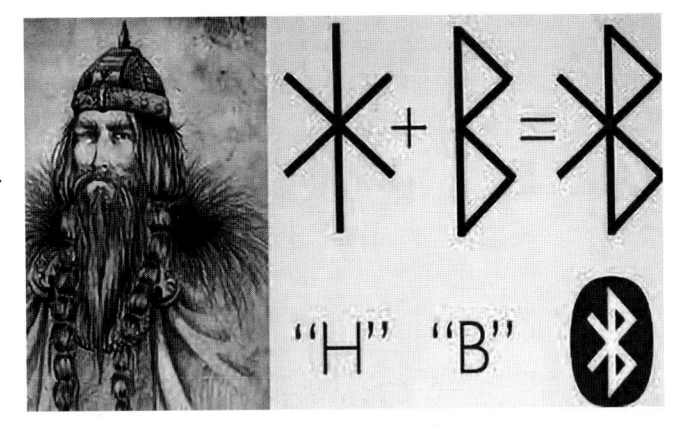

At first, Leif did not take kindly to his father's plan, feeling a spiritual kinship with the mutinous Fletcher Christian of the doomed voyage of the *Bounty*, who spent more time feuding with the crushing patriarchal rigor of Captain Bly, than serving his role in the crew's shared mission. To Leif, his father was obviously trying to punish him for failing to live up the expectations he held for his son's future. It could not be otherwise. His father had never bothered to ask Leif what he wanted.

Artist rendition of King Sweyn Forkbeard Haraldsson, who usurped the Danish Viking throne from his father Bluetooth in 985 AD. Forkbeard went on to invade England and on December 25th 1013 was pronounce the First Viking King of Denmark, Norway and England. (*Photo courtesy of online source "The Collector"*)

An Apprenticeship at Sea 35

His Danish Majesty's Ship (HDMS) *Hekla* (circa 1909), a Light Cruiser converted to a Submarine Tender and upon which Naval Apprentice Leif Bangsboll, age 13 served in 1932 The captain of HDMS *Hekla* at the time was his father, Lieutenant-Commander Frederik Bangsboll. (*Naval History and Heritage Command (history.navy.mil/85349 Hekla – Danish Cruiser)*)

First Lieutenant Frederik Leif Julius Sorensen (second row, second from left) with fellow officers of the Fynske Infantry Regiment, during Second Holstein War with Germany, 1864. (*Photo courtesy of the author's family collection*)

What Leif wanted was to get expelled from school and return to his grandparents, not end up stranded at sea, denied agency, forced to be at the beck and call of people he didn't want to be stranded with, and on a mission designed solely to humble him, crush his spirit and punish him for his perceived insubordination. He wasn't the one who abandoned his child at the entrance gate of Sølvgades school so he could get back to sea, tempting fate, until he was whisked up by the Valkyries. Yes, Leif knew all the fabled stories of Valhalla and thought them nonsense.

Frederik made it clear to the crew that his son was to be given no special privileges, that each man on the *Hekla* should treat him as their own charge, teaching and discipling Leif as they saw fit. The irony wasn't lost on them. Many of the sailors aboard the *Hekla* had also been present at Leif's baptism, and seeing how he was close to confirmation age, they could look at this as the next stage in the Royal Danish Navy overseeing Leif's growth into a man.

Leif certainly didn't interpret their actions that way. Everyone obeyed the commander's orders and put Leif through his paces. He was taught how to properly wash and iron uniforms, to shine shoes to a glowing gleam, to polish leather belts and brass buttons, to mend socks and repair the stitching on uniforms. Leif was also tasked with delivering and returning verbal and written messages to and from the ship's leadership, as well as organizing the ship's wardroom for meetings and, finally, the most detestable part, serving coffee at the captain's twice-daily meeting with the officers. It was beyond Leif to understand the point of all this labor – all this humbling and menial – that sent him to his hammock each night with sore limbs and callouses. Frederik understood.

Even though on the surface it might appear to Leif as mere indulgence in parental power, Frederik was trying to make the boy feel an attachment, a sense of duty to something larger than himself, forcing him to realize that other people were relying on him, that his time was also their time. Leif had spent far too long luxuriating in his own psyche, dwelling and focusing on his loneliness. This self-destructive path had driven him to educational ruin and lashing out at a fellow student. In Frederik's estimation, the only

Captain Frantz "Revolver" Sorensen-Bangsboll, Copenhagen 1889. (*Photo courtesy of the author's family collection*)

solution was to snap the syndrome and reorient Leif's mind by immersing him in an environment where he couldn't focus on his own needs, where he had to give over his body and mind to the needs of a group: the crew of the *Hekla*.

When Leif was not busy with the multitude of cabin boy duties and tasks assigned to him, his father ensured he was kept busy reading a broad range of books and classical literature. Though Frederik had withdrawn Leif temporarily from a formal academic setting, he ensured his son's education continued uninterrupted through a regime of reading and practical work experience. And that transmission of Leif's misspent energy wasn't limited to his role as cabin boy, Frederik was also intent on continuing his son's education. Every few nights, Frederik would leave works of classic literature: *Julius Caesar*, *Mutiny on the Bounty* and *Moby Dick* on Leif's bunk, and during their evening meal together, he would entreat his son with provocative questions. Frederik wanted his son to not only read but analyze and consider the dynamics and ethical overtones of human conflicts. Eventually, their literary exchanges grew in length and depth as young Leif was taught the value of critical thinking and how to appreciate the drama and moral dilemmas that these great works of art conveyed. Soon enough, Leif did not wait for his father to select a new reading for him, and he would, on his own, peruse the impressive selection of books that his father maintained in his cabin and make his own choice of readings, turning the tables and posing questions to his father regarding his selections.

Ship's crew, Submarine Tender His Danish Majesties Ship Hekla, 1931. Lieutenant-Commander and ship's Captain Frederik Bangsboll, seated, second row, fourth from the left. (*Photo courtesy of the author's family collection*)

The first book that Leif chose to read on his own was William Shakespeare's *Hamlet*. One evening over dinner Leif asked,

> Father, do you think the Danish prince was really visited by his father's ghost and told of his betrayal? Or was it just the Danish prince's grief manifesting in his imagination?

Impressed with his son's inquiry, Frederik considered the question and replied,

> Loyalty to one's family and to the sovereign of one's country should have no bounds. And if Hamlet, the young Danish prince, felt that his father had been betrayed, it was his duty to come forth and state his beliefs without remorse or regret and act upon those beliefs with determined certainty.

These discussions with his father kept Leif's young mind active, and his knowledge and appreciation for great literature expanded with each book he read. However, the greatest benefit of these literary ventures was the intimate daily discussions between father and son, which helped to heal their damaged relationship and foster a closer bond between the two. Frederik understood.

During one of their first, post-dinner meal discussions on literature, Frederik asked his son 'Do you think Brutus, Caesar's closest friend, was right to conspire against him and participate in his emperor's assassination?'

Leif would let the question linger in the air, like the smoke from his father's cigarettes and would eventually deign an answer, while showcasing a level of dexterity with subtext, both in reading and analysis, far beyond his age:

> I think tyranny is always tyranny, regardless of whether it's your friend, or a family member responsible. Tyranny by its definition, is always tyrannical. And I am against it.

Frederik quickly realized that Greek and Roman literature were pitfalls to be avoided at all costs, lest his son emerged from his Trojan horse and ransack the city of Troy – his ship – just to make his father look foolish. He decided to skip past several centuries of literature and left a copy of *Moby Dick* on Leif's bunk and repeated the dinner ritual again a few nights later. Thinking the sea adventure of Moby Dick might raise some interesting discussions between father and son. Frederik had no idea what he was in for.

'Leif, what do you think was the source of Captain Ahab's maniacal motivation for seeking out the death of the great white whale?'

I don't know father, perhaps Captain Ahab didn't want to be home. I've met other sailors who also want to sail to the end of the earth, chasing their fantasies or running from something in their past.

Frederik placed the cigarette back in his mouth to purse a smile at his son's insouciance. Truly, if Leif wasn't his child, he'd find him sterling dinner company with a wry and wrathful wit. 'Fine', Frederik thought,

> if you want to proxy our conflict through literature, I'll use it against you, and still make you think: then you must believe the crew of the Pequod should have mutinied against their captain? That it was within their rights.

Seaman Apprentice Leif Bangsboll, age 14, as crew member of the HDMS Hekla (1932). (*Photo courtesy of the author's family collection*)

'But they did attempt to', Leif said,

> but they couldn't. Ahab had hired paid hunters and brought them aboard to assist him. He also bribed the lower officers to keep the top men in line. It was tyrannical. Like me, here on the *Hekla*, everyone aboard the *Pequod* was trapped.

'That wasn't my question.' Frederik said, trying to expand Leif's train of thought beyond hating him. 'Should they have tried to mutiny?'
'No', Leif said,

> they would have been killed. Ahab should have had the decency to leave them at the next port or transfer them to another ship. The men who didn't want to be there, should have been allowed to get on with their lives.

Frederik tapped the tip of a new cigarette on the table, then struck it with a match, preparing to delve further. 'What does the white whale mean to you?'

And exhaled his first stream of smoke, fully expecting his son to compare him to the mythical tormentor.

'Nothing', Leif responded, 'I didn't finish the book. It bored me.'

'Nonsense', Frederik said, calling Leif's bluff, 'if you read to the chapter with Ahab's hunters and the St Elmo's fire striking the coin, you practically finished the book.' The smoke formed a scrim against his tight features. 'What does the white whale mean to you?'

Leif crinkled his nose. His own precociousness having trapped him in Frederik's net.

I read in the book's annotations that Herman Melville was an American. An American who believed it was his mission to create a work of authentic American literature. Free from European influences.

Frederik nodded. Leif was correct.

'So, couldn't the great white whale be Europe?' Leif asked. 'The only way Melville, and America could be free, was to kill their father, Europe, the place they left. Their white whale.'

Frederik was awestruck. He had never even thought about examining *Moby Dick* from that angle, not to mention it sounded as if his son might want to kill him. 'But the great white whale kills almost the entire crew of *Pequod*. Are you saying Melville realized that America had to end in failure?'

'Even when you leave home' Leif said, evenly, 'you always bring part of it with you. You can never kill the father.'

Frederik was amazed at the suppleness of his son's mind. It was a finely calibrated analytical tool, capable of complex thought, waiting for the right person, the right passion to unleash its majesty. He also hoped for a day where he'd be able to talk about books with Leif – one of his favorite topics – and not have his shortcomings be the central trope of the discussion.

Following the dynamic dissection of *Moby Dick* by father and son, Frederik gave Leif some space and waited a few days before reengaging in scholastic discussions. Following dinner in the captain's cabin, Frederik asked Leif a few general questions about celestial navigation. Leif was familiar with the essential navigational instruments of a sailor, such as the magnetic compass and sextant, along with navigational charts of the ocean, having been taught their use by his father during their voyage on the *Svanen*. To ensure that his son's nautical skills remained sharp, Frederik would often take Leif up on deck of the *Hekla* to practice their use. Leif would be asked to determine the ship's exact location by use of these mariner's tools and soon became quite proficient. Leif particularly enjoyed those evenings when the night sky was cloudless, and the magnificent full expanse of the universe was projected above them. Shooting a correct azimuth off Polaris, the North Star – often referred to in the Royal Danish Navy as 'the sailor's star' – and seeing his father's subtle, but clear acknowledgement of the successful calculation was immensely rewarding for the young sailor. It was often at times such as these, under the countless stars, that his father would convey his deepest thoughts about his love of the sea and the majesty of the earth. Frederik would extol man's ability to master celestial navigation of such enormous, seemingly endless, expanses of water that surrounded them but would always end his lesson with a warning:

> Leif, man is a clever beast. But no matter how smart and strong we are, we will never conquer the sea. The best we can claim will be to have harnessed a small portion of its awesome power, and that of the celestial bodies which guide us with tools such as that sextant in your hand, and the charts on my desk. We should be satisfied and proud to have endured and survived the challenges and countless dangers she throws against us.

Leif understood.

* * *

While assigned to the *Hekla*, Leif also learned less dire, but none-the-less important, and practical lessons. For example, he learned his way around the galley, often assisting the ship's cook in the preparation of the officers' meals. Master Seaman Manfred Olsen, the senior cook on the *Hekla*, had taken an immediate liking to the lad and truly enjoyed helping him hone his cooking skills and learn some of the tricks of the trade of a sailor's life. Leif's father had instructed him to watch, listen and learn from the old sea dog, and that is what Leif did. Known as Manny to the crew of the *Hekla*, he observed during his time with Leif that the lad did not seek special attention, nor did his father offer it.

'The boy will earn his way in life, on his own merit. I like that.' thought Manny. Coincidently, Manny had been a brand new cook's assistant aboard the *Grønsund* some fifteen years earlier and was present at Leif's christening. As a result, he was not only a culinary mentor, but one of Leif's forty-two designated godfathers. There were several other godfathers from the *Grønsund* serving aboard the *Hekla* who also kept a close eye on their godson, all of which proved to be a blessing for Leif, as he was treated with a degree of respect and a sense of belonging seldom bestowed upon a mere cabin boy: the most junior position aboard a ship. Life at sea could be quite harsh and lonely. And although they were considered part of the crew complement, these young boys were not considered to be true sailors – certainly not by the sailors themselves – and had to earn the right to be called a sailor.

Despite his unique position, Leif was still expected, as a cabin boy, to pull his weight with many ship duties, including cleaning and painting the deck, loading and repositioning stores, preparing meals and training to fight fires. Under the close watch of Manny, Leif learned many things related to the galley's operations but also many things about the ship and its crew in general. He learned the fastest routes to and from the captain's cabin to the bridge, and from the galley to all the ship's various storerooms. Through his daily work activities, he learned who the bosses were, which sailors were decent men and helpful, and which were to be avoided. But it wasn't until the autumn of that year when the *Hekla* put to sea that Leif began to truly learn what life was like as a sailor on the high seas.

The threat of fire aboard ship is always of great concern, and all hands on deck must be trained and prepared to leap into action in the event of such an emergency. Leif's firefighting duties, although simple were important, nonetheless. At the sound of the alarm, no matter where he was aboard the ship, he was to rush to the galley and assist the cook with securing all culinary items and shutting down the gas valves and steam lines to all stoves and ovens. Then, once the galley was secure, he was to rush to fire station number 2–5 located on the second deck and assist with fire hose positioning duties until the emergency was dealt with. Leif learned the importance of training and being prepared for any emergency. As it turned out, Leif, the young cabin boy would show his metal during a real emergency, in which a fire broke out in the galley and without hesitation, he saved his shipmate, friend and mentor Manny the cook from serious injury or even possible death. The ship's crew was impressed with Leif's brave actions, Manny was forever grateful and the ship's captain proud.

It was the beginning of September 1932, the *Hekla* had completed its annual training cycle, conducted in the relative safety of the Baltic Sea, close to its home port of Copenhagen. Now, the *Hekla* was four days out from Denmark on its way south and west across the Atlantic to the former Danish settlements at St Croix and St Thomas, West Indies. The *Hekla* was just south-west of the southern tip of England, when she encountered rough seas and Leif spent the better part of two days and nights clutching the sides of his canvas hammock and repeatedly staggering to the latrine to empty the contents of his stomach.

Within a week and after gaining his sea legs on the great expanse of the Atlantic, life aboard the *Hekla* became more enjoyable and more routine. Looking after the ship's captain offered Frederik and Leif an opportunity to rekindle their bonds of trust: a sailor to commander and father to son. Leif also continued helping Manny in the galley, where cooking became even more familiar and enjoyable work for the young man.

It was during one occasion while working in the galley preparing food for the midday meal that Leif noticed Manny whistling a lively tune as he moved about the galley. Feeling brave, but remaining polite, Leif approached Manny, 'My father says that whistling aboard a ship will bring bad luck to the ship and its crew.'

The cook stopped his food preparation for a moment, then looked at the boy and smiled. 'That is true enough', he replied, 'but go ask your father to tell you the rest of the myth and come back and tell me what he says.'

Disappointed by the answer, Leif left the galley. It seemed like the one time Leif was sure of himself about an aspect of sea life – in this case, the myth about whistling on board a ship – he once again found himself unsure of what was true and what was false. Now he would have to go back to his father and find out the rest of the story – nothing was ever easy when you were a sailor.

Later that evening in the captain's cabin, as Leif was taking care of his father's end-of-day routines: collecting his uniform shirt and trousers to be taken to the ship's laundry and setting aside the captain's shoes, which he would shine later that night, Leif asked his father if there was more to the sea myth about whistling on board a ship.

'Why do you ask, Jocom?' asked his father.

Leif explained his brief exchange with Manny in the galley earlier in the day.

'And what did Manfred tell you?' Frederik asked.

'He said I should come ask you, since you were the one who had originally told me of this superstition.'

'And right he was to do so.' Frederik said, calling Leif forward with a slight gesture of his hand. Leif came over to his father, who was sitting behind his large wooden work desk with papers and sea navigation charts strewn across it.

'Yes, papa?' said Leif.

Frederik came around the desk and with both hands gently holding his son's face, the ship's captain drew him closer and said,

> The myth is true lad, whistling aboard ship will most assuredly bring bad fortune to those who sail upon her. But that rule does not apply to the ship's cooks while they are in the galley.

'But why father? Why is it safe for only the cook to whistle?' demanded Leif.

> Well, Jocom, if the captain can hear the cook whistling in the galley, he knows that the cook is preparing the food for the crew and not eating the food himself.

Frederik's eyebrows rose in a gesture of *Do you understand?* The young boy's face lit up with a smile. With this new information, Leif collected his father's uniform and dashed off to the ship's laundry room. He couldn't wait to find Manny and tell him what he had learned and, even more so, he couldn't wait to be asked to help in the galley again so he could whistle, too.

Leif would get many more opportunities to help in the galley and he would frequently take that opportunity to practice his whistling skills while safely defying maritime lore within the confines of the ship's galley. However, on one occasion, when Manny allowed his young charge to take care of preparing the dessert for the crew on the day shift – known as the 'Dog Watch' – Leif nearly crippled the entire crew complement by a series of errors in meal production. Mistakenly adding three times more canned prunes than the recipe called for and then failing to dilute the condensed milk in the creation of a batch of fruit pies, Leif unwittingly fed the crew of the ship an extraordinarily rich dessert. As a result, approximately an hour after the Dog Watch had consumed their meal, and young Leif's delicious dessert, an epidemic of gastro distress hit the crew with a vengeance. The well-meaning but misguided cabin boy received an extra two weeks of kitchen duties as a punishment for his culinary error and Leif thought, 'Maybe whistling in the galley is not safe after all.'

Much as he enjoyed helping the ship's cook, Leif eventually found himself spending more of his free time in the ship's engine room with the engineers, learning about what made the ship function. It was noisy and hot, and always reeked of diesel fuel. And although it often involved back-breaking work, the environment struck a chord with him. Much of what Leif learned from the *Hekla*'s engineers would influence his future endeavors as a cadet at the in Copenhagen and guide the next chapter in his apprenticeship at sea.

In the meantime, the *Hekla*'s mission to the former Danish naval station in the West Indies was completed without incident. From there, *Hekla* sailed due north, past the eastern coast of the United States, around the Canadian maritime provinces of Nova Scotia, Newfoundland and Labrador. Up the Davis Straight *Hekla* sailed, amongst the enormous white and blue shaded icebergs that drifted slowly southward on the Labrador Current in the opposite direction; continuing northward to the first scheduled destination of Julianehåb (modern day Oaqortoq), and from there even further north to the small coastal village known as Qaanaaq in the native Greenlander language (or Thule pronounced 'Tooley').

Thule would become one of Leif's most favorite places in the world. It was a place of vast rugged mountains and fjords, frozen ice fields and enormous glaciers and, above all, wonderfully happy, kind people known as native Greenlanders. After a short, yet fascinating stay in Thule, the *Hekla* returned to Holmen Naval

Base; by then it was late October 1932 and the completion of Leif's first voyage with the Royal Danish Navy.

* * *

It was a time when Leif was able to spend a few weeks back home in Nærum, the seaside suburb of Copenhagen with Frederik – solely as his father now, and not as the captain. It was when they were home, away from the ship's busy activities and essential routines that Leif's father began to notice the positive changes that had come over his son. Leif was more focused and responsible, and more talkative and opinionated on many subjects. But most of all, Leif seemed happier than he had been for years. His first real working voyage and experience at sea, alongside his father, had been enriching for both son and father, and both were eager to return to the *Hekla* after their break ashore.

In the spring, Frederik, along with Leif sailed the *Hekla* into the Baltic Sea, for a month to promote good international relations with Denmark's neighbors, making port calls at Stockholm, Helsinki, Leningrad (modern day St Petersburg), Tallinn, Riga and Gdansk. For Leif, it was a culturally enriching trip, the foreign ports were beautiful and the residence friendly.

That summer, the *Hekla* rejoined the submarine fleet for training and exercises in the North Sea. During that time, Leif was given the opportunity to spend six weeks abord the Danish submarine *Neptune*, this time as a junior apprentice sailor, not as a cabin boy. The experience gave him the utmost respect for those submariners who serve below the waves. Life on the submarine was an odd combination of excitement – during the onboard, high-intensity operations and training exercises – intermixed with long bouts of boredom and the claustrophobic feel of life in a steel chamber below the surface of the sea. For Leif, the greatest challenges were getting use to the claustrophobically cramped work spaces, constant smell of diesel fuel and the pungent odor of sweat from thirty-five sailors, which was exacerbated by having to hot-bunk (alternating sharing the use of small bunk bed) and finally, eating meals that were mostly unidentifiable – it seemed that the secret to the *Neptune*'s cook's daily menu was to smother everything in gravy or sauce making the content of the meal a bit of a mystery.

By mid-July 1933, with its sea training completed, the *Neptune* made a port stop in Copenhagen before returning to its main operating base in Frederikshavn to undergo repairs and scheduled maintenance. With his brief sea duty aboard the *Neptune* complete, Leif disembarked at the Holmen Naval Base where he was enthusiastically met by his father. The irony of this role reversal was not lost on Frederik as he embraced his sailor son. Father and son spent the remainder of the summer together at their home in Nærum, during which Leif regaled his father with his recent experiences at sea – below the surface.

During this time – within the confines of the *Neptune* – dreams of an alternative profession began to develop for Leif, as thoughts of clean, fresh air and sufficient space to move freely were constantly on his mind.

* * *

In September 1933, Leif, now 15 years old, with eighteen months of rugged sea-duty under his belt walked with his father through the entrance of Sølvgades school once more. This time, Leif was bigger, stronger and worldlier in his views as a result of a year and a half at sea with the navy. Now he was prepared, even eager, to complete his schooling because he knew it was a means to an end for him. He had finally concluded that he wanted to be an engineer – a naval engineer – and to achieve that he would first need to graduate from secondary school.

At first skeptical of Master Bangsbøll's intent, the headmaster of Sølvgades school eventually relented and agreed to interview Leif as a prospective returning student. The headmaster quickly realized that this was not the same disinterested and undisciplined boy he had once known. Clearly, Leif had changed, and changed for the better. With the approval of the school's headmaster, Leif was re-enrolled at Sølvgades.

Over the next two years, Leif would excel at his studies, focusing mostly on mathematics and science as these subjects would be most important in his future maritime engineering program. Leif still enjoyed studying history, geography and even some of the literary arts. The maturing young man enjoyed rereading the many Shakespearean plays he had read while assigned to the *Hekla*. He was most fond of *Hamlet*, as the story was of kings and ghosts, and took place in his beloved Denmark. Leif would even get the chance to live his dream and play Hamlet, the melancholy Dane, in a school production of the eponymous Shakespeare play – albeit in a vastly truncated form. The Sølvgades school presentation of *Hamlet* suffered from a teen audience's attention span, necessitating half the script to be cut, not to mention, there weren't enough dormitory mothers to cover all the speaking female parts. However, even under those less than ideal theatrical conditions, Leif experienced the thrill of live performance, the vivacity of thinking on your feet, and improvising your way out of tricky situations, like when you or your co-star drop or downright forget half the lines in a scene. Little did he know that acting and assuming a new character, and improvising in a tight situation would be a skill Leif would need to rely upon in the years to come.

* * *

An Apprenticeship at Sea   47

During this time, Leif's father, recently promoted to naval captain, became the technical advisor to Admiral Wolfgang Vedel, commander of the Royal Danish Submarine Fleet. Subsequently, and as a direct result of Admiral Vedel's recommendation, Frederik was appointed commandant of the Danish Submarine School. Both of these assignments allowed Leif and Frederik to spend more time together, in a non-work environment. Frederik was proud that his son had faced the challenges of the sea, returned to complete his schooling, and seemed to be excelling. He also knew that this positive turn of events would have made Leif's mother proud as well.

* * *

During summer 1935, following his graduation from Sølvgades and before commencing his engineering program at the Danish Maritime Academy, Frederik offered Leif the opportunity to be a member of the crew aboard HDMS *Dannebrog*. Used primarily as a Royal Danish Navy training ship for cadets, the *Dannebrog* was a three-mast schooner built in the 1870s, an awesome vessel of a bygone era. With a sleek design combining wood and steel, three huge masts supporting massive canvas sails, and a modified steam-powered engine installed in the early 1900s, it was a sea-going marvel. In its prime, it could fly across the sea in a couple of weeks. With the modernization, it was less maneuverable in high seas but more capable at slower speeds and in calmer waters. With the addition of the new steam-driven propulsion system, the *Dannebrog*'s three top sails had been removed. This hybrid vessel, though more versatile, was neither a complete sailing ship, nor a fully motorized vessel. This distinction would have significant ramifications on the lives of the crew and passengers during their upcoming voyage.

Seaman Leif Bangsboll, (17) on board HDMS Dannebrog 1935 on route from Copenhagen to Thule Greenland to return Edward Shackleton and the Oxford University Ellesmere Land Expedition. (*Photo courtesy of the author's family collection*)

The *Dannebrog* was scheduled to sail to Greenland as Denmark's

His Danish Majesties Ship *Dannebrog* at anchor, Thule Greenland, 1935 as part of the Oxford University Ellesmere Land Expedition led by Edward Shackleton. (*Photo courtesy of the author's family collection*)

contribution to Edward Shackleton's Ellesmere Land Expedition of the Canadian Arctic and western Greenland, part of the University of Oxford sponsored Arctic exploration program. For this particular – and special – international mission, the *Dannebrog* would transport the necessary winter supplies, including tons of coal, to several ports in Greenland. The *Dannebrog* would then rendezvous with the Shackleton team to bring the explorers back to England, the final phase of their year-long exploration of the Canadian and Danish Arctic.

During Leif's final year at Sølvgades school, and after more than a year's preparation, the Shackleton expedition had departed London, England, on board the Norwegian Sealer ship *Signalhorn* on 17 July 1934. The expedition had originally been scheduled to be conveyed to Greenland aboard the *Dannebrog*. However, delays in the expedition's preparations precluded the *Dannebrog*'s use, as she was scheduled to resupply the Greenlanders with vital stores for the winter and her departure could not be delayed. As a result, Shackleton was required to contract the Norwegian replacement ship *Signalhorn* to transport the six members of the expedition and their ten tons of supplies to western Greenland.

The University of Oxford Ellesmere Land Expedition was a multinational effort with an ensemble of explorers, scientists, botanists and biologists who realized the importance of exploring and understanding the lesser-known Arctic region. Sponsored by the National Geographic Society and the University of Oxford, the governments of Canada and Denmark, as well as the Danish-

An Apprenticeship at Sea   49

Leif and crew member of the HDMS Dannebrog going ashore at Thule Greenland, 1935. (*Photo courtesy of the author's family collection*)

Greenland Administration, the expedition had the logistical support of both the British Royal Navy and the Royal Danish Navy. During its year-long scientific expedition, the assembled team, using dog sleds to survey and chart undocumented areas of the northern Arctic region between Canada and Greenland. As well, the explorers conducted botanic research and visited numerous villages along the western coast of Greenland.

Edward Shackleton, the youngest son of Sir Ernest Shackleton, the famed British explorer of Antarctica, was the expedition's organizer and surveyor, and was joined by Dr Noel Humphreys, the lead surveyor and botanist, along with Sergeant Henry Stallworthy of the Royal Canadian Mounted Police (RCMP). Filling out the complement of the exploration team was Mr Robert Bentham, an Arctic travel expert and geologist, Mr David Haig-Thomas, an ornithologist, and Mr Winston Moore, a photographer and biologist.

While Leif had been diligently applying himself to his academic studies during his final year at Sølvgades school in Copenhagen, Edward Shackleton together with his five colleagues and two native Greenlander guides were facing the perils of the Arctic. But soon enough their paths would cross very far from home.

In mid-June 1935, Leif, excitedly accepted his father's offer to sail on the *Dannebrog* and reported for duty on 1 July 1935. As one of only eighteen crew members and, yet again, the youngest of the group, Leif was thankful for the previous sailing experience he had gained under his father's tutelage aboard the

Leif at Thule Greenland with the villages' school teacher, nurse and child, 1935 prior to departing for England and Denmark. (*Photo courtesy of the author's family collection*)

Svanen during their adventurous trip to Bergen, Norway, his year aboard the *Hekla* and his time on the submarine *Neptune*. As the *Dannebrog* was a vessel of another era, knowing how to tie proper rope knots and rig sails was an essential part of Leif's duties on the ship. He worked hard to acquaint himself with the ship's routine and the idiosyncrasies that every ship possesses. Leif had a month to prepare himself for the voyage and had no difficulties doing so.

As part of those preparations, and as a prospective maritime engineer, Leif was keen to learn how the modification of a traditional sailing schooner into a 400-horsepower steam engine worked. Not surprisingly, he spent much of his time working with the ship's first mate and engineer, learning the workings of the vessel's propulsion and steering systems.

Upon the orders of the ship's captain, Lars Peterson – and this time with his father standing on the pier to bid Leif farewell – the *Dannebrog* set sail from Copenhagen harbor on 12 July 1935 – marking Leif's seventeenth birthday. Full of essential stores required by the Danish Greenlanders, the *Dannebrog* was scheduled to arrive in Thule, Greenland, by mid-August 1935. The plan was to deliver the winter stores, including 30 tons of coal destined for Julianehåb (modern day Qaqortoq) and Jakobshavn (also known as Ilulissat), and then to rendezvous with the Shackleton's Artic expedition in Qaanaaq (Thule).

The voyage to Greenland was completed without incident. The weather was fair, although the presence of so many massive white and turquoise icebergs kept the crew on constant alert as they passed Cape Farewell, the southernmost point of Greenland, and entered the Davis Strait, known to mariners as Iceberg Alley. Countless floating mountains of ice had calved-off hundreds of glaciers, which lined the coast of Davis Strait or had broken away from the Arctic ice pack and over the months and years had slowly made their way into the southerly current of the Davis Strait and eventually into the North Atlantic Ocean. Though dangerous to ships' navigation, they had become beautifully sculpted behemoths, worn smooth by the endless assault of wind and waves. They were a marvelous site to behold.

After depositing its cargo at Julianehåb and Jakobshavn, the *Dannebrog* proceeded up the western coast of Greenland to Thule, where, on 16 August 1935, she laid anchor a few hundred yards offshore. From their anchorage, the *Dannebrog*'s crew could see the leading edge and feel the cold air emanating from the massive Humboldt Glacier, which loomed in the distance as a backdrop to Thule. As well, Mount Dundas, with its dramatic volcano-like shape, stood prominently off to the north. The mountain appeared to have had the top half of its peak sheared off, flat as a plate. In fact, the mountain top had been ground-flat by the enormous and relentless power generated by the passage of ancient glaciers.

After only a few minutes at anchor, a single kayak came paddling out to greet the *Dannebrog*. Its occupant, wearing a traditional seal fur parka, was a local Greenlander who spoke Danish. He confirmed that the Ellesmere expedition had arrived in Thule two days earlier from their final staging base of Etah, located 80 miles north, and were waiting ashore, keen to meet the captain and crew. Raising the anchor, the *Dannebrog* slowly maneuvered closer to shore under steam power and carefully came alongside the pier that jutted out into the bay. There, the *Dannebrog* was moored under the shadow of Mount Dundas.

Captain Peterson went ashore and was formally met by the village doctor, nurse, school teacher and administrator, along with Edward Shackleton, Dr Noel Humphreys and Winston Moore from the Ellesmere expedition. After Captain Peterson spoke with his reception party, he ordered the crew to begin unloading the cargo from the *Dannebrog*. All the local Inuit and Danish Greenlanders of the village – about 100 people in total – came down to greet the *Dannebrog* and assist its crew. Rejoicing at the arrival of their mail and their winter provisions – including fine specialty items from Denmark – everyone was in a festive mood.

The extraction of the last 600 coal-laden burlap sacks, weighing 60 pounds each, from the *Dannebrog*'s hold was not a quick or easily completed task. With the assistance of some of the local Greenlanders, the crew went to work hauling coal bags up from the bowels of the *Dannebrog*. In no time, the white faces of the Danish crew were covered in sweat and blackened from the coal dust. This delighted the local children who taunted and teased the sailors to no end. Leif, being the youngest of the crew, enjoyed the company of the young children and played with them by chasing them and making frightening faces and arm gestures to both scare and entertain them. Silently watching from the pier where the *Dannebrog* was moored, Edward Shackleton noted the youthful enthusiasm of the young Danish sailor and his playful interaction with the children. Though he did not yet know it, other than Captain Peterson, this young sailor was the only one of the *Dannebrog*'s crew that had been to Thule previously. Leif was thrilled to be back amongst the expanses of raw, natural beauty of the Arctic. In addition to its natural grandeur, the Arctic was blessed with wonderful, kind people who were friendly, generous and courageously resilient.

As Shackleton watched the crew and local Greenlanders work to unload the ship as the children played, he mused on the fact that he was witnessing one of the fundamental realities of life in the Arctic and thought,

> To survive, one must cooperate with our fellow inhabitants and one must anticipate and adapt and be prepared for whatever the weather conditions demand.

Today the weather is mild and calm so work will continue until it is complete, and no one questions the long, grueling hours of labor. For tomorrow we may be inundated and prevented from working because of high winds, frigid temperatures and feet of new snow. Shackleton and his small team of explorers had just spent a year in the most inhospitable climates on earth and were living proof of these fundamental rules.

During the month of August 1935, at 77° north latitude the sun does not set. Though the breeze coming off the nearby glacier was cold, the five hours it took to unload the *Dannebrog* was completed by midnight, under the warm, bright sunlight of the Arctic summer night. As Leif assisted with the unloading of the *Dannebrog*'s cargo and subsequently the loading of personal items from the expedition and retrograde freight and mail from the villagers, he could not help but notice the fatigue on the faces of the six expedition members. Leif was eager to speak with them to hear what living in the arctic for an entire year was like; but that could wait he thought. 'There will be plenty of time for talk. We'll be sailing together for a month on their return journey to England.'

The *Dannebrog* remained moored in Thule for another two days to allow the crew to rest, enjoy some local hospitality and explore. Following a visit to the local schoolhouse, Leif trekked up Mount Dundas with several others of the *Dannebrog*'s crew. Surrounded by the marvelous expanse of white ice of the massive Humboldt Glacier, looking out across the glistening blue sea dotted with icebergs, and taking in the expanse of slate gray rocks that dominate the Greenland geography, all under the brilliance of a sunny, cloudless blue sky, Leif was in awe.

On the morning of their planned departure, the crew and the passengers were well rested from their three-day respite in Thule and were all eager to get home to England or Denmark respectively. Following his breakfast in the galley, Captain Peterson instructed Leif to advise their six expedition passengers that the *Dannebrog* would 'set sail at ten bells' that morning and that they should make their farewells to the villagers sooner rather than later. Leif found Dr Humphreys on deck with four others from the team and passed on the captain's orders. Dr Humphreys indicated that Shackleton was below deck in his quarters, and that Leif should go advise him there of their departure plan.

Knocking softly on Shackleton's cabin door, Leif heard the response, 'Enter!' Shackleton was at his small desk with many papers laid out before him and was scribing words into a notebook – his journal. He did not look up and continued writing.

'What is it, doctor?' he asked. Leif could not help but let out a small laugh at Shackleton's mistake. Shackleton looked up and said with a smile, 'Oh excuse me, son, I was expecting Dr Humphreys.'

That's quite alright, sir. The captain bids me to advise you, sir, that the *Dannebrog* will set sail this morning at ten bells and that if you wish to go ashore for any reason you should do so soon.

Leif added a polite node when he finished speaking and turned to leave.
'Wait a moment, lad.' Leif stopped abruptly and returned to the doorway.
'Yes, sir?' he asked.
'You're the sailor that was playing with the village children the day we were unloading the coal, aren't you?'

Ah, yes, sir, but I only strayed from my duties for a few moments to play. The children seemed quite entertained by my sweaty, coal-covered face. I think they thought I was some sort of monster.

'I meant no criticism. You're not much more than a child yourself – you should be allowed to play. What's your name, son?'
'Leif Bangsbøll, sir. But you can call me Jocom… it's a nickname my father gave me when I was little, but close friends call me that too.'
'Well Jocom it is.' said Shackleton. 'Jocom, please go tell Dr Humphreys that I will be up presently, I just need to finalize an entry in my journal.'

Leif replied with a crisp, 'Yes, sir!' closed the cabin door and ran up to the deck to pass on Shackleton's message.

As the sound of Leif scurrying up the ladder to the main deck faded, Shackleton looked down at his journal, at his last entry. He reflected on where his thoughts had been prior to the pleasant interruption by the young Danish sailor boy. Shackleton thought,

> The expedition members are eager to set sail for England, yet we all have our misgivings about leaving our Arctic home. We've grown close to the people of Greenland, especially our Greenlander guides, Inutuk and Nukapinguaq. They've cared for us for the past year like we were family. Clearly, we all feel a growing sadness at the prospects of the expedition coming to an end.

Shackleton picked up his pencil and began to write,

> *As we began to make preparations to depart from Thule, a remarkable change, and one for which we had obscure feelings of regret, came over our lives. No longer were we destitute white men living as the guests and friends of the simple Eskimos in the midst of this beautiful but harsh land. Our circumstances had altered magically by the arrival of the Dannebrog with all its resources, tangible emblems of European civilization. Somehow our Eskimo friends now seemed separated from us by a previously non-existent gulf ...*

Shackleton closed his journal and went up on deck to join his team who were now on the quay bidding farewell to their Thule hosts. It was an emotional parting of ways for the expedition team and their two Greenlander guides – for a year they had explored thousands of miles of rugged terrain of Greenland and Ellesmere land, they had lived together and survived the unforgiving arctic, facing great dangers, enjoying close comradeship and sharing their cultures.

At precisely 'ten bells', Captain Peterson gave the order to cast-off the *Dannebrog*'s lines and engage the steam engine to slow ahead to navigate out of Thule Bay. Once in the channel, with a brisk but steady wind whipping across the Humboldt Glacier behind them, the captain ordered the main sails to be dropped and the engine turned off. The *Dannebrog* was under sail and on its way home.

The return voyage to England would be scenic, but not without its challenges. The first part of the voyage was spent traveling south along the Davis Strait, joining the hundreds of icebergs in their mass migration southward. Next, the *Dannebrog* made brief stops along the coast at Godhavn (modern day Qeqertarsuaq), Holsteinsborg (modern day Sisimiut) and Julianehåb, primarily to pick up mail.

The *Dannebrog*'s unique design was explained to Shackleton during a dinner with Captain Petersen, the evening before the *Dannebrog* was scheduled to go round the southern tip of Greenland with the expanse of the North Atlantic ahead. Shackleton wrote in his journal that night that the captain had fondly referred to the *Dannebrog* as 'Denmark's bastard of the sea.' Shackleton also included comments from the captain that indicated,

> without the coal in the cargo hold, the little ballast gained by the Shackleton exploration equipment and the mail and a dozen barrels of dried fish being shipped back to Europe, the *Dannebrog* was riding high in the water and would perform poorly in high seas.

Shackleton prided himself on his ability to judge the character of people as he observed them in action and accordingly, he described Captain Lars Petersen, the commander of the *Dannebrog* as the epitome of a professional, seasoned sea captain:

> *He is a strong, rugged man of focused purpose yet with a pleasant personality ... like many men of the sea, he was a man of few words, but when he speaks, all in his presence seem to listen. The Danish sailors too, who were mostly young fellows between the ages of 16 and 22, were a very fine lot, friendly, polite and well-educated and seven of the nine could speak very good English. The youngest sailor, whose nickname is Jokim [Jocom] is a delight ... we get along quite well. On our first day of the voyage back to England, Jokim [Jocom] warned me of the traditional Danish drinking game the sailors like to play ... it's called: 'Hundebidde' ... literally translated as 'Dog Bite'. Thankful of the young Dane's warning, I managed to politely participate on several occasions during the voyage home, when offered the chance, but kept my wits about me in order to extricate myself from the festivities in a timely manner before things got out of hand.*

Once past the southernmost tip of Greenland at Cape Farewell, they steered east, where the sailing was clear for a week. In a thoughtful moment, Leif realized that it was here, at Cape Farewell, five years earlier that his father, then sailing with his friend and colleague Knud Rasmussen, had received the wireless message of the death of Leif's mother. Leif found it difficult to comprehend that so much time had elapsed – how had he managed without her? Since Rigmor's death, Leif had changed. Though not quite yet a man, he had seen and done so much already. He had traversed the seas in modern iron war ships, sailed in traditional wooden ships with masts, sails and rigging, and experienced the claustrophobic life aboard a submarine. He had faced the sea's perils and survived to tell the tales. He had been lost at sea and found again. He had danced on snow with local people in fur-lined mukluks and parkas, shared traditional meals of whale and seal blubber and witnessed the beauty of never-ending Arctic summer sunsets. He had sailed with brave explorers and met all sorts of adventurous people – and he was just 17 years old.

Letter from Edward Shackleton, leader of the Oxford University Ellesmere Land Expedition (1934–35) to Leif Bangsboll, 31 November 1935. (*Photo courtesy of the author's family collection*)

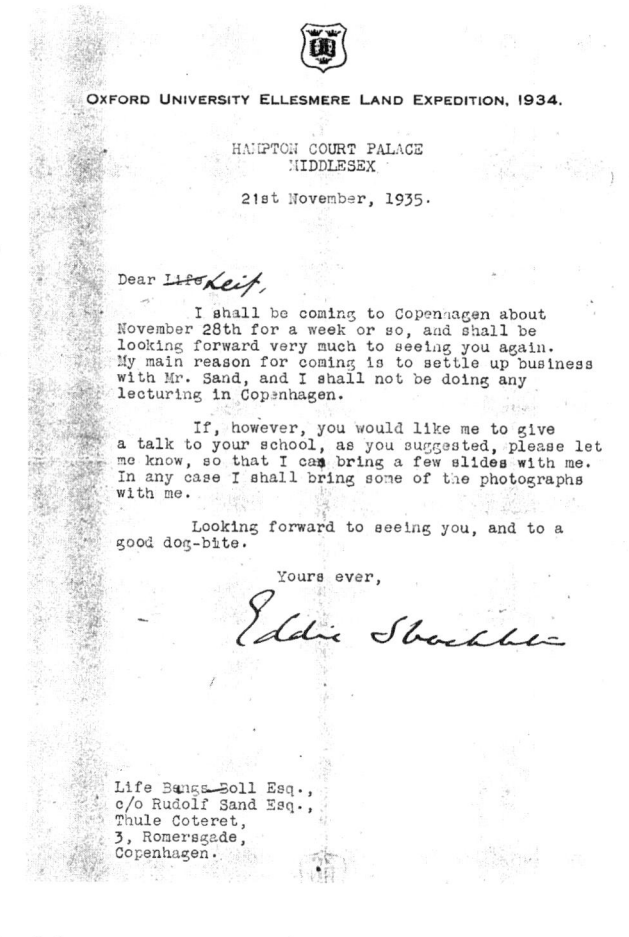

OXFORD UNIVERSITY ELLESMERE LAND EXPEDITION, 1934.

HAMPTON COURT PALACE
MIDDLESEX

21st November, 1935.

Dear Leif,

I shall be coming to Copenhagen about November 28th for a week or so, and shall be looking forward very much to seeing you again. My main reason for coming is to settle up business with Mr. Sand, and I shall not be doing any lecturing in Copenhagen.

If, however, you would like me to give a talk to your school, as you suggested, please let me know, so that I can bring a few slides with me. In any case I shall bring some of the photographs with me.

Looking forward to seeing you, and to a good dog-bite.

Yours ever,

Eddie Shackleton

Life Bangs-Boll Esq.,
c/o Rudolf Sand Esq.,
Thule Coteret,
3, Romersgade,
Copenhagen.

For the first week of their return voyage, the weather had been good, with calm seas, blue skies and fair winds. Then, with Greenland fading behind them and Europe much further ahead, the winds faded away and the *Dannebrog* was confronted by a wall of fog that stretched across their entire easterly view, horizon to horizon. Within a few minutes of encountering the fog bank, the ship was enveloped by the thick white mist. While not unusual at that time of the year in that region of the North Atlantic, precautions still had to be taken. Wary of icebergs and of other ships, Captain Peterson ordered all lights to be illuminated, and assigned a crewman to sound the ship's bell every minute in an effort to be seen or heard by any other nearby ocean-going vessels. The *Dannebrog*, now relying on its steam engine, needed to keep a minimum speed of 3 knots in order to be able to steer out of the way and avoid collisions with any icebergs or have any chance to avoid other ships in their path. The ship was virtually adrift, moving slowly but blindly in an eastward direction. The stress level of the crew had noticeably increased.

An Apprenticeship at Sea   57

As he stood on deck that first evening of fog, Leif saw that the dense haze and the ship's navigation lights made for an eerie sight. It reminded him of a story his father had told him one night on the *Hekla* when he was serving as his cabin boy. The topic of ghosts had come up in the conversation as father and son discussed the reading Leif had just completed of *Hamlet*. Frederik had gone on to tell his son the Scandinavian sea fable of the Clabowder Man, a ghostly apparition whose unwelcome appearance on a ship foreshadows the coming of disaster. Leif had been intrigued by the story as any teenage boy would be, but at 15 was too old to admit to his father that it had frightened him.

The following night on the *Dannebrog*, the second amidst the heavy fog, the story his father had recounted to him became all too real. A late-night occurrence, both frightening and fascinating, opened up a world of mystic possibilities to Leif. On that night in the fog, the *Dannebrog* was allegedly visited by the Clabowder Man.

Late that evening, Leif was resting below deck in his hammock, but was not yet asleep. There were several other crew members off duty and snoring in their shared crew quarters and the minute by minute sounding of the anti-collision bell was comforting, yet alarming and hypnotic. A diffused glow from the ship's navigation lights came through the porthole just off to Leif's left. Just as he felt the soft, alluring touch of sleep wash over him he was startled when the gray-green light coming through the porthole wavered. As he looked towards the porthole, the shape of a large hand appeared on the glass, and lingered there for a moment, as if someone were balancing or bracing themselves against the porthole as they walked along the deck. 'But the sea is dead calm', Leif thought, 'there should be no need to balance oneself.' Still half asleep he considered, 'Why would any of the crew be walking along the deck at this time of night?' A chill ran up his spine.

Leif was now fully awake. He left his bunk and went into the adjoining galley where several other, on-duty crew members were drinking coffee. He joined them and it was all just small talk about the fog and its delay of their voyage home. 'Two of the four on-duty crew are here in the galley', Leif thought, as the conversation continued around him,

> that leaves one at the helm and one manning the anti-collision bell. Could it have been one of the passenger's hands I saw? But surely, they're all in their bunks asleep at this late hour.

Leif thought it wise not to mention what he had seen through the porthole in the crew quarters. 'The others would surely laugh at my childish fears.'

After a few minutes of idle chatter in the galley, a sudden commotion of shouts emanating from up on deck could be heard. Instinctively, Leif and the other two crew members responded to the sounds and clambered up the ladder to the main deck. While moving briskly with the rest of his crew mates coming up from their sleeping quarters, Leif's mind raced with thoughts about the possible cause of the raised voice they had heard on deck.

> Has another ship been sighted? Are we in danger of a collision? Or, God forbid, has someone fallen overboard? In this fog we might never find them!

As the rest of crew from the sleeping quarters assembled on the deck, they all frantically looked forward and aft to locate the crew member who had raised the alarm. There, at midship, just forward of the wheelhouse stood Arne, the crew member who was manning the anti-collision bell. He was standing beside the ship's bell and looking towards the bow of the ship. As he heard the others approach, he did not turn to them or take his hand off the bell's rope but pointed forward with his free hand and spoke, Look there, lads', he said, 'who is that standing on the bow?'

All eyes followed Arne's gaze and his outstretched arm. There, shrouded in fog was the silhouette of man standing on the railing of the bow of the ship. The figure had its back towards the crew and had one hand holding a rope of the fore mast's rigging for balance. His other hand appeared to be shading his eyes as if he were searching for something in the depths of the fog bank ahead. The figure appeared to be wearing a long, dark raincoat and a sou'wester oilskin rain hat, common among sailors. With all the crew present, Leif considered that it must be one of the six passengers of the Shackleton team. Then the oldest, and senior member of the crew amongst them, yelled out, 'You there, come away from the rail – it's not safe up there!' The figure did not move.

Moments later, Captain Peterson arrived on deck, pushed his way through the crew members and stood in front of the gathering. Realizing that all ten crew members were on deck, and that by now the six passengers had joined them at the commotion, Captain Peterson moved forward several steps to address the intruder. For an instant Leif thought, 'the crew and passengers are all present, it must be a stowaway.'

Just as Captain Petersen took another step forward and prepared to speak, a billowing wall of heavier fog enveloped the bow of the ship, obscuring the view of the forward half of the vessel and the figure standing upon it. Seconds later, the fog dissipated momentarily and the bow reappeared. There was nothing there but an empty railing, ropes and rigging. The Clabowder Man had appeared and was gone.

Unsure of what they had all just experienced, but determined to control the situation, Captain Petersen began giving orders for the passengers to go back to their quarters and for the rest to get on with their duties or go back to their quarters. Leif made his way back to his hammock and lay awake the remainder of the night reflecting on what he had seen, 'I don't know who or what I saw, but I did see something.' He overheard his fellow crew members whispering from their bunks in the dark of the crew cabin. 'It was the Clabowder Man… the Clabowder Man.'

The next morning, the wind picked up, the fog dissipated and the *Dannebrog* was making good speed once again. 'See!' Leif overhead one of the other crew members exclaim. 'The weather has cleared and we are in full sail again. That omen of the Clabowder Man is nonsense!' And the *Dannebrog* sailed on, making good time.

As expected, the *Dannebrog* passed the southeastern coast of Iceland three days later, but as it did, the ship ran into a gale that even the experienced Captain Petersen found to be of unusually strong force and duration. Making matters worse, the storm had pushed sea ice southward into the shipping lanes and, as a result, the *Dannebrog* struck something – possibly a partially submerged iceberg, which broke the ship's rudder and damaged the propeller. Without engine propulsion, the hybrid vessel was tossed about in the high seas like a cork. Unable to steer effectively, the *Dannebrog* was caught up in sea currents that took it well off course, northward towards Scotland rather than on its southern bearing towards the south of England.

Seven days passed before the crippled *Dannebrog* limped into the harbor at Castle Bay on the Isle of Barra in the Outer Hebrides. It would take nearly a week to repair the *Dannebrog* before it was able to sail again. With the rudder repaired but the steam-drive still out of commission, Captain Peterson agreed to deliver the Shackleton party to the nearest landfall. With the winds up and the *Dannebrog* at full sails, Captain Peterson set a course for Oban, Scotland.

Two days later, as the *Dannebrog* lay at anchor in the Oban harbor waiting for the harbor master's boat to arrive to ferry its passengers and their belongings to shore, Edward Shackleton used the time to log his final *Dannebrog* voyage entry in his journal:

Disaster nearly overtook us during a tremendous storm about 700 miles off the west coast of Scotland – the propeller had been fractured by ice and half of the propeller was lost … causing great vibration and oscillation which bent the drive shaft … no engine/propulsion and with no top sails, the ship did not navigate well … skilful seamanship by Captain Petersen saved us, I'm sure. Captain Petersen was now rather anxious about our landfall options, and as we passed the southern end of the Outer Hebrides, the wind came up and he decided to put in to the little island of Barra, as the wind was beginning to veer us to the south-east. To the amazement of the local fishing people, the Dannebrog rounded the channel buoy like a racing yacht, missing the reef by a few feet, and at last dropped anchor in the safe haven of Castle Bay – thankful to a most skillful piece of seamanship by Captain Petersen and his young crew of Danish lads. Another tremendous gale came in that evening which would have most certainly been the end of us had the Dannebrog not been at anchor in the safety of the Castle Bay harbor. With the Dannebrog out of action, the expedition will go ashore at Oban, Scotland and we will make our way with all haste back to London by coach and train – I am thankful to be alive and look forward to being back on British soil.

And so, it was Edward Shackleton and his five companions from the University of Oxford Ellesmere Land Expedition to bid farewell to the *Dannebrog* and its crew. Though Shackleton's report did not include any mention of the alleged strange visitation of the Clabowder Man, Leif recalled that during their voyage, Shackleton seemed to enjoy hearing the sailors recount the Scandinavian myth and had mused at the timeliness of the *Dannebrog*'s misfortune with the bad weather and her broken propeller, which immediately followed the strange, fog-shrouded encounter.

* * *

Within the week, the *Dannebrog* was sailing into Copenhagen harbor. With the wonderfully exciting experience of sailing to Greenland behind him, Leif turned his attention to his next obligation: the engineering program at the Danish Maritime Academy, which was located adjacent to the naval yard at the port of Copenhagen. This would occupy all of Leif's time over the next two years, as he studied mechanical and systems engineering. During that time, Leif applied himself diligently in the pursuit of a career as a maritime engineering officer, drawing upon the many practical lessons he had learned from the engineering crews of the *Hekla, Neptune* and *Dannebrog*.

It was during his first year at the Danish Maritime Academy that Leif and his childhood friend and fellow Sølvgades school classmate, Jørgen Bech, were reunited once again. Jørgen had completed his first year at the academy, but unfortunately due to poor academic grades began his second year on probation.

Jørgen lamented,

Leif, I just don't think books and me are meant to be together. Ask me to replace a 100-pound piston in that old mock-up diesel engine in the classroom, I would have no problem, but ask me to write out the formula for transferring horsepower to torque or converting miles per hour to knots and it is all a jumble of numbers floating on the page.

Leif knew this was true. Jørgen was at the top of the class when it came to practical application but was failing miserably in all aspects of the academics of the engineering program. This was a problem that Leif could not solve.

Chapter 4

Friends at Last…

> 'They that go down to the sea in ships and occupy their business in great waters; these men see the works of the Lord, and his wonders of the deep.'
> 'Psalm CVII', *Bible*

After ten months aboard the SS *Bergensfjord*, traversing back and forth across the Atlantic, stopping in Scandinavia, northern Europe, and the east coast of North and South America, Leif was almost home. He stood on the deck of the merchant cargo ship, his hands clasping the iron railing, his eyes locked on the land mass he'd been longing to see: the familiar port of Copenhagen.

Home. He could smell it, the salty air blending with diesel fumes and a dash of decaying kelp. No other harbor in the world delivered the same olfactory tickle as Copenhagen. And Leif felt like he had seen most of them. The assistant engineer of the SS *Bergensfjord* was ready for a few needed weeks of relaxation, some quality time away from his ship and crew.

It was the 1 April 1939. Leif was almost 21 years old, a working man, a world traveler. He reflected, while watching the port grow closer, upon the paradoxes of time, about how the first year following his mother's death had moved like silt across the ocean floor, and the next six years were a chain of breathless events strung together like the drumming montage of a newsreel shown before a movie begins.

Leif thought about Sophie, the young waitress he had met while at Sølvgades and later dated during his time at the Danish Maritime Academy. Theirs had been a typical youthful relationship, caught up in the cliched dialectic of hot and cold. They would fight, not speak for weeks, and then when Leif returned to town, they would pick up right where they left off. There was talk of marriage, then talk of breaking up; there was talk of the future, and then talk of leaving each other in the past. The truth was they were basking in the other's light and it was relatively certain they wouldn't end up together. They were wild, running on teenage emotion, and determined to enjoy the other's company for as long as it lasted, and not a second more. And then Leif graduated and went to sea, duty called.

Sophie wouldn't be the sole remnant of Leif's youth to follow him into his life's next chapter. On his first day at the Danish Maritime Academy, Leif and his childhood friend and competing paramour, Jørgen Bech, were reunited. Their paths had diverged at Sølvgades school. When Leif, expelled from Sølvgades, went on his extended sea voyages courtesy of the Royal Danish Navy, while Jørgen's grades continued to hover just above the watermark of academic expulsion. But somehow, his impressive practical skills got him through Sølvgades school and one of the last billets at the Danish Maritime Academy.

The two old friends quickly rekindled their close friendship despite Jørgen being a year ahead of Leif. In fine Jørgen fashion, after the two had gone out for a celebratory beer after school, he confessed that after completing his first year at the academy, he was already on academic probation.

The academy didn't see eye to eye with Jørgen's views on instinct, and he failed out the following semester. Lucky, as he was – remembering the axiom that God protects drunks and fools – Jørgen landed on his feet, getting hired by a merchant navy company registered out of Panama. The once promising engineer would be a deck hand aboard a cargo vessel running between Copenhagen and ports on the east coast of the United States, which fit his ultimate plan. Jørgen wanted to gain enough experience to jump ship at the first opportunity, find gainful employment aboard an American steamer, and then enlist in the United States Navy.

Every few months, Jørgen would keep Leif apprised of his progress, dropping missives that he was enjoying transiting the Atlantic, but was finding access to America elusive. Until, just as Leif was completing his final exams, he received an ebullient letter from his friend that he'd finally managed to join the United States Navy and was writing from Grand Central Station in New York City:

Dear Leif,
New York is the greatest city in the whole world! Unbelievable! Endless tall buildings, an equal number of tall, beautiful women and so many bars – that never close! It's so much bigger than Denmark, you wouldn't believe it, even if I described it in detail. You have to see it for yourself.

Good news! The Navy has given me written orders and train fare to San Francisco. From there, I'll head south to Coronado Island in San Diego where the U.S. Navy's Gunnery School will train me.

But the reason I'm writing today is that when you write me back, you'll need to address the letters differently. The United States Immigration Office misspelled my name while processing my citizenship and now all my new documents, even my Navy enrollment papers, and military identification say I'm George Beck, not Jørgen Bech.

It's the strangest thing. When someone changes your name, even by accident, you start to feel like a new person. It's as if your whole past gets erased and just the random switch of a few letters lets your start over. This George Beck fellow is much more outgoing than Jørgen Bech. It seems women like him more too. George can also hold his liquor better than Jørgen. I guess it's kind of how America feels in general. A land where if you act the part correctly, everyone believes you, no matter if what's written down is a mistake. And this America has welcomed George Beck with open arms.

Your friend,

'George Beck'

Jørgen Bech wasn't the only one undergoing a meaningful identity change.

When Ensign Leif Bangsbøll fully matriculated from the Danish Maritime Academy, he was immediately commissioned as a junior engineer by a Norwegian shipping company based in Oslo. The next eighteen months were defined by a constant shuffling of contracts and assignments to sail aboard several merchant freighters and ships, and his latest assignment on the ocean tanker, the SS *Bergensfjord*, where he spent long and demanding, yet also boring and demystifying hours in the ship's bowels, surrounded by the omnipotent drone of laboring engine turbines and spinning drive shafts, becoming numb to diesel fumes and engine grease slick on his skin and embedded under his finger nails.

* * *

Now, as the *Bergensfjord* docked in Copenhagen, Leif had already begun to wonder if perhaps a life at sea acting as the master intelligence of the engine room required as much intelligence as he had originally imagined. It seemed that rote skills and pure stamina were the requisites. But that could wait. He quickly scanned the pier as he said his goodbye to some of the other crew members on deck. He walked down the gangway and onto the pier, there was only one thought on his mind: his father. And there he was. Frederik was waiting in the midday spring sun, dressed in a pair of corduroy pants, a wool sweater and scarf, and apparently patting himself down for his missing pack of matches for a cigarette.

Leif was not used to seeing his father out of uniform, dressed as a civilian. Parallel to Leif heading off to the Danish Maritime Academy, Frederik had been promoted to naval captain and technical advisor of the Royal Danish Submarine Fleet and would now bear the title commandant. His ascent up the hierarchy meant Frederik would spend considerably less time at sea, and only interact with sailors on inspections, making the navy's acknowledgement of his formidable talents bittersweet.

Frederik tried to find peace with his success, with being the only naval officer to deeply resent having an office on land, and audibly grousing whenever trouble at sea arose and he wasn't there to be part of the drama. After realizing the Admiralty wasn't going to change its mind and rescind his new title, he went about setting down roots, purchasing a cottage on Hegnsvej Street, conveniently located near the port, which meant he could meet Leif whenever he docked, plus take his own sloop on long sojourns along the Danish coast or far into the Baltic – hoping secretly that the hands of the Valkyries might reach down and summon him during a storm at sea.

'Jocom, let me look at you.' Frederik said, abandoning his search for a match, and embracing his son, long and hard.

Leif held his father tight but couldn't match the older man's grip. He wondered if he would ever be able to match his father's raw strength, honed on a warrior's ethic and long travails across the ocean.

Ending the hug and examining his son at arm's length Frederik said, 'You're too skinny.' He gave Leif a playful slap on the cheek. 'I'll take you home and fatten you up.'

Frederik had originally taken up cooking as another of his time-filling hobbies after the dreaded promotion. However, he quickly realized knowing his way around a kitchen was a necessity, for he was bound to *terra firma*, without a cook like Manny to tend to his culinary needs.

For Leif's return home, he had prepared a hearty soup: equal parts beef broth, barley, vegetables and ground chuck. 'It smells wonderful.' Leif commented as he dipped his spoon into the bowl. 'Clearly, you've mastered the kitchen since I last saw you.' Then, between swallows, Leif said, 'Father, I have a question.'

'You haven't been reading again and found my literary equivalent, have you?' replied Frederik.

'No', Leif said grinning, 'I'm thinking of going to the Royal palace tomorrow to watch the Changing of the Guard ceremony.' He took another sip of soup. 'For old time's sake.' He leaned in closer to Frederik. 'Would you like to come?'

'I'd love to.' Frederik answered, moved by the invitation. 'I remember when we used to take you. You must have made your mother and me go at least a dozen times a year.'

The mention of Rigmor rendered both Bangsbøll men momentarily silent and wistful. They both shared the same unspoken thought: 'My God, can it really have been nine years?'

Frederik took a deep draught of the soup and then tossed his spoon into the bowl and folded his arms. 'This soup does not compare to what Manny made us on the *Hekla* eh son?' He opened and closed his fist in stress.

> Two years now, I've been trying to cook, and everything I make tastes like piss and whatever spice I throw in. Piss and thyme. Piss and basil. Piss and pepper.

Leif couldn't help himself and began laughing convulsively. 'Better than submarine chow, I suppose?' Leif had to hold the side of the table, howling. 'Father. It is terrible.' He began to cry in mirth. 'Just dreadful.'

Frederik banged on the table with an open fist, then put his hand over his eyes, and burst out in laughter even harder than Leif. 'Let's say we forget this soup and go to the pub.'

Leif rose from his chair before Frederik finished his sentence. 'Yes. Let's.'

Frederik walked into the living room, looking for his coat. 'We can pick up Sophie along the way if you like.'

Leif laughed. 'We've broken up again.'

Frederik snorted in derision. 'Nonsense. She's probably already taken you back. You just don't know it yet.'

'If I bring Sophie', Leif said with a louche smile, 'then I can't meet anyone new in the pub.'

Frederik feigned outrage. 'Good god, you've become a true sailor Leif! What would your mother and sisters think?'

A moment of awkward silence followed, when Leif smiled and said, 'So true father – so true. I'll still take that as a compliment.'

Leif lowered his voice to a whisper, ready to broach a potentially delicate topic. 'Father. Have you ever thought about meeting… someone else?'

Frederik buttoned his coat, tied his scarf close to his throat and said with calm equanimity, 'Never.'

> Your mother was the only one who could ever understand me. Who could love me for me. Frankly, I'd rather save myself and someone else the trouble.

'Fair enough', Leif said, 'but maybe we should place an ad somewhere to help you find a cook. For your own good.'

'I may not be able to cook', Frederik said, opening the front door to the cottage, 'but I can still drink you under the table.'

At 0700 hours the next morning, Frederik, nursing a throbbing headache that beat a ruthless tattoo behind his eyes and his temples, called his office and advised his aide that he would not be coming in, then fell back into an aqueous sleep, the room spinning as if he had returned to sea, only to be awakened an hour later by his son, shoving his shoulder so they would have time to get breakfast before the Changing of the Guard ceremony. Frederik cursed Leif's youthful recuperative powers, angrily threw off the blanket and threatened to throttle his son for the entire time he performed his morning ablutions.

* * *

Both Bangsbøll men arrived at the Royal palace grounds, a large cobblestoned courtyard, approximately 200 yards by 200 yards, bracketed by tall, ornate palace walls done in the French Empire style and adorned with dozens of Danish flags. Leif stood on his toes, peered over the barricades, and took in the skyline expanse of bell towers and rows of red roofs. Then the crisp snap of snare drums and the sonorous whistle of flutes riveted his attention. The ceremony began.

The Danish Royal Life Guards were founded by King Frederik III in 1658 and their inception stemmed from a place of deep distrust. The king had been bitterly suspicious that the Roskilde peace treaty between Denmark and Sweden would have any longevity, and he was proven right, when the Swedes invaded, proving a piece of paper could do nothing to restrict aggression. To safeguard his city, the Danish king created the Royal Life Guards, and graced his new regiment with the motto: '*Pro Rege Et Grege.* [For king and people.]'

Leif watched as the Royal Guards entered the square in unified formation, each one impeccably dressed in the traditional blue and black regal uniform topped with bearskin hats. He checked his watch: 1130 hours on the dot. Every day at the appointed time, the parade of the Royal Guards stretched across the streets of Copenhagen's city center, picking up hundreds of onlookers along the way, all of whom tried to distract the stoic military men, to force the solemnity from their faces, and make them smile, laugh or react in any infinitesimal manner, before the half-hour cavalcade reached the Royal family's residence at Amalienborg Palace and the ceremonial shift change occurred.

Frederik and Leif stayed at the front of the pack, keeping up as the Royal Guards left Gothersgade Barracks, accompanied by their marching band, made up of thirty-six musicians and sixteen drummers, who added an extra layer of pomp to the proceedings and signaled the queen was in residence, for the artists only appeared when her presence filled the castle.

Directly at noon, the parade reached the Palace Square, where the watch being relieved stood at attention with pointed rifles and enacted the transition march, during which the flag, the distinctive mark of the command, was handed over by the lieutenant to the adjutant coming on duty.

Leif basked in the display, proud of his country's traditions and his family's deep roots to Denmark's past and present, but his enjoyment ran deeper than simple nostalgia. He was thrilled at the performative nature of the ceremony, the ritual acting out of history. Each one of the Royal Guards was playing a role far bigger than themselves, they were an embodiment of a storied history stretching back almost three centuries and carried their responsibility in the roles. It was akin to how Leif felt portraying Hamlet, as if he had been transported back to the seventeenth century, and could feel a spiritual connection between his body, Shakespeare's pen, and all the other Hamlet's throughout history, like he was a link in an unbroken eternal chain of poets.

'Jocom', Frederik said, interrupting Leif's musings and putting his arm affectionately around his son's shoulder, 'in honor of today's outing, I've made a surprise reservation for lunch for us.'

Chapter 5

In the Shadow of Brandenburg Gate

> 'By the pricking of my thumbs,
> something wicked this way comes.'
> William Shakespeare, *Macbeth*

Leif pondered whether his father had chosen the Holmen officers' club at the naval wardroom for their meal solely because his father was always looking for a reason to be at the naval yard – near the fleet. However, once they were seated at a table overlooking the harbor filled with naval ships waiting to be assigned, and alongside too, was the royal family's yacht, Frederik's rationale for choosing the officers' club became clear.

Frederik, in uniform, removed his navy cap, ordered his first cocktail, and lit the first of many cigarettes. 'Leif', he began, 'the king, like many other world leaders, has received an invitation to attend a military parade and state dinner in Berlin to mark the chancellor's [Adolf Hitler] fiftieth birthday.' He leaned in closer to Leif, blowing a plume of smoke away from his son's face.

> I expect the nations closely aligned with Germany or who are fearful of its growing power will attend to appease the chancellor. King Christian, on the other hand, like his British, French and American counterparts, is reluctant to accept.

Their cocktails arrived at the table. Leif took his first sip. Frederik placed his cocktail to the side, too focused to entertain diverting it with drink. 'The king does not wish to appear as if he condones Hitler's fascist totalitarian regime by his presence at the ceremony.' Frederik held his cigarette between thumb and index finger.

> King Christian also recognizes that Germany lies on our southern border, and we have continued trade and commerce with them. Hence, Denmark cannot outright reject the invitation.

He crushed his cigarette in the ashtray and immediately began fingering another one in his case.

It is because of this curious political ambiguity that I have been asked by the king to attend the chancellor's parade and celebrations as Denmark's representative.

Frederik waited for the weight of his errand to register on Leif before he continued, 'I would like you to accompany me, Leif.'

'Father', Leif said, moving closer to his father, elbows first across the table, pressing them against Frederik's, 'are we to be spies?'

Frederik shook his head. 'No. We are to be King Christian's representatives and present the chancellor with his birthday gift.'

'That's what spies are.'

'Leif. We are going on the king's behalf as…'

'Representatives.' Leif said, interrupting his father. 'But everyone knows that government representatives are spies.'

'I don't know that.' Frederik said, pointing to his chest. 'I know I'm one of the king's closest friends and because he trusts me …'

Leif replied, 'He's asking you to spy for him.'

Frederik smiled awkwardly, looked around at the other officers surrounding him. 'Now I'm even more pleased I chose this place.' He took the first sip of his cocktail. 'With your loose lips. Who knows who could overhear your nonsense?'

'It's not nonsense.' Leif said. 'Maybe you're not reading between the lines of the king's errand.'

'I know the king better than almost anyone.' Frederik said, tapping a fresh cigarette on the table.

Leif narrowed his eyes, teasing his father. 'Do you though?'

'This is ridiculous.' Frederik said, taking another hard glance at the restaurant's other diners.

'Let me ask you', Leif said, raising his index finger for emphasis, like when he was a boy, 'will the king expect you to provide a thorough debrief after your trip?'

'Of course.' Frederik said.

'Then you're spying.' Leif said validated.

'Are you coming with me or not?' Frederik nearly yelled, losing patience.

Leif couldn't hide his infectious grin. 'Of course.'

'Thank you.' Frederik said, considering the conversation finished.

'Perhaps I should bring Sophie.' Leif said. 'We may need to set a honeypot for a German officer.'

Frederik laughed. 'I thought you two had broken up?'

'True.' Leif shrugged. 'Shall I rope her into our mission anyway?'

Frederik ignored him, snapped his fingers at a waiter and requested two menus. 'We leave in two days' time by rail.'

* * *

Over piping hot coffee served in the train's dining car, Frederik educated Leif on the economic, political and military transformations that Germany had undergone in the past decade.

Denmark's political relations with Germany had been strained since the election of Chancellor Adolf Hitler in 1932, but even with his radical agenda and superhuman perseverance, the scope of his power had been relatively constrained. Until August 1934, when the untimely death of President Paul von Hindenburg, allowed Hitler to come into the full bloom of his political capital, which he was more than eager to spend. Germany changed nearly overnight into an inexplicable nation, one in which the people were enthralled and had taken to calling Hitler their Führer (or leader) and he had responded by ruling as a supreme authoritarian since.

Hitler's rise to chancellor wasn't the first time Denmark had engaged in open conflict with Germany, and unsurprisingly, a Bangsbøll family member – in this case, Leif's great-grandfather, Captain Frederik Leif Julius Sørensen, an officer in the Fynske Regiment of Fredericia, Jutland – played a lead role in the fighting. The Second Schleswig War of 1864 was prosecuted over disputed lands on Denmark's southern border, and Prussia-Germany would emerge victorious, assuming control over the duchies of Schleswig and Holstein with the signing of the Treaty of Vienna.

Following Germany's loss at the end of the First World War, these hotly disputed territories would be grudgingly returned to Denmark, according to the diktats of the Treaty of Versailles. The same brokered peace that seeded the ground for Hitler's eventual ascent to Führer.

The loss of its Danish – and Polish – lands, infuriated many Germans, especially Hitler, who was determined both existentially and martially to reclaim those lost territories and many more, while on his ultimate quest of reconstructing Greater Germany.

But the loss of their 'rightful' lands wasn't the only factor making ordinary Germans ready to wholeheartedly embrace fascism. They were disillusioned with the world and their standing in it. The monarchy had led the people into total war and left them vulnerable to a communist takeover, then the democratic government that followed the global inferno lacked legitimacy from the beginning, for the Germans had no prior experience with democracy as a concept let alone a hallowed institution, plus it had capitulated to crippling reparations and humiliation at Versailles, which destroyed the economy via war debts that led to mass inflation devaluing the Deutschmark to the point it took a wheelbarrow of currency to merely purchase staples. Not to mention, in the conservative nationalist position, democracy had opened the door to mass degeneracy, which had infiltrated Weimar in particular, but had infected the national stock and character with the disease of unfettered liberalism. Many demoralized Germans were desperate for a savior, for someone who would turn the tides of history, and return the nation to a time of great pride.

Frederik leaned across the table and whispered to Leif, 'Intelligence reports indicate Germany is rebuilding its military at an alarming rate.'

Leif carefully put down his knife and fork on his plate and said, 'Intelligence. Denmark is spying?'

'We're not.' Frederik said. 'Our British allies are, the French too. They seem to be the only one's worried enough to pay any attention to the goings on in German.'

The full scale, massive rearming of Germany's military was not only the root and branch of their 'economic miracle' granting full employment to all able-bodied citizens, but also a flagrant contravention of the terms of their surrender according to the Treaty of Versailles. However, mounting a standing army outfitted with fleet technology wasn't the only international violation Hitler had sanctioned. He'd also begun daring the victors of the First World War to react to his provocations by halting Germany's debt repayments and stuffing the savings into his air force and tank brigades, as if he was raising a red flag across Europe, seeing if anyone would blink.

'All of Europe', Frederik said grimly,

> Scandinavia, France and Great Britain are uneasy at the prospect of such a dynamic political and military shift in the continent's power. However, there seems to be no collective will to confront Hitler. No one wants to check the Third Reich's power until they step over some line in the stand. The problem is what is that line? And who is going to check them?

Frederik sipped his coffee until he reached the bottom of his cup.

> Everyone is still exhausted from the First World War and fearful of another. I suppose they're hoping if they keep their heads in the sand, they'll somehow ignore their way into avoiding a second. In that case, Europe best sincerely hope Hitler reads their reticence as temporary battle fatigue before unleashing the lion, and not a submission to the chancellor's unholy fusion of Arian race fanaticism and outright militarism.

Well before the lead elements of the chancellor's birthday parade were visible, the triumphant Wagnerian thrust of the military marching band's music dinned the ears of Leif and Frederik, who stood amongst the other dignitaries on the appointed viewing stand for special international guests, located adjacent to the

Pariser Platz. As the parade came closer, the cadence of thousands of leather jackboots striking the ground in a unified wave threw an ominous hum over the soaring instruments.

This lavish and unrestrained spectacle to commemorate Hitler's fiftieth birthday had been the brainchild of the Nazi Minister of Propaganda Joseph Goebbels, who had harnessed the extraordinary power of new media, radio and film, to cast a conjurer's spell over Germany, and convince them that fascism felt good, felt right, by bypassing their brains and shooting straight for their hearts, eyes and ears. Goebbels's parade was 4 miles long and traversed the wide avenues and boulevards of Berlin, with hundreds of thousands of jubilant spectators lining the route, cheering and shouting their devotion to the Führer in one voice, like a revanchist religious rite.

Frederik examined the dais, noted that the prime minister of Japan, Hiranuma Kiichirō, had been given prominent placement as the guest of honor, befitting his country's role as Germany's newest ally. As Frederik and King Christian had expected, King George VI of England had declined the invitation and did not send a representative of Great Britain in his place, instead dispatching a conspicuously curt letter of congratulations to the German chancellor, which undoubtedly was received as a grave insult. Nor did American President Franklin D. Roosevelt attend. America did not acknowledge the event, save for sending a *charge d'affaires*, another egregious snub by the Anglo alliance in Hitler's book.

Suddenly, the lead element of 20,000 newly equipped troops belonging to the Wehrmacht and the Nazi Schutzstaffel, known as the 'SS', turned the corner. Their jet-black uniforms adorned with the macabre Death's Head insignias, was profoundly enhanced by the Luftwaffe (German air force) flying hundreds of new combat aircraft over the soldiers in waves. Once the air display, designed to flex Germany's aerial authority had climaxed, hundreds of state of the art tanks rolled down the cobblestoned streets. The strident testament to modern Germany's military prowess was a mere prelude to the main attraction, the imminent arrival of the Führer himself.

Frederik felt queasy about delivering King Christian's gift, which absolutely dripped with symbolic irony. The king had decided it was proper to echo the 1864 victory of the Prussian-Germans that stripped the Duchy of Schleswig from Denmark and placed it in the possession of Prince Otto von Bismarck and King Wilhelm I of Germany. The occupation of Denmark's southern border had been a terrific source of pride for both men, and they enjoyed lording their power over their neighbors, until the Treaty of Versailles relocated the Danish border with Germany 40 miles south and returned control of the seized territories to the Danish sovereign. With a note of irony, the Danish sovereign's gift to the Führer was a painting of Schleswig's famous Glucksburg Castle on the

Flensburg Fjord. The message was subtle yet unmistakable. Even if you should prove successful at first, Germany always loses the long game of conquest. The Danes raised their patience against short-term Teutonic gratification.

From the beginning, Frederik had doubts regarding King Christian's desire to rouse Hitler's pique – but agreed to be a good sport and hand deliver the gift. However, his original doubts had become grave concerns. Hitler was clearly a man who no longer felt confined by the rules of international diplomacy. This bellicose paramilitary parade was not only a blatant breach of the terms of the Treaty of Versailles but it also threw down a gauntlet at the world's feet, no longer would Germany willingly comply with foreign-imposed limitations on their ambitions. This was no mere birthday celebration it was a birth. Frederik could feel it in his bones. King Christian had chosen satire, when only the gods could help them from Hitler's true intentions.

Standing at his father's side, surrounded by increasingly bewildered foreign leaders, Leif was hypnotized by the sight of Germany in thralled to an esoteric primitive urge dredged from the ooze of its previous national failure. The hardened granite soldiers' faces reminded Leif of a Homeric ode; their jackboots pounding the street were magnificent, as were the prancing horses. He began to reflect on the Changing of the Guard ceremony, Denmark's own display of performative nationalist nostalgia replete with crowds, music, conformity in costuming and ritual. But this – this was something far different; this was a distant Teuton past strapped to the back of a rocket hurtling toward a jackboot-stomping future.

Leif turned to his father and saw a look across Frederik's face he'd never glimpsed before: fear. Pure and deep. 'My God', Leif thought,

> now I understand why he asked me to come with him. It had nothing to do with spying, nothing to do with reconnaissance work for the king, as I'd imagined. Father asked me to accompany him because he couldn't face Hitler and his militaristic masses alone.

Frederik was speechless as he stood silhouetted by the huge, billowing red, black and white banners emblazoned with the Nazi swastika. He turned around, and took in the viewing stands for the public, which overflowed with countless cheering and weeping Germans, anxiously awaiting Hitler, who would deliver an impassioned oratory to the nation while facing the Brandenburg Gate.

He leaned over and whispered in Leif's ear with trepidation in his voice, 'Remember this moment, remember what you are seeing here.' After a moment's pause, Frederik added, 'Jocom, do you remember when you said Europe is the United States' great white whale?'

Leif nodded in recognition.

'Hitler is ours, Jocom. He is our Moby Dick. He is the part of Europe that we must either kill or die trying.'

A massive Mercedes motorcade made its way down the boulevard, and the crowd erupted in full-throated cheers and Nazi salutes. The Führer had arrived.

He exited from the backseat, flanked by SS officers glimmering in black, and drank in the adulation pouring from the stands, becoming charged, possessed by the cries of loyalty and devotion, while offering his own stern love in return, a series of stiff waves and a forced crinkle around the lips and eyes. Hitler ascended the dais, placed both hands on the podium, and began to address his guests and followers in a gruff yet still poetically resonant German, relishing his role as the container of Germany's rage, and comparing his role to a doctor, dedicated to the health of his nation and ridding the decaying organism of foreign – non-Aerian – bodies and filth. His voice, tone and hand gestures growing in amplitude as he insighted his adoring supporters.

Leif couldn't take his eyes off the man, mesmerized by the inhuman intensity of his speech. Then it finally struck him what he found simultaneously so enervating and unnerving about Hitler. He was performer of the highest caliber, almost an actor, an arch lunatic who had obliterated the subjective space between fantasy and reality and became his character, clearly one he'd trained his entire life to embody and inhabit, a tightrope walk that openly flirted with outright madness.

The only difference between an actor courting insanity to inhabit a part and Hitler was that only one of them had convinced an entire nation to join him in his apocalyptic delusion that Germany was his rightful bride, that he was the blessed patriarch who could somehow become the mythical Fisher King and bring fruitful crops and water to the blighted land by healing the open wound, even though he himself allegedly suffered from a myriad of physical and mental ailments, including irritable bowels, syphilis, Parkinson's disease, manic personality disorder and was addicted to amphetamines.

The only hope Leif could foresee was that Germany would awake from its fever dream and realize they were about to be dragged straight to hell by a tyrannical thespian who had taken the world as his stage and was delivering one final command performance that would surely end in death and destruction. Leif had no idea just how much desolation the grim reaper had in mind.

Chapter 6

Blitzkrieg

> 'Those who cannot remember the past
> are condemned to repeat it.'
>
> George Santayana

Leif would receive a rapid answer to his fateful question: how much destruction? And Frederik's dire premonitions of Hitler's true intentions would be unveiled for all mankind to see. In rapid succession, the free world would teeter on the verge of totalitarian rule.

On 1 September 1939, German forces invaded Poland by land and from the air. The twenty-one-year interregnum holding Europe together was vanquished in an instant: the Second World War had begun.

According to Hitler, the operations in Poland were merely a matter of 'reclaiming annexed parts of Germany' and protecting the welfare of his fellow citizens, who were existing in a fictional country cobbled together over coffee by the allies in Versailles, none of whom bothered to take ethnic composition into account, seemingly only occupied by enacting whatever new way to punish all Germans popped into their heads.

Outside of allowing Hitler a chance to double-down on the baseless excuses he'd been using since he 'diplomatically liberated' nearly the whole of Czechoslovakia in 1938, his capture of Poland put the world on notice, gave Europe a harsh awakening and humiliating primer on how the Führer intended to wage his war. His new war fighting tactic was what would become known as his 'blitzkrieg' strategy, a near-Napoleonic method of 'total war' that no military imagined Germany's war machine had up its sleeve.

The blitzkrieg employed massive aerial bombings up front to incapacitate the enemy's air defenses, railroads, communication lines and munitions dumps. Once the chosen country had been set ablaze and was reeling in shock, an enormous, mechanized land invasion with a commanding number of troops, tanks and artillery followed to ensure full capitulation. After all outward signs of resistance had been eliminated, the German infantry moved in to occupy and neutralize any remaining resistance. Poland would be overwhelmed in just under one month's time.

Within twenty-four hours of breaking the Poles defenses and collective will, Hitler already had deployed his security forces to erect bases of operations, and the SS 'Death's Head' regiments had begun to travel the country, domesticating and punishing the populace, and putting any enemies of the Nazi ideology in slave labor camps or worse: concentration and extermination camps.

The response of the Polish army to Hitler's Wehrmacht was an object lesson on what not to do and immediately established the new rules of war. Although the Poles had over 1 million able soldiers – compared to Germany's 1.3 million – the outmoded thinking of their commanders allowed the troops to be decimated within days by Hitler's titanic opening assault gambit, which used the cutting edge of modern mechanized military hardware, and followed the chaos with a quick, almost asymmetrical ground game. Ironically, this style encapsulates one of the great paradoxes of the Nazi regime, their rabid antipathy to the modern, wedded to an absolute faith and addiction to technology.

Although the continent should not have been surprised. When British Prime Minister Neville Chamberlain agreed to Hitler's reclamation of the Sudetenland in 1938, the die had been cast. Chamberlain believed the deal had averted another war that would engulf Europe in cataclysm, but his actions merely convinced Hitler that the British and French wouldn't resist further annexations of the east. Hitler also calculated, and correctly, that he could overrun Poland before the Allies could mount a sufficient response to his aggression.

Hitler's move into Poland was also a direct threat to the Danes, who knew that the former duchies of Schleswig and Holstein were being eyed by Hitler and his generals as ripe for reconquest. Another wrong committed by Versailles to be righted with their indomnable force.

* * *

It was under those increasingly surreal and dangerous conditions that Leif completed his tour abord the SS *Bergensfjord* and immediately signed a new six-month contract with a Norwegian shipping line based out of Oslo. He was assigned to an ocean cargo vessel, the *C.O. Stillman*. From January to March 1940, the *C.O. Stillman* sailed within the Baltic Sea, transiting regularly between the neighboring ports of Oslo, Stockholm, Helsinki, Leningrad (modern day St Petersburg), Gdansk and Rostock, while wondering daily if they would awaken to a world nashing it's teeth at each other's throats.

And Europe was at each other's throats, just not militarily. There had been no further battles, even a slight skirmish, since the commencement of hostilities in September 1939. The war had been confined to a matter of increasingly bellicose words, with national newspapers printing bold headlines and inflammatory articles shouting demands and issuing threats and counterthreats from overheated politicians and hawkish generals hailing from Germany, France and Britain, whose representatives went so far as calling Hitler's aggression a 'phoney war'. It seemed like the war had been frozen in its incubation, although no one in Europe and Scandinavia believed it, existing as if dangling from tenterhooks waiting for the next shoe to fall.

On the afternoon of 9 April 1940, just two days after departing Rostock Germany, the *C.O. Stillman* was navigating the English Channel toward Le Havre, France, when Leif and the other officers abord the ship were called to the bridge by the ship's captain. There was a crisis, an earth-shattering event unfolding in Europe.

Following the captain's announcement that Germany had just invaded Norway and Denmark, Leif and the other officers assembled in the galley with the rest of the crew. Huddled around the radio, they listening to a BBC radio broadcast, reporting that Norway and Denmark had been invaded and were now occupied by Nazi troops.

According to the BBC, Hitler claimed the British had violated Norwegian neutrality by laying ocean mines in the shipping channel the Germans were using to transfer iron ore from Sweden. As per usual, Hitler was deflecting. True, the British were trying to subtly sabotage Germany, but their actions had merely forced Hitler's hand to occupy Norway faster, a move he'd intended for months. From an operational standpoint he had to. If the British occupied those territorial waters, Germany would be without its major source of iron ore. The reporter continued,

> As Hitler's forces were on their way to Norway, his paratroopers landed at six of Norway's ports between Oslo and Narvik, while simultaneously, the German army moved to take control of the land directly between them and Norway: Denmark. On the first day of the invasion, the Danish king, King Christian X, ordered his troops to cease fire, realizing his army and naval forces would be quickly overwhelmed and slaughtered. The king saved his people but lost his country in less than twenty hours.

With this done, Hitler had added a second and third conquered nation to his delirium of a glorious, revitalized Germany.

Leif was horrified and stunned by the report. He felt hollow inside as if his stomach had shot down to the soles of his feet. His immediate thoughts went to his father. How could Leif be certain he was safe? There was no way to contact him. The captain of the *C.O. Stillman* told the crew that telephone lines were now controlled by the Nazis who prevented any communication outside the occupied company and the short-wave radio signals had failed.

Terror kept racing through Leif's mind, through his trembling fingertips.

> Hitler is going to finish making me an orphan. I'm going to be forced to walk this world alone. And I won't even know that I have no one until the end of the war.

Then an even more disturbing conclusion dawned on the young man: 'The war might not even last long at this rate, the Nazis are already getting closer to the heart of western Europe.'

Over the course of the next hour, Leif considered other crucial variables. He felt immense pity for King Christian, a family friend, who had sacrificed the sanctity of his country, for the sanctity of life. It was a brutal decision for a monarch to make, and he was proud Christian was Denmark's royal leader. He also understood why the king and Frederik had always valued the other's divergent council. Leif knew that in the same situation, his father would likely have not made the same compassionate call as his friend, that knowing the danger of the Nazis, Frederik would have led the men into battle. Better, in his mind, to die a Dane and dine in Valhalla, then live a day under Nazi occupation. Which is why you want a man like Frederik in the military and Christian on the throne.

Leif also knew that even though he loved his father, that King Christian had been correct to surrender, that the odds were insurmountable, that Hitler was taking Denmark regardless of the military's passion, and it was shrewder to save lives and fight another day, than add another laurel to Hitler's crown by bathing his triumph in the blood of innocents.

Finally, Leif reflected on Sophie. They might have shared a uniquely turbulent relationship, but he couldn't imagine never seeing her again. Sophie, the one person who could drive him so apoplectically with both love and anger.

By the time the *C.O. Stillman* arrived at the port in Le Harve, Leif realized he had to rely on the oldest method of connection possible: the post. He wrote a desperate five-page letter to his father, filled with everything that was on his mind, the pages and margins overflowing with love and fear, with memories they'd shared and plans they'd promised to undertake before the war. He hoped somehow it might reach Frederik, even though he had no earthly idea how the missive would arrive at Frederik's cottage. Finally, before he handed the message over to the port postmaster, he said a silent prayer to his mother, begging, pleading with her to take all the love she had for both her Bangsbøll men, and make sure, his father received his letter.

Leif wasn't the only one whispering pieties, asking heaven above for any kind of sign for the future. He, the captain and the remainder of the *C.O. Stillman*'s crew were without a country, unable to return, without orders and the ultimate fate of their employer unknown, but likely dismal and grim. Before shoving off from Le Harve, the captain gathered everyone in the galley and put the situation to a vote:

Gents, we can either part company here, go our separate ways and try and either survive in France or claw our way back home, which from what I've heard is unlikely. Norway and Denmark have been cordoned off by German troops.

He allowed the dire report to sink in on his crew, then continued,

Or we can continue on the last leg of the mission, sail the *C.O. Stillman* to New York, drop off our cargo, and wait it out in the United States – a safe distance from the war. And see if somehow, by God's graces, we hear something back from the home office in Oslo.

The vote was unanimous. Ten days later, the *C.O. Stillman* dropped anchor in New York harbor. For how long, nobody knew, least of all its crew. They were a ship without a country to call home.

* * *

To end the boredom of weeks at sea and the trek across the Atlantic, and to drown the pain of not knowing the status of their families and friends, and to douse the fear they might never be able to return home, the crew of the *C.O. Stillman*, Leif included, embarked upon what most young men would do to the remedy the situation – they went ashore to explore and carouse the streets of New York. Leif took the reins of the deployment, using the letters of his friend Jørgen Bech or 'George Beck' to guide their way, and despite the less than ideal conditions of their visit, they all had to agree with the academy dropout turned United States Navy recruit: New York was the greatest city on Earth. And the most expensive.

They exhausted themselves seeing all the tourist sites, including the newly constructed Empire State Building, the Statue of Liberty, the Public Library and both Washington Square and Central Parks. The visiting Danes had already seen more people and cars in their short time there than they would in a lifetime back home. Next, they went to a Yankees' game, a Broadway show, several jazz clubs, took in several movies and attempted to eat their individual weights in authentic pizza. Seven days later, the party was over. The crew of the *C.O. Stillman* had run through most their pay traipsing around Manhattan and decided to have one final night on the town.

The *C.O. Stillman* crew took it as a talismanic sign that the bars they passed on the way back to the harbor was called 'The Arrow' and outfitted with a nautical theme including massive, mounted fish lining the walls who looked as if they hadn't surrendered without a snarling fight. It seemed like the perfect spot for a company of 'dangling men' to spend their last night on land. Leif's comrades immediately befriended a gaggle of what appeared to be chorus girls in search of their next gig and nestled in with the troupe at the back corner of the room.

Leif parted company with the group, not in a mood to party, his heart heavy with pressing business. If he was going to leave a note for his father with the New York harbor master – in the hope of getting it passed to any ship heading in the vicinity of western Europe – he needed to finish it now. He pulled up a seat at the bar, grabbed his notebook and pen from his jacket, and began to write. He didn't care if he was conducting a monologue, the Germans were not going to take the dream of his father away.

'What can I get you?' the bartender asked.

Leif looked up. He was a man in his mid to late forties who maintained a paradoxical physique, composed of equal parts raw muscle and muscle that had gone to seed, coated with a visible outer layer of fat. The bartender's face was an equally discomfiting specimen, like a roadmap of crisscrossing stress lines giving contradictory directions, and atop the worry, dotting it like an exclamation point, was the left eye, which was made of glass.

'Whisky.' Leif said, then followed with the crucial proviso. 'Whatever's your cheapest.'

The bartender picked up on Leif's accent and halting English. 'You're pretty far from home.'

Leif nodded, and in true stereotypical fashion, began to unburden his troubles to the man pouring his drink. 'I don't have a home right now.'

The bartender placed a glass before Leif. 'What do you do?'

'I'm a maritime engineer', Leif said, 'aboard a Norwegian vessel.' 'We're pretty much marooned here thanks to Hitler. We can't go back to Norway. We can't connect with our home office.'

The bartender began to pour. With a flick of the wrist, he stopped the whisky stream. 'On the house wayward son. And it's not the cheap stuff.'

Leif toasted his guardian bartender and shot back the drink in one gulp.

The bartender placed a hand under his chin, leaned against the wooden surface. 'So, what the hell happened? Who'd you guys piss off? Customs?'

'The Germans.' Leif said. 'The Nazis invaded Norway and Denmark. The ship I'm aboard is from Oslo. To make matters worse, my father is trapped in Denmark. I cannot get home and he cannot get out.'

The bartender's face went steely and cold. 'I'm sorry for your troubles. You seem like a nice kid.' He pointed to his glass eye:

> This is a gift from the Germans. From the last time you all decided to go wild on each other, and we, Americans, had to rush in and save your asses from each other.

He tapped on his mirrored substitute eye and said,

> Never again, my friend. Never again. You people need to either learn how to police your own backyard or start speaking German. Because they obviously want to rule you all, and you can't hold them back without us.

Leif was taken aback by the man's blasé attitude toward the European theater. 'You must realize Hitler is a grave threat to the world, not just Europe.'

'Do I?' the bartender said.

> Not to our world. An ocean separates us and we can get along with the Führer just fine. We walked out on your continent a long time ago for a reason. We got no business solving European problems. This is America.

He leaned in close to Leif and said, 'Here's my penny's worth of advice. Stay here. Stay with us. Not for nothing, but you and I both know Hitler going to win.'

'I don't know that.' Leif said, infuriated, ready to jump the bar in spite of the man's calm passive aggressiveness.

'Calm down, son. Calm down.' He poured the young Danish sailor another drink.

> I'm just saying. We're the new world for a reason. We'll happily take you. Hell, I'll even let you crash in the office here and take you down to immigration first thing in the morning.

Leif stayed his nerves. 'I appreciate the offer. But my father is still in Denmark.'

'If he loves you as much as you obviously love him, he'd want you to stay here, to be safe.'

'Frankly', Leif said, biting down on his tongue to control his temper, 'if you suggest that you don't know my father and you don't know me.'

'Fair enough', the bartender said, 'but I do know America. And we're not going to stand being dragged into another war. You're on your own, kid.'

The bartender moved along to serve a new customer, leaving Leif to continue writing his note to Frederik. But he couldn't seem to find the words, particularly one's of hope, after that exchange. Could it be true? Would America leave Europe to devour itself this time? Did they feel their geographical advantages and plentiful natural resources excused them from global responsibilities?

Leif finished his drink, packed away his notebook, and left a tip for the bartender, who had given him both a free whisky and an unsolicited lecture in American realpolitik that haunted him to his bones.

Maybe the bartender had a point? Maybe he should stay? Had Denmark already been condemned? Had he already lost his father but was too sentimental to process the grief? For God knows, Frederik Bangsbøll, would not take kindly to Nazis running amok in his ancestral land, and may already be supping with Odin. Perhaps Leif should take a page from 'George Beck', try to get assigned to an American ship and start a new life, albeit under a slightly misspelled name. And frankly, if Leif had any inclination what his near future held in store, he might never board the *C.O. Stillman* again, and instead embraced life as a refugee here in America.

* * *

The *C.O. Stillman* would spend nearly a month at anchor in New York harbor – stranded in a state of physical and existential abandonment. It wasn't only the number marking their forlorn drifting that felt biblical, it was the isolation, as if they were all waiting for a sign, any sign that life was worth enduring, that there was some reason to believe. Soon enough the sign came in the form of a cable from the British Merchant Navy, authorizing the now stateless *C.O. Stillman* to berth at Portsmouth, England at its earliest ability. The captain and crew of the *C.O. Stillman* decided that they could not remain idle any longer. They raised anchor and set a course for England.

The Atlantic crossing was rough – the *C.O. Stillman* ran the gauntlet of a late spring gale, and with no cargo in its hold as ballast, the ship was tossed about like a cork upon rough waters. The foul mood of the crew was further legitimized by the equally grim turn of global events outside the steel walls and hull of the *C.O. Stillman*. As the vessel, thrashed along the literal tides of fate towards England, Hitler was invading the Netherlands, Belgium and Luxembourg, and within three weeks controlled them all.

The Ruhr Valley was both the Achilles Heel in Hitler's plan to conquer France, but also an essential aspect on his road to vengeance for the Treaty of Versailles. By 1922, four years after the treaty had been signed, Germany requested permission to suspend payment on its war debt – which had to be paid in gold – while its economy recovered from a spell of massive inflation. In response, France and Belgium invaded the Ruhr, a highly industrialized region of Germany, and took possession of the factories, intending to use these resources to make up for the unpaid reparations. The Ruhr had been an area of unrest ever since, consisting of German works and police constantly sparring with French and Belgium, with violence breaking out on both sides.

In order to possess western Europe, Hitler had to first possess the Ruhr, especially before England and France could arm themselves and test their mettle against the Wehrmacht, for the Germans knew they would likely lose the battle. All the sympathy and loyalty in Belgium and the Netherlands were with France and Britain, and if they threw their combined weight behind the French army, it could give Hitler considerable trouble. Hitler laid out his rationale in stark language to his generals:

> Breach of the neutrality of Belgium and Holland is meaningless. No one will question that when we have won. We shall not bring about the breach of neutrality as idiotically as it was done in 1914. If we do not break the neutrality, then England and France will. Without attack, the war is not to be ended victoriously.

The *C.O. Stillman* arrived in Portsmouth early in the day on 29 May 1940. After going ashore to register with the harbor master the captain of the *C.O. Stillman* met with the senior representative of the British Merchant Navy. Upon his return to the ship, the captain assembled the crew to give them the news:

> We're part of a new arrangement, gents. A deal has been struck between our now defunct employer in Oslo and the British. The *C.O. Stillman* is to be transferred, post-haste, to the British Merchant Navy for the duration of the war. You heard me right, gents, we have a new home port and thankfully before our food and fuel ran out.

The mood among the crew was positive elation, screams and hugs, grown men practically scaling up and down the galley walls in excitement. When the crew's elation abated, the captain continued, 'For those who wish to sign-on to this British offer, you are welcome to remain with the *C.O. Stillman*.' After a moment's hesitation, the captain continued,

However, the bad news is that there will be no back-pay coming for what is owned you. There's no more money coming from Oslo. The back half of your pay disintegrated when Heir Hitler paid a visit to Norway. Also, many of you can't go home without risking imprisonment or death. Let me repeat, let it sink in, gents: most of you are now stateless.

Chapter 7

Finding the *Folkstone*

'Not all those who wander are lost.'

J.R.R. Tolkien

On 30 May 1940, the day after the *C.O. Stillman* dropped anchor at the port of Portsmouth, its crew discovered that they had arrived at a particularly dire time for Britain and its Allies.

Gathered around the radio in the galley the crew of the *C.O. Stillman* listened to ominous news on the BBC broadcast. They were informed in wrought, somber sentences that not only were Belgium, Denmark and Norway now Hitler's prizes, but the German Wehrmacht had seized the moment: France had been overrun with a blitzkrieg, and a military disaster was unfolding for Allies in real-time. Nearly 500,000 Allied soldiers were trapped in and around a small port town on the western coast of France, Dunkirk, where a desperate rescue attempt was underway to save the stranded BEF and the tattered remnants of the French army from certain death.

The captain of the *C.O. Stillman*, no ideological supporter of the Nazis, even before they put his employer out of business, offered his vessel to assist with the ongoing evacuation on the shores of France. Unfortunately, the size and draft of the *C.O. Stillman* were too large for the close to shore mission being conducted. The Royal Navy needed smaller, shallow-hulled vessels and lots of them.

That first evening in Portsmouth, Leif and several other crewmen of the *C.O. Stillman* walked along the pier towards the center of the port town, looking for their first quality meal in weeks. During their

Ensign Leif Bangsboll, upon graduation from the Royal Danish Maritime Academy (Engineer), Copenhagen 1938. (*Photo courtesy of the author's family collection*)

stroll, while his crew mates bantered back and forth about which was the best bar in Portsmouth, Leif observed a bevy of hectic activity in the port, as many vessels were being readied for launch. He saw a coastal merchant vessel, also known as a 'coaster', moored along the quay and undergoing maintenance to its engine. As the *C.O. Stillman*'s crew walked past, Leif noted that the ship's spotlight, positioned up on the bridge superstructure was shining aft, illuminating the open hatches to the coaster's engine compartment, where several crew members were engaged in its repair.

Several hours later, as the *C.O. Stillman* crew made their way back to their ship for the night, having consumed a fine meal and some excellent local beer, Leif noticed that the repairs to the coastal vessel were still ongoing, while many of the other vessels had vacated the harbor. 'Gentlemen, I'll be along shortly, I just need to see what's going on here.' He pointed to the moored coaster vessel. His colleagues carried on towards their ship, mocking Leif's eagerness to get into another ship's engine room, especially so late in the evening.

Leif approached the vessel with a curious eye. After obtaining permission to come aboard the *Folkstone* from a crew member, Leif introduced himself to the *Folkstone*'s captain as the *C.O. Stillman*'s assistant engineer and explained the circumstances that brought his ship to be moored idly alongside at Portsmouth. The captain was vaguely sympathetic to his Danish visitor's plight but had more pressing concerns. The *Folkstone* was undergoing emergency engine repairs in the hopes of launching towards Dunkirk to assist with the ongoing evacuation.

Leif could quickly surmise that the *Folkstone*'s engineer was stymied by whatever was malfunctioning with his engine. He also knew that he could help and didn't want to stand idly by when lives were at stake. The New York bartender had taught him a valuable lesson: no one was coming to help Europe. In fact, even parts of Europe itself, weren't coming to save their neighbors and allies. It was up to people like him. 'I'm fairly proficient with a wrench, I think I might be able to help.'

'I already have a qualified mechanic and several able crew members, all familiar with this vessel, attending to our engine, thanks for the offer.' The captain turned to walk away and saw his crew staring at the uncooperative powerplant and looking forlorn, their greasy hands on their hips. The captain of the *Folkstone* turned back to Leif and said, 'Listen here', sticking a large wad of chewing tobacco into lower lip and then chewing like a cow with cud,

> we've got a rescue mission to get to, so, if you've got the tools and the know-how and think you can help, you get yourself into the engine compartment and sort this thing out.

Leif nodded. 'I believe I can.'

'Then get the hell to work.' the captain ordered as he turned and walked towards the ship's wheelhouse to study the sea charts of the northwestern coast of France.

Leif rushed back to the *C.O. Stillman*, grabbed his tool bag, and borrowed the most skilled member of his crew: his Filipino assistant, Armando. When he returned to the *Folkstone*, Leif reintroduced himself and Armando to the *Folkstone*'s captain, who then led the two over to the engine compartment.

The two *C.O. Stillman* engineers got right to work. They knelt down at the edge of the deck hatch, watched the other onlookers puzzled by the mechanical malfunction, then peered into the bowels of the engine compartment, noted the distinct smell of electrical smoke. Leif and Armando shared a glance and a nod, realizing they could already diagnose part of the problem.

The two men descended into the chaos. Leif introduced himself to the other engineers, who were at their wit's end, having spent hours at war with their inanimate antagonist.

'Mind if I take a look.' Leif said.

Martin, a British engineer, only a few years older than Leif, who was chain-smoking and covered in grease, wiped his hands off, and laughed, 'What the hell do you think we've been doing lad?'

Leif noted Martin's cigarette. 'Should you really be smoking down here?'

Martin sized up Leif. 'Helps me think, lad.'

'As I said', Leif repeated, 'I think we might be able to help.'

'Might', another crewman named Jack said, peering out from around the engine,

> might is what got us here. Might is what we've been doing. Dead is what our young soldiers are gonna be if we don't get this scow running.

He turned to Leif. 'If you can fix it, have a go.'

Leif turned to Armando looking for support and received it with a firm nod: yes. 'We can fix it.' Leif said.

The British sailors stepped aside, half annoyed, half curious at the young Dane's confidence in his own skills. Leif proceeded toward the engine manifold, examining the state of disarray. Immediately, to begin with the first principles, Leif ran his hand in and around the engine works to determine if anything was loose or misplaced, but he recoiled in pain from the intense heat emanating from the works. Not an auspicious sign, he thought, it's been overheating for hours. Leif went into his bag, pulled out a pair of thermal gloves, and beckoned Armando to bring their tools over. 'Armando, you smelt that electrical smoke too, didn't you?' Leif asked and then immediately added, 'Have a look at the solenoid connection in the engine initiator.'

Leif disassembled and inspected the fuel injector, the cylinder liner, the diaphragm and then the exhaust manifold, where Leif suspected the problem originated. Much to his surprise and dismay the cause of the smoke didn't have its origins there. He wiped the sweat from his eyes and the soot from his face, listening to the British mechanics gripe about how they'd tried all these tactics hours ago.

Leif lay prone on his stomach and examined the bilge-pump to see if there was a blockage. Nothing. Everything appeared to be in order. 'Then why the smoke?' Leif thought, puzzling, frustrated and becoming increasingly embarrassed by his critics. He should've kept his mouth shut, should've gone to dinner with the rest of the *C.O. Stillman* crew, not wading into a situation where young men's lives were at stake but he reminded himself, 'I'm committed to fixing this boat.'

Leif turned around and looked at Martin who had a cigarette affixed to his lip. 'Maybe it will help me think? Father is never without one and there are no problems he can't handle.' Leif thought.

'Can I have one of those?'

Martin approached Leif, handed him a cigarette and lit it with a match.

Leif coughed after his first drag. The smoke wafted into his already red and swollen eyes. He felt sick to his stomach and a wave of dizziness. This wasn't the answer, he thought it was a horrible idea. He handed the cigarette back to Martin, who passed it along to another willing smoker among the crew.

Leif stepped back and decided to begin again, to take a holistic view of the apparatus. He whispered to Armando, who slid on a pair of thermal gloves, and began to knock gently against the surface of the engine, so Leif could listen and ascertain if a hidden part had been dislodged.

The British crew began to laugh at this approach and one sailor joked, 'No one's home.'

'Shut up!' Leif retorted, losing patience, and raising a clenched fist to the crowd, without bothering to turn around. 'Hit it again, Armando.' Armando rapped against the engine and finally Leif heard the small catch he'd been waiting for. He smiled. He had it. He was the master intelligence in the *Folkstone*'s engine room.

He approached the open engine combustion chamber, stared at the cooling water supply-return, raised a shaft, and realized that the piston had been dislodged. Leif bent down, rifled through his supplies, and found a replacement part, then he set about dismantling that section of the engine in rapid succession. The British men stood in awe at the quick work, jaws slack at how Leif and Armando appeared more orderly and regimented than the engine itself.

Within an hour, Leif had replaced the piston, reinstalled the water circulator, fused the two, and instructed the disbelieving captain, to start the coaster's engine, and see if he and Armando's diagnosis had been accurate. Martin, the *Folkstone*'s engineer, acknowledged that the solenoid had signs of arching, noting it was probably caused by the misfiring of that piston.

The results weren't promising at first. The idling coaster was still billowing drafts of heavy black smoke toward the morning sky, now glowing a crimson red. Leif waited patiently and ran his hand through his hair while staring at the struggling engine. Momentarily, he felt gutted by his inability to save the allies at Dunkirk, at his inability to restore life to the coaster. He watched the British crew's faces turn, trying to process their own private disappointment. Leif raised his index finger as if he were about to make a statement, but just held it there, cocked his ear and said, 'Wait for it…'

Until he heard the burnt smoky cackle of the captain's laugh. It was a sound filled with joy, with disbelief, as the engine's exhaust system sprang to life, and the smoke turned from black to white and finally disappeared altogether.

The engine now purred as if it were brand new, and before Leif realized it, half a dozen disbelieving, joy-filled British sailors were all slapping him and Armando on their backs, grinning like fools.

'Bloody marvelous!' shouted the captain, above the drone of the boat's engine. 'We are mission ready and ready to depart at high tide.'

Leif and Armando exited the celebration, began packing their tools, ready to disembark the *Folkstone*, pleased with their success. When suddenly, the captain

British, French and Belgian troops on the beaches of Dunkirk – awaiting rescue, May, 1940. (*Photo courtesy of the online Pinecrest Stock Imagery*)

put an arm on each of their shoulders, and spoke through an orb of chewing tobacco, 'Come to Dunkirk with us. It should be bloody exciting.'

Leif and Armando exchanged glances, intrigued by the offer, but unsure.

'The round trip shouldn't take more than twenty-four hours.'

'Hell', Martin said, 'that's assuming we make it back at all.'

The *Folkstone*'s captain slapped his crewman a withering look. This wasn't the exact moment for blunt honesty.

'We could certainly use both of your expertise', the captain said, 'the *Folkstone*'s not the most reliable seacraft at time. She's temperamental.' He smiled at Leif and Armando. 'You boys have the magic touch.'

'Come on', another crewman said, mentally preparing for battle, 'who wants to live forever if it's a world run by Nazis.'

Leif wanted to tell the men the truth: 'I don't want to die without seeing my father again.' Then thought better of the idea. 'All these men', he thought, whether on the Portsmouth harbor or stranded on the beaches of Dunkirk, risk never seeing their fathers again. What makes me special in that desire?

* * *

No. It was best to keep his real reasons for declining their invitation private. 'You see', he said, 'I signed up for a year on the *C.O. Stillman* …'

'But it's just sitting there anchored.' Martin said. 'Besides, it's British property now anyway. Who's going to know?'

'Fair enough', Leif said, trying desperately to poke a hole in that line of reasoning, 'but I'm still an employee technically. And if I leave the ship, I'll be in dereliction of duty to both my captain and my employer.'

The captain held his tongue, about to say,

> Who cares about dereliction when there are British and French soldiers drowning in their own blood, just a few miles across the Channel from where we now stand.

But he didn't. Years of service had made him realize that you can't make a fighter, make a gilded warrior out of anyone, until the heart is ready. He offered his hand in thanks to Leif and Armando and saw them off the boat.

The two *C.O. Stillman* engineers had almost cleared the gangway back onto the pier, when Leif stopped his colleague and said, 'Armando… I think we made a mistake. I think we should go with them. Just in case they need us.'

Armando frowned. 'Leif, you said it yourself, we'd be in dereliction…'

'You and I both know that no one cares.' Leif said. 'They won't even notice we're gone. The *C.O. Stillman* isn't leaving this port for days, and even when it does, we likely won't be on it.'

'Leif', Armando continued, grave, 'I'm a Filipino. The Philippines is not at war with Germany. It... it isn't my fight.'

Leif reflected once again on the words of the American bartender, now coming out of his shipmate's mouth: 'It isn't my fight.' And both men, in their own way, were correct. Much like Frederik had scholarly observation years ago, Hitler, at this moment, was Europe's great white whale and Europe shouldn't expect any assistance in putting the Führer down.

Armando put his hand on Leif's shoulder. 'This Dunkirk isn't your fight either Leif. Your fight is in Denmark. Your fight is to live and be reunited with your father.'

The decision was in Leif's hands, only he could make it. 'I would rather meet my father in the hall of the gods in Valhalla', he said, 'than greet him again in this life as a coward.' He placed his hand atop his colleague's and said, 'Goodbye, Armando. Hopefully, I'll see you again tomorrow.' Leif turned back and made his return to the *Folkstone*.

Chapter 8

The Ensign

'A hero is someone who has given his or
her life for something bigger than oneself.'

Joseph Campbell

Traveling at full throttle, the *Folkstone* made rendezvous with convoy OB-160 assembling off the coast of Dover. Their guiding light and escort was a stalwart yet aging Royal Navy corvette brought down from Liverpool for the mission and tasked with leading the way for the twenty-five small coastal vessels, fishing trawlers and yachts from ports all across the south of England. As the convoy traveled toward Dunkirk, it would link up with additional boats, swelling its ranks for the rescue mission.

Once all vessels were accounted for, the ragtag flotilla proceeded north, along the southeastern coast toward the English coastal town of Ramsgate, where they turned east to cross the English Channel towards France, for an anticipated arrival time of sunrise the following morning, 2 June 1940.

British, French and Belgian troops being evacuated from Dunkirk, May, 1940. (*Photo courtesy of the online Pinecrest Stock Imagery*)

The weather was a mixed blessing. The blanket of low-ceiling clouds created an inhospitable atmosphere for the Luftwaffe. The seas were only moderately rough – a blessing to the small British flotilla through what was usually a rough part of the Channel at that time of year. Ironically, those same fortunate elemental conditions threw an ominous portent, a hovering atmospheric anxiety, over the already fraught operation.

And no other soul seemed to feel the tension more than the newly arrived naval ensign aboard the *Folkstone*. Like each of the other private vessels in the rescue convoy, each was assigned a Royal Navy sailor or junior officer. The young naval ensign who was assigned to the *Folkstone* provided official Royal Navy direction to the ship's captain and crew during the rescue mission. The ensign did not mingle with the crew, stayed mostly silent for the first half of the journey, and stood stone still beside the vessel's captain, staring off into the distant horizon, as if giving a series of talismanic signs everyone else aboard the ship were unable to interpret. He had been here before.

However, the ensign wasn't the only quiet crew member, all the men followed suit. The crew was young, save for the captain, each one barely an adult and either too afraid to talk or desperately avoiding knowing too much about the man beside them as they might be forced to watch their newfound colleagues die.

Leif was no exception. On his first quasi-military operation, fear clawed around the edges of his heart, gnawed away at his stomach, and pulsed behind his eyes in midnight black hammer throbs. 'How could my father have spent most of his career enduring this level of stress and suspense?' Leif wondered. It was true. Every day Frederik ran the risk of a life and death situation interrupting the smooth flow of basic naval endeavors.

As the *Folkstone* cruised smoothly across the Channel current, Leif tried to summon up his father's cool demeanor in the face of overwhelming odds. Leif tried to burrow into the bravery living in his own soul, drawing upon the same selflessness that allowed him to race into a burning galley to save Manny the cook. It didn't work. There was a huge difference.

Leif didn't have time to think when Manny's life was in danger in the galley of the *Hekla*, didn't have time to weigh the consequences of his rapid decision. On this trip to Dunkirk, seconds ticked by in slow motion, torturously slow motion, allowing Leif time to ponder his own potential demise or awful mutilation.

Shall I die in a blazing burst of gunfire from a German fighter aircraft or in a sudden blast of artillery explosions? Or maybe I'll die a slow, agonizing death – drowning in the gray waters of the English Channel.

Martin, the *Folkstone*'s chain-smoking engineer, walked over to Leif and whispered in his ear, 'Wanna' try another cigarette?'

Leif shook his head, unable to conjure up the sound necessary to articulate the refusal.

Martin stood beside his new Danish shipmate and silently smoked another cigarette with his nicotine stained fingers. His exhale seemed like a mere murmur against the Channel's wind and dissipated quickly.

Soon enough, the quiet would be obliterated. There was no need to rush its appearance, for when it came, it would be undeniable.

The lead vessels of the convoy soon became aware they were approaching Dunkirk when the distant horizon produced stacks of black smoke, curling, coiling, choking the heavens above. The harbinger of things to come.

The *Folkstone* was still too far from the coast to discern the precise source of the smoke, but they could all intuit that Dunkirk was under siege, another victim of Hitler's patented blitzkrieg tactics.

As the convoy progressed, the French coast appeared on the horizon, slowly at first as a thin dark line where the gray sky met the gray ocean – gradually revealing its dreadful, pathetic scene. Normally included azure water, a pristine coast and miles of pure sand with vacationing crowds. Not today. On this day, all the natural beauty had been ripped asunder, reduced to burning oblivion, sullied and soiled by the madness of war and the inhumanity excused in the name of nationalism. Only the dead and those waiting to die stood upon the sandy beaches.

The crew on the *Folkstone* lost their collective breath when they began to recognize and pass debris in the water – remnants of destroyed vessels, drifting in oil-slick waters. Then as the shore came into view, the smoldering steel remains of military vehicles stranded on the beach, destroyed and now an ominous part of the backdrop of the humanitarian disaster at Dunkirk.

To Leif, the smoking, inanimate remains resembled a horde of huddled prehistoric beasts that had been dipped in boiling tar and left out to fossilize. It looked as if the convoy wasn't only traveling into a warzone, they were also traveling back in time to the Paleolithic Age.

The ensign raised his binoculars, scanning ahead for a long moment, and then he lowered the instrument and quietly whispered, 'Sweet Christ save us all.' Everyone would soon share the same sentiment.

The convoy propelled further towards the French coast, until it was forced to stop short and rapidly change its course. A half-submerged vessel recently pulverized by German artillery was floundering in their path.

The *Folkstone*'s captain steered around the lifeless obstacles, desperately trying to avoid contact, while the crew stared at the wreckage with collective concern and realization of the seriousness of their situation. The only proof humans had once been aboard these ships were the corpses floating in the water, faces down or staring, sightless to the sky above.

Suddenly, the ensign looked over the bow, then whipped his head towards the preoccupied captain, 'Reduce speed to one third – we've got mines in the water.'

The captain acknowledged the instruction and the forward motion of the *Folkstone* was reduced. The ensign put his hand firmly on Leif's shoulder. 'Get another crew member up here – you know what to look for.'

Leif caught Martin's attention, who was still enraptured by smoking. 'We've got mines in the water – come with me.' Martin took the cigarette from his lips and tossed it overboard.

The pair rushed to the bow of the boat and scanned the ocean for either German mines, or recently bombed-out vessels drifting in the current, which might strike the *Folkstone* or detonate a mine and initiate a chain reaction.

'Look', Martin said, 'a survivor in the water.' Before they could react, a wave toppled the floating body, who's torso bobbed-inverted revealing the gore of his missing legs and recent demise – German artillery barrages were taking their toll.

The ensign called back, looking over his shoulder toward the ship's wheelhouse and gave the captain a wave, and instructed, 'Steady as she goes.'

Operation DYNAMO, the Allied evacuation from Dunkirk, France, 26 May – 4 June 1940. (*Photo courtesy of the online Pinecrest Stock Imagery*)

The captain nodded, then wiped the perspiration from his brow with the sleeve of his wool sweater and mockingly whispered, 'Steady? Steady my arse, there's nothing goddamn steady about this at all.' His cynicism was well-placed.

Minutes later, three strategic horn-blasts bleated from the corvette escort ship, signaling that the oversized leader of the convoy was pulling out of formation, that its role in the mission was over for now. The corvette would loiter at a distance, provide defensive fire for any approaching German aircraft and assist with the return voyage, with whatever remnants of the small-craft convoy were left to return to England. The flotilla of thirty small vessels would have to brave the beach alone.

As the drone of the corvette's engine retreated, a new sound immediately occupied the vacancy, ear-splitting screams from in-bound artillery shells launched from several German batteries located in land from the French coast began a new barrage.

The German artillery had decamped within such proximity to the convoy that shells were detonating several hundred yards offshore, churning the water amongst the convoy like the froth of a witch's brew. The extended line of rescue boats in the flotilla began to disperse as they moved ever closer to the beach and the awaiting Allied soldiers.

Before the *Folkstone* had time to adjust to the enemy's new onslaught, they heard a high-pitched whistle from above. Before they could muster a response, the surface of the water, barely 30 yards ahead, erupted with a massive torrent of water rising from the sea like the frenzy of a wounded whale breaching – revealing its rage.

Leif and the ensign instinctively tightened their grips on the bow's railing, while getting coated in a geyser of crashing water, stinging sharp against their skin, and bandying them about the surface of the boat's deck as if they were rag dolls.

The captain gripped the wheel white-knuckle tight, fighting the tension and torque, trying to hold steady and not capsize the vessel. His effort was a snapshot of desperate valor until 10 feet of spiraling water enveloped the sides of the craft, and the hull groaned and rolled from the shuddering impact.

Leif lost his grip, soared up with the surface on a wave and smashed into the ensign, who arrested his motion.

The ensign grabbed Leif to support his recovery. 'That was close!' the ensign said.

Leif wanted to respond that it was more than close, it felt like inches from a direct hit, but the ensign's face instantly calmed him. The visage was pale, but absent panic. The ensign offered a rationale for his eerie grace, 'This is my third pick-up in the past five days.'

Without warning, the two were tangled in an awkward embrace, balancing themselves against each other's arms and legs, when another German shell impacted the water, this time, only 20 yards off the *Folkstone*'s starboard bow, sending the craft reeling, undulating in the wake of the artillery shells explosion. The crew shouted curses at the violent momentum, threatening to suck them into the undertow.

The captain ripped the wheel to the right, trying to seek sanctuary from the German's line of fire, while screaming at the crew to pile onto the opposite side of the boat to stabilize the water weight and save her from capsizing.

The ensign said, 'The Germans are closer to the coast… Much closer than last time.' He winked at Leif. 'Means we've got to hurry.'

Leif stared into the ensign's pale blue eyes and once again his deliberations returned to his father,

This is exactly how Frederik Bangsbøll would react under intense enemy fire. He'd remain dispassionate to the unfolding chaos and try to plan his next move, while always assuring the safety of his men.

Even as Leif glimpsed the gaping void of annihilation, he felt calm in the presence of the ensign. The captain had piloted the craft out of immediate harm's way, the flood had subsided, the ensign rose to his feet, and Leif did likewise.

The ensign's eyes peered about 100 yards ahead, directly off the port bow. He didn't immediately share the discovery that had popped into his perspective with Leif, just instructed the captain, 'TURN HARD TO PORT!'

The captain yelled, spitting tobacco juice. 'That's worse than where we came from. She doesn't have many turns left.' Suddenly, Martin and several other soaked crew members rushed to the bow and jumped onto the rail. The engineer shouted to the captain, 'CAPTAIN, THERE ARE MEN IN THE WATER – TURN HARD TO PORT!'

The ensign turned to Leif, noted the direction of the floundering vessel and barked, 'Bastards. That ship was going home. It was carrying survivors from the beach.' Some of the crew shielded their eyes, others lowered their heads in prayer. Those weren't men they saw floating. It was detritus from a fallen rescue boat gutted by a direct hit from a German artillery shell, polluting the water with its innards and the remnants of its crew – darkening its shade of pitch. The ensign took a deep breath. 'You can proceed captain… no survivors here.'

The captain began to rotate the wheel back towards the beach, when he suddenly stopped, jerking the *Folkstone*, sending the crew reeling, literally and figuratively.

From the *Folkstone*'s wheelhouse the captain pointed and yelled, 'I SEE SURVIVORS IN THE WATER!' The crew rushed to the opposite rail, peered over, and shouted in joy and enthusiasm. They could pick out the survivors, still within the vicinity of the disabled craft, bobbing amongst the turbulent swells and debris, trying to hang onto the sides of the demolished vessel for survival.

The captain steered the *Folkstone* out of the convoy formation and proceeded to the steel husk of the stricken ship, stripped down by the blast. Pieces of the stern and hull stood intact, defiant, like a raised black flag, refusing to surrender. The ensign turned toward Leif and said, 'You smell that?' Leif sniffed the surrounding air. 'Diesel fuel.' The surface of the sea was coated with the fuel oil.

The ensign nodded gravely. 'We haven't much time before what's left of that craft blows and takes us all with it. We need to work quickly.' He patted Leif on the back. 'Get to it lad. Round up the boys.' Within minutes the deck of the *Folkstone* transformed into a rescue station replete with ropes, life jackets and Kisbee rings to throw to the survivors.

The *Folkstone* came as close to the floundering boat as it dared. The crew saw dozens of men clinging to the gunnels, while others swam against the ocean swells, struggling to stay afloat trying to not swallow the fuel oil fouling the sea or end up sliced or impaled by the drifting debris. The cruelty was doubled. Many of the men were already wounded, bleeding, screaming in pain, having survived Dunkirk, and now forced to fight for their lives again in the churning sea.

The *Folkstone* came to a halt. The crew began pitching life jackets and rope lines into the water. And as the survivors migrated toward the craft, German artillery sent another salvo of death and destruction, narrowly missing the *Folkstone*, but landing a direct hit amongst the convoy itself. Soon the rescuers would need rescuing.

The massed flotilla of rescue boats were thrown awry, some instantly flooded, others straining to squelch out fires, while the worst hit had their crews jump overboard for safety. A progressive line of explosions from the German batteries rippled across the ocean in a catastrophic current. The waves kicked up tens of feet into the air and crashed on the marooned soldiers, snapping down on their bodies, complicating the *Folkstone*'s already near-impossible task.

The ensign shouted encouragement to the stricken soldiers, begging them to swim, but the pitiable men were disoriented, shocked and frozen by the renewed German bombardment.

Leif took note of a floundering young soldier without a life jacket and bearing his heavy steal helmet, the brim of which was catching each wave and dragging the soldier away and under the water, pulling him further from the *Folkstone*'s reach with each successive wave.

The ensign spotted the boy as well, and without thinking, kicked off his shoes and dove head first into the roiling ocean. When he surfaced with fuel-oil in his eyes he called back to Leif to help direct him to the stricken soldier, for in the brief time he was underwater, another round of German artillery had scattered the soldiers who all wore the same expression: terrified, bloodied, their youth and innocence rapidly drained from their faces.

Leif scanned the ocean's surface complete with debris and bobbing heads and waving arms of frightened men for the young solider in the helmet. Suddenly, his attention was diverted, wrested to the right, where a fire had spread from one of the bombed-out would-be rescue boats, across its hull, and was rapidly making its way to the pooled fuel oil surrounding the boat. Once the blaze made impact with the flammable accelerants the boat would blow and envelope them all in an inferno. The ensign's shout broke Leif's focus: 'WHERE'S THE BOY?'

Leif adjusted his focus, scanned for the soldier, but became more concerned about the ensign, who had dove into the water without a life jacket. Now the ensign was at the mercy of the ocean, which was yanking him up and down, laboring his breathing with his mouth fouled by fuel oil. Leif whipped back and forth between the fire gaining on the fuel, and the ensign, all precious seconds from catastrophe. The struggling soldier tried to call out for help but was strangled by the chaotic elements around him and the dwindling consciousness and the gripping, cold, calm embrace of death.

Finally, Leif saw a hand rise above the churning surface of the sea, followed by the helmet-clad head. The soldier's face was drawn, desperate, near devoid of life. Leif yelled, pointed him out to the ensign. 'THERE… THERE HE IS, DIRECTLY BEHIND YOU!'

The ensign followed the direction of Leif's outstretched arm, but by the time he reached the soldier, the boy was on his way back down, a dead weight, the ocean's carrion prize.

The ensign filled his lungs, lunged for the back of the young soldier's uniform collar, and grabbed the fabric in his fist, until the sea clawed at the helmet once more, not ready to relinquish the boy.

The captain of the *Folkstone* watched the stricken rescue vessel across the way burst into flames, then shouted to the crew, still trying to pull the survivors onboard: 'I'VE GOT TO PULL BACK. TELL THE MEN TO KEEP SWIMMING TO US AND TO FOLLOW MY LEAD.'

Leif pointed to the spot where the ensign had last been seen and pleaded, 'CAPTAIN, HE ALMOST HAS HIM!' But the request was to no avail, the captain had undertaken the necessary maneuver to extricate the *Folkstone* from imminent danger. The soldiers in the sea tried to keep pace with the withdrawing *Folkstone*, not looking back, pushing forward before their former rescue vessel exploded. The ensign rose to the water's surface, holding the soldier close to his chest, still struggling with the chin strap of the tin hat.

Leif kept them in his sights, but he was losing visibility. The further the *Folkstone* moved to outpace the fire, the further the ensign was from sanctuary. He shouted to the ensign, hoping to be heard, 'TAKE OFF HIS HELMET!'

A wave crashed over them and they were gone, tugged under the ocean again. The young soldier's tin hat had been dislodged from his head by the impact of the last wave and sunk in a gentle, fluttering motion towards the ocean floor. Leif was overcome. It was as if he could read his relationship with his own father onto the brave ensign and suffering soldier and refused to let either of them die that day. Leif kicked off his shoes, tossed two life jackets onto the water's surface, and dove off the *Folkstone*'s railing.

The crew rushed to the bow, calling him crazy, while cheering on his efforts. It made them feel braver, more worthy, more human, just being in the vicinity of Leif's suicidal act of courage.

'The Dane is certifiably mad.' Martin said, smiling, watching his new friend confront the violently oscillating sea. Leif realized he couldn't fight the sea, and leaned into a surging, swelling wave, letting it drag him out to the ensign and his charge, who were locked in the same spot, relenting to the force and pull of the waves. Leif reached them, wrapped his legs around the ensign's to stabilize him and fastened the lifejacket to his torso before the man passed out from oxygen deprivation. Then he turned his attention to the boy, yelled at him to stop trying to swim, that he was only making it harder, and to hang onto Leif's life jacket while he pulled them both back to the boat. The soldier went limp, grateful for the rest, and placed himself under Leif's guiding hand. Leif grabbed the boy by the back of the collar, began doing the sidestroke, frantically trying to keep the soldier's head above water. His efforts were for nothing.

Just as the ensign regained his senses and cleared the stinging oil from his eyes, another German shell crashed in the water directly behind him. The concussion radiated out from the blast, through the sea water rupturing every organ in the ensign's body. At that same moment, Leif closed his eyes and inhaled a deep breath as the shell's explosion created a sinkhole effect in the surrounding waters, dragging Leif and the soldier into the center of the maelstrom.

Leif desperately held the boy tightly as they flailed together under water, hoping to ride the momentum to safety, but realistically expecting to perish from the pressure and lack of air. He began to lose visibility, to lose sight of the world above water, everything reduced to an aqueous smear. Leif eyes burned with sea salt and diesel fuel. He hoped his heart gave out before he drowned. He stared into the blurry face of the young soldier. There was no denying it. The boy must be dead. And Leif would be joining him soon.

Leif wished he had written to Frederik one last time before he boarded the *Folkstone*, wished he had told someone his father's name or given an address.

Leif wanted him to know that his son had perished in an honorable fashion of a bearer of the Bangsbøll name, that he had earned his place in Valhalla. That his deeds would be bandied around the dinner table of Viking gods, until Frederik arrived in due time. And as if Frederik had willed it, another German shell cracked against the water, and the explosion had such a massive reach, that Leif and the solider were expelled to the top of the water, thrust and nestled inside a wave, propelling them up and forward, depositing them just a few yards from of the *Folkstone*. Leif opened his eyes, the crew of the *Folkstone* were on deck hauling the remaining soldiers to salvation.

Martin saw Leif bobbing close to the craft and rushed over, soaked cigarette dangling from his lip. He quickly lowered a rope down to Leif, who tied it around the dead soldier. His sacrifice demanded as much. They dragged the boy up, then pushed his body over the gunwales, where he flopped against the deck with a sickening splat, and immediately upon impact, the body began to hurl up seawater. He was shaken, but still alive.

Leif prepared to climb back on board the *Folkstone*, extending his hand toward Martin for the rope, when suddenly he felt a sharp tug at his heel, and a force began to drag him back down into the ocean. Leif wrenched his head around, ready to fight, ready to struggle, but instead, he found another soldier, a refugee from the blasted boat, gasping for air, and digging his desperate fingers into Leif's calf for salvation. 'I'VE GOT ANOTHER ONE!' he yelled to Martin, and braced himself against the side of the ship, then tied the rope around the exhausted soldier's waist, and helped Martin raise him onto the deck, where the soldier joined the pandemonium on deck. Once aboard, Leif slowly surveyed the deck of the *Folkston*, which was a mass of wet, brown wool-clad bodies. The crew had performed admirably in their mission, managing to save most of the men from the waters who had survived the charnel house of Dunkirk.

Martin collapsed next to his new Danish mate, pulled out a cigarette, affixed it to his lip, and relaxed under the blue swirls of smoke. The captain advanced the throttle, brought the vessel around, and pointed its bow back to England, then crossed himself several times, begging divine intervention to get them out of firing range. The *Folkstone* was overloaded and riding low in the water. The captain had to keep the speed down otherwise the boat would capsize.

Leif closed his eyes, teeth chattering, chilled to the bone and in shock from the near-death experience in the sea. His first conscious thought was: 'I don't even know what that brave ensign's name was.'

Before his clothing had dried, Leif had reached a life-changing decision. He was going to find a way into this war – not just trying to rescue frightened soldiers escaping from the enemy – a real, fighting job!

It was time for this Dane to become a Viking.

Chapter 9

Sailing Over the Horizon

'Wars are not won by evacuations … and there will be dark days ahead. We shall fight in France, we shall fight on the seas and oceans, we shall fight with the growing confidence and growing strength in the air, we shall defend our island, whatever the cost may be. We shall fight on the beaches, we shall fight on the landing grounds, we shall fight in the fields and in the streets, we shall fight in the hills; we shall never surrender.'

Sir Winston Churchill

Everyone aboard the *Folkstone* was exhausted. From the twenty-one shocked, bruised, but grateful British soldiers rescued from the sanguinary slaughter at Dunkirk, to the successfully saved tugboat crew sunk by German artillery, to the *Folkstone*'s crew itself. Together, in an overloaded vessel, the *Folkstone* was beating a hasty but cautious retreat towards England and the safety of the harbor at Dover. Leif and the *Folkstone* crew thought about the young British ensign who had led their rescue mission and now lay in the dark depths of the Channel. It had all happened so suddenly.

Leif also had to be counted amongst the depleted amongst the *Folkstone*'s complement. He had witness death and destruction and had nearly met his maker in the sea off the coast of France. Wet and wrapped in an old blanket, which smelt like decaying seaweed, he sat with his back leaning against the bulkhead of the wheelhouse, listening to the hoarse tremulous voices of the British soldiers around him – jubilant in their survival but still weary of their futures. Leif listened to their banter while he scanned the early night sky, searching for the appearance of the azimuth off Polaris. The North Star, his father's constellation, the celestial body Frederik sought whenever he was lost, thrown off course and desperate for a guiding light. Like many of life's confrontations, more darkness was ahead before the appearance of his guiding light would present itself to him. For Leif felt asunder.

Upon awakening, as they approached the port of Dover, darkness had set in, the skies had cleared and the moon was coming up over the horizon. Leif stretched and his muscles ached and rebelled against further movement. He felt proud of his actions of this day, deeply content that at a moment that called for courage he proved able to deliver without prevacation. However, he felt overcome, as if he had taken the first step into a new world, that he had participated in a mission far bigger than a run to rescue soldiers in peril, a mission that would come to define his days to come in unforeseen ways. And if his father's steadying presence wasn't available, then he would continue to search for Frederik's astral avatar and hope it would reorient him in his father's absence.

One sailor lamented,

> At least the Norwegians were able to smuggle out a bunch of their naval ships and military aircraft to England before they got in Hitler's hands. Lord knows that mad man doesn't need any more air power.

When Leif heard Norway, he stopped skimming the sky for the North Star, and tilted his water-logged ear toward the soldiers sitting in a semi-circle near to him. Was this the sign from Frederik he'd been waiting for? Was his father trying to pass along information about a neighbor to help Leif divine the future?

With Dover's lights in sight, realizing they were now truly safe, the soldiers began to banter about the war situation. Even to the common soldier, it was clear that the greatest danger facing Britain was the massive superiority and strength of the Luftwaffe. It tore apart and razed anything in its sphere, veritably salting the earth with bombs, to clear the path for a land invasion. As the German high command was keenly aware, the Luftwaffe had to assert its unparalleled dominance of the skies to blaze the path for a successful seaborne invasion of Britain. While Britain knew that to keep Hitler's Luftwaffe at bay and overcome their vulnerabilities, it had to expand its air force and supply of qualified pilots far beyond their current levels. There wasn't a second to waste, neither a sliver nor shard, if England hoped to match Hitler in the skies above Britain.

* * *

As the *Folkstone* trundled across the waters of the English Channel, with each wave left in its wake, a plan began to form in Leif's mind. His commitment to the war effort would take a new turn, would venture into a new element, one possibly guided by his father's unseen hand, and a tacit understanding between father and son.

For as much as it might pain Frederik, he hadn't managed to raise a son who shared his mythic pull of the sea. Leif wanted to explore a new element, preferably outside the confines of a merchant vessel's engine room, where he would no longer retire to bed with grease under his nails and the smell of diesel fuel. 'Yes', he thought,

I'll take my abilities to the air. There are plenty of sailors, but Britain is desperately in need of pilots. And I'm still unable to return home. So why not? I'm a quick study. I learned how to cook from Manny and in a week and effectively found my way around the complexities of a ship's engine room during a semester off from school.

It was at least conceivable that he could become an air force pilot aiding the British cause. Leif spoke what he'd charitably call passable English and French and was fluent in Danish, Norwegian and German. And it wasn't as if his own country needed him, as if he could join the Danish military and fight for his homeland. Denmark was both neutral and under Nazi occupation. If he had any hope of seeing his father again, he'd need to find a country prosecuting the war that he could ally himself with. It might as well be the British flying a bunch of smuggled Norwegian hardware if they'd have him.

After disembarking the exhausted, yet truly grateful soldiers at Dover, to the awaiting convoy of army lories, the *Folkstone*'s crew were given sandwiches and hot tea by local residents before they set sail for Portsmouth. The captain and crew of the *Folkstone* had expected to moor at Dover overnight in order to go back for another load of evacuees the following morning, however, the Dover harbor master, under orders from Admiral Preston, the commander of the Small Boat Auxiliary Fleet, advised them that three more convoys, totaling 110 vessels were preparing to rendezvous at Dunkirk at sunrise. As a result, the services of the *Folkstone*, though greatly appreciated, would not be needed again. The final two hours of their very long day was spent mostly in exhausted silence.

It was almost midnight when the *Folkstone* came alongside the quay in Portsmouth. The crew was heading to the nearest pub, but Leif could not join them. He had much to do still. Leif bid farewell to his newfound shipmates and brothers in arms and made his way back to the still-anchored *C.O. Stillman*. After advising the captain of the *C.O. Stillman* of the past day's events and that he was resigning from the ship's company, Leif told him that he was destine for London and the Norwegian Embassy, where he would volunteer to join the Royal Norwegian Air Force. Leif was on the train to London the next morning.

Leif quickly learned that even in times of war, bureaucracy and 'red tape' are still in great supply. The diplomatic clerk at the Norwegian Embassy accepted Leif's application but told him that, given his circumstances, the administrative process would undoubtedly prove complex, and processing his application along with required visas could take months. 'Young man, the war could conceivably be over by then.' The clerk knocked on the desk and said, 'God willing.'

Leif held his tongue, leaving out how if the war terminated in such a collapsed time span, the Allies likely wouldn't be the winners. There was no point. He'd figured out the *modus operandi* of the mid-level bureaucrat. War or no war, those in his position didn't like to make decisions of any sort. If Leif wanted to be a pilot, he'd have to make it far easier for the diplomat to say yes.

He decided it was a prudent moment to introduce his deep connections to Norway, to his service aboard many of their merchant vessels, and to the high-ranking government connections of his former employer, the owner of the ill-fated *C.O. Stillman*, which was still at anchor at Portsmouth harbor. Leif waited for an answer.

The diplomat restated his position, but this time very slowly, and agonizingly offered his 'young Danish friend' the necessary paperwork with a forlorn sigh.

Leif stepped outside the embassy with a heavy heart, ready to toss the visa application in the nearest rubbish bin when an idea seized him, and he felt his mother's influence in his veins. Leif felt Rigmor's perseverance, her indomitable spirit, and her steadfast refusal to ever accept no as an acceptable answer to any obstacle, stiffened the young Dane's spine. Frederik may have been the parent at sea risking his life for king and country, but Rigmor, often alone for months at a time, a woman with an absentee husband, had developed her own methods of dealing with stubborn men, perfecting an uncanny ability of wrapping an individual around her finger and mercilessly entrapping them, long before they could ascertain what happened.

It was in this spirit, that Leif made his way to the Danish Embassy a few blocks away and found himself in an understaffed space harried by a severe diplomatic crisis at home. Hitler's occupation had seemingly sent out every Dane living in England to the embassy, all of whom were trying to ascertain the status of their stranded family members and friends and inquiring about refugee status.

Leif endured another protracted wait, and was finally granted another disagreeable, grumbling audience with an embassy official. The diplomat at the Danish Embassy repeated chapter and verse, and with little variation, the Norwegian's interminable spiel regarding issues of nationality, territorial neutrality and sovereignty, to which Leif, upon realizing that it was spineless men like this – and their spiritual cousins – who had allowed Hitler to rearm and run roughshod over Czechoslovakia, Poland, Norway and Denmark without raising a lick of resistance, finally said, 'The sovereign might want to know…'

The diplomat replied, 'That is a curious choice of words, sir: "sovereign".'

'Well, seeing that my father, is a close friend of King Christian, our sovereign, he might be interested in why I am not being accommodated.'

The diplomat chortled, 'You. You know our king?'

Leif nodded. 'My father, naval captain Frederik Bangsbøll of the Royal Danish Navy was a school mate of the Crown Prince, they've known each other for years.'

'That's all well and good…' the diplomat said dismissively, as if none of this helped Leif's case.

Leif finally decided to improvise, to take a risk as if he were back on stage and threaten the one thing this man obviously treasured above all else: his job. 'I'll have you thrown to the gutters of London if you don't give me what I ask.'

He locked eyes with Leif. 'On whose authority, young man?'

'On the authority of the king.' Leif met the man's glare. 'Do you want to take the chance?' He waited for the gravity of his threat to register, then raised his index finger for emphasis.

> My name is Leif Bangsbøll. My father's name is Commander Frederik Bangsbøll, commandant of the Royal Danish Submarine Fleet School at Holmen Naval Base, Copenhagen. Make a call. See if I'm lying. And considering your behavior, you had better hope that I am.

The diplomat was daunted by Leif's refusal to leave the embassy without the proper papers and a visa in hand. In response, he rose from his chair and slammed the officer door on his way out.

Thirty minutes later, the diplomat returned, all smiles, effusively apologetic and borderline treacly. It had worked. Leif had managed to extemporize his way out a sticky situation. He had no clue who the diplomat had consulted to confirm Leif's story, but the bureaucrat had clearly received unequivocal orders to process the paperwork immediately. Suddenly, all roads had been cleared, Leif's papers and visa were being processed with nary a diplomatic issue. 'You will be assigned to the Royal Norwegian Air Force as a pilot in training and will leave for Canada in eight weeks', the diplomat said, 'where you will embark on your training, Mr Bangsbøll.'

'Canada?' Leif asked. 'Why Canada? I thought I'd be training in England flying Norwegian crafts.'

The diplomat shrugged his shoulders, finding his forked tongue anew.

> My apologies, sir. The plans of the British War Cabinet are slightly out of my domain. My humble role is simply to inform you of your paperwork's progress and your imminent relocation.

Unsurprisingly, the embassy employee's insouciance did not bring Leif any closer to an answer. 'Why in the hell am I being sent to Canada for training? The war is here.' The answer would reveal itself in due time.

Knowing that he had almost two months until he was to be shipped out to Canada to commence pilot training with the Norweigian Air Force under the

Ship's crew identity card of Leif Bangsboll, Assistant Engineer M/S Esso Balboa, August 1940. (*Photo courtesy of the author's family collection*)

British Commonwealth Air Traiing Plan (BCATP), Leif took the trian back to Portsmouth and signed as short contract with the merchant ship *Esso Balboa* as its interim assistant engineer. The Esso Balboa was conducting short-haul shipping services along the south and west coast of the United Kingdom. This temporary assignment would help pass the time for Leif and keep him close to his Embassy contacts in London – should the situation change.

Chapter 10

A Transformations Begins

'It is not the strongest or the most intelligent who will survive change but those who can best manage change.'

Charles Darwin

Once the Luftwaffe's awesome aerial prowess was made manifest and undeniable, the British quickly realized that the RAF would be called upon to stave off or at least blunt and delay any German invasion of Britain. The RAF needed to provide their prospective pilots a safe refuge to train far away from Germany's reach. Canada, one of Britain's stalwart former colonies, stood up and offered the air force a new home. Safe from the ravages of war, Canada enabled the BCATP to operate without fear of enemy attack and where it would train thousands of would-be Allied air force pilots with the skills they would need to confront the mighty Luftwaffe.

But the collaboration between Britain and Canada went well beyond training pilots and had been in effect before the Luftwaffe inaugurated the war with their aggression in Poland. Since late 1937, British intelligence agents had been reporting Hitler's military build-up, and although the political climate of the day prevented quick punishment being doled out to Germany by its neighbors, the foresight of certain political players regarding Hitler's real intentions caught the attention of Prime Minister Winston Churchill and American President Franklin D. Roosevelt.

* * *

One of the main personalities behind this unconventional alliance was Sir William Stephenson, a Canadian Army officer, airman, entrepreneur, inventor, spymaster and the senior representative of British intelligence for the Western Hemisphere. Stephenson also sat atop the BSC office located in New York City, which maintained close ties to the highest levels of the American government and armed forces.

Immediately after the near disaster of Dunkirk, Stephenson was tasked by the British government to deliver military intelligence to the United States, and doggedly reinforce the necessity of armed support from America in the form of a lend-lease program, which FDR had been dragging his feet on delivering. It was a delicate political calculus for Stephenson.

The United States remained staunchly politically neutral in the conflict and public opinion refused to budge. And FDR, despite his reluctance, was a valuable ally, far more than what the Republican slate was currently offering. And if Britain pushed FDR too hard into the war, he might lose the next election, and Churchill could be stuck dealing with an isolationist, while London burned.

Although none of this came as a shock to Stephenson, who vividly remembered Versailles, where American President Woodrow Wilson talked an enormous game, spread dreams of decolonization and encouraged a nascent nationalism amongst all peoples, one that would grow to include the League of Nations. However, when push came to shove, Wilson could not get his own Congress to vote in favor of joining the institution that their own president established, preferring to remain untouched by global events that did not directly affect Americans. Nonetheless, Churchill instructed Stephenson to use all the tools of his trade to realize his objective: 'Our primary directive is that American participation in the war is the most important single objective for Britain.'

Stephenson understood the urgency of his task, and he had a special conduit that he believed could accelerate the lend-lease delivery. The two men had been collaborating in the shadows for well over a year, both literally and metaphorically and results were being manifested for Britain and within its allies.

For Stephenson was a veteran of the dark arts, the practice and application of espionage in the name of national security, or national interests, operating in the nebulous zone between the two. He was the strongest proponent and supporter of Britain's SOE, a hallowed secret wartime agency responsible for recruiting and training secret agents to perform reconnaissance work within enemy territory, and if necessary, execute sabotage operations. The SOE performed its role alongside Britain's secret intelligence service M16 and their sister counterintelligence agency, M15.

Stephenson would find his doppelganger and route to FRD's ear in an American counterpart who shared his storied past from the First World War, his enthusiasm for unconventional and asymmetric methods, and for Britain's ongoing survival. His name was Colonel William 'Wild Bill' Donovan. These two men, in tandem, would develop their own parallel method of facing Hitler's blitzkrieg from above, and it would not be restricted to harnessing their air, their approach would come from all possible corners, and like the Luftwaffe would soften up the enemy's underbelly for a lightning attack.

Donovan was a highly decorated First World War veteran, addicted to the unconventional. He possessed a sterling devotion to internationalism and democracy, a wealth of knowledge and experience into the nooks and crannies of American politics, and unlimited access to the ear of FDR, stretching back to 1905, when they both attended Columbia University studying for their undergraduate and law degrees.

* * *

In those Ivy League halls, where Donovan was a star American football player, the parameters of their unique friendship were shaped, a relationship that would grow in stature and respect with the First World War, in which Donovan cemented his reputation as the consummate warrior, earning the DSC, the DSM, and the Medal of Honor as a battalion commander in the 'Fighting 69th' Regiment. After Donovan's return from Europe, FDR, who was then assistant secretary of the United States Navy, made Donovan a member of the Office of Naval Intelligence, and the rumors swirled that Donovan was given this strategic spot to become FDR's 'personal intelligence agent'.

However, as Donovan's nickname presaged, 'Wild Bill' answered to no one, even the Democratic president, his friend for over thirty years. Donovan was a hardline Republican, outspoken anti-New Deal critic, unsuccessful New York State Gubernatorial candidate, vastly more successful Manhattan lawyer, and who unlike his Canadian counterpart, Stephenson, took a vastly different approach regarding matters of persuasion. Donovan was given to haranguing isolationist representatives on the Congressional floor, complaining he had more enemies in Washington than Europe, carrying a loaded weapon with him into the White House, and constantly whispering to FDR to find avenues into assisting with the war effort without undermining his reelection chances. Little things, like, giving Donovan enough rope to collaborate with the British in mapping out a critical 'shadow war', and running cover for his efforts from the White House.

In early May 1940, just weeks prior to the Dunkirk crisis, Donovan and Stephenson held a planning summit at the Waldorf Astoria Hotel in New York, far away from the prying eyes of Washington, and filled with Donovan's dreaded enemies who he considered no better than a cabal of fifth columnists. According to those present, the meeting was a smashing success and Donovan quickly reciprocated by flying to London, under heightened security, in order to firm things up on the British end of the intelligence partnership.

Immediately following Donovan's and Churchill's *tête-à-tête*, the British SOE was instructed to help Donovan establish its American counterpart, greatly expanding the Allies potential for irregular warfare, and beginning the 'intelligence blitzkrieg' that would do in the shadow, what Hitler was performing in the air and on the ground across Europe.

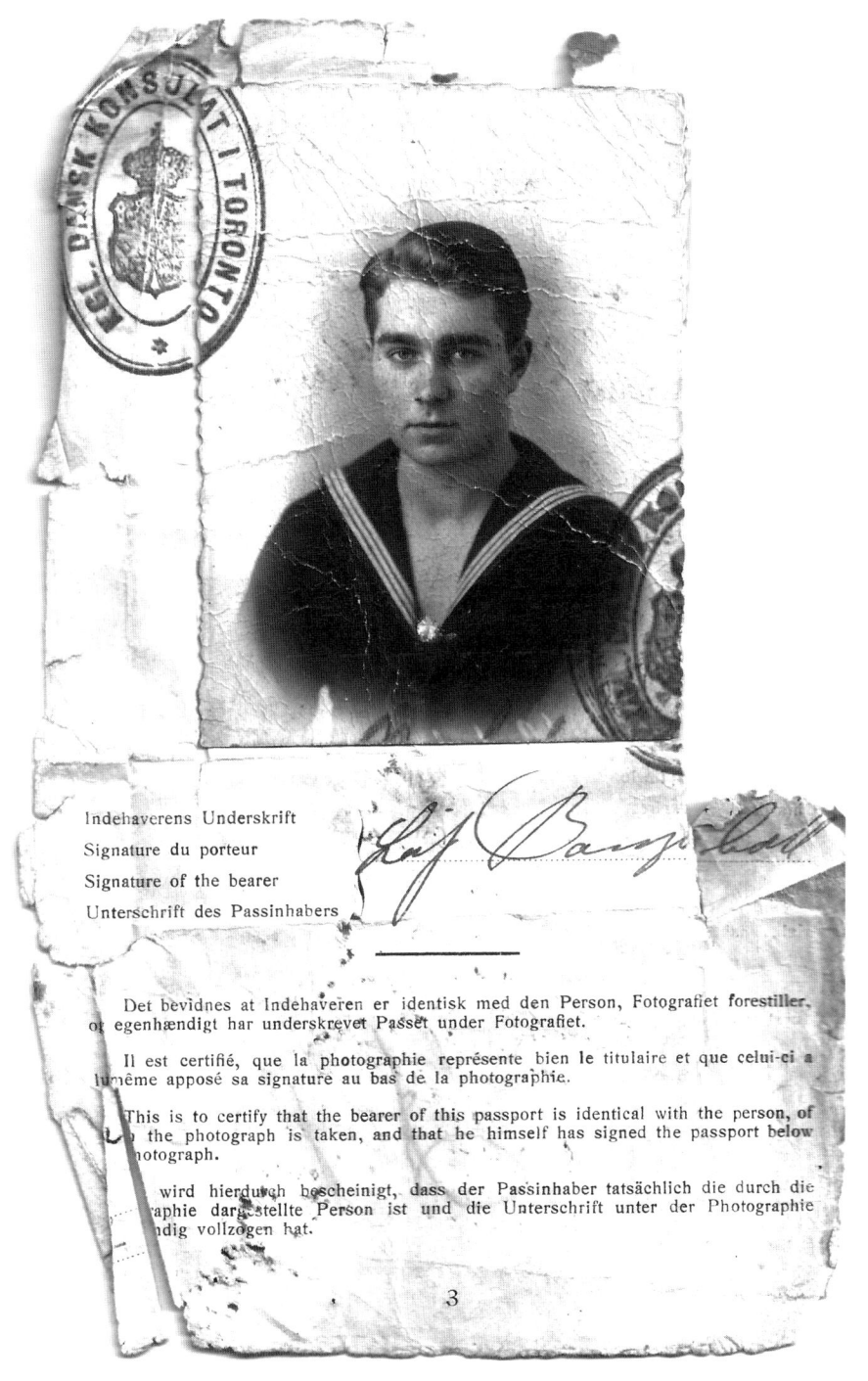

Danish Passport of Leif Bangsboll, with official stamp from the Consulate of Denmark, Toronto Canada, 1941, at the commencement of flying training with the Norwegian Air Force as part of the British Commonwealth Air Training Plan (BCATP). (*Photo courtesy of the author's family collection*)

Donovan's fledgling domestic intelligence agency would be named the Office of Strategic Services (OSS), a centralized clearing house that would engage in radically new forms of directed guerilla war, psychological and political subversion, and commando raids. Together, the British SOE and American OSS pioneered a unique and arguably never duplicated form of clandestine combat operations preceded by an ideological assault that would live on after the Second World War in the forms of an overhauled MI6 in Britain, and the CIA and United States Army Special Forces in the United States.

Both Stephenson and Donovan knew that incubating a secret army would require a sizeable commitment of resources and stealthy acumen to perform their objective, which according to Churchill was nothing less than to 'Set Europe ablaze by promoting sabotage and subversion behind enemy lines at every opportunity.'

Thus, in August 1940, when Stephenson made his desperate, post-Dunkirk visit to the United States, Donovan was able to push hard on FDR, citing the slaughter on the beaches, and the undeniable fact that Hitler now had the backdoor open to France. What more did the president possibly need to give Donovan? The answer was, access to the secret British training facility in Canada known only as 'Camp X.'

Stephenson returned home a hero, reporting back to Churchill that according to the agreed on lend-lease program, Britain would receive 50 naval destroyers, 100 USAAF B-17 bomber aircrafts, and 1 million modern rifles. While in return, the United States was given access to many British naval bases around the globe and shared use and administration of Camp X, where Americans would be able to develop OSS personnel with British and Canadian assistance, under the watchful glimpse of Donovan.

Camp X had been constructed on a 200-acre expanse of rolling hills located on the north shore of Lake Ontario, directly adjacent to the camouflaging farming town of Whitby, Ontario. Who would believe an enormous secret Allied training apparatus existed in the lush rolling hills adjacent to the picturesque shores of Lake Ontario? However, there was another reason behind Camp X's strategic placement. Placing critical technical infrastructure in Canada allowed for cryptic communication patterns to travel safely between SOE and OSS leadership, bypassing Britain's circuits, which were constantly bombarded by Hitler's codebreakers, and avoiding the eager eyes of American politicians and military intelligence, both desperate to catch Donovan and FDR in the act, and serve their sins to an isolationist public, and even more importantly, for those same selfish individuals to protect their own jobs, because the OSS was a direct threat to the already entrenched intelligence services serving the president.

* * *

A Transformations Begins   113

Norweigan Air Force technicians paint "Denmark I" on the aircraft of their Danish pilot-in-training, Flight-Sergeant Leif Bangsboll at Canadian Forces Base Moose Jaw, 1941. (*Photo courtesy of the author's family collection*)

Leif, now a member of the Royal Norwegian Air Force, arrived in Halifax, Nova Scotia from England in mid-September 1940, a pitstop before his ultimate, and yet unknown destination at Camp X. From Halifax, Leif was sent to Ottawa, where he met his Canadian Army liaison officer, Major Raymond Massey, and received three days of orientation briefings, before he became the lone Dane amongst a throng of Norwegian pilot recruits given their transfer orders and train tickets to Canadian Forces Base Moose Jaw – in the midst of the vast Canadian prairies. There amongst the limitless prairie landscape Leif and his Norwegian colleagues would commence their basic flight training.

Moose Jaw's unimpeachable status as the sunniest, perpetually clear-skied location in Canada was another boon to the training process, which would rarely, if ever, be interrupted by inclement weather. The greatest challenge to the trainees was maintaining overall spatial awareness while flying over the checkerboard prairie fields that stretched across a horizon absent any distinguishable landmarks to provide a point of reference at altitude. The trans-Canada railway and scattered roadways running east-west were the only discernible topographical markers.

Leif held two advantages over the other recruits when it came to spending the day in the cockpit of a Curtiss P-36 Hawk. First, the engine and technical aspects of the craft were relatively streamlined in comparison to an ungainly fuming diesel engine belching oil and steam while hauling hundreds across the sea. From its exterior, the Curtiss appeared sleek, being one of the first monoplanes to make extensive use of metal in its construction. However, under the hood, Leif's bailiwick, the Curtiss was relatively conventional. The radial engine was mounted at the front of the fuselage and powered by a three-blade propeller assembly. On either side of the aircraft were low-mounted straight wings with rounded tips. Leif's cockpit was set above and behind the wing assemblies, and the surrounding canopy was heavily framed with a single, rounded vertical tail fin. And the undercarriage provided two single-wheeled main landing gear legs plus a small tail wheel for ground maneuvering.

Leif, now a flight sergeant, also found flying over the vast Canadian prairies less daunting than his fellow Norwegian recruits, many of whom had never left home, and were unaccustomed to endless open spaces. On that front, there was only one person to thank for his comfort behind the Hawk's controls: his father. Soaring across the awe-inspiring Canadian landscape reminded Leif of looking over the deck of a ship and seeing nothing but a miraculous tapestry of blue for countless miles, reminding one of their humbleness in the grand scheme of the universe. 'As above so below', Frederik would say, 'with human influence absent in both spheres.' Leif felt the Curtiss responded to his feeling of confident, yet humble belonging in the air, as if they had fused and become sympathetic metal, agreeing to undertake this quest together and keep each other safe.

However, Leif could not translate his success with the Curtiss to his experiences with the Norwegian recruits and the Canadian administration at Moose Jaw, that was a situation which reminded him more of the pecking hierarchy at the Sølvgades school in Copenhagen, than a group of recruits being shaped by their officers to go into battle as a cohesive unit.

To begin with, there was the issue of petty nationalism between the sole Danish trainee and the Norwegians, who viewed their own homeland as superior for attempting to fight and the Germans, unlike Denmark, which immediately surrendered and dissolved the military. Leif had the opposite problem with the local Canadian training staff who refused to grant him any sort of individual autonomy, and just referred to him as another cog in 'the endless lot of Norwegians and other foreigners'. In essence, Leif thought, 'this is the worst of both worlds.' His fellow soldiers were exclusionary, and his instructors wanted to melt everyone down into an anonymous stew of Scandinavians, which in all fairness to the military seemed to be the point. You can't have mission focus if everyone's griping about whatever patch of land they hailed from. However, if you're the only trainee from Denmark it did ruffle one's feathers.

It also didn't help that unlike his father, Leif didn't thrive in a strictly martial environment, he didn't enjoy being a node in a hierarchical organization. His antipathy toward authority didn't mean that Leif lacked the capacity to lead; Dunkirk had taught him that he possessed the requisite fortitude to command others and save lives. However, what Dunkirk also taught him was that he needed to have the latitude to take risks, to apply his intelligence in a non-linear fashion, to entertain the possibility of improvisation.

These personal insights also began to inform Leif's political education. He realized that hidden within the heart of totalitarianism rested a great fear of humanity, that the innards of its stifling bureaucracy were lorded over by those who not only didn't trust their fellow citizens but viewed them with a mix of terror and apathy. German citizens didn't believe that Hitler had brainwash Germany with old hatreds filtered through new media, erased his own people's history and attempted to bend Europe to his will because he fervently believed. The only thing the Führer had absolute faith in was himself, no one else measured up or could be trusted, thus he could sleep soundly at night through world domination.

* * *

By March 1941, Leif had completed his basic training courses at Moose Jaw and received orders transferring him to the Royal Norwegian Air Force's OUT located in an enclave of Toronto called 'Little Norway' in order to complete his advanced pilot training. Leif quickly realized that this 'advanced training' was by and large a repeat of Moose Jaw except all the training flights would be solo and longer in duration, involving flying over large bodies of water of the great lakes and over vast forests of Ontario. All this would strengthen Leif's resolve and control of the Curtiss by flying over terrain, which was similar to European landscape – where he hoped to soon fly and fight the enemy. However, Toronto offered other pleasures and distractions for the young pilot.

In his second week at Little Norway, at sundown, after a full day of aerial maneuvers over Lake Ontario, Leif and several other pilots he had befriended were permitted to leave their base located adjacent to the sprawling Toronto harbor and delve into Toronto's thriving night life and teeming social scene. It was the perfect antidote to military life. This side of Leif, stifled during the day could emerge, the side that relished singing and dancing, that enjoyed unrehearsed intimate conversation. Toronto allowed his inner *bon vivant* to bloom and afforded him the chance to fully come into his own as a maturing adult.

Flight-Sergeant Bangsboll, preparing to take-off for a training flight from Little Norway airfield, Toronto Canada, 1942. (*Photo courtesy of the author's family collection*)

A few weeks after his arrival in Toronto, Leif began casually dating a woman whose prominent Toronto family was generationally wealthy and highly connected in the business community. In a mark of the family's status, Leif's girlfriend was attending Havergal College and they had a particularly desirable address on Forest Hill Road.

The only problem in the burgeoning relationship was the debutante's father, who was distinctly un-charmed by Leif, by his habit of keeping his daughter out all night, and most of all, that he was a transient Scandinavian earmarked for war and potential death. How could Leif possibly be serious about his daughter? He might be dead within a month or two.

'For Christ's sake', he thought, 'I'm trying to protect both of our reputations.' Prior to Leif's arrival he had been trying to marry her off once college was over. How would it look if she was seen traipsing all over town, singing and dancing with a young Scandinavian pilot harboring a death wish? What good could come out of it?

Leif had to give the devil his due. The girl's father was partially right. Nothing good would come out of the relationship. In fact, Leif never intended anything more than a casual fling, and let it be noted, neither did the debutante. However, it didn't mean that the patriarch's behavior didn't stick in his craw. Who did he think he was? Leif internally rebelled against the moral snobbery on display that pretended to make virtue its highest order of existence, while simultaneously plotting to marry his daughter off to the highest bidder. And Leif intended to make his point crystal clear.

Leif knew one of the main reasons the debutante adored him, much to her father's chagrin, was that Leif made a good first impression in his well-fitted uniform and was considered a 'hot shot' pilot, and a foreign pilot added to the intrigue. She liked him because he was willing to sneak her onto the base to show off the Curtiss waiting on the tarmac to take flight the following morning. So, in order to impress her, to reinforce why she wanted him, plus add a little excitement to the relationship, and not to mention to provoke her father, Leif decided to conduct his own 'training mission' from Little Norway airfield.

Leif used the landmark of the prominent clock tower of Upper Canada College as a fixed navigational point, a directional reference that merely happened to be located across the street from the debutante's Forest Hill estate. After stabilizing the craft, he regaled his girlfriend with several loud and low fly pasts. She melted under his romantic and impetuous gesture, rushing to the home's third floor balcony, cheering him on, calling his name, and waving her arms to keep beckoning him back. She was impressed. Her heart belonged to Leif – her beloved aviator and showman, the performer of her dreams – for the foreseeable future.

Her father did not have quite the same reaction to Leif's impromptu aerial visit. He reported the incident to the city police and to Leif's Norwegian CO, barking demands of arrest and swift imprisonment.

And despite being one of the top student pilots, Leif was given a rather explicit and demeaning verbal dressing down by his CO and given additional

Flight-Sergeant Bangsboll, Norwegian Air Force with Lieutenant - Junior Grade (JG)., United States Naval Reserve (USNR), Judith Bullock in New York City, 1942. (*Photo courtesy of the author's family collection*)

work duties as punishment – washing aircraft nightly and having his weekend leave privileges suspended. He accepted his guilt with a degree of pride. Despite these imposed restrictions, Leif would keep seeing the beautiful young socialite until his next assignment.

As his pilot training with the Norwegian Air Force at Little Norway airfield in Toronto, Canada neared completion, Flight-Sergeant Bangsboll had to

Flight-Sergeant Bangsboll, Norwegian Air Force with Lieutenant Junior Grade (JG) Portia Williams, United States Navy Reserve (USNR), New York City, 1942. (*Photo courtesy of the author's family collection*)

complete one final, long-range navigation flight. He chose the destination of New York,... New York City to be precise. While there, reacquainting himself to the city he had visited two years earlier, when his ship, the C.O. Stillman was at anchor. While having a drink at the popular United Services Organization (USO) Club on Broadway, Leif met a girl. Her name was Portia, Portia Williams. Portia was a Lieutenant (JG – Junior Grade) in the United States Navy Reserve (USNR) and was visiting New York City from Washington D.C. with her close friend Judith Bullock, also with the USNR. The young Dane fell hard for pretty Portia, but alas, their romantic relationship was not destine to be.... immediately upon return to Toronto a meeting with an American Colonel named Donovan would change the trajectory of his military career. Leif's friendship with Portia, Judith and Judith's husband Edward Thompson would last for years."

Ironically, that next assignment would happen rather quickly and quite unexpectantly. It all started at the mess, with much alcohol being consumed. There was a squadron party at the Little Norway officers' mess in honor of a visiting high ranking American officer. Late in the evening, with everyone well into their cups, the entire dinner table was in stitches listening to the tale of Leif's recent impromptu flyby of his Toronto girlfriend's home, and no one was laughing harder or was more intrigued than Colonel Donovan of the OSS.

Chapter 11

Preparing for War in the Shadows

'We need people with PHD-level minds who can hold their own in a bar fight.'

Colonel William Donovan

Donovan had not arrived at Little Norway airfield by accident. Donovan never executed an arbitrary action, would not enter any situation without all the angles figured out well in advance. His every move calculated and evinced no waste of effort.

The colonel was making a series of targeted stops across Canadian bases, focusing on BCAPT flying schools that housed a plurality of displaced European

Flight-Sergeant Leif Bangsboll resigns from the Norwegian Air Force after receiving letter from the United States War Department assigning him to the Office of Strategic Services from Lieutenant Colonel Ole Imerslun Reistad, Commanding Officer of Norwegian Air Force Training Center, Little Norway Airfield, Toronto, Fall of 1942. (*Photo courtesy of the author's family collection*)

soldiers, sailors, aviators, scientists and engineers, particularly those who could speak multiple languages, such as French and German, which were particularly prized, and necessary elements to staff up the expanding roster of his OSS.

Donovan had been primed in advance to respond to Leif. During pre-dinner cocktails, Lieutenant Colonel Reistad, Little Norway's camp commandant, had briefed Donovan on the young Dane's strong flying skills, extensive linguistic capabilities, and his unique resume, highlighting Leif's years with the Royal Danish Navy, his experience as a cabin boy aboard a submarine tender while barely a teenager. Leif's training as a maritime engineer, his voluntary participation in the evacuation efforts at Dunkirk, and ending with his dogged initiative to enlist in the Royal Norwegian Air Force to fight the war in Europe at all costs was clearly evident to Donovan.

Donovan liked what he heard, but what solidified his interest was the flyby story. The young Dane had an obvious attraction, susceptibility to being a showman with bravado, a risk-taker and a romantic, all qualities that made him a handful for the military but an ideal candidate for the OSS's peculiar needs. As the party in the officers' mess wound down, Donovan approached the confident, yet polite, and surprisingly modest young Scandinavian pilot, and arranged for them to share a formal interview the following morning, right before Donovan returned to Washington.

Leif was at a loss. He had only attended a very few interviews in his life, and they were all related to gaining employment as an engineer on commercial maritime crafts, where his obvious skills with a diesel engine spoke for themselves. On top of which, 'what was this OSS?' Donovan had been cagey about the organization, merely mentioning that he'd like to talk about it with Leif. 'How to prepare?' Leif thought. He was desperate to make a good first impression with this important American army officer.

Leif replayed the dinner back in his head, trying to remember the colonel's behavior, and Leif's only lasting impression was that outside of a formalized magnanimity, one could sense Donovan was studying everyone at the table, sizing them up, while everyone else obliviously, swapped stories. 'That's interesting', Leif thought, making his interviewer more intimidating. What Leif didn't realize was that his quick psychological distillation of Donovan was exactly why the head of the OSS wanted to have a sit-down meeting with the young Dane.

When Leif arrived for their 0800 hours meeting, Donovan was wearing his Class A uniform festooned with rows of ribbons, representing the many medals he had earned, including his Medal of Honor earned in the First World War. The colonel's gray hair was slicked back and parted with the same precision as his military uniform and he was pounding tobacco into the bowl of his pipe with his thumb. He extended his free hand in greeting and gesture for Leif to sit: 'Feel free to smoke if you like.'

'I don't smoke.' Leif replied, watching the first plume from Donovan's pipe waft towards the ceiling.

Donovan smiled, while pushing smoke through his nostrils. 'Do either of your parent's smoke?'

'My father, like a chimney.' Leif said.

'My children don't smoke. That I know of. Which I suppose is a rather large proviso.' Donovan puffed harder and made the tobacco glow amber. 'They don't like that I smoke so much. Do you get along with your father?'

'We're very close, now.' Leif said.

'Now?' asked Donovan. 'That implies you were not always close with him' Donovan added.

Leif replied, 'My father and I had some divergent views on his parental skills when I was young.'

Donovan asked, 'And your mother? What of your relationship with her?' Donovan asked.

Leif answered, 'She died when I was young, while my father was at sea.'

Donovan inquired further, 'I'm sorry to hear that sergeant. Is your decision to join the air force, not the navy an of rebellion against your father the sea captain?'

'Was it?' Leif thought. 'Could it be?' Leif had never considered that as a possibility. And what kind of interview starts with that as a question?

Leif said, 'I believe that I've spent enough time at sea to earn my father's respect in that regard.'

Donovan then remarked,

> Yes, I'm aware of your unique up bringing sergeant… cabin boy on a war ship at the age of 13, duty time spent on a submarine, a sailing voyage to Greenland and most recently, an impromptu trip to Dunkirk. Yes, I think you've demonstrated your sea worthiness son.

'Okay', Donovan said, getting what he needed from the conversation, 'then you just don't like smoking and your once-tense relationship with your sea-faring father is now a good one.' Donovan opened Leif's personnel file, flipped through the pages. 'Why do you want to be back into Europe so desperately?'

> I want to help free Denmark from the Nazis. My father once told me that Hitler was Europe's 'great white whale' and we would have to destroy him to be free. You know, like Melville's book *Moby Dick*.

'So, you're a patriot and a well-read, want-to-be soldier with a father, who you weren't close to, but are now?' Without waiting for Leif's response, Donovan added, 'It sounds like your father enjoyed reading and quoting the classics.'

> Yes, my father ensured that reading all the classic materials was part of my upbringing. And yes, secretly, at the time, I doubted his concerns about Hitler and the Nazis. I couldn't see yet what he could. I thought he might even be letting his experiences with the Germans in the First World War influence his thinking. After all, at that time, Hitler had only annexed ethnic Germans out of Czechoslovakia.

Leif noticed Donovan scribbling a note on his file with a fountain pen and said,

> My father was right. Hitler has dragged all of Europe, and potentially the world with him, into his personal God damn regime unless he is stopped. He's made the choice clear: it's either his apocalypse or the one we make destroying him.

'Your father is a wise man, he saw what few of us did', Donovan said, cracking the knuckles on his right hand, each joint like an exploding drum, each pop unnerving Leif. 'Is your father', Donovan scanned Leif's file to verify the rank 'the commodore, still in Copenhagen?'

> Yes, as far as I know. I have not been able to contact him since the Germans invaded. All outside contact inside is impossible. Given my current training, I thought it wise not to contact him – in case the German's were to intercept our correspondence and I put him in further danger.

Donovan tried to suppress a smile crinkling in the corners of his mouth. 'Would it be safe to say you've been trying to find any way back into Europe, to see if your father is safe.'
Leif hadn't heard his rationale broken down so simply. 'I suppose that is true.'
Donovan drew the pipe stem into his mouth. 'And yet you don't smoke.' He rested the pipe on the side of an ashtray, clasped his hands together on the desk. 'But you do enjoy reading classic books, like your father, correct?'
Before Leif could respond, Donovan announced, 'Flight Sergeant Bangsbøll, I can give you a chance to get back into Europe, to get into the war. Now let me tell you what you would have to do for me.'
Leif stiffened himself in the chair.
Donovan began,

> It will take more than our military to defeat Germany. We need men and women trained in the strategies of irregular warfare. The Nazis lack this skill. They are tanks and fighter-bombers, bulldozing their way across Europe. But we can defeat Hitler, as long as we have the right people familiar with the occupied countries planted inside them.

Pointing at his own chest, Donovan continued,

> That is my purview, the Office of Strategic Services. We will insert these special operatives behind enemy lines. And to survive they must possess the courage and physical stamina to operate in hostile, deadly territory as spies, saboteurs, insurgents. OSS officers will face the constant threat of capture, torture and death for months, maybe years on end. To survive that, one must possess absolute loyalty to their country and a willingness to die to defeat their enemy.

Donovan removed his pipe from the ashtray, propped it in his mouth again: 'Do you think you possess those requisite qualities, Flight Sergeant Bangsbøll?'

'I am willing to sacrifice my life to liberate Denmark and the rest of Europe.' Leif said.

Donovan parried back. 'Even if it means never seeing your father again?'

'If we don't win, I'll never see him again anyway. What's the alternative?' Leif replied.

Donovan's face was bereft of emotion. However, Leif assumed he answered properly because the colonel resumed talking.

'On our initial recruiting drive, 4,000 volunteers signed up to be part of the OSS and only 50 were deemed acceptable to begin training.'

'I understand, sir.' Leif said. 'You are looking for…'

'I'm looking for', Donovan said, interrupting, 'a person with a PHD level mind who can hold his own in a barfight.' He smiled for the first and last time in the interview. 'Which has turned out to be a tougher search than I'd imagined.'

Leif remained silent. He could read Donovan's mood.

'If you are willing to be part of the OSS', Donovan continued,

> you will first take a semester at Georgetown University to improve your English, then complete United States Army basic training and attend Officer Candidate School, followed by parachute training. If you complete all these requirements successfully, you will be sent to an undisclosed training location to undergo the additional, highly specialized training

at a secret location, that will mold and transform you into a field-ready OSS operative.

Donovan then added, 'You know, secret agent training', sensing that Leif had not fully comprehended the phrase 'OSS operative'.

Donovan struck a match against the table, relit his pipe: 'And that all must happen before you can be sent into Europe to possibly perish at the hands of the Nazis.'

Leif started to answer, 'I under…'

'I'm not finished', Donovan reasserted, cutting Leif off once again.

Besides being physically and mentally prepared for war. I need free-thinking leaders with nerves of steel. Agents who can improvise, think on their feet, in situations where the best laid plans go awry. Some of these things just can't be taught – they must be instinctive… they must be able to transform themselves and act the part – whatever part we need them to play.

'Yes, sir.' Leif answered, without hesitation. That part he knew he could handle.

'You're awfully certain of yourself.' Donovan said, searching for a crack in Leif's reaction when pressed for more. 'Why do you think you have these special talents?'

Leif wasn't certain he should confess to Donovan that it was because he'd played Hamlet several times and adeptly managed to improvise his way into getting a visa from an uncooperative embassy bureaucrat. 'I can and will do anything you ask of me.'

Donovan sized up Leif. 'How do I know that? How do I know you can artfully dodge your way out of any situation thrown before you?'

Leif hesitated and gulped, a nervous thirst in the back of his throat. Silence.

'Very well', Donovan said, taking a last look at the young Dane, 'you are dismissed Flight Sergeant Bangsbøll.'

Leif rose, flattened the creases in his clothing from sitting, made his way to the door, when he realized that he would never see Europe again if he left the room under these circumstances. He could be authentically himself, risk failure in Donovan's eyes, or he could stay silent and absolutely fail. Leif turned back and looked at Donovan.

'Prince Hamlet…' Leif said. 'I know I can do all that you ask because I played Hamlet.'

'Hamlet?' Donovan said, chewing over the information. 'Were you any good?'

'Yes sir.' Leif said, standing at attention. 'Very, very good, I was convincing and compelling, sir.'

Donovan nodded and smiled. Satisfied, Donovan said, 'Thank you, you are dismissed.'

Leif remained in limbo regarding the success or failure of his interview with Donovan, right up until his graduation from Little Norway's final phase of pilot training. Following the graduation parade, Leif was summoned to the commandant's office and handed a letter sent by the Office of the United States Joints Chiefs of Staff, which contained orders that he was to immediately report to OSS headquarters in Washington DC to commence his indoctrination training into the United States Army. The commandant then handed Leif his release papers from the Royal Norwegian Air Force. He was going to become an American soldier and a secret agent: 'an operative', Leif mentally corrected himself.

First though, he had to get through his English course at Georgetown, his basic training at Fort Benning, Georgia, complete officer training and log in his jump hours at Fort Bragg; all of which would occupy the next eight months of his life.

Chapter 12

Camp X

'Every soldier must be a potential gangster.'
Major William Fairbairn

Once he had completed his training in the United States, Leif received orders sending him back to Canada. This time he was sent to Special Training School No. 103 – Camp X, where, despite the rigor of his military training he had just completed with the United States Army, this training would drive him past what he believed was mentally and physically capable of any human being.

Now Sergeant Bangsbøll, United States Army, Leif took the train from Baltimore to Toronto with a connection to Oshawa and then a taxi from Oshawa to Whitby and then to his destination – a remote plot of land on the shore of Lake Ontario. Before any introductions were made, each trainee was ushered into a private room, and given a series of psychological intake evaluation, which included a battery of Rorschach, word association tests and a detailed clinical history, all of which made Leif feel as if he were a test subject in some rudimentary consumer study. He'd never been asked the question 'Why?' so many times in one sitting, never realized it could be that exhausting and render him ready to nap.

Instead of sleep, the recruits went to dinner in the cafeteria, an antiseptic space stacked with tables and chairs kept handy for Allied government visitors. This was the first time the twenty recruits – eighteen men and two women – had laid eyes on each other, and they were all too worn down from relentless psychoanalysis to rustle up much enthusiasm to engage in small talk.

The lethargic dinner came to an apathetic conclusion, and the trainees were escorted to their respective quarters. The men were to be housed in a long, single-floor dormitory room lined with identical beds, foot lockers and nightstands with a goose neck lamp bolted to the surface. 'It' very familiar.' Leif thought, thinking about his Canadian barracks in Toronto and Moose Jaw before that.

Later that evening, while sitting on his squeaky, saggy bunk in the barracks, Leif pondered his future. But thinking about the future, immediately triggered a memory… it had struck him like a bolt. It had been almost three years since

Aerial view of Camp X, near Whitby Ontario, on the shores of Lake Ontario, circa 1942. (Achieve photo obtained from internet). (*Photo courtesy of online Pinecrest Stock Imagery*)

Hitler had declared war, had been two and half since he'd had his own quarters, had a hot, solitary shower and a decent meal. Moreover, it had been two and a half years since he'd been home, seen and slept in his own bed, and last seen his father's face. Maybe it was the psychological testing earlier that had softened him up, but when he sat on the corner of his single bed, he nearly burst into tears of overwhelming loss and the passage of time.

His incoming emotional release was halted when an instructor entered the barracks and informed them that lights out was 2300 hours, and they should all rest up, for tomorrow the real training started. The man's voice was the last sounds Leif remembered before he drifted to sleep, almost the minute his head hit the pillow.

Sometime later, without warning, Leif was jolted awake by voices shouting outside the barracks, totally disoriented, unaware of how much time had lapsed.

SOE/OSS agent trainees practice clandestine amphibious assault on the beach at Camp X 1942, on the shores of Lake Ontario. (*Photo courtesy of the author's family collection*)

Then it came, the ear-shattering sound of an explosion in the communal quarters. His first thought was 'the ship has been struck by a torpedo; I must rush to the engine room.' He wasn't sure if he was back aboard the *C.O. Stillman* in hostile waters and his last three years had been a hallucination or if he was a teenager again, cabin boy of the *Hekla*, and Manny was about to burst into flames. He threw off his blanket, leapt to his feet, and scanned his surroundings, while still trying to rub the sleep out of his bleary eyes.

Leif realized he was still on land, still in a dormitory surrounded by seventeen men, some still in bed, some upright like him and terrified, and others streaming out into the hallway investigating the source of the blast. Before anyone could fully get their bearings, they heard: '*STEH AUF! STEH AUF! DU SCHWEIN ES IST ZEIT, DICH ZU LEHREN GEHEIME KRIEGER ZU WERDEN!* [GET UP! GET UP! YOU PIG, IT'S TIME TO TEACH YOU TO BECOME SECRET WARRIORS!]'

Someone was screaming in a foreign language outside their barracks. 'What the hell?' Leif wondered aloud. Then the horror began to dawn on him.

> The worst had happened. They're speaking German. They're calling us pigs. My God. They've found us. Canada wasn't far enough from the Wehrmacht; they've made it to our shores.

Leif shouted 'RUN' to his fellow trainees and bolted toward the door. His hand was about to grab the knob when the entrance was busted open with the butt of a rifle, and a man dressed in all black, wrapped in a balaclava, and with camouflage paint spread under his wild eyes, faced the trainees: '*RAUS! GEH RAUS SIE SCHWEINIES*! [OUT! GO OUT YOU PIGIES!]'

Then the German unclipped an object from his webbing, tossed it across the room, where it bounced around the floor with a series of dull metallic thuds. Everyone in the room was mesmerized by the slow spiral, until a trainee yelled,

'GRENADE… GOD DAMN IT… GRENADE!'

Leif and the other men didn't hesitate, sprinted full speed toward the exit, throwing the intruder to his side. And just as the last trainee made it passed the door frame to safety, the grenade – a training grenade – exploded. Very loud, but no shrapnel.

The trainees plowed through the exit leading to the courtyard and dashed into the cold Canadian night, wearing nothing but their underwear, never stopping to look back.

Only when several gunshots cut through the crisp air, did they all pause momentarily, shocked, trying to decide what to do. Each questioning themselves if they would die on their feet or on their knees. Was the fate grimmer ahead or behind?

'Alright, lads', they heard, 'the fun is over.'

'Come on', a second voice shouted, 'get yourself in two lines. We haven't got all morning.'

The trainees stood stunned, reluctant to obey and ready to start running.

'Get into bloody line for Christ's sake!' a voice shouted and fired a few more rounds into the air. 'It was a damn training exercise.'

All the men exhaled in relief. It was just a drill. And when they faced their instructors, they also saw the black-clad German intruder grinning behind the balaclava.

'Those were real bullets fired but only a training grenade. One tenth the strength. Loud, but doesn't produce shrapnel.' he snorted.

'It appears that we've got some real work with this lot!' the other instructor replied.

The trainees were cold – some swinging their arms repeatedly across their chest or cupping their hands to their mouths to fight hypothermia. An instructor separated himself from the pack and addressed the group,

Good morning gentlemen. Welcome to the first day of your training at Camp No. 103, affectionately known in certain circles as Camp X. I'm Sergeant Sykes of His Majesty's Parachute Regiment and Commandos. I'm one of your instructors for the next twelve weeks. Your other instructor this morning [while pointing at the fake German in the face paint] is camp Sergeant Major de Relwyskow.

This exercise was designed to teach you to always expected the unexpected. And there's a lesson within the lesson. If you wish to disrupt a target, do it as quickly and aggressively as possible. And do not remain behind once the deed is done. Additionally, never forgot to toss in some noisy explosives, they add chaos and give you valuable time to escape.

Sergeant Sykes examined his watch, tapped the face, showed it to the trainees.

It is 0430 hours. You have exactly five minutes to don your PT gear and join the sergeant major and I for a brisk 5-mile run. Light and easy on your first day.

He clapped his hands and motioned the trainees away with fingers, 'Off you go, lads. Dismissed.'

As the trainees walked back to their quarters to get dressed, still desperately trying to assimilate to what had happened to them, Leif heard one of them ask, 'What the hell was he shouting when the explosions went off?'

They were shouting 'Get up you lazy pigs. It's time to start your training to be secret warriors.' Leif said.

The same trainee gave Leif a friendly shove in the shoulder. 'Yes. I imagine it is time.'

Leif thought, 'Lesson learned.' He could speak and understand German fluently, since he was a child, but when the bomb went off, it was as if his mind went blank. Quick explosions work as a memory eraser. 'I will have to be more in control in such situations.'

As promised, a typical day for agent trainees at Camp X began with a 5-mile run, then two hours of gymnastics and obstacle course training, followed by a timed swim in Lake Ontario, sometimes paired with parachute jumping practice from a 90-foot tower. The training exercises also pushed the notion of simulation to the breaking point, a place where the simulation dissolved and became real.

Only weeks before, an instructor had been drilling his class in the live-fire training area on the Camp X obstacle course, when he slipped into a trench, and while crawling out became entangled in barbed wire and was struck in the head with a bullet, killing him instantly. The loss was a tragic but sadly valuable reminder that you train like you fight and fight like you train. There were no blanks in war and no blanks during training at Camp X. After the instructors considered the body primed, they moved on to the mind.

There were in depth lectures on weapons handling, primers on making primitive explosives, the art of personal disguise, which proved to be Leif's favorite. They were taught how to compose and decode messages, setting up dead drops on hostile terrain, and the art of making yourself undetectable while tracking your prey.

After a base level of physical condition had been achieved in all the trainees, hand-to-hand combat classes started. Their instructor was the legendary Major William 'Dangerous Dan' Fairbairn of the British Army, famous within the SOE for his unrivaled panache and skill in silent killing. The major, who at first glance appeared ready for retirement, had honed his techniques as a senior officer on the Shanghai police force, back when it was the bloodiest city on earth riddled with violent gang warfare. His intimate history with violence had given him a harsh yet simple perspective on defense. Quoting a passage from the British *Handbook of Irregular Warfare*, Major Fairbairn told the gathered students: 'Every soldier must be a potential gangster.' Adding,

> The *Queensbury Rules* do not apply in a struggle of life and death. Use your initiative to seize the advantage through the swift and violent execution of maximum force to your enemy's most vulnerable regions. The aim is simple: kill your opponent as quickly and quietly as possible. There's no glory in killing. You must dive into the gutter and win at all costs. Do not play fair; fair gets you killed. You kill, you live.

Next, to provide a vivid example of his principles in action, Fairbairn asked for a volunteer, handed the young man his pistol, and asked him to play the role of an armed sentry and squeeze a shot off at his teacher. While the student was confused by the request, Fairbairn disabled the man – easily twice his size – in seconds, by stabbing his extended and flexed thumbs into the volunteer's neck, right in the hollow behind his ears. The trainee, weighing at least 200 pounds, went down like a bag of wet cement. Fairbairn put his fingers to the volunteer's neck, verified his pulse, then addressed the class,

> He'll be fine in five minutes. But remember this. Incapacitating your enemy is only a temporary solution. Best to kill him and get it over with. Save yourself the trouble.

'Can you believe that guy?' said Bill Whitaker to Leif. Whitaker, who hailed from New York, was a recent law school graduate with an undergraduate degree in psychology. He'd been selected by the OSS for his fluency in French and Italian and his deep familiarity with both countries having studied abroad. Leif sat down next to Whitaker at a long cafeteria table, starved and ready to eat lunch. 'No', he said, laughing and unwrapping his sandwich, 'I can't believe him at all.'

'Fairbairn's something else, isn't he?' Ross Smith said, from across the table. He was another American trainee from Virginia, and with a rather murky background, involving some sort of high-powered familial connection to electoral politics and international intelligence through his British mother. 'I heard about him when I was down in Maryland.'

'The man must be 70.' Whitaker said.

'He's the best at what he does.' Ross said smiling and continued,

At the outbreak of the war, he was in his mid-60. He walked down to the British War Office and volunteered for active duty. They told him he was too old. Then Dunkirk happened and Fairbairn contacted them again and pled his case. Again, they told him he was still too old.

But Fairbairn refused to be taken lightly. He told the War Office he'd teach their soldiers to fight so each one was worth ten combat ready men from the enemy side. He arranged to have two burly British Army infantry majors attend his demonstration, or as he called it his 'talent show', wherein he'd illustrate how a trained, unarmed solider – Fairbairn himself – could efficiently neutralize his targets using properly applied hand-to-hand combat.

Before the demonstration Fairbairn put his arms around the two army officers volunteers and whispered,

Boys, I'm sure you'll understand, but I've got to convince these dunderheaded generals that I, a gentleman of 65 years of age, can deal with tough men as yourselves.

He rolled up his shirt sleeves, removed his watch and said, 'Apologies in advance, but I may have to put one or both of you in the hospital to prove my point.'

'And he basically did.' Ross continued, while Leif and Whitaker listened slack jawed, although not entirely surprised. 'Thirty seconds later. Both of those men were flat on their backs, barely conscious.' Ross raised an eyebrow,

Needless to say, under a special wartime service requirement of the realm, Fairbairn was immediately re-enrolled in the army and on a ship to Canada with instructions to report to this camp as its senior instructor.

'It makes sense', Leif said, 'it's not as if a man like Fairbairn can just retire. The skills he can teach us are invaluable.' As soon as the words passed his lips, Leif thought once again of Frederik and his promotion crisis. His father and Fairbairn handled being out of action similarly, which is to say, poorly. Men like Frederik and Fairbairn didn't care for delicacies like pay raises, prestige or a removal from danger due to time served and a chance to set down roots. Fundamentally, the two were chemically incapable of existing in a state of peace or to be precise, they found tremendous inner peace through strife. And if Leif was correct, he imagined his father was trying – or had already managed – to insert himself into the war effort. There was no way in hell that Frederik would sit idly by while Nazis occupied his homeland. He would fight; he would fight dirty.

As would Leif. Not only was the OSS honing his physical prowess through Fairbairn, but they also continued to expand his skill craft when it came to espionage, schooling the trainees in subversion and counterintelligence. They were taught how to hotwire vehicles and open locked doors without leaving visible traces of forced entry, the art of setting up improvised drop points in occupied territories and observing your target without leaving yourself vulnerable to surveillance.

'Eyes in the back of your heads, lads.' De Relwyskow would repeat.

To enforce the lesson, the instructors would add or remove objects from the classroom and around the camp, then cold quiz the trainees on what changes they observed in their immediate environment. The perception drills might have seemed like overkill, but the rigor slotted into place when the trainees reached the next stage: demolitions.

Under the camp's explosive instructor, they learned how to construct fuse and time delay bombs, then were taken onto the obstacle course and instructed how to place them in strategic wartime targets, like on locomotives, bridges, ships and factories. Suddenly, the training became clear, if anyone on the enemy side caught you strapping explosives to valued infrastructure, you'd be shot dead or captured in a heartbeat.

The training also gave Leif the distinct impression that when you're a field agent, you're virtually alone, with maybe one or two additional agents in direct support. As an agent you must rely on your wits and training, be totally self-sufficient in the tools of your trade, and vulnerable to your personal weaknesses and shortcomings. You win or lose, you live or die based upon your own decisions, on your ability to achieve the mission objective.

But Leif had no idea how truly alone OSS agents were, until halfway through the three-month program, when the trainees arrived at their first class of the day, and could immediately sense the mood was palpably different, somber, foreboding even.

'Take your seats.' De Relwyskow stood before the class, his uniform freshly pressed, his spine stiff, shoulders square, and his face visibly trembling behind a stern mask. After grasping the trainees' attention, he gave a quick nod to an instructor standing at the back of the classroom, who quickly locked both classroom doors, entrance and exit. The already present tension in the room rose.

De Relwyskow spoke, not in his usual booming voice peppered with color expletives, but softly and deliberately, making his audience lean forward to hear him,

> In the next phase of training, you will be shown what resides in the darkest, coldest depths of the human soul. You will go places and discuss matters you will never want to see, hear or speak of again. Understand, we must take you down these roads so you can understand and prepare yourself for what may come… what you may be forced to do. Man is best left an enigma. You will be forced to understand him better than most.

With another nod from de Relwyskow's head, the other instructor drew the shades, then wheeled an 8-millimeter film projected into place, plunged the room into darkness and beamed the first shaft of light against the blank screen.

The initial seconds of the black and white film were out of focus, grainy, unsteady, kept switching angles, as if the image was struggling to find room to be born. Then, as the shot steadied and came into focus, the trainees could make out a dimly lit room with a single lightbulb dangling from a cracked ceiling. Directly below the bulb, was a young man seated in a chair, head hung low, shoulder slumping. A voice, alternating between German and French barked off screen, demanding answers about the identity and the purpose of the man in the chair, whose ankles and knees now trembled in fear.

The camera pulled out further, encompassing more of the room, and directly framing the man's face, which had been beaten, pulped around the eyes and mouth, and drained of color. His arms were tied behind his back, his right shoulder was dangling and dislocated, and a lap restraint had been jammed between his legs. It was undeniable. He was a PoW being interrogated – tortured.

The source of the off-screen face strutted into the frame, making his presence known. He was a uniformed Gestapo officer, and not only acknowledged the camera's presence, but seemed turn up his performance in its presence. He approached the PoW, smacked him awake on the swollen cheek, then when he had the man's attention, shouted off-screen for a medical tray to be wheeled over.

After his delivery arrived, he inspected the surface and produced a metal implement. He held the pliers up to the light, letting the camera pick up the glimmering instrument then braced the PoW's wrist with his free hand, and began running the tool over the flesh of his fingers.

The Gestapo agent repeated the same question as a mantra, like a ritual screamed at a sinner, and before the barely conscious PoW could summon the energy to answer, he drove the pliers head under the middle finger nail and ripped the nail out with the precision of a surgeon. The PoW screamed in pain and fruitlessly struggle to free himself from his bonds.

The trainees in the classroom flinched, started to sweat and feel their stomachs tighten. They all tried to look away, to avert their eyes from the film, like it carried contagion. Now they understood why the doors had been locked. 'Suffer through it, lads', de Relwyskow said, 'this one did.'

The next six minutes of the film preserved on celluloid examples of barbarism and inhumanity. After removing three more fingernails, the Gestapo agent became further frustrated and turned up the intensity. He demanded freezing water be thrown in the PoW's face to strip him of the luxury of passing out, while his henchmen moved on to move drastic methods, arriving in the frame bearing heavy ropes. They beat the PoW about the head, stomach and across the legs. Leif heard more than one bone snap. Finally, at their wit's end with the PoW's recalcitrance to talk, the Gestapo agent demanded a hammer.

Mercifully, the image sputtered out abruptly before the hammer was produced. The film was just a small segment of a prolonged session of vile conduct by the Gestapo, conduct that violated law and conscience, that had no place being utilized even in war.

'This film', de Relwyskow said, as the lights went up exposing the ashen faces of his trainees,

> was produced by the Nazi secret police, the Geheime Staatspolizei, otherwise known as the Gestapo. This monstrosity we just watched was smuggled out of occupied France by the resistance. It's now a training aid we use.

He reflected on the OSS's decision to show all recruits the footage. 'And a rather grim one at that. Sorry, lads.'

Although nauseated by the proceedings, Leif understood the point, it would be cruel and unethical of the OSS to not bring the stark reality of the evil that the Allies, and more personally, future agents faced from the Nazis. 'You have to go in with eyes wide open', Leif thought, 'even if it makes it worse.'

'This would be the appropriate time to consider withdrawing from the program', de Relwyskow said, tossing down the gauntlet, forcing their hands and continued,

You must ask yourselves, factoring in this new information, this accursed knowledge, if you are still willing to continue with your training. Are you prepared to undertake a mission that will put you in danger of potentially experiencing what you've just watched?

He cleared his throat, nodded for the inspector to open the doors,

I'll be calling each of you into my office, one by one, and I expect your decision. Resign from further training here at Camp X without repercussions. Remain and accept the risks.

He approached the classroom desk, grabbed his pen and clipboard, ran his fingers down the roster, and selected the first interviewee, 'Sergeant Bangsbøll, follow me.'

Chapter 13

A Chance Encounter

'Sometimes our lives have to be completely shaken
up, changed, and rearranged to relocate us
to the place we're meant to be.'

Unknown author

Over the course of their training assignment at Camp X, the group of twenty trainees of which Leif was a part, lost three fellow trainees for various physical injuries, academic or practical application deficiencies or personal reasons. In early June 1943, Leif completed his training along with the seventeen other remaining agents, ten of whom were American OSS agents and seven who were agents with the British SOE.

Initially, upon graduation, the OSS had Leif scheduled to return to OSS headquarters in Washington DC, prior to attending Officers Candidate School [OCS] in the autumn of that year. However, with Leif having completed his training with impressive results, the commandant of Camp X contacted the director of the OSS in Washington and, after a brief discussion during which the commandant outlined the academic and technical merits Leif had displayed during the course, Leif was subsequently authorized to remain as an instructor for Camp X's next serial of agent trainees. This arrangement suited Leif personally, as this would give him the opportunity to continue his work at Camp X, which he enjoyed, and would bridge the time leading up to the commencement of his OCS training scheduled for October.

After graduating from Camp X, Leif received a three-day leave pass and took the train into Toronto to enjoy the sights and sounds of the city, spending much of his time carousing with his former colleagues, the Norwegian instructor pilots from Little Norway airfield – it was familiar and felt like a little piece of home. He purposely avoided reconnecting with his former girlfriend from Forest Hill, as he was sure her influential father would make trouble for this former flyboy if he dared come around again. Given his new, clandestine line of work, Leif knew that discretion was the better part of valor. The following week, Leif was back at Camp X working on the training schedule with the other instructors, preparing for the upcoming course that was programed to begin in two weeks.

Though he had just transitioned from being a trainee to becoming a trainer, Leif felt confident in his newly acquired abilities and he sensed that the other, more experienced instructors, trusted him and felt he was their equal, or at least working hard to achieve that distinction.

Like all the OSS/SOE agent trainees, Leif's experience at Camp X had been life altering. Having the good fortune to be selected to remain at the top-secret camp as an interim instructor for the subsequent course only reinforced the sense of heightened awareness of his surroundings and feeling of enlightenment that Leif now felt about his chosen profession of arms. Leif was evolving as a man and as a warrior – how could he not?

One of his first realizations of just how this evolution was manifesting itself as a specialized war fighter came during the two weeks between his graduation from Camp X and the start of the first and only course he would be instructing at the camp. Leif, who would oversee, amongst other things on this course, exposing the students to interrogation practices at PoW Camp No. 30, in nearby Bowmanville. Leif planned to meet with Captain Smyth, a Canadian Army intelligence officer who was responsible for interrogations at PoW Camp No. 30 and for coordinating the visits and training sessions of the trainees and staff from Camp X. In preparation for the upcoming serial of new trainees, Leif planned to meet with Captain Smyth at a café in Oshawa, which was midway between Camp X in Whitby and PoW Camp No. 30 in Bowmanville. Their plan was to review the course calendar, confirm visit dates and discuss any intelligence finds that the captain and his staff may have recently uncovered during interrogations of German and Italian PoWs at Camp No. 30.

When Leif arrived at the café, he was wearing civilian clothing, Captain Smyth, wearing his Canadian Army uniform, was already seated at a table for two, located in the middle of the café. There were a dozen patrons seated in scattered locations around Smyth's table. Standing in the doorway, and without hesitating or proceeding further, Leif got the attention of a waitress and pointed to an empty table on the far side of the café, a table which was adjacent to the entrance to the kitchen and motioned that he and his colleague would move to that table. With a smile and a gesture of 'okay, whatever' the waitress led Leif to the new table and walked over to the army captain and let him know that she had a better table for him and his recently arrived colleague. Without thinking much of it, Captain Smyth grabbed his note pad, coffee mug and cigarette pack from his table and joined Leif, who was seated with his back to the corner of the café, facing the entrance. Unconsciously it felt better, more secure – it felt right Leif thought. After a few minutes of socially appropriate small talk, the two men got down to business, going over their respective calendars and discussing recent intelligence 'finds' that Captain Smyth and his team of investigators had gleamed from their German and Italian captives. From time to time, during their discussion, café patrons would leave and new patrons would arrive – Leif quickly assessed each newcomer. Captain Smyth seemed oblivious to his surroundings. Despite the knowledge that he was sitting in a café in Oshawa, Ontario in Canada – thousands of miles from the dangers of the battlefronts of Europe and the Pacific – as trained, Leif found himself consciously searching for any possible threat or anyone paying too much attention to them. The discussion between Leif and the captain went well and within an hour they had completed their exchange of information and had a plan in place to bring the Camp X trainees to Camp No. 30 on week six of their ten-week course. Then, just as the two men were wrapping up their meeting, which had unfolded without incident, a series of loud noises – jarring bangs – were heard in close proximity to the café. 'Gunfire?' thought Leif. Instinctively, his right hand swiftly moved across the table and hovered just above the handle the knife in his table setting. Sensing a possible threat, he was prepared to transform the utensil into a weapon if a threat was to present itself – preparing himself for what may come next. The seconds passed, and then another bang was heard and Leif realized the source of the noise was just an old Studebaker car across the street backfiring. Slowly, Leif's hand withdrew from its ready position over the knife. 'No threat, relax.' he said to himself. Leif lit a cigarette. Captain Moore seemed oblivious to it all.

* * *

The next time Leif felt the evolving development of his warrior/secret agent instincts was on the Friday afternoon of the week following his meeting with Captain Smyth. Nine of the expected twelve students scheduled to attend the next serial of training at Camp X, where Leif would be an instructor, had already arrived at the camp and were allotted their bunks, being interviewed and having medical and psychological tests, while awaiting the commencement of their training on Monday morning. The three remaining trainees were to arrive from New York City at Toronto's Union Train Station that afternoon. They had been delayed by severe weather in New York state, so Leif volunteered to take an unmarked staff car from the motor pool and pick up the three inbound trainees himself in the hope of getting them to Camp X as soon as possible. Leif knew that it was important to enable these new trainees to complete their in clearances, including a rigorous medical and psychological assessment prior to the commencement of the course, early – very early – on Monday morning.

All Leif knew about the three inbound trainees was that one was a British Army lieutenant affiliated with the SOE and the other two were United

States Army lieutenants assigned to the OSS and were traveling on the same train from New York City. Their joining instructions told them that they would be met by a driver from the Travelways Bus and Taxi Company. Before leaving Camp X, Leif, dressed in civilian clothes, went to the supply room and tore a flap off a cardboard box and made a rudimentary sign with bold letters saying 'Travelways Bus and Taxi Company'. The train arrived at 1800 hours and by 1815 hours, Leif, with sign in hand, had three unique specimens standing before him. Leif thought of them as specimens because he was already sizing them up. Identifying the British officer was most obvious and easy. Clearly the chap with the swagger stick, Sam Browne belt and fine brown leather gloves was clearly the British army lieutenant, concluded Leif. But what could Leif make of this new, British streetrainee from just simple observations. Firstly, he spoke with precise British grammar; 'well educated' Leif assumed. Secondly, he waved the swagger stick around like it was a tool to emphasize each point he was making. 'A school teacher?' thought Leif. 'No, a professor, a mathematics professor, who was used to having a long, wooden pointer to trace mathematical formulae across a blackboard for his students to follow along', concluded Leif. Quickly moving onto the two American officers – one wore a wrinkled, ill-fitting uniform, his rimmed officer's hat was askew and his shoes were scuffed and had not seen polish in far too long. Under his arm he carried a book, a novel entitled *The Great Gatsby* by F. Scott Fitzgerald, Leif observed. Despite Leif's love of books and impressive record of books having been read, he had not read this American classic yet. But he knew enough about it to recall that it was about the rich and famous of the American elite, living in a world of jazz music and excesses in the early 1920s. The disheveled United States Army officer also carried a copy of *The New York Times* under his arm. It was open to the theater section, detailing the reviews on the current Broadway shows. 'An actor or possibly a musician?' surmised Leif. Finally, the third trainee, and the second American army officer in his game of who's who. 'This one is easy.' The uniform looked smart and well-fitted, his shoes were highly shone and his hat squarely placed upon his head. His uniform jacket also bore two medals, both unknown to Leif, but that was no surprise, because he too was new to the ranks and awards of American soldiers. And yes, that was it, he was a soldier, or had recently been one. This man had recently commissioned from the enlisted ranks to an officer. Leif noted the army officer's shiny, gold-colored second lieutenant bars on the tops of his shoulder and faded remnants of what once were sergeant stripes that had been sown but recently removed from the sleeves of his uniform jacket.

Leif surmised,

So, he's a recently commissioned officer from the enlisted ranks. What special skill would the OSS and SOE be looking for from a soldier? An explosives expert, or skilled radio operator.

Leif chose to shake hands with this enlisted/now commissioned army fellow first to test his theory. The second lieutenant's hands were strong, Leif noted, and calloused – hardened more than most. 'He's a man that works with his hands. An explosives expert?' Leif concluded. After greeting the other two trainees, Leif led them to Front Street to his waiting staff car parked just outside the train station's main entrance. They loaded their suitcases into the boot of the car and were off. Leif thought to himself, 'I wonder how unaware of the of the magnitude of the commitment they had made to undertake the OSS/SOE training that awaited them?'

The drive to Camp X took ninety minutes, during which, all of Leif's assessments were validated. Sitting in his staff car with him, he learned that he had a British engineering professor from the University of Cambridge, an American actor, who had just recently graduated from the Julliard School of Performing Arts in New York and a former sergeant from the Ordinance Corps all heading to Camp X to learn to be secret agents for the Allied cause. Leif drove on contently, knowing that his skills of observation were improving, just as his Camp X instructors had told him they would – if he practiced them until they became second nature. 'These hidden skills, that you don't realize you have, are just waiting to be tapped-into' their instructor had said. Apparently, the instructor was correct.

Leif would enjoy being an instructor and would fit in well with the rest of the Camp X staff and instructors. However, he was surprised to learn that Sergeant Major de Relwyskow had been temporarily transferred to Camp Peary in Virginia, to assist Major Fairbairn with running a similar, secret warrior training program for the Americans. The OSS were in the process of duplicating the British-Canadian SOE training facility with their own, American version, but needed the expertise of some of the Camp X, SOE senior staff to do so in a timely manner – there was a war going on, after all. Upon completing his work at Camp Peary, de Relwyskow was reassigned by the SOE to special operations in Burma. Sadly, he would be killed in action against the Japanese. As for Major Fairbairn, within the year, he received orders to return to London, assigned to SOE headquarters where he worked supporting agents in theater. Fairbairn would be promoted to lieutenant colonel and retire soon after the end of the Second World War having contributed significantly to the war effort with the SOE and as the oldest active SOE instructor and staff officer.

Though disappointed at de Relwyskow's absence from Camp X, as Leif truly admired him and had looked forward to working directly for the sergeant major, he took solace and a degree of pride in being assigned some of de Relwyskow's course duties – in particular the lead for 'midnight ambush' that the sergeant major had so spectacularly performed on the first night of Leif's course. With the self-imposed pressure of meeting or exceeding the expectations of the Camp X instructors and its leadership, Leif, at precisely 0400 hours, delivered an impressive show for the students and fellow instructors alike on the new trainees' first morning of their course at Camp X. He did so by adding a full magazine of live rounds from a Tommy gun to the inventory of explosives (non-lethal training grenades) and the shouting of orders in German to magnify the chaos that he and the other instructors levied upon the new trainee agents. The sudden machine gunfire terrified the unsuspecting students. However, Leif was careful to have the Tommy gun pointed up and towards Lake Ontario when firing, where the rounds fell harmlessly into the expanse of the great lake. The detonation of several training hand grenades added to the bedlam. Recalling his experience as a new trainee, where the female students had been excluded from the harsh early-morning assault, Leif, now as an instructor, made sure to include the four female trainees enrolled on this course in the early-morning lesson – there would be no favoritism on his watch; they all needed to maximize their training experience.

It was only, after the dust had settled, and the ringing in their ears from the auditory assault that the students regained their wits from the shock of the late-night ambush when the three trainees – one British and two American lieutenants – who had only recently arrived at Camp X, recognized their instructor who had led this, initial, ungodly midnight lesson. It was none-other than their driver, the Travelways Bus and Taxi Company employee who had picked them up from the train station in Toronto: Sergeant Leif Bangsbøll. The three duped trainees now understood that clearly, things are not always what they seem around Camp X, and that is exactly the message that Leif and the other instructors wanted to convey.

The first six weeks of the course progressed smoothly, only losing one trainee to a broken leg from a fall on the obstacle course. And like on Leif's qualification course at Camp X, midway through this serial, the trainees were ready to be taken to PoW Camp No. 30, located 15 miles away, on the outskirts of the town of Bowmanville to learn interrogation techniques and strategies to endure and survive if they were so unfortunate as to be captured.

It was late August when Leif was assigned the task of escorting the trainees to the nearby PoW camp for their inaugural visit and training session. The objective was to familiarize the trainees with some of the interrogation methods the Allies employed on German PoWs – nothing remotely like what the Gestapo use in their torture chambers. The trainees had all viewed the Gestapo interrogation film earlier that day and then spent the afternoon observing interrogation sessions at the PoW Camp No. 30. By the end of the day, the trainees looked exhausted and pale. Leif understood that this was an important but stressful phase of training but he also knew what needed to be done following this experience.

* * *

After the long and emotionally stressful day of interrogation training, Leif brought the trainees to the NCOs' mess hall for a well-deserved drink. It was Friday, 1700 hours, and the bar was busy. Smoke hung heavily in the air, and from the far end of the crowded room, emanated the sound of someone playing a lively piano tune. The dozen trainees with him that day quickly established a prominent position at the bar, all to the chagrin of some of the regular patrons. After the first round of drinks he had ordered for his students arrived, Leif paid the bartender with a healthy tip and quietly slipped away from his now rowdy trainees and made his way towards the sound of the piano.

'I wonder if this could be Mrs Henry?' thought Leif, as he navigated through thick haze of cigarette smoke and the throngs of uniformed men and women, and the drone of dozens of competing conversations. The side of the piano came into his view and there, sitting with perfect posture, wearing a flower-patterned dress, with her hands dancing across the black and white ivory keys, was the glamorous yet innocently kind, Margaret Henry. Margaret was smiling at the mingling audience gathered around her piano and moved her head gently to the rhythm of the song as she played. After a few moments, their eyes met and Leif and Margaret smiled warmly at each other. Leif moved forward and took up a position leaning casually on the piano while watching Margaret perform. He raised his glass in a gesture of a toast to the pianist. Margaret smiled again and nodded her reply to Leif's toast without missing a note.

A minute later, Margaret finished the song with a bit of dramatic bravado upon the keys and the crowd cheered in response. She stood up and politely waved and nodded as the applause enveloped the room. Mouthing the words, 'Thank you... thank you...' she basked in the moment. Then, to Leif's happy surprise, she reached over and gave him a long, warm hug as if they were long-lost friends. 'Sergeant Bangsbøll, how delightful to see you. I thought you had been reassigned back to the United States.'

'That was the plan but I have been kept on to...' Abruptly he stopped. He had almost said, 'to instruct at Camp X', but caught himself and continued. 'I've been kept on to study how the Canadian Army operates their prisoner of war camps. I expect to be sent back to the States later this year.' Leif trusted Margaret, but the important work he was involved with was secret and strictly on a need-to-know basis.

Margaret seemed pleased, and said,

> Leif, you must come back for another visit to Oshawa, it has been over a month since we've had the pleasure of your company and my husband Clifford does so much enjoy chatting with you.

'I enjoyed my visits very much as well, in particular the time spent talking with your husband.'

'Well then', said Margaret, 'we shall expect you for supper this Sunday evening, 5 o'clock sharp. Bring along one of your colleagues if you would like – we'll have plenty of food.'

'I cannot turn down such an offer, Mrs Henry.' Leif graciously accepted. 'It will be my pleasure to attend. Please give my regards to Mr and Dr Henry.'

'Wonderful!' enthused Margaret. 'Now Leif, would you be a dear and order me a drink? Rye and water please. I must get back to work.' At that, Margaret sat back down at the piano and began to play to the delight of the mess members.

It had been a chance meeting, eight weeks earlier, during Leif's first visit to PoW Camp No. 30 as a trainee from Camp X, that he had met Margaret Henry, who lived in nearby Oshawa, was an active volunteer with the Canadian Red Cross who frequented PoW Camp No. 30 to distribute Red Cross care packages to the German PoWs. Margaret was also involved with organizing and hosting social events for the Canadian soldiers who guarded the PoWs. An accomplished pianist, Margret often regaled the mess members during functions at the officers' and NCOs' messes, which were located adjacent to the PoWs' compound.

Whether it was his Danish charm and Scandinavian accent or his well-fitting American army uniform that first impressed Margaret, we will never know, but whatever the reason, Margaret took a liking to this young Dane and invited him and a guest of his choosing for dinner the following Sunday.

Chapter 14

A Reason to Return

'Every new beginning comes from some other beginning's end.'
Lucius Seneca, Roman philosopher

Leif and his Camp X colleague Ross Smith arrived promptly at 1700 hours that Sunday evening at the Henrys' large, two story, red brick home at 231 King Street East. Framed by tall oak trees, with a sprawling lawn covered in yellow and red leaves, the autumn sunset spangling their red veins and crinkling corners. The two soldiers stood on the large front porch of their Canadian host's home. Leif gave the rocking chair a slight push, and rang the bell, while anticipating his first home cooked meal in months.

The Henrys' youngest son, John, 13 years old, could be heard clambering down the stairs, and making a dash towards the front door and the mysterious dinner guests on the porch. John threw the door open quite dramatically to inspect the dinner guests in their dashing uniforms.

Leif offered John his hand in greeting, but the young teen ignored pleasantries and immediately peppered his uniformed guests with questions: 'Have you killed any Germans?'

Leif was taken aback by John's bluntness. 'No. I haven't.' Leif looked to Ross with a puzzled expression and a nod of his head to respond. But before Ross could utter a word, the young, inquisitive boy continued his interrogation: 'Did you bring a gun with you?'

Leif shook his head. 'No. I didn't realize it was going to be that kind of dinner.' Exasperated at his failed expectations, John led the two 'boring' dinner guests into the sun room where Margaret made introductions to her husband Clifford and their eldest son, Robert, who was 18. Pre-dinner cocktail orders were taken and a few minutes later Dorothy-Jean, 16 years old, made her entrance into the room – hair was done, makeup on and dressed for an occasion. She said,

Hello Sergeant Smith – nice to meet you. And hello again Sergeant Bangsbøll, it's good to see you again. So, you're a soldier and an awfully long way from home – Copenhagen, Denmark, I understand. That's very intriguing. May I ask…

At that point Margaret cut in, surveilled her young daughter for a moment and then explained that Dorothy was attending high school in Oshawa and that Peggy, their oldest, who had just recently secured a job working as a model for an advertising firm in New York City, was upstairs packing, and would be joining them later.

As soon as Margaret left to tend to the dinner preparations, Dorothy, recommenced her flirtatious assault,

> Father, did you know that the Danish flag is called the Dannebrog and it is the oldest flag of any nation? Isn't that right Sergeant Bangsbøll, or may I call you Leif?

Before her father or even Leif could respond, Dorothy went on to pronounce several other 'fun facts' about Danish culture that she had learned at the library, earlier that day – clearly in preparation for this evening's dinner guests' arrival. And just as Dorothy was to introduce her next Danish fact, her older sister, Peggy, arrived and delivered a cold beer to their guests and a whisky and water for her father. Peggy turned to her younger sister and said, 'You're needed in the kitchen Dot.' Using Dorothy's nickname, which she despised. Narrowing her eyes and glaring at her older sister, Dorothy got up and went to assist her mother in the kitchen. Before Dorothy was out of ear shot, Peggy apologized for her 'little sister's immature behavior', and immediately sat down on the sofa between Ross and Leif. A few minutes later, after hearing all about the latest in ladies fashion trends, and Peggy's upcoming plans to take the train to New York to start her modeling job, young John came running into the sun room to announce that dinner was served.

The evening was a welcome distraction for both the trainee agents and the Henry family. After dinner, Leif and his colleague joined Clifford for a nightcap and a cigarette on the back veranda, which overlooked the large and heavily treed backyard. As they sat enjoying the warm Canadian summer evening with the fragrance of lilac bushes saturating the air, the men talked about all manner of subjects late into the night. Leif enjoyed those tranquil hours with Clifford but sensed that he was not the man he once had been. Clifford was a First World War veteran, and although he was only 49 years old, he appeared and acted much older. Leif thought Clifford could easily pass for Margaret's father.

Later in the evening, Clifford's father, Dr Franklin Henry, a dentist, arrived home. He had been called out on a medical emergency before the two dinner guests had arrived, and now joined his son and the two young men on the back porch. After the introductions, Dr Henry lit his pipe and joined in the discussion, which now revolved around the Allies' progress in the Battle of the Atlantic.

Clifford declared, 'According to the newspapers, fewer of our naval convoys are being hit by those damn German U-boats.' Ever the optimist, Dr Henry added, 'Mark my words gentlemen, we've turned a corner in the war on the Atlantic; we've got those Nazi submarines beaten!'

Margaret, while doing the dishes at the sink, watched the four men through the kitchen window and thought that the time spent with these charming young soldiers might have a positive influence on her husband, and be a little encouragement for her father-in-law as well. She brought out a small meal for Dr Henry and joined the men. The conversation changed to more pleasant topics and they spoke well into the night.

Following a delightful and relaxing evening at the Henry home, Leif and his colleague, Ross, drove their staff car the twenty-minute journey back to Camp X, arriving shortly after midnight. They were over an hour late for camp curfew. The next day, Leif was brought before the camp adjutant to explain his breach of curfew regulations. Before Leif had the chance to explain, the adjutant indicated that he assumed the cause of his late return was directly attributed to alcohol consumption and local women, in keeping with so many other similar student infractions. Unwilling to disclose the true, benign reason for his late return to camp, Leif just smiled and agreed with the adjutant's assessment and accepted the seven days confined to camp that he received as his punishment. Leif considered the punishment to be inconsequential but made sure that his colleague who had accompanied him that evening received no blame in the matter and was not punished for his involvement in the evening's curfew infraction.

Leif was invited back to the Henry home on several more occasions during his prolonged assignment at Camp X, occasions that fostered a close relationship with the entire Henry family. Cognizant of his secret, Leif was careful not to let the Henry family, nor anyone else for that matter, know his true reason for being in Canada. Instead, he conveyed vague and fictitious stories about being just a sergeant with the United States Army on assignment to work as a liaison officer to the Canadian Army and RCAF at Camp Borden, the RCAF at Base Trenton and the national headquarters in Ottawa – all these installations were in relatively close proximity to Oshawa, Whitby and Bowmanville, which supported his cover story. Leif understood that in times of war, it was essential to limit exchanges of information about his true mission. Despite this understanding, Leif deeply regretted lying to the Henry family. 'Someday, when this whole dreadful affair is over and the war has been won, I'll tell them the truth.' Leif promised himself.

During these most welcome visits, Leif learned much about the Henry family. Margaret Henry (née Daignan) grew up in the small Ontario town of Niagara-on-the-Lake. She was a kind and gentle woman but was a force to be reckoned with. Always the epitome of a dignified lady, she was intelligent, beautiful and generous; attributes that could be disarming to any man. With the arrival of wartime activities to the Oshawa area, she directed her energy towards her efforts as a volunteer with the Red Cross and to extending social opportunities to the Canadian and Allied military personnel, who were serving away from home. Margaret's pleasant nature and focused concerns were for the well-being not only of the Canadian soldiers on guard duty at Camp No. 30, but also for the welfare of the German PoWs. She understood that they were the enemy and that Germany had started this horrible war, but she knew that these young Germans had no part in starting this war. They were simply caught up in it and answering the call just like her husband, Clifford, had done in 1916.

Margaret's husband, Russell Clifford Henry, was a kind and good man but, regrettably, a broken man. Having withdrawn from the University of Toronto during the Christmas break in 1916, he joined the 116th Canadian Infantry Battalion on 5 February 1916 to fight for king and country. On 24 July of that year, Lieutenant Russell Clifford Henry of Oshawa, Ontario, went off to war to fight for the Empire.

He and his battalion sailed from Halifax, Nova Scotia to Portsmouth, England, on the SS *Olympic*. The 116th Infantry Battalion, along with the 34th Regiment to which Clifford had been assigned, would go on to serve with distinction throughout the First World War and received battle honors for such notable engagements as Vimy Ridge, Ypres, Passchendaele, Amiens, Cambria, Hill 70 and Flanders. Clifford was repatriated to Canada after eighteen months in combat. He came home a different man.

Leif had not seen combat yet, but he had studied the First World War while at Sølvgades school. He could only imagine the physical and emotional scars that were heaped upon a young officer like Clifford, who spent so much time on the frontlines – in the trenches of France and Belgium. It must have been hell on earth.

Clifford had physical and emotional scars from the First World War. A severe case of trench foot – a painful and debilitating ailment that was common to First World War trench warfare caused by prolonged, wet, cold and unsanitary conditions – had crippled his circulatory system. He was also suffering from the lingering effects of exposure to German gas attacks. As a result, he would have medical problems for the rest of his life. Worse still, the once strong, ambitious young man was now a fragile shell of his former self. Enduring the horrid conditions of life in the trenches, the trauma of prolonged combat and the constant exposure to the horrors of trench warfare continued to haunt Clifford for throughout his life. Labeled as 'shell-shocked' at the time, post-traumatic stress disorder is what they would call it today. As a result of this now recognized mental illness, Clifford began to rely on alcohol to escape his discomforts and eventually became an alcoholic, which only weakened his tenuous hold on a productive life. It was a difficult time for his wife, Margaret, but thankfully, her father-in-law, Dr Henry, a wise man, had the good sense and sufficient financial resources to care for both Clifford and Margaret and their growing family. Fearful that his daughter-in-law might give up on her marriage to Clifford because of his condition, Dr Henry made certain financial arrangements to guarantee Margaret and her four children's well-being for as long as she remained part of the Henry family.

Though her husband Clifford supported and encouraged Margaret's efforts to extend comfort to the Canadian and Allied soldiers working at the PoW camp, he could not understand nor support his wife's Red Cross activities with the German PoWs; he had seen too much in the First World War to consider a German as anything but a vile and dangerous enemy. Margaret was not deterred by her husband's views and continued her Red Cross work with both Allied and enemy soldiers. Furthermore, her husband's condition had been part of her inspiration to regularly invite one or two young Canadian or Allied soldiers for Sunday dinner. It was always a formal affair in the Henry household and provided her husband the opportunity to meet and talk with the young soldiers. She believed that these conversations might help him deal with the demons that tormented him.

Leif felt the healing undertones of his talks with Clifford as well. On his last visit to the Henrys' home in late September 1943, just before returning to Washington to finalize his OSS training, Leif made a point to express his sincere appreciation to Clifford and the Henry family for their friendship and generous hospitality.

Leif saved his final farewell for Margaret.
Mrs Henry, having lost my mother at a young age, I feel you have come into my life and have become my new mother. Your kindness to me and the other Allied servicemen and women and even to the German prisoners has been wonderful, and so greatly appreciated by us all.

During that final farewell, Leif was made to promise Margaret, Clifford and Dr Henry that if the opportunity ever arose, he would come back to visit the Henry family again.

'Yes of course.' Leif assured them. 'Once the war is over and won.' As it turned out, it would be more than two years later before Leif would return to see the Henry family again – and reacquaint himself with the woman who was to become his future wife – Dorothy.

Chapter 15

Veritas

'Soldiers, I love them for their virtue's sake and for their greatness of mind. If we may have peace, they have purchased it; if we must have war, they must manage it.'

Robert Devereux, 1600

For nearly a century, from John Buchan to Graham Greene, and from Ian Fleming to Robert Ludlum and Tom Clancy, the concept of the secret agent has been portrayed and usually with great misrepresentation by

Second Lieutenant Leif Bangsboll, United States Army (standing center) with Lieutenant Junior Grade (JG), United States Navy Reserve (USNR) Portia Williams to his left, along with Lt (JG) USNR Judith Bullock seated beside her husband Second Lieutenant, US Army Edward "Shorty" Thomson (just married), along with Nell Riddick (far left) and her date Lt Buck Lee, United States Navy (USN) at the Robert E. Lee hotel, Lexington, Virginia, 24 April 1943.

these fiction writers and Hollywood movie makers. The true 'secret' agents of the Second World War were referred to as just 'agents' or 'field operatives' and though incredibly brave and extremely skilled in their profession, did not resemble the stereotypical James Bond-esque characters portrayed in popular books and movies. Real agents did not drive expensive sports cars nor attend glitzy cocktail parties in stylish tuxedos with a beautiful *femme fatale* to aid them in the execution of their mission assignment. An actual agent was trained to blend in and remain anonymous and unremarkable while conducting clandestine activities.

Agents needed unified minds and bodies, physically and psychologically fit, with brawn and bruising cognitive skills, but not necessarily to defeat heavily armed and giddily named henchmen. An OSS agent required those attributes to think on their feet, to adapt to changing circumstances, to anticipate second and third order effects of decisions, and then take decisive action, which sometimes translated to beating a hasty escape or outright flight. And while remaining letter-perfect in physique and mental dexterity, there was one last ingredient in the brew, perhaps most pressing: an agent needed to lie and be a consummate actor, a preternatural performer. A successful synthesis of these disparate elements, the ability to be of the crowd and far removed from the chaos, would earn one the distinction of becoming a legendary 'gray man'.

Lieutenant Leif Bangsboll (standing, fifth from the left) with OSS colleagues, London England 1944. (*Photo courtesy of the author's family collection*)

Upon arrival in Washington DC, Leif would be educated in the third pillar of espionage, the ability to interact and socialize effectively within and amongst the enemy's hierarchy, mixing with military and government officials. An agent had to protect their cover, while extracting information from targeted individuals and conveying false leads to others. From the moment his airplane touched the tarmac, Leif would no longer be able to use his own name. He was rebaptized, reborn, as 'Agent Alexander Hudson', and the acronym 'OSS' would never be uttered aloud again. While on the job, Leif and his fellow agents referred to the organization by a given code name, 'Veritas', which translates to 'The Truth.' The gallows irony required no further elaboration.

Although the James Bond character and some of the high-tech tools of his trade depicted therein were unquestionably an exaggeration, the OSS and SOE did create and issue a few clever devices to enable their agents to enhance mission performance. Things such as miniaturized shortwave radios and cameras concealed in briefcases or in modified books, cufflinks that were miniature compasses and, of course, invisible ink pens, water-soluble message paper and even emerging microdot technology to store imagery or documentation in miniaturized form. OSS and SOE scientists developed explosives that could be disguised inside mundane objects including candles, bread and even horse manure – fake or modified manure – which could be placed inconspicuously on a roadway and detonated as an enemy convoy or patrol passed. Agents were also given shoes with hollow heels to hide lock-picking tools. Razors were frequently concealed in the toe of a boot, which when extracted and elongated could be used as weapons in a close-quarter fight. On the ballistics front, agents were issued a single shot spring-loaded assassin's pistol that could be clipped under a table, successfully obscured by a cloth or dinner plate, and when activated would fire a bullet at the target one minute after being engaged. The time delay would allow the agent to activate the weapon and excuse themselves from the table, leaving the victim unaware of their pending fate and allowing an escape before a bullet was shot into in their unfortunate dining companion.

Of course, there were less-exotic weapons like brass knuckles, switchblade knives and daggers, garrots made of piano wire, all easily hidden inside a waist band or belt for an effective silent kill. However, Leif, echoing the sentiments of Major Fairbairn, believed there was no substitute in a fight for the most lethal weapon that all agents possessed: their homicidal hands. And Leif had large, strong hands.

* * *

Leif was not the only one who had gained a considerable educational upgrade in espionage since late 1942, Donovan's fledgling OSS was still at war with the entrenched intelligence bureaucracies, political isolationists and internal pushback coming from the White House, but the organization finally had an office. And Donovan had been given a title to match his new quarters. The colonel was now known officially as the Coordinator of Information (COI) and his staff occupied the former naval war department's observatory buildings on E Street, north-west of the Lincoln Memorial. The location, known to locals as 'Navy Hill', was perfect for OSS personnel. They were in proximity to downtown Washington DC, close enough to the Capitol to receive real-time updates about the military and political battle unfolding in Europe and the Pacific, but far enough off the beaten path that their comings and goings were unlikely to be observed by the civilian public, and most importantly, the prying eyes of foreign assets.

For Leif, now a Second Lieutenant in the United States Army, along with his fellow agents on the last leg of their journey to becoming practicing field operatives, Navy Hill's contiguity to the downtown nightlife scene fit the bill, for it was at government-sponsored social functions they were expected to ply the tools of their trade, particularly at the famous Round Robin bar at the Willard Hotel on Pennsylvania Avenue and the Old Ebbitt Grill on 15th Street North West. Leif often referred to this time of his training as attending 'charm school', where in the role of Alexander Hudson, civilian mechanical engineer, he infiltrated Washington DC's cloistered velvet rope of secrecy and debauchery. Before attending an event, Leif would stand before the mirror for hours, practicing facial expressions, greetings and reciting back his cover story. Alexander Hudson worked for a private American firm with business affiliations in Scandinavia under contract with the USAAF.

After a few weeks in 'charm school', Leif's side trip to Washington DC fell into place and suddenly, its purpose made sense. The program was about far more than becoming comfortable with your alternate identity before being cleared to enter Europe. The OSS was testing your ability to maintain cover when alcohol and sex were tossed into the equation, the grinning hand grenade of transgression, for Donovan was sending his troops into situations where there would be plenty of chances for both temptations. The colonel and his minions would have female OSS agents or call girls sent down from Baltimore, planted at social functions, restaurants and bars, and given instructions to target the trainees and see if they could get them to lower their guard – to break character and reveal their cover stories. It was during this time that a new, lighter definition for the OSS began to be circulated among the agents: The 'Oh So Social Club'. During this strange phase of their evolution as agents, Leif watched several of his cohorts fail the final litmus test and be removed from duty, either sent back for additional training or given non-operational orders, such as being an analyst or permanent mission support officer. If the action was serious enough, the agent would be removed from the OSS entirely.

Leif had three advantages aiding him to minimize interpersonal pitfalls. First, he possessed a herculean tolerance for alcohol, one that rivaled even his father's, who was known throughout the Royal Danish Navy for having a veritable wooden leg. What it took Leif to get intoxicated – or even loosened up – would have sent the average social drinker to the hospital. Secondly, he had a deep personal motivation to return to Denmark. He desperately wanted to locate his father and liberate his homeland from Hitler's grasp and would not allow anything or anyone to distract him. Finally, perhaps his greatest armor of all in the face of temptation, was his growing love for Dorothy-Jean Henry, which erased interest in any other woman.

Leif's time in Washington DC was not restricted solely to 'charm school' loyalty tests designed to ferret out personal weakness, he was also sent on training exercises, including mock special operations and sabotage-demolition training at Area B or RTU-11 in the Catoctin Mountains of Northern Maryland – a site that would later become the heart and soul of the CIA and be christened as 'The Farm', their version of Camp X.

Leif and his fellow agents were also given live action training in the application of saboteur techniques. These exercises served a dual purpose: to troubleshoot an agent's weak points before being sent into the field and testing the security of vital regional infrastructure, including transportation nodes in the Washington DC area, as well as the port of Baltimore, the Philadelphia shipyards, and the Pittsburgh railyard.

OSS agents were given instructions to breach the security of these facilities, photograph critical apparatuses of the operations and, in some cases, to plant 'dummy' explosives on essential port and railyard components. These assignments were invaluable runs for occupied Europe, where agents would secure locations or disable an enemy ship in port. Blocking a port channel with a disabled vessel or destroying a train would be prohibitively expensive to The Reich (German Empire) in terms of both time and labor, not to mention the financial strain under wartime austerity of constantly repairing or replacing vital national properties.

One specific training assignment involved Leif and two other agents disguising themselves as longshoremen and using false identity cards produced by the forgery section at OSS headquarters to sneak into the Baltimore City shipyard and plant six 'dummy' explosives at various critical port infrastructure, including three ships and in the lobby of the port authority office itself, which shared space with the Baltimore port police station. Obviously, when the exercise was completed, and Leif led the port security officials to the OSS's handiwork, lessons were learned.

Based upon Leif's success in avoiding the allure of alcohol and women, his ability to seamlessly blend into his environment, and his overwhelming competence at staying in character, Agent Alexander Hudson, was classified as a versatile, multi-lingual asset with high intuitive skills and a decisive, though at times methodical approach, all qualities that made him ideal for complex direct engagement with enemy forces. And after reading Leif's report, Donovan immediately recommended the young Dane's file to be expedited for early deployment to work with the OSS's counterparts in Britain – the SOE – in preparation for Alexander Hudson to assume his role as an operational agent. Leif was overjoyed, his transfer to London would place him one step closer to the war and realizing his dream of returning home.

* * *

Leif, as Agent Hudson, was assigned to the SI branch to work under another American, Captain William 'Bill' J. Casey, who would eventually become the director of the CIA. Casey's aggressive tenure lasted from 1981 to 1987 and encompassed the height and ultimate winding down of the Cold War, a feat Casey's CIA achieved by bogging the Soviets down in several ill-fated proxy wars stretching from South and Central America to Afghanistan.

But before Casey would get his hands on that assignment, he oversaw the OSS's department that was a beehive of activity, involved in preparing over 200 agents to be deployed into occupied Europe in advance of the Normandy invasion. Everyone at the SI was operating according to the explicit orders of Winston Churchill to the OSS and SOE: 'Set your agents loose and set Europe ablaze.'

For Normandy to be a success, the SI needed to have all cylinders firing round the clock. They needed to coordinate airdrop deliveries of weapons, ammunition, explosives and radios to resistance forces across Europe, but especially in France and Belgium, which were not merely the main invasion sites, but also boasted the largest, most committed, and seemingly most arson and carnage chapters of the resistance.

Leif's role was to serve as a liaison between the OSS and SOE in a mission support capacity, bridging the gap between the two agencies, and ensuring the Jedburgh missions, joint American and English operations, went off without a hitch. And if Normandy provided an Allied beachhead, for which everyone hoped and prayed, Leif's job would get busier, for the OSS and SOE would begin looking to place officers in previously overlooked areas such as Italy, the

Balkans and Scandinavia, where powerful anti-Nazi underground networks kept popping up and were spoiling for a fight.

However, outside of their unflagging unity in prosecuting the war, the office culture struck Leif as a bit odd and eerily reminiscent of his flight school training where he was surrounded by chauvinist Norwegians who belittled his Danish heritage. There was a deep professional rivalry between the agents of Britain's SOE and their American counterparts, and Leif was SOE's favorite target to tangle with and single out for special attention. The British attitude baffled the young Dane. Not only had the SOE given their blessing and helped train OSS candidates, but Leif wasn't even an American yet, he was a European. The SOE agents did not see it that way. His accent and his heritage were immaterial; it was the flag he was fighting under. Guilt by association. But perhaps, the greatest irony, in Leif's opinion, was that most of his British colleagues did not even see themselves as European. They were British.

To further test Leif's mettle and impress Anglo superiority upon the young Dane, the SOE agents invited him to a special warfare exercise run by an SOE commando school near the town of Arisaig on the rugged and isolated, west coast of Scotland. The training would span two weeks and call upon advanced survival techniques necessary to endure in the cold, harsh, low-visibility climate of northwestern Scotland. Agents were required to live off the land and travel by foot for over 100 miles across the notorious Scottish moors and mountains – some of which had legendarily swallowed up and buried whole parties – conducting mock ambushes and sabotage missions along the way, and practicing clandestine, nocturnal amphibious landings on the coast.

Leif performed admirably, escaping exhausted with the expected lacerations, sprains, bruises, along with some impromptu wrapping and binding, but he did not bowl over the SOE, who impressed him with their ferocious drive. No, Leif's survival skills were not what finally caused the deep thaw at the office. That happened the night the commando training mission wrapped up, when everyone decided to drink away the past two weeks by interspersing pints of British ale and Scotch whisky. And as they got progressively more inebriated, the British realized Leif was no typical Yank.

Not only could he match them pint for pint, shot for shot, but Leif appeared to know more about European history and literature than all of them combined. In addition, he was fluent in five languages, including German, which he showed off to the SOE by moving the party into a secluded corner, away from listeners who might mistake Leif for a Wehrmacht officer and tear him limb from limb. The agents were flabbergasted, few of them had been able to master the tortured machinations of the German tongue enough to pass muster with the enemy. Then, Leif regaled them with his experience as a merchant maritime engineer who had participated in the evacuation-rescue mission of their fellow British soldiers from Dunkirk, an early-war failure turned into pyrrhic victory that remained close to the heart of all Britons. He closed by mentioning that as a Royal Norwegian Air Force flight sergeant, he had earned his pilot wings with the BCATP, leading Leif to round off his drunkenly rendered resume, with: 'See, gents, me… an average Yank, has done more for the British war effort to date than any of you.' From that point forward, Leif was one of them; he had established his bona fides with his British colleagues beyond any doubt.

* * *

There was one SI officer who had befriended and been drawn to Leif immediately, one who did not require a two-week test of wills to prove his worthiness, likely because she felt as out of place as the young Dane. Her name was Lieutenant Nicole Weatherby – known in the office as Agent Natalie Simons.

At the outbreak of the Second World War, Nicole had been a 23-year-old librarian from Bristol. She had studied languages at the University of Oxford and was blessed with a near-perfect eidetic or photographic memory. If she read it, she could recall it verbatim. Nicole was initially commissioned into the WAAF, but her leadership skills and razor-sharp intellect separated her from the pack, and she was immediately brought to the attention of the SOE, who quickly reassigned her to SI, where she was invaluable as a translator and codebreaker analyst.

Thus, after months of leaning on each other as their only office comrade, when Nicole found out she was about to be para-inserted into Norway as a radio operator codebreaker, Leif was adamant they must celebrate. The entire time they'd been colleagues Nicole had been dreaming of dining at one of London's swankiest restaurants, the Criterion, a cavernous, neo-Byzantine spot that remained popular and packed even during the darkest days of the Blitz. Leif promised Nicole they would dine there, that he would get a reservation.

The Criterion's *maître d'* turned down Leif's request for a reservation with a dismissive sniff, informing the young man that such an inquiry at short notice was patently absurd and offensive to them both. Leif rested on arm on the man's podium, leaned in slightly and attempted to ignite a charm offensive, explaining that he was a serving Allied officer, working in Britain at the behest of their monarch and the pleasure of the United States, and that he wished to take a young female British air force officer, about to be placed in harm's way, out for a glamorous dinner at the restaurant she requested. Point of fact, the Criterion should be flattered.

'Sir, being a Yank', the *maitre d'* scoffed, hardening his position, 'you may not realize but this is one of the most popular and finest dining establishments in all of London. I can't give you a reservation on short notice.'

'Sure, you can.' Leif retorted. 'If not you, then who?'

The *maitre d'* enjoyed being reminded of his power. 'Correct. And I choose not to expedite your request.'

Leif felt thrust back to the Norwegian and Danish embassies, dealing with stifling and cowardly bureaucrats who held all the power and refused to wield any of it. This *maitre d'* was cut from the same shrewish cloth and there was only one way to deal with such people.

'Two cartons of American cigarettes for a 9.00 pm reservation for two.' Leif said, drumming on the podium, and resorting to a simple bribe, the only language the *maitre d'* was fluent in.

The man scanned his surroundings. 'I might be able to secure you a table later in the evening, once the theater crowd clears out.'

Leif smiled, pleased he'd successfully sized up the *maitre d'*, and could secure Nicole's table.

> Okay. Two cartons of American cigarettes and a pairs of silk stockings for your favorite friend. But then I want the 9.00 pm table near the dance floor, the one close to the piano stage.

Leif knew the street value of such scarce items in war-ravaged Britain, as did the *maitre d'* who leaned over his podium, uncapped his fountain pen and readied himself to write Leif's name in the reservation book. 'Alexander Hudson', Leif said.

'Young Mr Hudson', the man said,

> I don't know who you are. I don't know what it is you exactly do, since you seem a bit… slippery for a commissioned officer. But whatever efforts you are applying your considerable talents toward, I have no doubt you will be a smashing success against the enemy.

Leif smiled, calling himself Alexander Hudson in these circumstances seemed existentially correct, like for the first time, he was fully inhabiting his character. Agent Hudson possessed capacities for moral ambiguity, negotiation and sarcasm that Leif Bangsbøll lacked. He would willingly flout the law, break it if necessary, to get what he wanted, and could deal with criminals on their own terms to succeed in his mission. Leif's encounter with the *maitre d'* may have been a piddling event, but in that moment, he realized that he had truly become an agent.

The Criterion was located just off Piccadilly Circus in the heart of London's theater district and promised Leif and Nicole a brief respite from the demands of war, particularly as she was about to be thrust into the middle of the conflict. He was excited to retire Agent Hudson for a few hours and just have dinner with a friend. Although that dinner was a large question mark floating over the evening. As a result of government imposed food rationing, the menu at the Criterion was far less elegant and expansive back then. However, the restaurant assured all diners that the available food was still exquisitely prepared by the renowned chef. Leif stood before the entrance, peering inside, scoping out his reserved table with Hudson neatly inscribed across a placard, and waited for Nicole to arrive. His thoughts drifted to Clifford and Margaret's daughter, Dorothy, and how he wished she could be with him in London.

Since he'd grown up absent any female presence or influence, Leif habitually found himself drawn to the kindness, the company, the sheer wonderment of women, but Dorothy was different. She was the one, his person. He did not want to let a second pass without her at his side. She was not filling an absence; she was the only presence he desired. Whereas Nicole – as Leif was quite aware – filled a more predictable and diagnosable role. She was a substitute for his younger sister, who would have been Nicole's exact age, had she survived.

Leif waved to Nicole when he spotted her rounding the corner to the Criterion. She began to rush over, and he quickly discerned why she was late. Leif had never seen Nicole dressed in anything but basic office casual clothing and without a hint of makeup, but tonight, she looked almost like a movie star, wearing a cocktail dress, her hair teased up and her cheekbones highlighted with blush – she was beautiful.

Before either one of them could speak a word of welcome, the unmistakable sounds of air raid sirens sounded in the distance. The two agents stopped dead in their tracks, looked at each other, listening intently. The warning signals had started at the east end of the city, and grew like a chain reaction, sirens from other districts began to join in, creating a cacophonic tidal wave sweeping westward, rolling toward Leif and Nicole, and the hundreds of thousands of other Londoners.

'Run Leif!' Nicole shouted. 'The Convent Garden tube station isn't far.'

For that was all one could do when bombing was imminent, seek the closest site located underground, and hope your location was deep enough to survive the onslaught.

Nicole extended her hand toward Leif as she ran, and they raced with their fingers intertwined toward the long, narrow stairwell that would usher them into the bowels of the underground tube stop.

Paradoxically, Leif and Nicole were fortunate to have been so close to the underground station when the sirens started – they would miss the mad onrush that would follow. Soon, thousands would be pushing, racing and bulldozing their way toward safety. It always struck Leif just how desperately people wanted to live at all costs. Most were orderly and considerate of others. However, some would literally toss aside the well-being of their fellow citizen for an added sense of safety, an extra second of breath, a snatched minute of mortality on this mortal coil, regardless of what had to be done to get it. Peril showed everyone who they were in a mirrored handful of dust.

Out of breath but almost giddy with adrenaline rushing through their veins, Leif and Nicole reached the underground platform, deep below street level. They were joining several dozen partygoers already in the station, who had huddled themselves in small enclaves dug into the walls with sandbags, hoping to avoid the fallout if a bomb caved the station ceiling.

The two agents squeezed into an available space and before they had a chance to exchange a word, the next German bomb detonated above them. They felt the ground shudder, bricks in the arched ceiling of the tube shed sentiment from the enormous impact. Thankfully, the blast was still relatively far away, but if this was a preview of the enormous firepower coming their way. 'Was there a chance that Convent Garden tube station could withstand a direct hit?' thought the couple simultaneously.

Another explosion followed quickly on its heels, this one closer, causing the lights to flicker and rats to rush across the platform, scurrying between the Londoners legs and feet, trying to chart their own path to safety. Nicole drew her body into Leif, and they held each other tightly. More people began pouring down the stairs seeking refuge, jostling over with one another, most silently praying, some crying and others shouting, adrenaline-fused expletives at the Germans, about how they should 'bring their goddamn, bloody best because they could take it.'

Nicole and Leif locked eyes, unable to speak over the din of the air raid warning and human noise. The Germans struck again, lobbing another bomb seemingly into their heads. Seismic cracks showed in the underground platform; the stairwell shook and groaned in agony, sending people over its sides, falling over one another. A last kick to the explosion plunged half the station into total darkness. Nicole grabbed Leif by the back of the head and kissed him, long and deep, holding him in place and closing her eyes.

Another explosion rocketed through the air, doing further damage to the structures already made vulnerable by the prior blasts, and a small electric fire started at the switches at the end of the tracks, threatening to engulf several abandoned trains. Smoke drifted through the tunnel, powered by the vacuum effect of the explosions above.

Nicole slowly ended their kiss and said, 'I'm sorry.'

Leif grinned, stunned by her overpowering affection. 'It's quite alright.'

'I love someone else', she confessed, 'but I didn't want to die without feeling one last touch of love.'

Without thinking, Leif confessed, 'I'm in love with someone else as well.'

'What's her name?' Nicole asked.

'Dorothy-Jean. She lives with her family in Canada. She's… she's still in school.'

'Mine is Maxwell. He's in school too – an Oxford lecturer.' She laughed. 'He was one of my professors actually.'

Just as randomly as the air raid had started, it ended and the lights flickered back on. However, everyone stayed still, frozen in abeyance, letting the time pass, until they felt secure to rise.

Nicole was the first. She got up, brushed off her dress, and tried to instill some order in her hair. Neither she nor Leif looked exactly Criterion ready. 'I didn't hear any German airplanes. Those must have been the new flying bombs we've heard about, the V-1 Rockets.' She placed a hand on Leif's shoulder to steady herself and slipped her shoe back on. 'Hitler is stepping things up. He means to crush us, punish us, break us.'

Indeed, Hitler did. The V-1 rocket, known as the Vergeltungswaffe, or 'vengeance weapon' was specifically designed to embody its name, to terrorize British citizens and undermine morale. The newest incarnation of the 'Buzz Bomb' or 'Doodlebug' – the moniker assigned by Britain and its Allies to the prior V-2 rocket – had made its terrifying debut.

The V-1 was the bandied about sequel to the legendary V-2, both designed by the father of Nazi aeronautics Wernher von Braun. The V-2 was a triumph of innovation, of screaming death across the sky. It was the world's first large-scale liquid-propellant rocket vehicle, or in layman's terms the first modern long-range ballistic missile. But the V-1 was a true cut above in aerial terror. Once launched, it could fly unmanned at the speed of sound and when its fuel supply was exhausted, it crashed down, exploding on impact.

The Germans preferred method of launching the V-1 was either catapult ramps or aircraft, and once propelled the V-1 carried an 850-kilogram explosive warhead at 360 miles per hour with an average range of 150 miles. Hence, the cruel demoralization of the V-1. One was aware of its presence long before they touched down and wreaked havoc.

Once Leif and Nicole surfaced and reached street level, the air raid sirens had been replaced with fire engine and ambulance sirens responding to the impact disaster zones across the city. Central London had largely been spared that night, but the V-1's had reigned destruction on several outlying neighborhoods, which had gone up in flames.

Nicole pointed to her disheveled experience. 'I think we may have difficulty getting a table at the Criterion.'

'Shall we get you home, then?' Leif asked.

'Absolutely not', she answered, 'I'm still famished and need a drink more than ever. Shall we go to the Café de Paris? It's close by and they're a lot more accepting of sartorial eccentricities.'

Leif smiled and said, 'I know the place.' He and grabbed Nicole's hand and moved off in the direction of the Café de Paris.

The Café de Paris was housed in the basement of the Rialto Theatre on Coventry Street, and despite the late hour and the recent scare, the club was packed with patrons, many in uniform, and bristling with energy, soaking in the live entertainment. Leif couldn't help but be heartened by the display. Londoners were a courageous and resilient people, living amongst the constant threat of German bombings and letting them roll off their backs. Come what may, that was the attitude.

The minute Leif and Nicole arrived, they went to the bar and ordered drinks, shouting over a jazz band playing on a temporary stage, an unfortunate necessity, since the former space had suffered both crippling damage and an equally debilitating loss of life, at the hands of a German air raid. Three dozen revelers and café staff had been killed, as was the band who refused to stop playing during the air raid. The owner, a Dane named Martin Poulsen refused to be cowed by the Germans, and within a year of the disaster, the café had opened its doors again.

Leif and Poulsen were part of a small network of Danes in London, some of whom were long-time residents, some of whom had left Denmark while there was still time before Nazi occupation, and others who were serving in the Allied military like Leif. Upon hearing Leif and Nicole were at the club, Poulsen came over to see his fellow countryman, and when he found out why they had stopped by – the air raid that had interrupted their dinner plans – Poulsen set them up with a prime table close to the band and a bottle of complementary champagne.

Leif and Nicole shared a wonderful evening for two young people living in a time of extreme hardship and danger, a situation that would get far worse before showing any signs of improvement. But that night, they felt alive and electric, felt like themselves before the war with the unmistakable excitement of the war. They knew their efforts with the OSS and SOE were a small but critical part of the greater, nobler effort, but it felt good to be Leif and Nicole, to let their guard down and retire Agent Hudson and Agent Simons for a time and speak of regular life, to focus on post-war dreams.

164   An O.S.S. Secret Agent Behind Enemy Lines

Several days later, Nicole departed from RAF Harrington and flew across the northern region of the English Channel and the North Sea aboard a modified B-24 Liberator bomber, from which she parachuted into occupied Norway in the dead of night. Soon after landing just north of Narvik, Nicole and her SOE partner, Agent Thomas Maddison, encountered a German patrol.

The local Norwegian Resistance cell reported the incident. Agent Maddison was killed in a firefight with the enemy and Nicole was wounded and taken as a PoW. And through the resistance's internal spies, confirmed her imprisonment and interrogation at the hands of the Gestapo. Upon hearing of Nicole's apprehension by the enemy, the SI branch searched high and low for evidence of a security protocol breach or international sabotage, desperate to understand what went wrong, but it was to no avail. A leak was never uncovered, and Niccole died of her wounds or was tortured to death, only the Gestapo knew. The SI could only assume the untimely presence of the German patrol near the Narvik drop zone was just unfortunate luck on the part of the doomed SOE team.

Leif knew the risks. Just as Nicole and Maddison did. But losing someone so smart and beautiful, kind and brave as Nicole – someone so very lovely – was like a punch in the gut for Leif as he remembered, 'We had one wonderful night in London together.'

Tragically, the SI losing their two agents would not be the last piece of unfortunate news to strike the Allied effort in quick succession. One of the boldest and most ill-fated Allied operations of the Second World War was about to unfold in the Netherlands, just as Leif was preparing to be inserted into occupied Denmark. It was a foreboding precursor, which resonated amongst all the Allied troops, especially those so close to their embarkation towards Hitler's Fortress Europe.

* * *

Operation Market Garden, which was the largest airborne operation of the Second World War, with the stated goal of delivering 35,000 British, American and Polish troops behind enemy lines in the Netherlands was underway. The mission objective was to capture a series of bridges, a move that would allow the Allied Armed Division to conduct a large-scale pincer movement into Germany from its northern flank. Against all odds, initially the mission appeared to be a runaway victory. The lightly armed Allied airborne units were able to seize several bridges between Eindhoven and Nijmegen. There was even talk among the Allies, 'Had they caught the Nazi war machine by surprise, even more than they'd anticipated?'

Unfortunately, Clifford Henry was not on hand to advise the Allied commanders of his experience with the Germans, for the cunning adversaries had set a trap. They allowed the Allies a fast roll through their territory, inflating their cockiness, hoping their guard would drop, for they had the entire 9th and 10th Panzer divisions patiently positioned at the most strategic location the Allies hoped to take: the bridge at Arnhem.

The German Armored Division easily overwhelmed the Allies lightly armed airborne units, inflicting heavy losses: 17,000 troops killed, wounded or captured, and allowing the Nazis to commandeer nearly 100 tanks and 400 glider aircraft. After mercilessly mauling the Allied airborne units, the Germans retook all the Dutch territory that the Allies mistakenly believed they'd won. The Allies' objective of ending the war by Christmas 1944 was dashed. Operation Market Garden was one of the largest fiascos of the Second World War.

* * *

It was under those two foreboding clouds that Second Lieutenant Bangsboll was informed his deployment date had been moved up and he'd be dropped into Denmark posthaste. It was then, in early evening in mid-September 1944, Leif was working late at SOE headquarters, familiarizing himself with the details of his upcoming parachute drop into occupied Denmark and the associated Danish Resistance network contact information of those he would be soon working with, when he heard a faint, almost tentative tap on the door frame of his open office door. There stood a skinny, young man, no more than 20 years of age, wearing an ill-fitted tweed jacket and sporting a broad, large-tooth smile.

'Sergeant Alfred Keller.' the voice said, offering his hand. 'Damn, I mean Toller. Bjorn Toller. That's my codename and it's what you should get used to calling me. I'll be your partner in Denmark.'

'I've been expecting you Bjorn', said Leif. He did not extend his hand to his new partner. 'But you're late, why?'

'Yes, about that, I'm not accustomed to this big city and though the underground train is just an amazing thing, it's so damn confusing at times. I just arrived from Boston, three days ago and have not really got my bearings yet', replied Bjorn, half apologetically.

'Well, don't expect to get too comfortable here', warned Leif, I expect we'll be moving on soon.'

'I'm here to learn. What do you think, Jørgen?' Bjorn said. 'Care to get a pint?'

'I've still got some work to do here.' Leif lamented.

'Jørgen', Bjorn said warmly,

we're about to embark on a life or death mission together. That requires implicit trust that we have each other's best interests at heart. I don't know you from Adam and vice versa.

He smiled. 'Come on. Look at it as an early bonding session.'
'Of course, you're correct.' Leif nodded. 'I know a perfect place nearby.'
Leif put out his hand again to reintroduce himself. 'Bangsbøll. Leif Bangsbøll.'
Bjorn chewed his lower lip briefly. 'I think I prefer Jørgen Bech.'
Yes, Leif had now assumed the codename, Jørgen Bech.

The two agents left the headquarters together, walking the darkened, air raid prepared streets on central London with Leif delivering an extended lecture on the storied genealogy of the 'Bangsbøll' name, that lasted almost the entire trip to the pub and didn't end until Bjorn admitted 'Bech' was the vastly inferior name.

The Ship and Shovel pub, one of Leif's favorite haunts, located near Charing Cross, was wall to wall with customers and cigarette smoke, which the low, wood-beamed ceiling seemingly sucked in and kept lingering above people's heads, like a permanent atmospheric cloud. Whenever the kitchen door opened, as if to complete the stereotypical features of a London pub, the acrid haze had to battle for supremacy with the smell of fish and chips.

'I'm German by birth.' Bjorn said.

> But I grew up in southern Jutland. I'm fluent in both Danish, German and English, and I guess that's part of why the army and OSS selected me for the mission.

That made sense to Leif, who had spent most of his life close to Copenhagen, not the large western peninsula that was Bjorn's home. A home that also happened to share a southern border with Germany, through which it was moving reserve units of its army and supplies headed to the frontlines to support the war effort.

'I wasn't there when the Nazis invaded Denmark.' stated Bjorn.

> Our whole family had moved to Boston in 1937. My father had been lured over by a professorship at Harvard, and I was subsequently accepted into Boston College. When I graduated in 1940, I joined the United States Army.

'Why did you volunteer – America wasn't even in the war at that point?' Leif said. 'If your loved ones weren't in danger?'

Because those Krauts royally pissed me off. That's my family's home. You don't get to bring your blood and soil empire into my homeland without a fight. No Sir!

Bjorn took a sip of his beer. 'I volunteered for service in the army, and they forwarded me to the OSS.' He noted Leif's reaction. 'I'm going to assume you have people left in Denmark?' Bjorn asked.

'My father.' Leif said, lowering his eyes. 'At least, I hope he's still alive. I haven't been able to communicate with him in years. I've kept writing the whole time, but… who knows?'

'With a son like you', Bjorn said, 'there's no way he isn't fine. You don't just happen upon the gumption to do something this crazy.'

Leif changed the subject. 'Did you train at Camp X?'

'No', Bjorn said,

I originally trained with the army Signal Corps; I'm a communications specialist. After that, the OSS sent me to some secret camp in the mountains of Maryland where they taught me how to blow stuff up. That's my thing: radios and bombs.

He dipped into his shirt pocket and pulled out his cigarettes. 'That's why you're the front man in this op, and I'm mostly behind the scenes.' He sparked the cigarette and offered one to Leif, who declined.

Although, in the interest of mission integrity, I'm registered as an actuary with your maritime insurance company. Do I have to know accounting or attend company meetings?

Leif shrugged. 'You may have to. An actuary is an important job.'

'Christ. That's bloody disappointing.' He crushed out his cigarette in an ashtray. 'How do you do it, Bech?'

'Do what exactly?' replied Leif.

'Lie all the time.' Bjorn said.

You don't even flinch when I call you by your persona. Half the time I forget who I am and what the hell I'm doing here. Let alone be an actuary.

'I lie', Leif answered, 'because I need to live.'

'I'm not sure I understand that logic.' Bjorn said. 'They seem like two diametrically opposed values.'

'Yes. In a normal world.' Leif said.

But we aren't being tasked with being normal, those aren't the given circumstances. This world has gone mad, and we must respond in kind. Remember, Bjorn Toller, we aren't regular soldiers. We are actors. We exist between those terms. Almost like magicians. We dissemble. We constantly try to distract attention and focus it elsewhere, so we can apply our trade in the shadows.

Leif looked to Bjorn's face for a flash of recognition and received nothing in return. He'd have to boil this down materially, less abstraction.

Sometimes that trade can involve heavy explosives and sabotage. Other times it can involve disguise, deception and counterfeiting. But all these options are united by lying. Lying so we can live. And Hitler's Germany will not.

Leif saw a light in Bjorn's eyes. His acting lesson was bearing fruit, helping his colleague find the motivation he needed to become a consummate performer.

'They lie. We lie. And if we lie badly', Leif said, 'they will catch us. And kill us. Torture us to death.'

Bjorn snapped his fingers, sold. 'It's us against them.'

'Yes.' Leif said, vigorously nodding in agreement. 'Use that. That's how you lie. That's how you become a great performer.'

Bjorn rose to get two more pints from the bar. 'I'm already finding it easier to keep my stories straight.'

The following morning, Leif and Bjorn were briefed by an OSS operations officer named Major Forsyth on the current geopolitical solution and how it related to their mission. The Allies had made substantial progress in their assault against Germany across western and southern Europe, and a cornerstone of that success had been the OSS and SOE Operation Jedburgh. Allied agents and the august French Resistance had deeply collaborated to raise absolute hell during the build up to Normandy, softening up the enemy's underbelly for the incoming invasion by weakening German morale with a relentless campaign of industrial sabotage, subversion and propaganda.

However, as the failure of Operation Market Garden had demonstrated, it was time to redirect some of the OSS's and SOE's focus on to Operation Carpetbagger. The Allied offensive drive needed to drive further into occupied the Netherland, Denmark and soon Norway, if they wanted to keep up the momentum gained in western Europe and cut off the Nazi hydra before it could nest in Scandinavia and refuel for a final showdown.

'Agent Bjorn Toller will be inserted first.' Forsyth said.

> It is crucial he establish the maritime insurance firm in Aarhus and begin to make overtures to the resistance forces on the ground, before we insert Agent Bech.

Bjorn leaned over and whispered to Leif, 'Guess we know which one of us is the fresh meat. Never risk the front man.'

Forsyth cleared his throat. 'Do you have a question, Agent Toller?'

'No question, sir; just damned happy to go in first.' Bjorn said, then turned to Leif again.

> You're going to have to make sure of two things. One. That I have the vaguest idea of what a maritime insurance company does, and two, how one can be the actuary of one. Otherwise, I'll be dead by dawn.

Leif put his hand on Bjorn's shoulder. 'Relax. I promise that by tonight I'll make you into a walking, talking, lying actuary.'

At the crack of dawn, Sergeant Alfred Keller, fully in character as Agent Bjorn Toller the actuary, was driven to the small port of Grimsby on the east coast of England, where he boarded a fishing trawler to cross the North Sea and rendezvous with a Danish fishing boat off the coast of Denmark, a few miles from the town of Esbjerg, from where the Danish Resistance had made arrangements to have him transferred to Aarhus, where he would file falsified documents legally creating a maritime insurance brokerage office.

There, Bjorn would await the arrival of his partner and team leader, Leif undercover as Jørgen Bech. Bjorn would not have to wait long.

Chapter 16

Escape and Evasion

'Few men are born brave, some become so
through training and force of discipline.'

Flavius Vegetius, AD 378

The date was 1 October 1944. Leif knew that sleep would be a commodity in short supply in the weeks to come and certainly during the first few days of the mission. With this in mind, Second Lieutenant Bangsbøll, United States Army and OSS field agent, codenamed Alexander Hudson, but now using the alias Jørgen Bech, tried to take advantage of the expected two-hour transit time from central London to RAF Harrington. But sleep would not come. Whether it was the lack of proper shock absorbers and springs in the 5-ton cargo truck the United States Army had furnished for his transport to RAF Harrington or the fact that Leif's nerves were on edge because of his impending first operational mission, he did not know.

Leif had risen early that morning, as was his custom. Working with both the two sister spy organizations of the American OSS and the British SOE involved rigorous training schedules, which always seemed to start well before the break of dawn. As such, he had taken his breakfast at the Hotel Metropole's café and left his military duffle bag with his uniforms and other, meager personal belongings with the hotel's concierge. He checked out of the hotel by 0700 hours. Arrangements had been made by the OSS support staff to pick up and store Leif's belongings during his expected prolonged absence. Dressed in a brown tweed jacket with tie and beige slacks, carrying a well-weathered brown leather suitcase, he walked from the Hotel Metropole, just off Trafalgar Square, to his designated pick-up point in front of the Royal Academy of Arts on Burlington Arcade, located just west of Piccadilly Circus. As he turned the corner onto Burlington Arcade, Leif could see the truck, painted in the standard olive drab green with a large white star on the door designating it as a United States Army vehicle. The American truck was a familiar site, like so many similar American military vehicles and personnel that had arrived in Britain over the past two years. The truck had a large green canvas covered cargo compartment and was parked adjacent to the gallery's delivery entrance. The United States Army private who was sitting behind the wheel of the truck and could be seen through the open driver's side window, was smoking a cigarette and reading *The Times*. Leif stood for a moment, suitcase in hand looking up at the young soldier and cleared his throat to get the driver's attention. Bringing the newspaper down and leaving the cigarette in the corner of his mouth, the driver said, 'Ah, good morning. You must be Mr Hudson?'

With a smile, Leif nodded.

'Nice to meet you. You're early, sir.'

'Yes, it appears we both like to be punctual, private.' said Leif as he lifted his suitcase waist high in a gesture of 'Where can I put this?'

The young private motioned for his passenger to jump in, so Leif walked around to the passenger side as the driver leaned across the cab of the truck to open the passenger door. Leif pulled himself up into the cab of the truck, placed his suitcase between himself and the driver and settled in for the drive. The driver, who usually worked alone with his load of military equipment, wooden crates and supplies in the cargo compartment, was unaccustomed to having a passenger sitting up front with him. He glanced at his passenger with a nod and asked, 'Ready?'

'As ready as I'll ever be, private. Let's go.'

The driver put the truck in gear and moved slowly into the street, which was sparsely occupied by only a few other automobiles and lorries going about their early morning business. Glad for the company for a change, the young private was full of commentary about his experience in London and how the war was a whole lot more interesting than his life back in Iowa. Leif listened politely and refrained from sharing much of anything about himself, save to say, he was a civilian businessman, working in London, providing some sort of products to the USAAF and had business at RAF Harrington for same. Transportation had been arranged for 'Agent Hudson' by his OSS handlers for him to travel on the regular supply run from the City of London to RAF Harrington.

After navigating the network of narrow streets of London for fifteen minutes, they approached the motorway slip road and Leif leaned his head back, complaining about staying out too late the night before. The driver nodded and said that London's night life, despite the frequent air raids, was everything a single man could want. Leif had, in fact, retired relatively early the previous night, but to avoid further conversation with the driver, he slouched down further and closed his eyes. As far as the driver was concerned, it wasn't until the truck pulled off the motorway onto the winding side roads of the English countryside close to their destination two hours later, that his passenger awakened. However, since he was unable to get any real rest, Leif fell back on his training and surreptitiously observed the entire journey while feigning sleep.

As part of his OSS/SOE training at Camp X, back in Canada, Leif had been taught to be observant, to always assess his surroundings and to memorize essential facts and landmarks.

Sergeant Major de Relwyskow had taught the trainees that 'You won't know what details will become important to you later in the mission, so pay attention to everything.' He emphasized the need to maintain constant mental awareness of their surroundings.

Leif mentally reviewed their travel route – central London to the RAF base just north-west of the town of Kettering was a distance of 85 miles. They had departed London via the London to Northampton sideroad and traveled north-west for an hour and fifteen minutes, traveling on average at 50 miles per hour, he estimated. They had exited the roadway at Northampton then took the road towards Kettering, continuing north-west for twenty minutes, then passed by a road sign for the town of Peterborough, which indicated was 12 miles north-east of their position.

* * *

Leif smiled to himself. He knew of another Peterborough, in the province of Ontario, Canada, named after its sister city in England, like so many Canadian towns and cities. Peterborough, Ontario, located approximately 60 miles north-east of Whitby, Ontario, where the Allies' top-secret, spy training facility, Camp X was located. The Peterborough sign, combined with the mental exercise of tracking his current movements, reminded him of the first escape and evasion exercise he and half a dozen of his fellow Camp X trainees had been subjected to the previous year.

Leif recalled that during the third and final month of training, just as he and his fellow trainees entered the mess hall for breakfast on a Sunday morning in June 1943, they had been immediately confronted by several burley RCMP constables. The trainees were denied their morning meal, searched and relieved of their military identification and any money they had on their person. They were blindfolded and their hands were tied behind their backs, then they were brusquely loaded onto a canvas covered cargo truck with an MP guard keeping watch and driven away from Camp X. The trainees, dressed in civilian attire, which was standard practice during weekend training, were driven for three hours. The truck made numerous turns and traveled over various types of paved and gravel roads at various speeds to disorient the students. They were finally dropped off on the side of a tree lined road. Unbeknownst to them, they were just north of the town of Peterborough, Ontario at a place called Fowlers Corner – 60 miles from Camp X.

As the bindings and blindfolds were removed, their instructor, Sergeant Major de Relwyskow described their task,

> My dear distinguished agents-in-training, you are to make your way back to camp as quickly as you can, by such means as you deem necessary and appropriate but must report for duty no later than 0800 hours Tuesday morning.

Looking at his wristwatch, de Relwyskow continued, 'You have just under forty hours to complete this task. Oh, and by the way', he said, as he climbed back into the cab of the truck, 'we have advised the local authorities, including the Royal Canadian Mounted Police, that you six rascals are German prisoners of war who have escaped from the Bowmanville prison camp.' He paused for effect. As the truck began to pull away, he stuck his head out of the open passenger window and added with a huge grin on his face, 'We also told them you were armed… and very dangerous.'

In summer 1943, the Bowmanville PoW camp held over 800 German and Italian PoWs. The locals knew of the prison camp and were always on guard for possible escapees. They were also aware of the existence of Training School No. 103, located just a few miles west of Bowmanville, although none among them knew its true name or purpose. The regional RCMP director was one of only a few outside of Camp X staff, the OSS, the SOE and the Canadian Army headquarters staff who knew the true nature of Camp X, and of this particular military escape and evasion training being conducted this day. If or when the Camp X trainees/escaped German PoWs were caught, the RCMP director would eventually arrange their release and subsequent return to Camp X. However, such exercises were not without some real danger. An over-exuberant or startled police officer on alert to armed and dangerous German PoWs on the loose might shoot first and ask questions later. After all, to them these were real PoWs and the enemy.

The six agent trainees – five men and one woman – stood by the roadside where they had been unceremoniously dropped off by their instructor and wisely chose to move into the adjacent woods to regroup and discuss their situation. Reviewing the facts as they knew them, they shared what intelligence they could, which was very little. They had been on the road for three hours, but in what direction had they driven? They each offered up their perceptions, options and courses of action to be considered. Given that Camp X was located on the north shore of Lake Ontario – a large body of water that ran in an east-west direction – they surmised that they must have traveled in a northern direction, and that if they now traveled south, they would eventually run into Lake

Ontario and could then adjust their direction of travel east or west from there to get back to the town of Whitby and Camp X. Initially, they also agreed that they had to separate and travel independently to avoid suspicion. However, Leif suggested that their lone female should pair up with one of the five men and travel as a couple as that would probably be least conspicuous. They drew straws for the co-traveler. They all shook hands with each other and wished each the best of luck. Then they each chose a direction of travel and departed in ten-minute intervals.

Leif was the third to depart, and thirty minutes later, after walking in the westerly direction he had chosen, was confronted by his next major decision of the ordeal. As he stood at a quiet intersection of a country road, he saw a road sign that indicated that the town of Oshawa – which he knew was just east of Whitby – was 57 miles south of his current location. Alternatively, the town of Lindsay was 10 miles north-west of where he stood. Logically, he should turn left and head south towards his objective. Leif now had only thirty-nine hours to get back to camp. After a moment's contemplation, Leif turned right and walked north towards Lindsay and in the opposite direction of his final destination. Leif had a plan.

One thing Leif's training at Camp X had taught him so far was to never limit yourself to the known facts or the apparent obvious constraints of the situation that one was confronted with. It was essential to always consider options or courses of action that the enemy might rule out as too unlikely or too risky – hence why he had chosen to walk in the opposite direction of his objective. Fortunately for Leif, his ten months of flight training at the Island Airport in Toronto (Little Norway) and at the airfield in Orillia, Ontario, with the Royal Norwegian Air Force (as part of the BCATP) had made him quite familiar with this region – from the air at least. Orillia was approximately 70 miles north-west of Lindsay, his current destination. Leif had flown over this area several times when conducting navigation flights between Orillia and the RCAF base at Trenton, Ontario. The Trenton air base was also located on the north shore of Lake Ontario, about 70 miles east of Camp X. The plan formulating in his mind was all coming together.

Though he knew where he was, and where he had to get to, the question now was, how would he get there? And, more importantly, how would he get there without being arrested? It was 1700 hours when Leif located the bus stop just off Main Street in the quiet little town of Lindsay. He took the chance to enter the general store and paid for the bus ticket to Orillia at the pharmacy counter using one of the three $10 notes he had kept hidden in the lining of his shoe. The money had been there for over three months, kept just in case of an emergency. Leif was thankful that the MP's search had not been overly thorough and that his secret stash had remained unnoticed. He had always assumed he would need the emergency cash for a taxi after a late night of drinking when he was on leave. This current situation seemed like a reasonable time to break into his emergency stash.

The next bus for Orillia was due at 2000 hours. He had three hours to kill and three hours to remain unnoticed by the public and the local law enforcement agency. Leif wondered if news of the escaped German PoWs had reached this small town. He had to assume it had and was determined to stay out of sight until nightfall. Getting on the bus without being noticed by the police would be a challenge. But that could wait, he needed food. He had not eaten since the previous night's dinner. The exercise planners and course instructors had chosen their exercise start time deliberately, preventing the students from having breakfast, knowing that hunger would soon become another stress factor for the escapees to deal with. However, as Leif reconsidered his needs, he chose to forego any attempt to buy or steal food – it was too risky.

At 1950 hours, from the shadows of the park down the street from the bus stop, Leif saw the gray coach bus pull up and park in front of the Lindsay general store and pharmacy. He had used his time waiting for the arrival of the bus wisely. He had carefully assessed the most probable route the bus would have to exit town towards Orillia and situated himself about a quarter of a mile from the bus stop, assuming that the police would be watching all the passengers board the bus and intercept and question anyone who might fit the description of an escaped German PoW. His plan worked. The bus departed Lindsay's general store at 2000 hours sharp and had traveled only a quarter of a mile when the friendly and unaware bus driver pulled over as Leif stood on the side of the road waiving his bus ticket above his head. Leif apologized for being late for the bus's planned departure. He explained to the driver that he was a Royal Norwegian Air Force pilot on leave and needed to get back to his squadron in Orillia. Whether the bus driver knew of the BCATP and the Norwegian airfield in Orillia or not, he accepted Leif's story at face value; this airman's command of the English language was pretty good and there certainly was a Scandinavian tone to his speech. He let Leif get on and closed the bus door behind him. Leif took a seat near the back of the bus – he was on his way.

Arriving at the Orillia bus station just after 2200 hours proved anticlimactic. Everything in the small Ontario town was closed for the night. Unfortunately, as a result, a meal would have to wait a bit longer. Familiar with the town and the proximity of the Norwegian run BACTP airfield, Leif walked in the dark, with just the crunching noise of his shoes on the gravel beneath his feet and the occasional rumbling of his empty stomach as his companions. As he approached the main gate of the airfield, Leif considered options of how to get past the guards and onto the base without his military identification. However, getting onto the Norwegian airfield proved much easier than Leif had anticipated. It was shortly before 2300 hours when Leif saw the headlights of a car approaching, driving up the long country lane that led to the main gate of the airfield. The car slowed down as it approached, but the headlights temporarily blinded Leif, preventing him from seeing who was in the vehicle. Suddenly, a familiar, Norwegian voice called out from within the car, 'Leif? Leif Bangsbøll? Is that you?'

Captain Niels Sanderstrom, Royal Norwegian Air Force had been one of Leif's flight instructors during his time with the Norwegian pilot training program the previous year. Relieved at the warm reception, Leif learned that Niels and his two Norwegian companions who seemed quite hungover had just returned from a two-day furlough in Toronto. Clearly, it had been a wild couple of days for his Norwegian brothers. Now, with his own personal escort, Leif had no difficulties getting onto the airfield.

Interested in what Leif had been up to over the past year, Niels took him to the officers' mess for a night cap and a desperately needed meal for Leif. As they stood at the bar with beers and sandwiches, they chatted about the past year's activities. Niels recalled only that Leif, immediately following graduation and wings presentation, had received some secret orders. His student had been assigned to the USAAC as some sort of exchange or liaison officer. Leif had, in fact, been released by the Royal Norwegian Air Force at the request of the American government, enrolled as a sergeant in the United States Army. Over the next hour and a couple more beers, Leif explained that he had not been assigned to the USAAC, but rather he had been recruited by the OSS and was currently a sergeant in the United States Army undergoing training as a special agent at a place called Camp X, not more than 100 miles south-east from where they stood. Once Leif had explained the circumstances of his sudden appearance back in Orillia as a result of the escape and evasion exercise, a plan was soon hatched to get Leif, this 'German PoW escapee' back to Camp X before the exercise deadline.

Early the next morning, Leif and Niels went to the camp headquarters. The CO and commandant of the flying training school remembered Leif but was initially reluctant to provide any tangible support to this young Danish lieutenant, despite his previous affiliation with the Royal Norwegian Air Force and the enthusiastic support and recommendations of his senior instructor. However, once Leif politely reminded the commandant that it was his new American boss, Donovan's generosity and influence that had arranged for the expedited delivery of the new, modern Curtiss Hawk 75-A trainer aircraft, which replaced the school's aging Northrop Gamma A-17 almost nine months earlier than scheduled, the commandant paused to reconsider and had a change of heart, if only to get this troublesome Dane off his camp. The commandant authorized Captain Sanderstrom to conduct an unscheduled navigation training flight that afternoon, during which his co-pilot, Sergeant Bangsbøll, United States Army/OSS agent-in-training would be flown to Whitby and back to his current assignment at Camp X. At that point, Leif and Niels departed the commandant's office and headed to the flightline and the airfield operation office to make the arrangements. While conducting their flight plan, Leif reminded Niels, that for security reasons, their destination could not be registered as Camp X. 'Just indicate the Whitby Regional Airfield as our destination.'

An hour later, Niels and Leif were taxiing towards the end of the runway in their almost new Curtiss Hawk trainer aircraft. Once airborne and vectored towards their destination, Niels offered Leif the opportunity to take the controls for old times' sake. More modern than the Northrop trainer Leif had been trained on, the Curtiss Hawk was a delight to fly, thought Leif.

'Oh, how wonderful it is to feel the sensation of flying again!' he exclaimed to his companion through their intercom. 'I can't tell you how much I have missed the freedom of being in control of an aircraft in flight.' As a fellow pilot, Niels understood exactly what Leif was saying. To a pilot, flying is everything. Thirty minutes later, with the northern shore of Lake Ontario on their portside and the expanse of the lake to the south; with the shore of New York State clearly visible on the southern horizon, Niels suggested that he should take back control of the aircraft for landing and Leif responded with a reluctant 'Of course, you have control.' Niels began the descent and approach to the Whitby Regional Airfield. On final approach, only a few seconds before touchdown, Leif called out, 'OVER SHOOT! OVER SHOOT!' Niels, as any competent pilot would do, immediately complied with the over shoot call, pulled up the nose and advanced the engine throttles and advised the control tower accordingly.

'What was that all about Leif?' asked Niels.

Leif pleaded,

Niels, just give me control of the aircraft for another two minutes and the aircraft is yours for good. I'd like to convey a quick aerial message to the directing staff at Camp X… to let them know I'm back.

With a knowing smile on his face, Niels said, 'You have control.'

Niels instinctively tightened his shoulder and lap harness in anticipation of what was coming next. Less than a minute later, Leif did a controlled high speed low pass (very low) – no more than 50 feet above and directly over the Camp X headquarters building, where he knew some of the instructors and the camp commander would be working diligently in their offices. Pushing the power throttle forward and pulling the control stick back as hard as he could, the aircraft nose quickly came up until they were almost vertical… 1,000 feet, 1,500 feet, 2,000 feet, then Leif slammed the left rudder hard over and pulled a tight bank to starboard. The Curtiss Hawk responded beautifully and within seconds the aircraft was diving on a reverse trajectory. And just as Leif had planned, this aggressive and exhilarating maneuver allowed them the opportunity to buzz Camp X a second time.

By the second pass, a dozen uniformed and civilian-dressed personnel had vacated the camp headquarters building and were standing in the open compound looking up into the sky at the offending aircraft, which had violated Camp X's sacred and secret airspace. Standing in the midst of the other dozen or so onlookers, all with their heads craned skyward, the camp commander, Lieutenant Colonel Cuthbert Skilbeck, looked back at Major Arthur Bushell, the adjutant and quartermaster of Camp X and shouted, 'WHO THE HELL IS THAT SON OF A BITCH?! I'll HAVE THAT PILOT'S ASS FOR THAT DAMN STUNT!'

Five minutes later, the Curtiss Hawk landed at the nearby Whitby municipal airfield and taxied to its designated parking spot on the ramp to be refueled.

'Well Leif', said Niels, 'you certainly have not lost your knack for flying – that was quite a show.'

'If you think that was exciting', Leif replied, 'you should come back with me to the camp, as I think there may be some fireworks coming at me for my little improvised air show.'

Twenty minutes later, after bidding farewell to his former instructor and now accomplice, Leif marched smartly up to the front gate of the Special Training School No. 103 and reported to the sentries,

> Sergeant Bangsbøll, agent-in-training reporting for duty. Request you advise my instructor, Sergeant Major de Relwyskow, of my return.

It had been just twenty-seven hours since he and his fellow 'escapees' had been left at the side of the road outside of Peterborough.

The other five trainees did not fare quite so well as Leif; one student was caught by local police, attempting to board a bus in Peterborough less than an hour after being released on the side of the road. The result was a mission failure. Two other escapees, who had crossed paths several hours after being released, had decided to travel together and were picked up by an RCMP patrol as they casually hitchhiked down Highway 115 towards Oshawa. Another mission failure. One ambitious student was caught attempting to hotwire a farmer's truck. The farmer and his shotgun waited patiently until the local constable showed up to take the would-be thief away. Another mission failure – but good initiative shown. The runner-up to Leif was the only female in their group. She had been paired up with the male agent who attempted to steal the farmer's truck but had managed to avoid being seen or captured by the armed farmer. She continued on her own and was eventually able to talk her way onto a Greyhound tour bus. She explained to the bus driver, amongst tears and sniffles that her boyfriend had just left her to join the army and she had to get home to Oshawa. With the promise to send payment to the driver once she got home to her 'poor, sick mother', she was allowed to board the bus. She was apprehended as she stepped off the bus at the Oshawa bus station by two MP officers who had been assigned to stakeout the Oshawa bus terminal to look for the escapees. Armed with a photograph of all the escapees, the MPs had no difficulty identifying the young female agent. Another mission failure, but an excellent effort on her part.

Fallout from Leif's impromptu airshow was far less than expected, as Major Bushell and all of Leif's instructors realized what the young Dane, now referred to by his fellow students as 'The Danish Duke' had accomplished. Not only was he one of the few students in Camp X's short history to successfully complete the escape and evasion exercise but he did so in record breaking time. Add to that, the deputy camp director of Camp X, Mr Pat Bayley, who was responsible for operations of the camp, was suitably impressed with the method and sheer ingenuity of success by the young Dane that he made sure no record of the incident was recorded on Leif's official file, save to say that he successfully completed the escape and evasion exercise with impressive aptitude and guile.

All five of the other 'PoW escapees' were eventually released by the authorities and returned to Camp X within a couple of days. The student who attempted to steal the farmer's truck spent the longest time behind bars – two days, because the local constabulary believed that regardless, if the fellow was an Allied soldier in training or an actual escaped German PoW, he had attempted to steal a citizen's vehicle. Eventually, with a personal call from the regional RCMP chief, the car thief was released, and a military driver was sent to pick him up and return him to Camp X. Nothing but his pride was damaged.

* * *

Jolted out of his daydream, back in the United States Army truck, transiting central England's countryside, Leif's thoughts returned to the present. He smiled at the memory of his Camp X adventures, then turned his attention back to the journey at hand. The truck he was traveling in had continued west on the Kettering side road from the town of Kettering towards the RAF base. This part of Britain, like so many others, was beautiful – broad, green valleys framed by rolling hills, with fields and pastures divided like a great quilted blanket. Mercifully, the ravages of war had not touched this place. Opening one eye, Leif looked at his wristwatch and thought, 'RAF Harrington should be close by.' A couple of minutes later he felt the truck decelerate as it approached the main gate of RAF Harrington.

Chapter 17

Agent Alexander Hudson

'Courage is not the absence of fear,
but the capacity to act despite our fears.'

Senator John McCain

A week after Agent Bjorn Toller has been successfully inserted into Denmark, the United States Army transport truck bearing Leif pulled up to the main gate of RAF Harrington, 80 miles north-west of London, located in the picturesque, rolling hills of Northamptonshire and home to the 801st and the 492nd Bombardment groups of the USAAF. It was 4 October 1944.

Though annotated on the daily delivery and access log, the arrival of the United States Army truck was immediately confronted by two British MPs

Lieutenant Bangsboll, AKA Agent Alexander Hudson, outside SOE headquarters, London England July 1944. (*Photo courtesy of the author's family collection*)

holding Lee-Enfield rifles at the port-arms position. The uniformed soldiers ordered everyone out of the vehicle and inspected the inside and undercarriage of the truck, and when they were satisfied with the absence of contraband, one MP moved on to verifying Leif's identity papers, while the other searched the driver head to toe, causing a few crusty barbs to be thrown back and forth.

Following this standard reception protocol, the MP acknowledged that 'Mr Hudson's' paperwork was in order and ushered Leif and the driver through the gate, and pointed to the end of the airfield, toward the bomber group headquarters, where the driver was to drop off his passenger.

* * *

Leif had been to RAF Harrington once before, six weeks earlier, to conduct parachute refresher training in anticipation for his up-coming mission into Denmark. Leif grinned – that had been a memorable day; after completing two successful training jumps in the morning with three other agents, Leif had decided to complete one more practice jump in the afternoon, before heading back to London. On this occasion, with only a solo jumper ('Joe'), the crew from the 492nd flew its Liberator bomber over their designated drop zone, located 15 miles north-west of RAF Harrington, flying the same route, just as they had during the morning's training jumps. However, as a result of a series of unrelated and uncontrollable factors during the final moments of the drop sequence, including a near mid-air collision with

Lt Leif Bangsboll (AKA Agent Alexander Hudson), conducting parachute training at RAF Harrington, August, 1944. (*Photo courtesy of the author's family collection*)

a flock of geese that forced the pilot to aggressively pull-up and increase the planned drop altitude of 3,000 feet to almost 5,000, was further exacerbated by unexpectedly high wind gusts. All of which resulted in Leif missing the intended drop zone – a large military training area, by over a mile. Upon landing, a local farmer, with a shotgun in hand, thinking this foreigner, clad in an American combat uniform might be a German spy, took Leif as a PoW and called the local police. Fruitless, were Leif's assurances that he was an allied soldier – conveyed unfortunately with his heavy Danish accent. 'Sounds like a German to me!' thought the farmer, as he held Leif at gunpoint on his porch until a local constable and two MPs from RAF Harrington arrived. Though the MPs knew that this was one of their own, they played the game and handcuffed Leif and treated him as if he were the enemy, thanking the farmer for his vigilance as they took Leif away. Having the local populace on guard for potential German spies was a good thing. Keep calm and carry on…

* * *

The truck continued along the flightline as Leif watched the brown weather-stone headquarters building grow closer and noted the bomber group's motto displayed in bold letters above the main entrance: '492 Bombardment Group – Any place. Any Time. Anywhere.'

Leif thought, We shall see if that's true soon enough.' Hopefully very soon. The young Dane had been waiting over three years for his chance to contribute to the war effort, which also happened to be wrapped inside a pressing personal issue: his father's condition.

Upon entering headquarters, Leif was informed by the duty officer that all OSS and SOE agents were housed separately from the air crew and military personnel – quarantined to a certain degree, in their own unit, where they would be surrounded by intelligence experts and handlers. He put the final signatory flourish on Leif's clearance form, then handed him the keys to his room, and said,

> Welcome to RAF Harrington, Mr Bech. Your room is on the second floor of the transient quarters, the building across from the officers' mess.

Leif made certain to smile at the sound of 'Mr Bech' nodded his head in thanks to the duty officer, then put the keys in his jacket pocket, picked up his suitcase and left the building.

'Jørgen Bech', he thought, that's correct. I'm no longer Alexander Hudson, support agent, I'm now Jørgen Bech, operational field agent.' Leif reviewed his cover story – maritime engineer running a fictitious branch of an actual maritime insurance brokerage firm whose head office is in Copenhagen. I have been sent to open a new field office in Aarhus, Denmark.

The selection of operational field agent identity – or *'nom de guerre'* as OSS and SOE agents called it – were typically created and issued by the OSS intelligence section. For example, Alexander Hudson, the American aviation parts supplier from New York, and all his accompanying paperwork, had been birthed in a document forging office in an undisclosed location, without any input from Leif.

'Agent Hudson' would not be following Leif to his new location, that persona was deemed a tad too generically Anglo to pass muster in Scandinavia and would necessitate new paperwork. However, three weeks ago, when it came to create Leif's new persona, he spoke up to contribute. He told them he wanted to be Jørgen Bech. This agent, Jørgen Bech, may have been born in London less than twenty days ago, but its genius stretched back much further – back to February 1942.

Two letters Leif had written to his childhood friend the real Jørgen Bech in December 1941 were returned still sealed and stamped 'undeliverable return to sender'. In the wake of Pearl Harbor and the corresponding dates of Leif's messages, he couldn't help but imagine his Sølvgades school friend turned transplanted United States sailor, had likely perished on that grim day. When he joined the OSS, Leif used their back channels to the United States Department of War to investigate his friend's fate and learn the truth, and unfortunately his worst presentiments were true. The death of sailor First Class Jørgen Bech – known as 'George Beck' to the United States Immigration Office and the United States Navy – had been aboard the USS *Arizona* on 7 December 1941; it was confirmed in stark black and white.

Leif had been devastated by the loss of his one true friend, who despite his faults and obvious eccentricities – which made him even more endearing – had been one of his oldest and closest friends and the last remaining person outside of Frederik who had memories of Leif's mother. But learning of Jørgen's death proved revelatory in another way. It caused Leif to realize his old way of looking at the world, his pre-OSS thought patterns had been replaced, when after mourning Jørgen death, Leif decided to become him.

Leif outlined his idea to his SI, Director Captain Casey, explaining that he knew the deceased very well, knew sufficient details about his old friend's life that could prove useful in terms of building believability and specificity around the persona. He wouldn't have to build a character from the ground up, wouldn't have to study and memorize facts cooked up in a forgery lab. He knew Jørgen better than anyone else.

In addition, Jørgen left a relatively blank slate behind with virtually no social connections, which was precisely what was needed when assuming a person's identity. He was an only child, had few significant personal attachments and his parents, upon his death, had sold their property in Copenhagen and permanently relocated to their summer home in the village of Ronne on the island of Bornholm, a relatively isolated hamlet on a small island in the middle of the Baltic Sea. Not to mention the bald, ugly fact that Jørgen had been killed in a conflagration so far from Denmark, meaning there was no grave marker and his United States Navy death records as Seaman First Class George Beck further distanced himself from the new Jørgen Bech, Danish businessman.

Captain Casey was impressed by Leif's ingenuity but had one question. 'Why don't you tell me the actual reason why you want to use this Bech's identity?' Leif should have figured Casey wouldn't be easily satisfied. Although he was becoming an astute judge of human motive, it would take a great deal more practice before he could outshine someone like Casey, a true artist in the field of clandestine and emotional subterfuge.

Leif thought for a moment and then asserted,

> I never got to say goodbye to Jørgen. We shared a lot of special childhood memories together. This will be my way of keeping him alive a little bit longer – in spirit at least. So, I can lay him to rest in my own time.

Leif smiled and added, 'I believe Jørgen would be honored to have his name associated with the Danish Resistance as a secret agent to help liberate his homeland.'

Casey nodded and paused reflectively for a moment before he picked up the telephone and instructed the OSS and SOE documents branch that Leif would enter Denmark as Jørgen Bech and instructed them to begin preparing the necessary papers immediately, and that Leif would provide the necessary details regarding Mr Bech's identity.

As Leif walked the length of the airfield toward his room in the transient quarters building, he watched the traffic of B-24 Liberators gearing up to leave or returning from missions. He knew these aircraft well, having assisted with over 200 OSS and SOE agents being delivered by them to locations behind enemy lines. The original Liberators aircraft were designed as heavy bombers, but these B-24s had been specifically modified to meet the war effort necessity of dropping personnel and cargo, including radios, weapons and explosives. At the height of the Second World War, over 18,000 B-24s were soaring in the air, especially in Norway, Denmark, the Netherlands and the Balkans, performing an invaluable service to Operation Carpetbagger, the namesake of Leif's mission, and the very reason he was at RAF Harrington.

Leif unlocked the door to his room in the transient wing. He hit the wall-mounted switch and an overhead light flickered then fully sprang to life, casting a harsh, muted light across the already subdued room décor, which was sparse and antiseptic. He sighed, followed the old, creaking floorboards to the foot of his bed, where had laid down his suitcase, and glanced at the words 'Property of the RAF' stenciled onto the fabric of his pillow and blanket.

It felt as if Leif was back in the Royal Norwegian Air Force or Camp X, where trainees were gifted the accommodations of interchangeable cogs in a machine and Leif thought, 'Another impersonal space.' Perhaps RAF Harrington felt even more bloodless because for the past six months, the SI office had put Leif up at the famed Hotel Metropole between Trafalgar Square and the River Thames. Granted, Leif admitted, a hotel is a standardized living space by its very definition, but the Hotel Metropole had character, some of it due to its rather advanced age and schizophrenic design, a combination of French and American styles, with enormous luxury rooms.

The only saving grace for Leif was this room was the final temporary stop before going home. Finally, three and a half years later, and a totally different man, he would step foot back on his own soil. 'But to what', he thought, 'this is either a celebration or a sifting through of remains?'

Several hours later, as Leif reclined on his bed with his hands interlocked behind his head, his thoughts were interrupted by a knock at the door, followed by a voice softly saying, 'Mr Bech.' Leif moved to the door, curious who was using his recently christened codename and *nom de guerre*, he pulled the door partway open. An American corporal, assigned to the OSS Operations Center, identified himself and handed Leif a sealed envelope addressed to 'Mr Jørgen Bech'. Leif thanked the young soldier, closed and locked the door. The single page, typed written note stated,

SECRET:
Operation CARPETBAGGER Update 00469/10/44

Confirmation received that Agent Toller of the Hudson team has established contact with local Resistance network and has set-up office and safe houses in the designated area of operation (AOO).

Agent Bech to be inserted in AOO within 36 hours to commence operations.

Director of Operation, Operation CARPETBAGGER, RAF Harrington 1930 hrs, 4 Oct 1944

Leif reached into his pocket and withdrew the matchbox and struck the match to destroy the message. The countdown was on.

Chapter 18

Operation Carpetbagger

'If the theory of war does advise anything,
it is the nature of war to advise the most
decisive, and most audacious actions.'

Carl von Clausewitz, 1812

With Bjorn's successful insertion into Denmark confirmed by the OSS operations center, Leif was summoned and the intelligence officer, Major Forsyth, gave him a full brief on his mission:

> Upon landing by parachute near the town of Skive Denmark, in central Jutland, you will initiate contact with the local Danish Resistance reception party. Under their guidance, you will commence operations in and around the town of Aarhus, where you will establish yourself as the OSS lead for Allied operations under the guise of Jørgen Bech, an insurance broker and ship parts supplier as part of a major Copenhagen based company.

False identification photo of Leif Bangsboll, AKA Agent Alexander Hudson, OSS Agent, soon to become Agent Vejlby Bech, Maritime Engineer and OSS field agent in occupied Denmark (September 1944). (*Photo courtesy of the author's family collection*)

Leif nodded. He knew this already. But he didn't feel Forsyth was the kind of man one could rush. He had a hardened layer of bureaucratic crust that even a man about to be dropped into a warzone could not chisel away.

> Your mission is two-fold, Bech. You are to collect intelligence on German activities in Jutland, using all means at your disposal. Denmark is being used as a staging area for supplies being sent to front line German units in France, Belgium and Germany. Which ties directly into the second part of

your mission. Whenever and wherever opportunity presents, you are to aggressively pursue counterinsurgency operations to disrupt their resupply of German units and to soften the target for our eventual invasion. You must exhaust, terminally disrupt the German forces and their local resources.

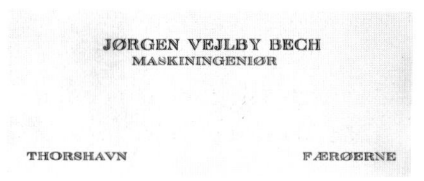

Forged business card of Jorgen Bech, Maritime Engineer and OSS field agent, Oct 1944–May 1945. (*Photo courtesy of the author's family collection*)

'Now we're talking', Leif thought, 'a material and psychological assault.'

As our sole OSS team in Denmark, you should maximize coordination of intelligence and force employment with the Danish Resistance command network. Compare notes and talk shop, so to say. Their primary contact to us goes by the code name Gold. He makes himself scares – the resistance in and around Copenhagen has been infiltrated by the Gestapo before.

'Sir', Leif said, raising his index finger for punctuation, 'I just want to be clear: When you say, "conduct counterinsurgency operations whenever and wherever" – what precisely do you mean?'

Forsyth finally showed an emotion – frustration.

Bech, what the hell do you damned well think I mean? Your orders are to set the place on fire, however you goddamn well can – disrupt, distract, and destroy the bastards where they live and breathe.

Leif smiled, that was exactly what he wanted to hear. 'When do I leave, sir?'
'We're just holding out on weather.' Forsyth continued,

We need cloud cover over England and the Channel, and preferably clear skies over Denmark and Jutland. That way our bombing raids into France and Germany will keep the Luftwaffe and German air defense busy, while we drop you in. Under those conditions, a lone B-24 flying towards the Danish coast has a decent chance of getting through unscathed, maybe even undetected. Which is most definitely what you want, Bech.

Forsyth concluded,

A password phrase will be given to you and communicated to your Danish Resistance reception party just prior to your departure. Get some rest – you'll need it.

'What I need is to leave now', Leif thought,

> to try and find my father. But I'll see it your way. It doesn't do me any good to get shot down because we took off in the wrong kind of weather.

Leif spent the rest of the evening reviewing in his mind all his mission details – his cover story, logistical facts of the insertion plan, names of contacts and key locations within Jutland to ensure the information was committed to memory. As Leif mentally juggled all the critical details, two names kept reappearing in his mind: Carl Bruhn and Tommy Sneum. As part of Leif's pre-mission planning conducted while at OSS headquarters in London, he had inquired about previous Carpetbagger missions into Denmark, to see if there were any worthwhile lessons learned. He could only find files on two such missions into Denmark run by the SOE. Agent Carl Bruhn had parachuted into Denmark on 28 December 1941 and had been killed during his jump due to a parachute malfunction. Agent Tommy Sneum, entered Denmark, posing as a fisherman in summer 1942 via a Swedish fishing boat. Sneum was able to operate with the Danish Resistance for only two months before his cover was blown and he had to be extracted back to England as a stowaway aboard a Danish troller just as the Gestapo closed in on him and his resistance network. Leif and Bjorn would be the first OSS agents deployed into Denmark. Leif recalled an English phrase he had recently learned: 'Third time is a charm.' These were sobering facts for Leif to ponder. It was late in the evening when he turned off the light in his small room in the transient quarters at RAF Harrington. Sleep did not come easily.

The next day Leif's prayers were answered. Just as he was finishing dinner at the officers' club, he was advised by the OSS duty officer that he was to collect his belongings and report to the OSS Operations Center within the hour. Upon arrival there, Leif received his final briefing on the mission plan and underwent his final inspection – a thorough search of his person was essential and conducted with great vigilance, during which all items in his possession were scrutinized to determine if they were consistent with his cover story. Forged Danish identity

The true Jorgen Beck. The caption on the back of the photo, written by Jorgen states: Leif, Good luck and fair winds, your good friend Jorgen, August 20th, 1941. (*Photo courtesy of the author's family collection*)

B-24 Liberator bomber of the 492nd Bombing Group, Special Operations Wing at RAF Base Harrington, England, circa 1944. (*Photo courtesy of online Pinecrest Stock Imagery*)

cards, doctored German travel authority papers, business cards, Danish currency (Kroners) and fictitious family photographs were pored over for any mistakes. They confiscated and replaced his cigarettes and lighter both English brands, which would tip off the Gestapo in an instant. Replaced with a small box of wooden matches manufactured in Denmark and a fresh pack of Spanish cigarettes. Even something as insignificant as a suspicious (British) brand name on a piece of clothing or a ticket stub from the London Underground left in a pocket, could prove fatal to an agent being searched by the Germans authorities. Finally, after the search was deemed satisfactory, Major Forsyth appeared and told Leif, 'The weather over the Channel is clear and conditions over the drop zone appear ideal: moonlit with scattered clouds.' Forsyth extended his hand with a pack of Lucky Strikes and offered Leif a cigarette, which he lit for the young agent, and said, 'I'll walk you to your jeep. It's waiting for you on the ramp side of the hangar.'

Five minutes later as Forsyth and Leif compared opinions about their favorite bars in London, Forsyth said the words Leif had been waiting to hear: 'OK, it's time, off you go.' Leif dropped his cigarette onto the gravel path and extinguished it with the toe of his shoe. He shook hands with Forsyth and climbed into the passenger seat of the jeep, noting that his parachute and small leather suitcase had already been stowed in the backseat. Forsyth gave the driver an all-clear signal to proceed, and before Leif knew it, the jeep was speeding down the dark airfield to a remote parking spot at the far end of the taxiway, reserved for a B-24 Liberator bomber with tail number of 42-63980, which was awaiting its 'cargo'.

Before the jeep had come to a complete stop near the nose of the aircraft, Leif, his adrenaline pumping, launched himself out of the vehicle. 'Thanks for the lift', Leif said to his young driver, adding the very British phrase, 'cheerio!' The driver replied, 'Good luck, sir.' The driver pulled away and parked the jeep about 100 yards away, facing the aircraft. He would remain there until the aircraft was airborne. Aware of the aircraft's dark looming presence before him, Leif, carrying his parachute over his shoulder and suitcase in his free hand, approached the aircraft. As he hunched over, passing under the port wing of the bomber, he noticed the name of the aircraft, which had been painted just below the cockpit window: *Lucky Playmate*. And just below the letters was the image of a curvy, bathing suit-clad model with her legs crossed seductively over the aircraft's stylish *nom de guerre*.

Leif thought,

> This leaves open all kinds of possibilities for an ironic death. Three years of training only to be shot down or crash in an airplane watched over by a bit of 'Lady Luck.' Yes, a little luck tonight would be welcome!

Before entering the black behemoth, Leif took one last look down the long, dark runway. The lights, outlining the runway were off and would not be illuminated until just prior to their take-off roll. It was a cool evening, but he felt himself perspiring.

Leif approached the open belly hatch of the massive black aircraft and craned his neck to peer inside and then lifted his parachute and small suitcase onto the aircraft's fuselage floor. The B-24s assigned to support Operation Carpetbagger had been modified to accommodate the special needs of its 'cargo'. The usual green and brown camouflage paint applied to most Allied aircraft was replaced by flat black to reduce the aircraft's visibility at night, since virtually all special operations were midnight runs. Most B-24 Liberator's also had their belly gun turrets removed so a hatch allowing equipment containers and agents to be dispatched via parachute could be installed. This new belly hatch had become known as the 'Joe Hole', a term inspired by the aircrew's nickname for their passengers. In the clandestine world of the OSS and SOE, real names were dangerous, and anonymity was as essential as loaded weapons. For the crew of the *Lucky Playmate*, tonight's mission was to deliver one 'Joe' along with four containers of military equipment to the Danish Resistance in central Jutland.

Walking back from the cockpit, the air despatcher saw Leif's head appear through the Joe Hole and snapped his fingers, pointed to a vacant jump seat, and told him to come aboard and strap-in.

Leif placed his belongings against the fuselage, adjacent to his intended seat and called out to the air despatcher, while buckling up, 'Any place, anytime, anywhere – right?'

'You got that right, Joe', the air despatcher said, 'that's our motto and we aim to please.'

The airman and special agent exchanged a smile of solidarity before the air despatcher closed the hatch. Leif's stomach tightened as the separational door snapped into place, marking his point of no return. The next time that hatch opened he would be dropping into Denmark.

Leif's mind raced, overloaded with adrenaline and a degree of anxiety. He tried to stem the flow, but crucial information kept flooding his synapses, like an explosion behind his eyes – code phrases, contact names, street addresses. Then, inexplicably, a quote from one of his favorite Shakespeare plays, *Julius Caesar*, piece he and Frederik had studied together, popped into his head 'Cry havoc and let slip the dogs of war...'

The first of the *Lucky Playmate*'s four Pratt & Whitney engines roared to life, and it took an additional five minutes for the three remaining turbines to reach operating temperatures. Then the black bomber, with its running lights off, sped down the runway, barely visible to the air traffic controller in the nearby tower. Next came liftoff and the hydraulic pump below Leif's feet kicked in to raise the wheels and close the doors around the undercarriage – they were airborne.

Leif was surrounded by noise and vibrations as the aircraft climbed towards its planned flight altitude of 8,000 feet, the air temperature was dropping and he shivered – his tweed jacket was no match for cold air at altitude. Fortunately, the flight would not be a long one.

The fuselage space was narrow and Leif was not comfortable. To give himself some room, he rested his feet on one of the four aluminum resupply cylinders stocked with equipment for the resistance force, dozens of rifles, machine guns and pistols, a dozen wooden crates containing thousands of rounds of ammunition and several hundred pounds of plastic explosives, detonation cords, blasting caps and fuses. Two crates of grenades along with four wireless radio sets and six combat first aid kits. All the tools of the trade for Leif and his partner, Bjorn.

But Leif's mission support equipment went beyond weapons, explosives and radios. A substantial amount of money was present in the haul, including Danish Kroners and German Reichsmarks, as well as hundreds of single ounce gold bullion plates, worth over $100,000. Leif and Bjorn would need the currency to pay for logistical and administrative requirements in support of Operation Carpetbagger, not to mention bribes. If there was one thing the OSS and SOE knew, it was that information was not free.

The *Lucky Playmate*'s flight path took the B-24 over the beautiful pastoral hills and valleys of Yorkshire, passing by the cities of Sheffield, Gainsborough and York, and directly over the ancient fortifications built on the River Trent in Lincolnshire by his great ancestor King Swyen 'Forkbeard' Haraldsson, the first Viking king of England. Had Leif known that fact, he would have considered it a very good omen.

The flight over the Channel was smooth and uneventful, and the weather over Denmark was just as forecasted: moonlit with a few clouds. The reflection of the moon shimmered off the water beneath them and made the Danish rivers glisten like liquid silver which facilitated their navigation towards the drop zone.

The *Lucky Playmate* had been airborne for ninety minutes, when Leif saw the air despatcher get up from his station. A moment later, at the five-minute pre-drop warning, the co-pilot illuminated the red 'jump light', which tossed an eerie emergency glow over the cargo compartment. In response, the B-24 Liberator throttled its engine back to initiate slow down and descent for phase one of the mission.

The aerial despatcher moved to the aft of the aircraft's cargo compartment to inspect and prepare the containers for dispatch. Leif helped him hook up the static lines of the cargo containers and remove the restraints that secured them to the aircraft floor. It was hard work because of the nature of the limited space within the fuselage and the constant oscillation of the aircraft, which made agile motion a struggle.

With a thumbs up signal the airmen opened the belly hatch/Joe Hole and were immediately greeted by a hurricane blast of wind. Under ideal circumstances, the heavy drone of the engines and the wind emanating up through the opening complicated the process, but this was unforeseen, it was as if the wind was fighting them, cancelling out all possible communication between the two, and intentionally trying to toss them around the fuselage of the craft – thwarting their every effort.

In anticipating the jump light switched from red 'standby' to green 'go'; time was of the essence to make the drop in that exact spot, so the Danish Resistance could rendezvous with their supplies quickly. But Leif and the despatcher were at war with the 'Lady Luck' and the atmospheric conditions battering the aircraft. Moving the cylinders was normally a one-man job, but with the bestial wind, it took Leif and the despatcher concentrated effort to drag the cylinders over, one by one, to the Joe Hole, fighting for balance the entire way, as the co-pilot shouted the warning through the intercom: 'thirty seconds!'

When the green drop light illuminated and the last cylinder had been dropped through the aircraft's Joe Hole, the despatcher closed the hatch, went on the intercom and advised the pilot the first phase of the mission was complete. The green jump light was replaced by the red glow of the stand-by warning light.

'Damn, that was a rough one – thanks for the help!' the despatcher said to his clandestine passenger.

Leif was satisfied. 'We got the supplies through. The resistance will have what they need to fight the Germans.'

The despatcher laughed. 'True enough, but the next time I open that hatch, you'll be jumping into that maelstrom, not me brother!'

'Cry havoc, you can say that again', Leif thought, 'Lady Luck had brewed up a tempest for his return home to Denmark.' Suddenly recalling the scene with the three witches in Shakespeare's *Macbeth*, Leif thought 'Boil, boil, toil and trouble…' And as an unabashed theater and literature lover, Leif hoped this memory wasn't foreshadowing his mission.

With the first phase of the drop completed, the *Lucky Playmate* began to circle the drop zone for the second pass: phase two. This was Leif's cue to prepare. As the craft levelled-out from its long arching turn and lined up for the drop run, Leif donned his parachute and retrieved his suitcase, securing it to his waist and legs with straps, then carefully maneuvered back to the hatch, positing himself near the edge.

The despatcher appeared, this time wearing goggles, ready to open the Joe Hole. Then came the call, 'Thirty seconds!' over the intercom from the pilot which was the air despatchers signal to open the Joe Hole.

Leif readied himself, this would be his first combat jump, and a jump without his usual kit – no rifle, helmet, heavy jump boots, pockets crammed with extra ammo, no first aid kit or maps, no food or even a canteen of water. Surprisingly, the lighter load gave him pause. With these wind conditions, he would be much lighter and more likely to drift further. The OSS commander at RAF Harrington had dressed him in a non-descript fashion, tweed jacket, sturdy khaki brown dress trousers, dark leather shoes, which had been tied tightly to prevent the slipstream from ripping them off during his descent. Also tied to his person, or to be more precise, strapped to his waist and leg, was a cumbersome worn leather suitcase containing his belongings and most of his money. His service revolver of choice was a Walther PPK, not the standard issue Browning HP 9 millimeter that most OSS agents carried. Leif had deliberately chosen a German made handgun, knowing that if he was found in possession of an Allied weapon such as the Browning in Denmark, his identity as OSS/SOE agent would be quickly exposed. This was strapped to his calf, just above his right ankle.

The red light still hadn't pulsed green. Leif and the despatcher waited, suspended in time, leaving the OSS agent additional and unwanted moments to reflect on being dropped into occupied territory in civilian clothing. If caught by the Gestapo, he would not be treated like a conventional PoW under the Geneva Convention. Officially, no government would protect him, nor claim rights to his person. Bearing that fact in mind, Leif felt his hand crawl up the seam of his tweed jacket lapel to locate the small bulge of a hidden L-tablets: cyanide.

He swallowed hard at the idea and as if on cue, the green light flashed on, and the air despatcher gave Leif a thumbs up, shouting, 'GREEN GO!'

Leif dropped into the maelstrom of noise, wind and darkness, instinctively shouting the airborne war cry 'GERONIMO!' as he vanished into the void. Leif immediately felt the blast of the cold wind cutting against his flesh. He felt stranded, mentally wanting to fight the current, until, come what may, he committed to immersion in the destructive element and let his body fall through space as trained. As Leif plummeted toward earth in the darkness, he resisted the temptation to look up toward the departing B-24, to watch it disappear into the night above him. Leif felt the seconds tick by as if in slow motion. 'One-one-thousand… two-one-thousand… three-one-thousand… four… BANG!' The parachute opened with a distinctive snapping noise and a mighty jerk of deceleration – instantly pitting his stomach towards his knees. With a sense of floating rather than falling, Leif scanned the darkness below as the sound of the aircraft's four engines began to fade into the distance above him. Several stiff gusts of wind shoved him laterally, revealing new shapes below, large, rectangular areas that Leif interpreted as fields. 'A pale straight line must be a road, the glimmer of a river and dark, irregular shapes, which must be trees.'

Another bruising draught tossed him to the left, prying open his field of vision. He could see lights from farmhouses, and the faint tracings of barns in fields. His eyes, adjusting to the darkness, began to process his expected landing site. But Leif continued to drift to the left – faster, heading toward the glimmering reflection of a river or stream that laid beyond the sprawling fields. He decided to stop struggling against the wind, try to use it, twist his torso in the gusts, and let nature carry him back to the farmland, away from the water.

And it worked. He was floating around 200 feet above the field, scanning for the most hospitable landing ground, when another gust of wind connected from behind and propelled him forward into a path of a line of trees. He was along for the ride now. It was too late for him to redirect course. Seconds from impact with the tree line, Leif went back to basics. He pulled down hard on both rises to slow his fall. He lifted his feet and pulled his kneed to his chest so that he was almost in fetal position, while watching the tree line rapidly approach from the corner of his eye. He was saved by speed. He cut through with such force against the treetops that they spun his body to the right, rocketed him on a new trajectory, and just as he began to recover and straighten out, a large dark surface rushed into his field of vision.

He assumed it was the ground and instinctively went through his jump training drills to soften his landing – feet together, knees together and slightly bent, hands up, pulling down on both rises as hard as he could. He landed on the balls of his feet, knees and then shoulders, rolling onto his side, as he thought, 'Now that's a landing! I wish my instructors at Fort Bragg could have seen it.'

* * *

Leif staggered to his feet; the ground was soft – unnaturally soft – and sloped upwards. He unbuckled his parachute. And that was when the truth hit him. He hadn't landed on ground. Not even close. He looked down at the foundation below his feet and cursed his situation. Yes. He was standing on the thatched roof of a large barn – at least 15 feet off the ground. 'Shit', he thought. 'Shit!' He rolled up his parachute through heavy breaths, trying to troubleshoot an escape from this mess before anyone noticed him.

Leif scanned his immediate surroundings. Other than the dim light emanating from the window of the farmhouse adjacent to the barn roof he was currently occupying, everything else seemed normal. Except that he needed to find a way down fast. At the bottom of the far side of the barn was a large pile of straw, and judging from the smell, cow and horse manure. No matter, it seemed like the smartest place for Leif to break his fall. He threw his parachute and harness down first, then his suitcase and stepped off the roof onto his belongings and manure pile below – using the same parachute landing technique as his first jump of the night.

Rolling off the manure pile with relative grace and agility, Leif barely had time to pick himself up from his second jump of the night, when the silhouette of a man emerged from the side of the farmhouse. He stepped out of the shadows holding a rifle at the ready position. Leif thought about running or even pulling out his pistol. But the man was only 15 feet away and the gun was pointed directly at his chest, looking for a reason to hollow it out.

'Welcome to Jutland' said the figure from the shadows, the words belying the weapon in his hands, 'it seems like I've made a new friend from Germany or maybe England. Or are you just a valkryie fallen from the stars?'

Looking around cautiously, Leif wanted to de-escalate the situation, so he began to nonchalantly brush off the straw from his clothing and replied in perfect Danish, 'I am a friend of Denmark. Who might you be?'

Lifting his shotgun slightly higher in a threatening gesture, the farmer retorted, 'I believe I will be asking the questions tonight, friend of Denmark.'

Chapter 19

The Network

'All warfare is based on deception…
Offer the enemy bait to lure him
where you want him.'

Sun Tzu

The Danish farmer who had confronted Leif on the evening of 6 October 1944, was Mr Olaf Gustovson, 'Uncle Olaf' as many locals referred to him. He was a good and honest man. Olaf was in his late seventies but still spry for his age. He was affable, but too old to be an active, anti-German resistance fighter. However, he was a true patriot and a reliable supporter of Jutland's Danish Resistance network. He had been made aware of the evening's OSS insertion mission and was ready to assist if needed. As luck would have it, he was needed.

Following their initial introduction, Olaf lowered his weapon and assured Leif that he had no ill intentions – just ensuring he wasn't 'one of those Nazi

SOE / OSS supply containers being loaded onto a horse-drawn wagon by Danish Resistance members, Denmark, circa 1944. (*Photo courtesy of online Pinecrest Stock Imagery*)

fellows'. Once an equilibrium had been established between the two Danes, Olaf used his rifle to point Leif towards the town of Skive, his destination that evening. Olaf reassured Leif that the resistance reception party was close by. Leif looked at Olaf and then at his watch. It was 2330 hours.

'What are you waiting for soldier, go find your colleagues', Olaf said, and again motioned the shotgun in the direction of the adjacent field, 'I will dispose of your parachute.' He then added, 'If for some reason, you do not meet up with your reception party, come back here and we will shelter you.'

Leif replied, '*Tak* [Thanks in Danish]' and moved off silently into the darkness of the field behind Olaf's farmhouse with his suitcase in one hand and his gun in the other. Leif had walked 200 yards, his eyes now adapted to the darkness, when he spotted a large, white shape contrasted on the dark soil of the fallowed field. It was a parachute, draped over one of his resupply cylinders, which he had seen from the air. Leif ran to the cylinder and immediately disconnected the parachute and began to roll it up, while scanning his surroundings. The resupply cylinder and landed 20 yards from the edge of a field that was outlined by trees and hedges. Though it would be difficult to detect from an adjacent road because of the vegetation, that same vegetation blocked Leif's view of any

Olaf and Ragla Gustavsson, whose farm Agent Bech landed upon when parachuting into occupied Denmark on the 6th of October 1944. Olaf, a member of the Danish Resistance would assist Agent Bech and become a life-long friend. (*Photo courtesy of the author's family collection*)

potential approaching danger. He did not like standing in such an open, exposed area, so he knelt and began to scrape away the loose earth in order to bury the parachute. Just as he completed concealing the parachute, Leif was alerted by a sudden noise. People, he was sure, were nearby.

Leif instinctively stopped and turned towards the approaching threat, hearing what to his trained ear sounded like several people crossing the gravel road and moving through the tree line. Before he had time to react, Leif clearly heard the distinctive sound of a rifle's bolt action being manually brought back and then forward, inserting a bullet into the firing chamber. Someone nearby had just prepared their weapon and was ready to fire it.

Leif froze in place, instinctively lowered himself further behind the aluminum cylinder to make himself a smaller target while he drew his gun up and forward to the ready position. Several seconds passed when a voice from the darkness of the tree line spoke, '*Hvern er du*? [Who are you?]'.

This was clearly not the code phrase Leif was hoping to hear. Using the designated mission code phrase, the OSS handler had given him prior to boarding their aircraft earlier that evening, he responded to the shapeless voice emanating from the darkness.

'Onward to Valhalla' he said and waited, moving his index finger onto the trigger. A few agonizing seconds past and then the voice from the darkness responded with, 'Where Odin awaits his Viking sons.'

Hearing the proper response code phrase, relief washed over Leif. He relaxed his tense muscles, slowly stood up and lowered his weapon. The perspiration from the stress and exertion suddenly began to cool on his skin in the damp night air – he had arrived and was safe for the time being, his rendezvous with the Danish Resistance party a success.

The leader of the reception team came forward to greet Leif with a hardy handshake and introduced himself as Captain Toldstrup of the Royal Danish Army and leader of the resistance reception party. After verifying that Leif was unhurt and had disposed of his parachutes. 'Good', Toldstrup said, switching tones, becoming all business like, 'we've located two of the resupply cylinders. Can you confirm a total of four were dropped?'

Leif replied,

Yes. I helped dispatch all four. The containers were heavy and fell faster, but the winds were higher than expected – tell your people to look west of the drop zone. They probably drifted in that direction.

'Very well', Toldstrup said, putting his arm on Leif's shoulder, 'we need to get you out of sight now. We will proceed to the safe house, while my men search for the remaining containers.'

Leif hesitated and said, 'I have been seen by a man at that farm over there, pointing off to his left.'

Toldstrup assured Leif,

> Yes, I know, he came and found us and directed us towards you. His name is Olaf and he's loyal to Denmark and a member of the resistance. He's too old to participate in such late-night activities, but nonetheless, he is trustworthy and does much good, behind the scenes work for us.

He continued, 'Did you happen to meet his dear wife, Ragla?' Before Leif could answer, Toldstrup added with a grin, 'Of course you didn't' she would have shot you first and asked questions later.' The remark triggered subdued laughter from the four remaining members of Toldstrup's reception team. With the introductions completed, the OSS agent and the five Danish Resistance fighters moved off silently into the darkness towards the nearby town of Skive.

The cross country trek towards the village of Skive and their safe house took half an hour. The exercise and fresh air – Danish air – invigorated Leif. The safe house was a small isolated one-room fishing cabin on the banks of lake Flyndersø, just south-west of the town and designed with function, not form in mind. In the main room, a fire crackled inside the hearth, sending an orange glow into the room. At the makeshift kitchen table, sat a graying man in his mid-fifties casually dressed in a wool turtleneck and corduroy pants, gutting a fish with a long, bloodied knife and tossing the innards into a rubbish bin.

When Leif entered, the man rose, apologized for not offering his blood-soaked hand and introduced himself as Vagn Bennike, chief of south Jutland's resistance. Bennike then asked one of his two bodyguards standing in the corner to get a bottle of Akvavit and went back to preparing the fish to serve his OSS visitor.

> You know Bech, I have only been with the resistance for a year. I was a major in the Royal Danish Army – an engineer and demolitions expert. I spent two humiliating years under the boots of our German occupiers. I just wanted to keep my wife and children safe and hoped the war would be over soon and things would go back to the way they were.

Bennike went silent. After another round of warming alcohol, he continued,

> I tried to hold out under the German occupation. I only had another year to finish out my service – but I could not stand the kowtowing any longer. I wasn't proud, but I have a family to think about and my military income was my only guarantee of a home and livelihood for my family.

Bennike and Leif finished their meager but delicious meals and got down to business.

'I know it's not glamorous or inspiring', Bennike continued, 'or the least bit patriotic. But in times of austerity and privation, we must make do with only the basics of necessities.'

Leif reached across the table and took one of Bennike's cigarettes from the pack, while nodding in sympathy.

Benneke laughed and pointed at the two bodyguards.

Ironically, the resistance had their doubts about me because I was a family man. They worried I'd resigned my army position to be a plant, to infiltrate the resistance network. They subjected me to countless loyalty tests, talking to my friends and former colleagues, even following me on a long weekend trip with my wife and children. Eventually, they realized I was serious and gave me this cell to look after.

He pulled a cigarette out and rolled it between his fingers, weighing his next words.

I'm very good at what I do, Bech. Even your demolitions expert Toller was impressed. But I'm not a spy like you. If you want something blown to hell, I'm your man. But I'm not a planner and I certainly don't have the ear and firepower of the OSS and SOE in London.

He raised his glass.at I'm trying to say is… I'm very happy to meet a man of your talents and connections. We needed that equipment you dropped to us tonight.' They clinked glasses to toast their new partnership.

'In terms of the situation on the ground', Leif said, once the introductory mood had passed. 'What are you finding in terms of German troops, Gestapo agents? Numbers? Activity?'

There's been a marked increase the more trouble the Wehrmacht has in western Europe. They're consolidating their hold. Which translates to more random searches, picking up people for interrogation in broad sweeps, many of them innocent and not part of the resistance. Anything that creates a climate of fear that makes people less likely to resist.

Leif absorbed the information. It was slightly more dire than he'd been led to believe. 'When do I meet Gold?'

'Gold doesn't want to meet you yet', Bennike offered, 'he meets very few people and never before have they proved their mettle. You'll meet Gold when he decides you're worth meeting.'

He put his hand on Leif's shoulder. 'You must be exhausted. Get some rest, then I'll take you to Aarhus to see your colleague, Toller.'

Leif thought, 'Bjorn Toller. It's been two weeks since I last saw him in London. I wonder how the actuarial business has been treating him?'

Three hours later, Leif was awakened by Bennike with a soft shove and the welcome appearance of a piping hot mug of coffee. They needed to move. It wasn't safe for either of them to stay in this location much longer and they had a morning rendezvous with Bjorn before their business opened shop.

* * *

It had only been a few years since Leif had lived in Denmark, but what years they had been. After the drive into Aarhus and a quick breakfast at a café, he felt as if he were in a foreign country. His homeland had been subjugated by hostile, alien forces and was paying a heavy psychic toll. It broke his heart and was a stark reminder of the stakes in this battle that was playing out beyond the fields of obvious combat. He could see it on the streets. The once charming, innocent and carefree lifestyle of the Danes had disappeared. The streets looked familiar; nothing was out of place except the presence of German soldiers from time to time. But a hostile, foreboding feeling blanketed the air. It went beyond the checkpoints, the unlawful searches, and the German soldiers marching the streets. It was the Danes themselves. When you alter a people's reality, you alter the people. And Leif's people were now constantly frightened, suspicious, meek and cowed. The jackboot of fascist tyranny had broken their spirits.

The Nazis had doled out the gradual slide into fascism in stages, in cruel drops of new reality. They knew that if they cracked down immediately, tore off their masks and showed the horror underneath, they make have risked outright rebellion and guerilla war. Thus, when the Wehrmacht first occupied Denmark in 1940, they were relatively benign in their approach. But by August 1943, the country had transitioned into a draconian police state lorded over by the Gestapo and kept in check by 200,000 German troops. In that same year, the Germans also dissolved the Danish Parliament and disband the remnants of the military. Life as the Danes knew it had ended.

It made Leif realize that in war, danger, death, and destruction were not the exclusive domain of combatants. The Danish people were in a precarious position, trapped between the resistance and the German occupation forces, both of which threatened their safety. The retaliatory actions of the resistance, meant to save these very Danes, could also place them in harm's way. The blowback of their success could lead to average citizens being rounded up and punished to further demoralize an already broken society. The bloodletting was a vicious cycle.

'Taking the life of an enemy in battle', Leif thought, 'would inevitably occur, and was expected.' Yet in the clandestine world of the OSS and SOE, ambiguity ran rampant, agents and resistance fighters would be forced to make conscious decisions to take lives take lives of the enemy and sacrifice lives of citizens, to root our traitors and collaborators and act like assassins. He shook his head in dismay and reminded himself that whether on a field of battle or in the shadows, the sacrifice of the few for the greater good of the many was a fundamental necessity of war.

Leif and Bennike pulled up to the newly leased and operational office of the front maritime insurance brokerage company, where the resistance leader took leave of the young OSS agent, not wanting to risk further public exposure. Leif peered into the office window. There were two desks overflowing with folders, paperwork, pens and typewriters, with freshly installed ribbons jammed with contracts waiting to be finished, and even nameplates on their desks reading Jørgen Bech, Manager and Bjorn Toller, Accountant. Tacked to the walls behind the furniture were calendars, one for each partner, inscribed with meetings, travel times and events crossed out on completion.

Leif entered, picked up a pamphlet explaining insurance risk rates, and waited for Bjorn to notice him. Bjorn was intently reading the local paper and raised his coffee to his lips when he saw Leif standing in their lobby. A broad smile spread simultaneously across both of their faces.

'Thank Christ you're here', Bjorn said. 'I'm a horrible actuarial.'

'Nonsense.' Leif said, shaking his hand with a firm greeting. 'What are your five principles of insurance policies? You know, the code you live by as an actuary.'

Bjorn dropped the handshake and stood at mock attention and said, 'Indemnity, insurable interest, utmost good faith, proximate cause and subrogation and contribution, sir!'

Leif laughed. 'Like I said, I knew you were a born performer.'

Bjorn pulled out a cigarette and offered one to Leif. 'Do you know I got invited to a bloody business conference next week?'

They shared a loud round of laughter, imaging the absurdity of Bjorn hanging out with a bunch of real actuaries.

Leif motioned around the office. 'How does this all work?'

Bjorn took Leif through the stages of how he'd incubated and pulled off this deception. The key to their successful covers was that he'd enlisted an actual maritime insurance company based in Copenhagen and with an office in Aarhus as their sponsor. These Danes, sympathetic to their cause, would act as their back office, while appearing to the uninitiated as their fiercest competitors.

All Bjorn, and now Leif, had to do was meet with the interested parties, ascertain their overarching needs and then close the sale. After that, the paperwork and the specific tasks would be handed over to the actual brokerage company in Copenhagen, which would handle all their necessary brokerage and claims processing. After that, Leif would only need to follow up to make sure the clients were satisfied with the work, adding a further verifiable layer to his cover story.

'This facade is important', stated Leif, 'but the majority of our time must be spent on building a strong network of reliable soldiers and training them in the art of sabotage and small arms handling.'

Bjorn agreed, 'We'll teach them how to unleash hell.'

With that, Leif and Bjorn went to work molding Bennike's resistance network into fighting shape. A handful of the recruits had military training, but most were committed citizens, dedicated anti-fascists desperate for a way to vent their rage at their occupiers. There were twenty of them in total – seventeen men and three women. The female factor provided an extra layer of capability in the cell, since many were employed as administrative clerks, hosts, waitresses or escorts, and could gain access to vital information thought non-violent means. Whatever the group's individual rationales for resisting, Leif and Bjorn were prepared to give them an explosive outlet for their passions.

Bjorn had secured the use of a large, abandoned farm on the outskirts of Aarhus, which became their designated training area. There, Leif channeled his inner 'Dangerous Dan' Fairbairn and taught the recruits close-combat tactics, how to rely on their hands as their deadliest weapon and enlisted poor Bjorn to recreate his OSS instructor's infamous move where he used pressure points behind the ears and plunged his colleague into five minutes of unconsciousness. Then Leif moved to the basics of weapons handling, a necessity, because even the most experienced hunters in the cell had not handled much in the way of British and American weaponry and needed to gain experience before engaging in potential, life or death situations. With so many Germans around, live fire practice was not advisable.

While Leif prepared them for physical standoffs with fundamental combat skills, Bjorn schooled the new resistance fighters in the fundamentals of the art of sabotage, showing the cell how to handle explosives and prepare proper demolition with various time delay devices. He took great pains to emphasize timers and blast caps, two areas where you did not want anything to go awry. Many rookies made the mistake of underestimating how long it would take them to escape a blast site and kill-radius and ended up being injured or dying from their own handiwork.

* * *

After a month of training, Leif and Bjorn felt their resistance cell was ready for some real field work. Unfortunately, they still hadn't heard from Gold. So, in fine OSS/SOE fashion they decided to begin planning to whip up some trouble of their own, announce their presence to the Gestapo in Jutland with a literal bang. To educate themselves on potential attack sites, Leif, Bjorn and two of their most able trainees took a series of business trips together to Vejle, Fredericia, Horsens, Herning and Kolding, all south of Aarhus, traveling along the main railway line that the Wehrmacht heavily relied on to keep supplies and reserve troops moving into Germany, France and Belgium.

After their prolonged reconnaissance mission, Bennike informed Leif via shortwave radio transmission to Bjorn that Gold wanted to meet; he'd been receiving reports from his regional commanders that the new OSS agents were making significant strides in training and their fighters near operational status. Meeting arrangements were made at a small, local restaurant in Horsens, a main railway stop between Copenhagen and Aarhus. When Gold arrived, he introduced himself to Leif as a prospective new client for the maritime insurance company and expected Leif to sell his services. They spoke in veiled business terms which cloaked their saboteur intent.

> Mr Gold, I'm terribly pleased to meet you. And I want to assure you that my firm has access to dozens of resources that will help your business prosper beyond your projected goals and objectives.

Gold replied,

> That is heartening to hear. From what Mr Bennike has told me, your company has already initiated many improvements to our local business community, which has, up until now, lacked action and vigor.

Leif studied Gold's face framed by wire-rimmed glasses, immaculately parted hair and a tight bow of a mouth, like an adornment on a patiently wrapped package. In normal times, Gold was the cut of gentlemen you'd expect to be seated next to at an opera or a new haute cuisine restaurant. But today, he and Leif were talking about raining down death and destruction.

> My marketing research department informs me that our competitor from Berlin intends to send an important shipment to Germany by train in the very near future. It would be most advantageous to Denmark's local merchants if you and your company could prevent that transaction from happening.

Leif nodded in acceptance while suppressing a smile. Gold was lowering his defenses.

> Of course. I will try and provide you with as much advance notice of the competitor's travel date. But you and your office must be prepared to respond quickly once the transaction has been set. It's important we show Denmark's local resolve in the face of such competition.

'It will be our pleasure', Leif said, 'we realize the importance of showing our resolve to our competitors.'

The dinner was good – simple. War rationing was limiting supplies. The waitress arrived with the bill. With a quick, yet subtle motion of the hand Leif grabbed the bill and stated to Gold, 'My first business expense.'

Gold smiled and said, 'Thank you Mr Bech, would you do me the pleasure of accompanying me to the train station? I will cover the gratuity.' Gold insisted. He left a large tip on the corner of the table for the waitress and then lit a cigarette, stood up and began walking out of the restaurant, with Leif in tow. It was a short walk to the train station, just enough time for Gold to provide the final details of the mission along with some background information for Leif to consider.

As they reached the street corner across from the Aarhus train station, Gold said, 'It has been almost a year.' There, they stood enjoying their cigarettes – a bonding exercise cementing their partnership.

> It has been a year since the two most productive and notorious Danish resistance fighters, Brent Hviid, codename Flame, and Jørgen Schmidt, codename Citron, were ambushed and killed by the Gestapo in Copenhagen.

Gold continued,

> It is imperative this new, ambitious mission be successful. A visible defeat of the Germans on Danish soil will bolster the people's spirits, drawing them to our cause, and will shake the Wehrmacht's confidence.

Leif added,

> And just as important, a successful sabotage campaign will draw vital German resources away from the front in order to attempt to quell our resistance activities. Every German soldier sent to Denmark to counter or control us, is one less soldier facing the Allied forces in Central Europe.

Leif nodded solemnly and added, 'I understand the importance, Mr Gold. I assure you.'

Gold stubbed the cigarette into the ground and said, 'Mr Peterson, my chief of staff, will be in touch when we have more information to share.'

Now that Leif had gained Gold's trust, he wanted to ask him about his contacts in Copenhagen, to see if the resistance leader could be of any help in unearthing Frederik's status and location. Being back in Denmark had doubled Leif's desire to find his father, but he knew Gold couldn't be put in that position, one that was dangerous for all of them. If Gold were ever picked up by the Gestapo, and placed under torture, who knew what he might say. And the Germans would consider picking up an OSS agent and his father, a senior naval officer who had connections to King Christian to be quite the bounty.

Gold noticed the saddened expression on Leif's face. 'Are you alright, Bech?'

Leif reached into his pocket for another cigarette. 'Fine, Mr Gold. Fine and fit. I have not seen my father in over three years, and I worry for his safety.'

Gold held Leif by the back of the neck in a fraternal, not threatening fashion.

> Wherever your father is, your reunion will have to wait. You're a young man for all this chaos. But it is important work and we shall overcome the Bosch. We just need to do it together. If your father is as grounded as you, he will do fine.

Leif nodded in agreement. 'Thank you, sir.'

Gold had one more bit of intelligence to share.

> There is another situation that needs to be brought to your attention Bech. It involves the imprisonment of eighteen members of the Danish Resistance being held at Gestapo headquarters in Aalborg. Most of them were captured during a botched resupply mission from London. Intelligence reports indicate the PoWs will be transferred to a prison camp in Germany – something that is being referred to by our agents as a 'concentration camp'. This move is expected within the next six weeks. We need options to liberate them.

That night, Leif and Bjorn began formulating a plan to sabotage the German supply train. While, in the back of his mind, Leif also contemplated the fate of the resistance members in the Gestapo's prison.

The next day, over morning coffee, Leif outlined his plan.

> We are going roll up both plans together. We will use the attack on the supply train as a diversion for the prison break. Who is the resistance leader for Aalborg? Do you know him?

'Fletcher, Hans Fletcher', replied Bjorn and adding,

> he's a good man. And I understand that five or six of those prisoners in that prison are his men – captured two months ago during an SOE resupply mission that went wrong.

'Even better', Leif said, relaxing his breathing, 'some of the prisoners will know Fletcher and trust him immediately. There's no time to waste.'

'But Fletcher barely knows us.' stated Bjorn emphatically.

'Confidence', Leif said, raising his index finger for emphasis, 'is one of those intangibles in this business that can never be forsaken.'

'Just for my own understanding', Bjorn said, 'we are going to blow up a German supply train as the diversion for a prison break… a German, Gestapo prison?'

Leif said, emphatically, 'Yes. Exactly.'

Bjorn sat back in his chair and sighed, 'This is going to be an interesting war…'

Chapter 20

Miss Sophie

'Perhaps I should not insist on this bold maneuver, but it is my style, my way of doing things.'
Napoléon Bonaparte, 1813

Though it had only been a few years since Leif had lived in Denmark, he felt, upon his return, as though he were in a foreign country. The once charming, innocent and carefree lifestyle of the Danes was gone. Though the streets were familiar, there was a fearful, foreboding mood across the land. It was not just the checkpoints and the presence of German soldiers in the streets; many of the Danish people themselves were different: constantly frightened and always suspicious.

Leif learned quickly that in war, danger, death and destruction are not the exclusive domain of combatants. Not only would the presence of the Wehrmacht and the Gestapo pose a threat to the Danish Resistance network, but all the people of Denmark would be suspect and, whether innocent or complaisant, could be caught between the opposing forces of the resistance and the German occupation forces.

Leif also realized early on that difficult, morality challenging choices would be an almost daily occurrence. Taking the life of an enemy combatant, he realized, would inevitably occur in war and to do so in the heat of battle was expected. However, in the clandestine world of the OSS and SOE agents and resistance fighters operating behind enemy lines or within enemy occupied territory would have to make a conscious, deliberate decision to take the life of an enemy, traitor or collaborator, much like an assassin. These premeditated acts were more complex and less reactive in nature, and thus created an array of difficult choices and ethical dilemmas. To cope, Leif focused on the simple rule that the sacrifice of the few for the greater good of the many was a fundamental necessity of war.

During the first week of November 1944, after one month in occupied Denmark as Jørgen Bech, Leif found himself confronted with a most unfortunate and untimely situation. It had happened during a scheduled meeting with Hans Fletcher, a local banker and one of his resistance cell team leaders. Fletcher and his resistance team had been ambushed by the Germans in September, at an SOE supply drop and now had a dozen men held in custody in the Aalborg prison. Leif and Fletcher met at a local café known as the Bygholm Park Inn. Within minutes of their initial meeting Leif happened upon an old friend. More precisely, an old girlfriend he had dated back when he lived in Copenhagen, whom he had not seen in four years.

Leif had entered the café with a copy of the local newspaper under his left arm. The position of the newspaper was a simple signal to Hans Fletcher, the team leader that he was meeting, that everything appeared normal – that he was not being followed by the Gestapo or local police. Leif stood just inside the café doorway, scanning the premises and the other dozen or so patrons, searching for his colleague. Fletcher was already seated and reading his own copy of the newspaper, the signal to Leif that he too had not been followed and that all appeared normal. Fletcher was waiting for Leif in a booth at the far side of the café, beside a window facing the back alley of the café.

'Good morning, Mr Fletcher.'

'And good morning to you, Mr Bech', Hans replied, 'I'm so glad you could join me.' The formality helped support the appearance of a routine business breakfast meeting.

Fletcher, a well-respected banker, had assumed a senior level leadership role in the local resistance a year earlier. He had been given orders by Gold to provide Leif with any assistance he needed. Fletcher had been impressed by Leif's and Bjorn's organizational skills and the intensive combat and explosives training they had provided to inexperienced freedom fighters during the previous few weeks. Commensurate with the increased training, came an expected increase in plans for new, more aggressive sabotage missions against the Germans occupying their region of Denmark. Flectcher was eager to hear what Leif had to tell him about his upcoming plans. Leif sat down and after a few moments of polite idle talk, Fletcher caught the attention of their waitress who was behind the bar drying glasses. With a small notepad in her hand, the waitress came over to take their breakfast order.

As Leif scanned the menu he heard a female voice utter his name as she approached their table. 'Leif? Leif, is that you?' the female voice asked.

Leif did not look up, but instead continued to read the paper in front of him. His training took control; the instinct to look up towards someone calling him by his true name was stifled – barely, thanks to the mental discipline he learned during his OSS training. Again, the waitress said from a few steps closer now, 'Why, Leif Bangsbøll, it is you!'

Leif continued to look down towards his newspaper but could now see the shoes of the waitress as she stopped and stood beside them. Slowly and under control, Leif let the newspaper descend to the table between himself and Fletcher. Fletcher, taken aback by the unexpected encounter, looked to Leif and then to the waitress and then back again to Leif, without speaking a word. There was fear and confusion in his eyes. Before Fletcher could say or do anything, Leif smiled calmly at him and stood up to face the waitress whose voice he recognized from a time and place far away. After a brief moment of sustained awkwardness, Leif reached out to embrace his old girlfriend, Sophie Halverson.

'Leif, when the war broke out you seemed to have disappeared!' she exclaimed. 'I thought you had gone to America to join Jørgen.' Before he could reply, Sophie continued, 'What are you doing here in Horsens?'

Leif smiled and leaned in towards her. 'It's a long story Sophie.' he whispered as he embraced his former girlfriend.

Leif and Sophie had met during his first year at the Danish Maritime Academy in Copenhagen. Their mutual friend, Jørgen Bech, had introduced Leif to a few local pubs and cafés within walking distance of their dormitory at the academy. Sophie had been a waitress at the Mayflower Café, one of Jørgen's favorite establishments, located just outside the academy property. Leif and Sophie had quickly become friends and had numerous dates – nothing serious, but serious enough now to possibly compromise Leif's mission.

The immediate problem, as Leif assessed it, was to protect his identity, cover story and the local resistance network at all costs. Clearly, Sophie remembered who Leif was and would not understand how or why Leif had taken on the identity of their mutual friend, Jørgen Bech, without a detailed explanation, which Leif was not prepared to do – certainly not there in the café – in public view.

Thinking quickly, Leif held their embrace a few seconds longer and whispered in Sophie's ear that he was having an important financial meeting with Mr Fletcher, the Horsens banker, but would come back to see her later that evening. Holding her gently by the waist, he took a step back and said, 'Sophie, what time do you finish work today? I'll come back and we'll go for dinner and we can get caught up then.'

Dazzled by the unexpected encounter with her former flame, Sophie replied, 'Yes, of course! I finish work at 6 o'clock.'

Leif let his hands drop slowly from her waist and added, 'Dear Sophie, Mr Fletcher and I must complete our important business meeting. We will have coffee, please.' And he turned and sat back down and looked back at Fletcher to resume their conversation as if nothing unusual had occurred.

After a moment of awkward silence, Sophie turned towards the kitchen to get their coffee turning back several times to look at Leif, as she did.

Hans stared at Leif and in a hushed voice said, 'My God Bech, she knows you – the real you.'

Leif returned his stare and replied, 'Relax, Hans, coffee is coming and we will sort this out at the proper time and place. Give me a moment to think.'

Leif picked up his newspaper and pretended to read it. Externally he looked calm, while internally, his mind and heart were racing.

A few minutes later, Sophie returned with their coffee and after a brief exchange of polite smiles, Sophie moved on to serve another table of customers. Leif lowered his newspaper in front of him, and spoke softly, just enough so Fletcher could hear him.

> If, and more likely, when she learns that I am using Jørgen Bech's identity as my cover name, it will certainly lead to more questions, and more questions means trouble. I'm not sure if I can trust her… she is very excitable.

Fletcher leaned forward and spoke softly but deliberately in return.

'Bech, look at me', he instructed and Leif put his coffee down, folded his newspaper, placed it on the table and looked up at Fletcher.

> You don't understand. The resistance, me included, believe this woman, Miss Sophie Halverson, to be a collaborator and susceptible to Nazi influence.

As Fletcher's words sank in, Leif stared at the banker/resistance cell leader. Both men realized then and there that this unfortunate encounter was now a situation that they would have to deal with in no uncertain terms. The whole intent of Leif being assigned outside of Copenhagen was to minimize the likelihood of anyone recognizing him as anyone other than Jørgen Bech, a maritime engineer and insurance broker. This chance meeting with Sophie, in this unexpected place and her being labeled as a potential Nazi sympathizer or collaborator could have serious consequences for all of them.

As they drank their coffees, Fletcher went on to describe the case that had been built around Miss Halverson. Soon after the German invasion and occupation of the capital, Sophie had been sent by her parents from Copenhagen to live with her aunt and uncle in the village of Horsens. Though the Halversons considered Horsens and the peninsula of Jutland in general safer than Copenhagen, Jutland was, in fact, the main entry way from northern Germany into Denmark and was the main transit route for German troops and supplies. The Horsens region was a major hub of German military transportation and, as such, a focal point for Danish Resistance activities. Sophie's cousin, Sven, and eldest son of her aunt and uncle, had joined Fletcher's resistance cell the previous year. Sven had been a good soldier and had recently been arrested by the Gestapo during an OSS resupply drop mission that went wrong. Sven was still being held in Horsens prison, awaiting transfer to a German work camp. It was believed that in her desperation to free her cousin, Sven, Sophie had begun dating a German officer stationed in Horsens in the hope of using their relationship to influence the young officer to help obtain her cousin's release.

'Our fear', said Fletcher, 'is that Sophie is desperate enough to say or do anything that might help free her cousin or lessen his punishment at the hands of Nazis.'

With this information, Leif realized that his cover story and his entire mission was in mortal jeopardy because of Sophie's previous knowledge of him and the real Jørgen Bech. If she was as desperate to save her cousin as Fletcher had suggested, one word to the German military – or worse to the Gestapo – of Jørgen Bech's existence as a cover for Leif Bangsbøll, and he would be arrested. More importantly, thought Leif, the local resistance network and OSS command link would be compromised. Silence ensued as the two resistance leaders pondered the situation. After a few minutes, Leif said to Fletcher, 'I'll pay for the coffees, you wait for me outside the café, we need to make a plan.

Fletcher and Leif finished their coffee and after a brief farewell, Fletcher departed and Leif walked over to Sophie who was standing by the entrance to the kitchen. Leif gently took her hand and squeezed it, and quietly said that he looked forward to seeing her again later that night. He looked into her eyes and paused… 'Right here at 6.00 pm, alright?' asked Leif. Sophie smiled and nodded. There was nothing left for him to do but hope that she would not say anything to anyone about their unexpected meeting between then and their meeting later that day – nine long hours from now.

Fletcher was waiting for Leif outside the café smoking a cigarette. Leif casually joined him and lit his own cigarette and said, 'We need a plan; a plan for tonight.'

'Do we have to kill her?' asked Fletcher timidly.

'I don't know', replied Leif honestly, 'but that is one option we must seriously consider.' Leif looked into Fletcher's eyes to gauge his take on the matter. Fletcher nodded reluctantly. As Leif's mind churned, various options flashed by like a broken film reel. Leif threw his half smoked cigarette into the gutter and turned to walk away and then stopped and looked back at Fletcher and said, 'Does the resistance have any reliable doctors within its ranks here in Horsens or in the immediate area?'

Fletcher replied, 'Well, of course we do.'

Leif looked at Hans and smiled.

I have an idea. I'll meet you at your office this afternoon at 4 o'clock. We will need a car, a safe house to use for a couple of days and the names of your trusted doctors in the region – a psychologist would be preferable.

Fletcher nodded hesitantly and Leif turned and walked away. Fletcher, a simple banker by trade, remained in place momentarily, mind spinning and hands shaking, recounting the tasks that Leif had just given him. Life as a resistance cell leader had just become much more real – complex, as well as intriguing and far more dangerous. Fletcher turned and walked in the opposite direction towards his office at the bank where he would make some urgent telephone calls.

Leif planned to arrive at Sophie's place of work precisely two minutes before Sophie was to finish her shift to minimize his exposure to possible surveillance. Both he and Fletcher had returned in Fletcher's car, an Opel sedan, shortly after 1600 hours and sat in the car a half a block from the café to observe patrons coming and going. Nothing suspicious was seen. If the Gestapo had been advised by Sophie and were waiting for him, Leif would know soon after entering the café. It was a risk he knew he had to take.

Fletcher was certain that Sophie was vulnerable and susceptible to coercion by the Germans and that she was desperate enough to do anything to save her cousin Sven. She had been seen on numerous occasions in the company of a German officer named Captain Manfred Trautermann – fraternizing with the enemy. It was Fletcher's opinion that Sophie was a willing collaborator, looking for a bargaining chip to offer the Germans for her cousin's release or at least, a less severe punishment. Secondly, Sophie had recognized Bech by his true identity: Leif Bangsbøll, and she could destroy his cover story with a casual misspoken word to her German boyfriend about running unexpectedly into an old friend who was using a false name to hide his identity, which would lead to his immediate arrest and probably far worse. The potential ramifications for the Horsens and regional resistance network were grave as well. Anyone who had any contact with the imposter Jørgen Bech would be hunted down and questioned by the Gestapo. For that matter, anyone who had any contact with Sophie Halverson would also be assumed to be a potential member of the resistance – the Gestapo did not care about human rights and laws. Eventually, the Germans would get someone to break under interrogation or torture and the local network would disintegrate like an egg dropped onto the floor. Imprisonment, torture and death would be the fate of many.

As they sat in the car, Leif and Fletcher reviewed their plan, a plan which either would unfold or unravel within a few minutes of Leif's walking through the café entrance. The two resistance men discussed the potential sequence of events. If Leif stepped out of the café with Sophie, carrying his hat in hand, this would indicate that Leif believed all was in good order and that they were not being watched by the Gestapo – the plan would proceed. If, however, Leif stepped out of the café wearing his hat, that would be the signal to Fletcher that they were compromised, and that the Gestapo had been advised and were present. With that latter signal, Fletcher was instructed to drive away and immediately alert the resistance leadership of the situation. Fletcher would explain that Leif's identity had been compromised, that he was or would soon be in German hands. Fletcher would immediately cut all ties with Leif and warn Bjorn, who would then advise the OSS leadership in London.

Leif nodded to Fletcher and said, 'It's time. Hans, we must do what needs to be done… the good of the many must prevail over the needs of the few.' Leif exited the Opel and crossed the cobblestone street towards the café. Time seemed to slow down for both Fletcher and Leif. One man walked towards the unknown and the dangers that may be present; the other watched his colleague and compatriot enter a potential gateway to hell on earth: a Gestapo trap.

Leif entered the café unmolested and within five minutes stepped back out with Sophie, his hat in hand – the signal that all was good. Fletcher breathed a sigh of relief, realizing that his whole body was tense and his brow and upper lip were covered in sweat. He observed from a distance as Sophie and Leif casually spoke for a moment, then turned to the right as planned and began to stroll away from Fletcher.

Fletcher sat in his car waiting another two minutes and then put the Opel into gear. He caught up with Sophie and Leif a few streets away. He slowed down as his vehicle came alongside the couple. He leaned over and rolled down the passenger window and greeted the two warmly, offering them a lift. With a smile and a nod of his head towards the car, Leif looked at Sophie expectantly and said, 'Shall we?'

With a casual gesture of his hand towards the rear passenger door, Sophie shrugged her shoulders and smiled innocently then moved towards the car. Leif opened the door for her and thought to himself, 'She is like a child and so naïve.'

Sophie had no idea what circumstances she had got herself into. To Sophie, Hans Fletcher's sudden appearance was nothing more than a pleasant coincidence – he was a well-known banker and a business acquaintance of Leif's. As she entered the car, Leif moved behind her and reminded himself that this woman was no longer a friend but a potential enemy and was dangerous – mission ending dangerous. Furthermore, he reflected, she was caught up in circumstances that made her desperate, and desperate people often made poor choices. There was a dangerous combination of factors at work in this situation and Leif knew that he had to take the initiative. He had to take bold, audacious action.

Horsens was a small town, and after five minutes of turns and twits the Opel had reached the outskirts of the town. It was a dark, cloudy evening and Sophie had difficulty identifying their exact location, let alone their possible destination. A few moments later, the Opel turned onto a side road, in a northwestern direction from Horsens towards the town of Skive. Sophie asked Fletcher where they were going. He did not reply. She turned towards Leif, her trusted companion with a questioning expression on her face, oblivious to the gravity of her situation. Silence. As the car continued along the dark country road and there was no response from Leif either, fear slowly gripped Sophie, her right hand moved instinctively towards the car door handle. Leif grabbed her left wrist firmly and spoke in a stern yet composed voice.

'Stay calm, Sophie', he said, 'if you ever want to see your family again, please stay calm.'

He gave her a moment to let those instructions sink in and then added,

If you cooperate, you will see the end of this war and will be reunited with your family – I promise. However, if you panic or try to escape, you will force us to take more immediate and drastic measures.

'Panic? Attempt to escape? Cooperate and see the end of the war?' Sophie stammered. Her voice began to rise. 'WHAT THE HELL ARE YOU TALKING ABOUT LEIF?' she demanded. 'LET GO OF ME AND STOP THIS CAR IMMEIDATELY – I WANT TO GET OUT!'

Leif's grip on Sophie's wrist tightened as the Opel continued along the dark side road transporting two silent, determined men and one young, frightened and confused woman, whimpering and unsure of what was happening to her.

It took them nearly twenty minutes to get to the safe house on the outskirts of the town of Skive. Given the sensitive nature and short notice of this mission – justifiable kidnapping in their minds – Bech and Fletcher had decided to call on one of the elder statesmen of the Danish Resistance network, Olaf Gustovson, a farmer who lived in the community of Skive, the same farmer who had unceremoniously greeted Leif at gunpoint, just two months earlier, when Leif had parachuted into Denmark. Since their initial encounter, Leif had learned that Olaf Gustovson was a highly respected man in the region, and though still agile at the age of 76, did not have the physical capability nor the aptitude to participate in more operational resistance missions. Olaf was a gentle man at heart, but a loyal Dane through and through. Leif was not surprised to learn that Olaf was willing to provide a safe and secure location to hold their PoWs until arrangements could be made to accommodate her on a more permanent basis – in a psychiatric hospital.

When the three travelers arrived at Olaf Gustovson's farm, Leif immediately escorted Sophie, sobbing and inconsolable, into the barn adjacent to the farmhouse. Ironically, this was the very same barn that Leif had landed on top of back in October during his parachute drop into Denmark. Meanwhile, Fletcher, who knew the Gustovson well, went to the farmhouse to speak to

Olaf and his wife of fifty-five years, Ragla. 'We will need to keep the young women, a collaborator here for two or three days at most.'

Initially, the plan was to shackle Sophie to a barn support beam with sufficient slack in her bindings to allow her to move a few feet and rest comfortably on the bed of straw but Ragla would not allow it.

> Regardless of what she may have done, the child will not be treated like an animal. She will stay here in our home, in the guest bedroom and that is final. She will be safe and comfortable here under our roof.

When Leif entered the farmhouse and was advised of the change of plans, he thought briefly of challenging Ragla's decision, but quickly realized he would not win such an argument. Ragla had made up her mind. After all, it was her home, and she and her husband were taking the risk and the responsibility of holding Sophie. He had to trust them. Fletcher indicated that he needed a couple of days to make arrangements with the two local doctors who would be required to sign Sophie's committal papers. The Gustovson's assured Leif and Fletcher that the girl would be safe and secure under their watchful eyes.

Two days later, Sophie was transported to the Skive psychiatric hospital. Sophie, the collaborator, would spend the remainder of the war at the sanatorium. The hospital's director was a trusted resistance member and ensured them that Sophie would be safe and cared for and would have access to only the most trusted medical staff who were either resistance members or at least dedicated supporters of the resistance. Sophie could rant and rave as much as she wanted about being 'falsely accused and abducted by the Danish Resistance', but it would do her no good. Sophie would be taken out of the equation and would live to see freedom once the war was won. It was a much better option than the alternative.

Orchestrating Sophie's disappearance in November 1944 was not a simple endeavor. Sophie's employer and friends were told that she had returned to Copenhagen due to the sudden illness of her mother. Meanwhile, Sophie's aunt and uncle with whom she had been living in Horsens, were told that even though Sophie had been trying to free her cousin she was considered a collaborator with the German occupiers and that time spent in the sanatorium was certainly better than the alternative: death. They were understanding of the circumstances and dutifully corroborated the story that Sophie had returned to Copenhagen to assist her father with the care of her ill mother.

Initially, Bech and Fletcher were most concerned about what Captain Trautermann's reaction to Sophie's sudden disappearance would be. The German captain and Sophie had dated more than a few times, so her unexplained absence would likely raise questions. However, their concerns were laid to rest when one week after Sophie's disappearance, Trautermann walked through the door of the Bygholm Park café where Sophie had worked and inquired as to her prolonged absence. The new waitress behind the counter innocently, and as far as she knew truthfully, told the young officer that Sophie had returned to Copenhagen to care for her sick mother. The German soldier considered this information as he looked around the café, then shrugged his shoulders, looked back at the new waitress, ordered a coffee and a pastry, and inquired, 'What is your name, miss?'

With Trautermann's attention drawn away from Sophie's whereabouts, both Bech and Fletcher had no further concerns about any inquiries regarding Miss Sophie, the naïve young woman whose actions almost branded her a traitor and who narrowly escaped a death sentence.

Sophie was safe from and forgotten by the Germans. And Agent Bech was free to continue his mission without fear that Sophie would reveal his true identity.

Chapter 21

Desperate Times, Deliberate Measures

'Desperation is sometimes as powerful an inspirer as genius.'

Benjamin Disraeli

With Sophie Halverson safely out of the way, Leif turned his attention back to the upcoming, two pronged mission to sabotage a German supply train and free a group of Danish Resistance members, including Sven Halverson,… from a Gestapo prison. The planning and coordination of such a complex and dangerous mission would call on all the cunning and bravery that Leif and his band of resistance fighters could muster.

At the end of Leif's briefing, he concluded with a well-known phrase from Greek mythology and the story of Daedalus and Icarus: 'We'll kill two birds with one stone.' Though not entirely accurate as a metaphor, as the origins of the phrase are believed to confer the impossibility of using one stone from a sling to kill two birds. None the less, both Gold and Bennike understood the juxtaposed meaning of Leif's chosen metaphor. Gold thought, 'This new OSS agent is good.'

Gold and Bennike were enthusiastic about Leif's plan. They sparked to the audacity and the element of surprise and distraction, always crucial elements in guerilla activity. Yet the most enthused was Fletcher, the resistance commander, who would get the dual good fortune of being responsible for rescuing his imprisoned comrades and doling out righteous punishment to the Nazis who killed, captured and tortured his people, his friends. If Leif's plan worked, Fletcher would have piquant revenge served cold.

It was the violent variable and the oscillating unknown, and Leif knew it was going to require more than a motivated resistance cell to execute a double pronged attack of this magnitude. On his first mission as Jørgen Bech, he was going to lead his people into the lion's mouth and order them to blow a German supply train off the rails, while another resistance cell attacked a Gestapo headquarters in an attempt to free fellow Danes who faced certain death. And it needed to happen in four days.

Leif knew he would need serious Allied support, specifically RAF support for the prison break plan to succeed. He knew who he needed to immediately contact,

Captain Casey, his former boss at the OSS's SI branch in London. Within the hour, via shortwave transmission, Leif outlined the given circumstances on the ground, the ticking clock and then laid out his plan. Casey – in a preview of his tenure as CIA director – loved it. Casey understood the tactical situation and embraced the bold plan and whether successful or not, these brazen attacks would infuriate the Germans and would undoubtedly draw more German troops away from the frontline – perfect.

Leif wasn't surprised. Casey thrived on risk and potential for disaster. It was easy getting him to agree on a plan that would make anyone else in his position – or right mind – fear for their career and personal standing. The only arms Casey would potentially have to twist belonged to the RAF. Using his connections with the British SOE to influence the RAF's Bomber Command, the stars aligned – the RAF had available resources and their pilots were positively elated at the chance to strike directly at the Gestapo – reports were widespread amongst the Allied intelligence about the atrocities being committed by these sadists.

The RAF would initiate a precision bombing raid on Gestapo headquarters located in the Danish coastal town of Aalborg with a flight of de Havilland DH98 Mosquito bombers, a low altitude flying craft used for fast supply transports or night raids. The Mosquitos most famous act – or infamous depending on which side of the war your sympathies laid – occurred on 13 January 1943, the tenth anniversary of the Nazi Party's seizure of power, when a prolonged Mosquito attack obliterated the main Berlin broadcasting station while Hermann Göring was invoking the inevitability of 1,000-year Reich and ripped his speech off the air.

After solidifying London's support and air raid for the ambitious undertaking, Leif turned the rail demolition plan over to Agent Bjorn Toller. His partner had three days to locate the best possible ambush location along the railway line and prepare the resistance team in demolitions, then one night to pre-position explosives on the railway tracks.

To best simulate the task before them, Agent Toller located a vacant and remote stretch of railway near the remote village of Jelling. The railway had not been torn up yet by the Nazis to recycle the iron and feed it to factories fueling their war machine. Bjorn drilled his team with up to the minute communications technology, including walkie-talkies operative for up to a mile. Then under dark of night, he had them practice laying explosives on the railway lines with only torches to guide them. To add real time tension and ingrain the potential for accidents, during a final dry run with his demolition team, Toller had arranged for Leif to suddenly appear out of the woods, shouting in German and firing off live rounds into the air. While the demolition team was still in a state of shock, Bjorn would start timing their recovery and then, based upon their results, explain how many of them would be dead.

Leif had an ulterior motive in making the trip to Jelling with Bjorn. Of course, he wanted to support his partner's efforts in whatever way possible, but Jelling was also the site of a historic shrine that held sacred meaning to Leif and the entire extended Sørensen-Bangsbøll clan.

* * *

It was in Jelling that King Harald 'Bluetooth' – Leif's ancestor – had in the tenth century erected two massive boulders with carved rune stones etched upon them. The first Jelling stone was to honor the king's parents, Gorm and Thyra, and the second was to celebrate his personal victory in winning control over all of Norway and Denmark. Many regard Bluetooth's rune stone as the country's 'Birth Certificate' because it marks the first time Denmark as a proper territorial designation appears, after the region's religious conversion from Norse Paganism to the Christian faith.

Leif, as a proud Dane, not Bech, the homeless OSS agent – who was currently the property of the United States Government – walked amongst the ancient monuments and felt a powerful connection to his past, one that went beyond shared history, and into his soul, his unconscious chemistry, stirring his blood. Like his ancestor Bluetooth, Leif was fighting for the existence of his people against crushing and potentially deadly odds.

Suddenly, he felt overcome with emotion, a pain in the center of his heart that drove him to his knees. It was fear, a final surge of weakness, a profound realization that he held many lives in his hands and that their continued ability to draw breath on this earth depended upon his tactical ingenuity. Him. A man of barely 25 years old.

Warm supplicant tears welling in his eyes. He called upon his blood lineage, the shared DNA across a millennium to guide him in his quest, then asked his mother and father for blessing. He would need his mother's artistic soul and his father's innate warrior instincts to find success in this potentially suicidal endeavor. Suddenly, he swore he felt and heard Frederik's words pass his lips, 'When the times have gone mad, the only guarantee for success is to be more insane than the times.' Leif rose to his feet, ran his shirt sleeve over his reddened eyes. 'Very well father', he thought, 'I will find my victory in the heart of this madness.'

* * *

To that end, Leif spent the next twenty-four hours performing a reconnaissance mission, riding the train along the planned ambush route of central Jutland, to determine the best location to attack the train. He was careful to maintain his guise of being on a business trip, stuffing his valise with signed contracts, which served him well when the Gestapo appeared at a stop to inspect papers and interrogate passengers. Leif submitted to a search of his person and briefcase and was quickly deemed unsuspicious by a clearly disappointed agent.

After spending the day traversing the main railway line in central Jutland, Leif decided on an isolated location of the railway line for the attack where the track made a relatively sharp turn about ten minutes south of the switching yard at Kolding, close to the town of Fredericia. The ambush site lent enough distance from the switching yard that the train would be at full speed and more likely to cause maximum destruction when it derailed.

Leif forced himself to sleep the night before the raid by mercilessly pounding both mind and body with Akvavit, but he still woke at the crack of dawn, and when he saw Bjorn at the maritime insurance office, it was obvious his colleague had tried the same approach. Neither of them looked fit to stand, let alone make business calls or process a claim, yet that is what the job entailed. To hold themselves above suspicion in Aarhus and its surrounding cities, their routine needed to appear entirely undisturbed and clockwork the morning before they attached the enemy. That said, the last thing they were up to involved insurance.

Leif spent the day activating his network of local operatives and informers, assigning them posts at specific points along the train's route, and paying them handsomely for their time. Bjorn then fitted them with short-wave radio equipment, so they could keep him updated on the German supply train's location and speed at regular intervals. Bjorn assembled the explosive packages and placed them in four separate canvas bags. Meanwhile, Fletcher assembled his team of assaulters who would attack the Gestapo prison in Aalborg.

The night was cold and crisp, a mid-December cold front pushing toward a Christmas frost, with an accompanying biting wind that burned against skin. Things were already off to an inauspicious start, technologically. One of the radio Bjorn dispatched to their people watching the switchyard had frozen after a few minutes of exposure, and the harsh wind gusts had rendered others mostly inaudible. For the first fifteen minutes, the twenty-strong resistance team didn't even know if the train had left the station, until finally, at the halfway mark of the train's journey, an informer's voice broke through the speaker on Bjorn's radio, announcing the locomotive had just passed their observation point, and then silence.

Leif, remembering his journey up and down Jutland, calculated that even with an unexpected stop, the train must be getting close, and it was time to set the explosives. Bjorn demanded, 'We need confirmation of the train's location.'

Desperate Times, Deliberate Measures 223

But Leif disagreed, 'The train is coming – get your demolition team going.'

Bjorn did not move and stared at Leif, restating his position with a slightly raised vice: ' Jørgen, we need confirmation that the train is on its way or we will waste this opportunity!'

Before Leif could respond or take a step forward to confront Bjorn, the radio crackled to life with a woman's soft voice: 'Ten-minute warning. This is your ten minute warning of the target headed your way.'

Leif and Bjorn looked at each other and the tension broke as they exchanged nods of recognition. Leif was correct that the train was only minutes away; Bjorn was right to demand confirmation but to also remind his headstrong partner that they worked better as a team.

Under Bjorn's supervision, the resistance cell sprang into action and laid two lines of charges on the outside rails of the curve in the railway line. When activated, the placement of explosives and the sheer force of the train's momentum would ensure it derailed and crashed into a ditch to the far side of the tracks. Leif assembled his assault team of twenty well-armed fighters who would be at the ambush site to protect the demolition team and respond to any threats from the surviving Germans who might be on board the train.

'It entering the curve', a voice squawked from Leif's radio, '1,000 yards from your position.'

Leif took a long inhale and listened. The sound of the on-coming locomotive could be heard, getting louder every second. Leif counted to twenty, stepped from his concealment in the tree line and looked down the track – the single light of the approaching locomotive grew larger. Leif turned and called towards the dark tree line, 'WAIT BJORN…WAIT…WAIT'…seconds passed aganizingly slowly until Bech shouted, 'NOW BJORN, NOW!' He shouted over the noise of the oncoming train. Bjorn pressed down hard on the 'T' handle of the plunger, which send an electrical charge racing through the copper wire to the explosives.

The resistance team saw the sudden flash of flames before the volcanic noise reached them. Leif's explosives ripped out 20 feet of railway just in front of the locomotive. It was dark but they could see the shapes of the locomotive and the first few railcars careen off its path. There was a fury of sparks and sounds of twisting metal as the locomotive plunged into the adjacent ditch dragging with it a succession of railcars, which tumbled, and flipped over, before coming to rest in a tangled mess with a cacophony of sounds of metal and wood bending and breaking in a defiant struggle of inertia. The end result was a massive, smoldering pile of bent steel, splintered lumber and shattered equipment.

Despite the darkness of the hour, as the dust and smoke began to clear, Leif could see that the ambush was not fully successful and that the resistance faced an unexpected and titanic problem. Only the first ten or so railcars had been derailed and destroyed. There appeared to be many more rail cars still upright on the tracks. Someone in Gold's intelligence network had miscalculated the number of railcars – this train was not twenty cars long; it was forty or possibly even fifty cars long! Now silhouetted by the fire emanating from the pile of crashed rail cars, Leif estimated that at least thirty, fully laden rail cars remained on the tracks and undamaged by the explosion and the derailing of the locomotive and the first portion of the supply train.

It was time to improvise. Leif knew very well that the resistance had to move in and destroy the remaining railcars before the German guards on the train could recover and mobilize an organized response. The shock of Bjorn's explosives wouldn't keep them stunned and restrained for long.

Leif, organizing his team of twenty, and leading them forward, down past the smoldering track wreckage towards the remaining rail cars still upright, shouted, 'ADVANCE, WE NEED TO TAKE THEM HEAD ON!' When they reached the intact railcars, he instructed his people to open fire, unloading full clips, stopping only to reload and recommence firing.

The hailstorm of Danish bullets punched gaping holes in the exterior of the railcars, shredding the wood and metal. The Germans guards, most of whom were unaccustomed to combat, or at least use to the quiet but begrudging cooperation of the Danes, quickly decided to abandon the train and retreat from the hail of Danish gunfire. Most of the German soldiers ran to the far tree line to seek cover, desperately seeking refuge from the relentless gunfire of the Danish Resistance. Those who remained on or near the train were mowed down by the resistance. Yet not every German surrendered to the resistance's onslaught. Many, now in the protective cover of the tree line, put up a spirited fight, returning heavy gunfire. And their attempt to hold the resistance force at bay was effective for a short time. They made it nearly impossible for Leif to advance his position, to get his people closer to the undamaged railcars. Leif sensed the futility in prolonging the firefight. The Germans wouldn't quit and Leif didn't want to risk his men getting injured out in this unprotected field. 'TOLLER!' he shouted, 'GRENADES AND MOLOTOV COCKTAILS – WE MUST DESTROY THE REST OF THE TRAIN!'

The resistance members threw everything they had at the railcars that remained on the track as Leif emptied his machine gun's clip to cover their withdrawal. Bjorn demolition squad pulled the pins and lobbed a dozen explosives and Molotov cocktails onto and under the remaining railcars, and they began to burn. Meanwhile, Leif and his team continued to fire and empty their ammunition clips towards the German defenders.

Suddenly, the German return fire lessened and then ceased all together. The battlefield's atmosphere went deadly quiet, save for the lapping of flames on the railcars. Then a torrential tattoo of German profanity and warnings could be heard emerging from the far side of the train. The German soldiers were bolting away as fast as they could – rushing deeper into the protection of the woods, away from the train. Leif squinted, assessing the German's sudden retreat. 'What the hell is making them run like that?'

Leif and Bjorn locked eyes – they suddenly understood the situation and shouted orders to their Resistance fighter.

MUNITION CARS! THE LAST RAILCAR MUST BE FILLED WITH MUNITIONS. PULL OUT! RETREAT! GET THE HELL AWAY FROM THE TRAIN!

Leif corralled his armed response team and they all rushed into woods on their side of the tracks and raced into the underbrush – putting as much distance between them and the conflagration of burning railcars, seeking anything to shield them from the inevitable blast and possible projectile shrapnel sure to come.

The first explosion erupted into a riotous chain reaction. Of the remaining thirty railcars of the shipment, twenty were carrying munitions and began to be ripped apart in a succession of blasts that launched them in the air or tore their insides out sending white-hot shrapnel in every direction. What remained of the railcars came to rest on their sides or severed into mewing metallic limbs, tossed asunder, each like a prehistoric beast in their last moment of life. The effect rippled like tipped dominoes and, within a minute, the remnants of the supply train was engulfed in fire and secondary explosions.

Leif looked up from his impromptu refuge of an oak tree at the edge of the tree line and watched the flames coil in a mix of orange, yellow and blue, the colors colliding like clashing tongues, while in the background a symphony of destruction, as the German munitions continued to rumble, cook-off and explode. The conflagration would burn until well into the next day.

Though the execution of the mission was somewhat different than planned, Leif had been the prime conductor, the moving force behind this chaos and felt the ungodly power of destruction in his vein's. His blood was pumping, his smile was wide and guilty and his prayer at the rune stones had worked. The young Dane had unleashed a higher form of madness against the already mad enemy. 'This is why', he thought, 'I was sent back to Denmark. This is what I was meant to do. This is what my people have done for centuries. We build new life upon the ashes of conquest and destruction.'

'Bech?' Toller's voice sounded through Leif's walkie-talkie from his position some 50 meters away, safe too within the cover of the forest. 'We've got to get out of here and fall back to the safe house.'

'We're on our way!' Bech said, giving the order to his group of resistance fighters that it was time to leave. Leif waited to ensure all his team were on the move ahead of him in their withdrawal – silhouetted by the inferno behind him, the shadowy figures of his colleagues spirited through the forest towards the safety of their waiting vehicles parked just ahead and the security of their safe house some 15 miles away.

Within minutes of the ambush and just as Bech's resistance team arrived at their safe house, reports from the Danish police and railroad officials at Fredericia and Vejle were received by the Wehrmacht regional headquarters, who, in turn, filled their radio airwaves with frantic messages to various German units in the area to converge on the ambush scene and set up roadblocks throughout the region. The Gestapo were also advised. Their headquarters in Aalborg was suddenly abuzz with activity, preparing their response to the bold Danish Resistance attack. And while they were reeling, attempting to process this completely unexpected visceral assault by the once ineffective Danish Resistance, dispatching Wehrmacht units and Gestapo agents to the blast site – phase two of the plan was about to be unleashed.

Fletcher felt the anxiety raising in his throat and looked at his watch, saying to himself, 'Come on, come on.' Unaware if Leif's ambush of the train and diversion had been executed as planned, Fletcher waited. He and his team of a dozen men crouched in the shadows of an alley two streets away from the Gestapo headquarters in Aalborg listened. First for the encroaching British aircraft, their cue to cut the telephone lines to the Aalborg prison and then for the bombs to make impact, their signal to commence the assault on whatever remained standing of the headquarters.

Moments later, four de Havilland DH98 Mosquito bombers, flying below radar detection, a few feet above the surface of the Baltic Sea, approached the quiet seaside town of Aalborg. A mile off shore, they pulled up in formation, to gain safe altitude to clear the sailboats in the harbor and buildings on the waterfront in preparation for their bomb release. Seconds later the Mosquito bombers unleashed fiery hell on the unsuspecting Gestapo headquarters and its staff and prison guards – direct hits. Debris was still falling when Fletcher shouted his order to attack. He and his men wasted no time approaching the now smoldering partially standing building, with weapons cocked and revenge at their fingertips.

The wounded Gestapo members and Germain prison guards, all in shock, many bloodied and suffering from lacerations and or broken bones, did not immediately capitulate, but mounted a feeble last stand at what remained of the prison's main entrance. The Germans were summarily overwhelmed by the unscathed and well-armed resistance fighters, who surrounded the remnants of the prison. The German defenders were felled without mercy and the resistance force raced into the wing of the building still standing, which contained the majority of prison cells in order to free the twenty Danish captives. Two detainees, of whom, ironically, had no association with the resistance, and were merely grateful local fisherman who had been arrested earlier that night at a local bar for drunken and disorderly conduct. Dazed and bewildered the Danish PoWs followed the instructions of their Danish liberators. As the resistance shepherded their grateful comrades-in-arms to safety, Fletcher was satisfied for the first time in months. He'd got his rightful retribution, redressed the wrongs, and felt justified and confident that he could lead his people once more.

A few of the escaping PoWs sustained minor injuries during their rescue, but remarkably, only one of the imprisoned inmates, Harald Sandbaek was seriously injured by the British air raid. Sandbaek, a long-time resistance member, was transported to a safe house on the outskirts of Aalborg for immediate medical attention and was subsequently secreted to the small port town of Grenaa for more extensive medical treatment. Concerned that the Gestapo would learn of his presence, as soon as he was able to travel, Sandbaek was smuggled onto a Danish fishing vessel and transported to Sweden where he remained until the war's end.

When Leif received the call from Fletcher that the Aalborg prison break had been successfully completed, Leif and Bjorn ordered their resistance teams to disperse and return home while they went back to the maritime insurance office to place a telephone call to Gold. The resistance leader was relieved and pleased with the fruits of Leif's operation, particularly the ruthless, pragmatic efficiency with which it had been executed. The German supply train, much larger than anticipated had been destroyed, the Danish freedom-fighters had been rescued and the resistance hadn't suffered any serious casualties.

Gold said,

I'm particularly impressed by your ability to think on your feet, Bech. This was a smooth bit of jazz you played, when the train turned out to have twice as many railcars than expected with twice the number of German guards I expect.

Leif explained that 'the men did well; they followed orders and did as they were trained.'

'Not many have the ability to switch tactics without hesitating.' Gold said, a warmth in his voice, a fatherly approval Leif always desired. 'And I apologize, my intelligence about the train was inaccurate.' Gold added. 'It won't happen again.' After a pause, Gold laughed, a genuine show of mirth straight from the belly, overtook the telephone line.

> The Germans had no idea what hit them tonight. They never expected such a brazen and brutal attack within the confines of occupied Denmark. You crushed them, humiliated them. This is supposed to be their land.

Gold's tone turned serious, cancelling his earlier exuberance: 'Of course, you realize what that means, don't you Jørgen?'
Leif was silent, swallowed hard. 'We changed the rules of the game, tonight.'
Gold continued,

> Upped the stakes on our occupiers. They are going to respond in brutal fashion. You need to be prepared, Bech. You made a declaration of war against our German occupiers. Like they say in American western movies: There's a new sheriff in town.

'I'm prepared, Mr Gold', Leif said, 'for whatever they throw at me.'
Gold's warning didn't take long to materialize. In fact, it took less than twelve hours. For Leif, the previous night's excitement would pale in comparison to his adventure the following day.

* * *

The next morning, despite being exhausted from the previous day's activities and to maintain an appearance of business as usual, Leif kept to his daily routine and walked from his modest apartment towards his office on Kannikegade Avenue in the port district of Aarhus. On his way, Leif stopped at a local café as he had done over the past few weeks and enjoyed a coffee and a small breakfast. Outwardly he looked calm but inside he was anxious to learn of the full results of the previous night's attacks and rescue mission. Leif knew that Bjorn would already be at their office, using his network of informants and shortwave radio to update the details on whether their mission had been a success. However, just a few streets from the café and just a short distance from his office, Leif was confronted with his own sudden – and potentially – deadly situation.
As he walked along the busy street, which was crowded with local Danes on their way to work, a German staff car with several officers and a troop truck full of Wehrmacht soldiers pulled up and blocked both ends of the street. The German troops scattered across the street ordering all the pedestrians,

Desperate Times, Deliberate Measures 229

approximately forty people in all, to move towards a vacant lot and to line up facing the wall for inspection of their identity papers.

This security routine was common throughout occupied Denmark. However, Leif assumed this particular German action was in direct response to the previous night's sabotage incidents and the attack on the Gestapo headquarters.

It was at that very moment that Leif realized he had made an extremely foolish and unprofessional mistake. The leather briefcase he was currently carrying for work had been used the previous night to carry some of the explosive charges he had used for the train sabotage mission. Inside the briefcase were, aside from some insurance company papers, two spare blasting caps, a chemical delay detonator, some electrical wire and a set of wire cutters – all clearly incriminating items and which, if found, would undoubtedly lead to his immediate arrest.

As Leif was forced to move with the crowd towards the vacant lot, he systematically scanned his surroundings looking for something that would offer at least momentary refuge from his situation. His mind was racing. Escape was impossible; there were just too many German soldiers in close proximity. In front of him, the pedestrians began to line up against the nearest wall at the edge of the vacant lot as instructed by the German soldiers. Leif walked towards the middle of the group of local civilians, stepping over piles of rubble where a building had once stood. As he approached the side of the large old red brick building, Leif continued to scan for possible courses of action. Then he spotted something between the many moving legs of the assembling people. He could see two ground-level basement windows in the brick wall they were facing – one window just off to his left and one to his right. He immediately selected the window on the left, which was furthest from the street and which had one of its four panes of glass broken and was missing a glass panel. This was his only hope. Trying to act nonchalantly, he casually adjusted his position in the line up so that the window was positioned directly in front of him, Leif placed his briefcase down on the ground and put his hands on the wall as they all had been instructed.

'Please God, don't let the window be locked.' Leif knew his next move must be completed quickly and seamlessly, without being observed by the Germans. He looked over his right shoulder towards the oncoming German soldiers who were inspecting the identity cards of the civilians at the far end of the line, while he simultaneously placed the toe of his shoe against the leather bag and began to push the briefcase forward, slowly scrapping along the dirt covered ground. The shouts of the German soldiers helped hide any noise Leif's bag made as it scraped the gravel covered ground. After a moment his leg felt resistance as the briefcase came in contact with the window. Cautiously looking first to the left and then to his right, Leif saw that the German soldiers were just a few yards away now, roughing up the civilian just four persons down the line. Leif applied more pressure with his foot against the briefcase, but it would budge no further. He had only seconds and tried again. Suddenly the window gave way. Hinged from the top and opening from the bottom, the window swung opened and the brief case tumbled through the opening with a muffled thud as it struck the floor inside the basement. The window swung shut to its original position.

Leif immediately looked again to his right – there was no reaction from the German soldiers. The sounds of the people milling around and being questioned had masked the briefcase's fall. Less than a minute later, Leif was handing over his false identity papers and answering all the soldier's questions using his politest formal German dialect. The Germans had not noticed the clandestine disposal of his briefcase and, thankfully, none of the Danish pedestrians closest to Leif noticed or mentioned the surreptitious act either.

A Gestapo officer, wearing a long, black leather coat approached and snapped his fingers at the soldier holding Leif's identity papers. Immediately the soldier complied and stepped back to allow the Gestapo agent access to his prey. The secret police officer leafed through the papers for what seemed like an eternity and then looked directly at Leif to verify the photograph matched the person. 'You are from Copenhagen?' he asked. 'Why are you here in Aarhus?'

Leif, again using the formal and politest form of German dialect, explained to the Gestapo officer his new insurance company's work opportunity that had brought him to Aarhus. Shuffling through the identity papers including his firm's letter of introduction to the Aarhus Chamber of Commerce once more, the officer appeared satisfied with Leif's identity and alibi for his presence, and Leif was given permission to proceed. Leif walked away from the scene, towards his office. As he rounded the next corner, Leif glanced back and saw several men from the crowd being detained and escorted to the waiting troop truck, while he, for now, was safe.

Leif walked the additional distance to his office and by the time he reached the doorstep his heart rate had almost returned to normal. The sweat on his back and under his arms felt cool and made his shirt cling to his upper torso. 'That is a mistake I will never make again.'

Leif, nervous throughout the day that someone might come upon his abandoned leather valise, left work early and retraced his route and retrieved his briefcase from the basement of the abandoned building, adjacent to the vacant lot where the Germans had searched and questioned him and the other local Danes that morning. After which, Leif walked through the narrow side streets of Aarhus towards his apartment, he mentally reviewed the advancements that the local resistance network had made since he and Bjorn had set up operations in Jutland.

> If last night's successful missions are an indication of what we are capable of planning and executing, then we just might make our German visitors very sorry that they have stayed in Denmark so long.

* * *

Sophie's cousin, Sven, was one of the eighteen imprisoned resistance members freed during that bold move against the Gestapo headquarters in Aalborg. For their own safety, the escapees were immediately relocated to distant and remote locations far from the towns of Aalborg and Horsens. Sven moved to Frederikshavn, on the north coast of Jutland, to live with a friend of the family for the duration of the war.

Sophie's aunt and uncle continued to maintain communication with Sophie's parents in Copenhagen to assure them that Sophie was alive and well. They told her parents that she was in hiding from the Gestapo as she had assisted in the resistance-led prison break mission that freed their nephew, Sven, and seventeen other Danes. It was a lie, but a good one to preserve the integrity of the story and keep Sophie's parents from making further inquiries that might jeopardize their daughter's safety and the resistance network's security.

Both Fletcher and Leif had agreed that for everyone's safety, Sophie's included, that Sophie should remain in the Skive Sanatorium until Denmark was liberated. She endured her incarceration in there and was released shortly after the end of the war. Her six-month stay in the sanatorium ended quite routinely when the two physicians who had committed her signed her release papers on the request of Hans Fletcher, the local resistance leader. Waiting to greet Sophie in the reception area of the hospital were her aunt and uncle, and her cousin, Sven. Content just to be free and thrilled at the sight of her cousin alive and well, Sophie accepted her imprisonment and subsequent release with quiet indignation. Eventually, Sophie would learn the facts of Leif's involvement in this strange wartime situation. Leif and Sophie never saw each other again.

Chapter 22

Christmas on the Run

'It is not for myself, or on my own account chiefly, that I feel the sting of disappointment, No! It is for my brave officers, for my noble-minded friends and comrades. Such a gallant set of fellows! Such a band of brothers! My heart swells at the thought of them!'

Lord Horatio Nelson, 1804

In early December 1944, Allied intelligence reports began to emerge, outlining a subtle but substantial assembly of various Wehrmacht units, including a Panzer division near the eastern boarder of Belgium. Dismissed by virtually all Allied intelligence experts as well as American commanders in the region, as just a defensive regrouping by the Germans, the threat was largely disregarded. Then, on 16 December 1944, a sudden and massive German counteroffensive began sweeping across Belgium, punching through the northern flank of the American front, by way of the dense Ardennes Forest – thought impregnable by the Allies. The sudden appearance of not only one, but two Panzer armies, the 5th and the 6th along with the 7th Army of the Wehrmacht put the Allies on the defensive and threatened their hold on western Europe. Additional German resources were being drawn in from across Europe, including Denmark, to support the German operation coded named Herbstnebel, meaning 'Autumn Mist'. The Battle of the Bulge, as it would later be known, was underway and was quickly going very badly for the Allies. If the Germans were successful with their objective of reaching the port of Antwerp, with their armored columns, it could prevent or significantly delay any chance of an Allied victory, leading to an extension of bloodshed and possibly force the Allies to consider a truce on Hitler's terms.

On 17 December 1944, unaware at the time of the German offensive in eastern Belgium, Leif received a communication from Gold, the regional resistance leader, indicating that an urgent and very large and important German supply shipment was scheduled to transit southbound from Copenhagen, through Jutland on 21 December 1944 to Germany, in order to resupply German troops embattled in the counteroffensive against the Americans in Belgium. Leif's orders were do everything in his power to prevent the train or any other

German resupply trains in Denmark from reaching German units engaged in this new and massive counteroffensive to the south.

Leif knew the German supply train would originate from the Kolding rail yard, which was the nearest station to the main German supply depot in Jutland. Leif spent a full day conducting reconnaissance missions under the guise of a business trip, to determine the best possible location for this ambush and the most effective placement for demolition charges to prevent the train from reaching its destination. Leif selected an isolated location for the attack, 10 miles west of Kolding and 2 miles east of the town of Lunderskov where the railway line turned south towards Germany. The location was far enough from the switching yard that the train would be at full speed and, therefore, more likely to cause maximum destruction when it derailed.

On the evening of the planned attack, Leif's network of local operatives and informers provided progress reports of the German supply train's location and speed. When the train had just passed the outskirts of Kolding, Leif gave the go ahead for the demolition team to plant their explosives. Four distinct and separate charges were used, all on the outside rails of the curve in the railway line, which would ensure the train would derail and crash into the ditch on the outside portion of the curve for maximum effect. Leif had also brought additional resistance teams to be close at hand in case the demolition team ran into trouble – as it had the previous month's supply train attack.

At approximately 2000 hours on 21 December 1944, on a dark remote area of the trans-Jutland railway line, the German army's supply train began to navigate a long curve. Just as it passed 100 yards after his position, Leif ordered the detonation of the explosives. With a sudden flash of flames and thunderous noise, the explosions ripped out 30 feet of rail just in front of the train. The locomotive careened off its path and plunged into the adjacent ditch, pulling with it a succession of railcars, which tumbled and crumpled with a deafening roar. The result was a massive, smoldering pile of bent steel, splintered lumber, shattered equipment and broken ammunition cases.

Wanting to ensure the complete destruction of the German supply train, Leif moved forward from his place of concealment in the tree line and yelled, 'GRENADES! THROW YOUR GRENADES NOW!' The dark tree line suddenly revealed dozens of Danish Resistance fighters moving forward towards the disabled train. Several resistance members had brought Molotov cocktails – crude but effective explosives – which upon striking the wooden railcars created a conflagration of flames, which quickly spread to adjoining railcars. Despite the sudden and violent assault by the resistance forces, the surviving German guards put up a spirited yet brief defense. Like their previous ambush of a German supply train, as soon as the resistance fighters' grenades detonated inside a railcar, which was loaded with ammunition and began to detonate the munitions, the Germans' will to fight quickly evaporated. The German soldiers who survived the initial assault retreated into the woods on the far side of the train. With Leif and several others methodically firing their machine guns into the woods this ensured that the retreating German soldiers did not change their minds. Meanwhile, the other resistance team members dispatched the remainder of their explosive charges into the remaining derailed railcars. A series of explosions followed as Leif and his raiders observed and began to withdraw, silhouetted by the orange glow of the flames and sounds of exploding ordinance burning behind them. Leif could not contain his obvious pleasure; his grin was wide and his blood was surging. 'Come on friends we must clear out of this area immediately.' Leif said. 'Those Krauts won't retreat for long and reinforcements will be called in to help search for us.'

Later that night, back at his office in Aarhus, Leif telephoned Gold, who was relieved and pleased with the outcome of the sabotage mission – the German supply train had been destroyed and the resistance had suffered no losses. Leif and his small band of shadow warriors needed to disappear – for the time being at least.

Unbeknownst to Leif, at the same time as his assault on the German supply train, hundreds of miles south, in the Ardennes Forest of Belgium, German and American forces were in a pitched battle over the strategically important city of Bastogne. The road through Bastogne led to the port of Antwerp, the largest deep-water port in Europe and an essential resupply route for the Allies' war effort. Only the American 101st Airborne Division and components of the 10th Armored Division stood in Hitler's way. Thanks in part to the work of Leif, Bjorn and their Danish Resistance forces, the needed shipment of German war supplies from depots in Denmark would never arrive and ultimately the Germans' last offensive of the war would grind to a halt.

However, as this historic battle raged on south of him, Leif was about to experience one of his most memorable and fondest wartime memories: Christmas 1944 – on the run from the Gestapo.

* * *

With their successful attack and destruction of the German supply train outside of Vejle completed, Leif ordered his teams to disperse, dissolve and disappear until the New Year. At the same time, the regional commander dispatched orders to provide potential safe houses for Leif's team in numerous locations throughout central Jutland. The responsiveness of the Danish Resistance network would be tested.

Leif and three of his team members were spirited out of Aarhus in the back of a postal van arranged by Bennike. Two hours later, early the next morning, they arrived at their safe house near the small village of Rønninge. The post van had a false wall within which Leif and his three resistance colleagues hid silently as they passed through a succession of German roadblocks. By midday, Leif and his colleagues were received cautiously by the owners of the safe house – a farming couple who would host the hunted for the next week. Leif, knowing the danger that the farmer and his family were in for helping the resistance, was polite and used his charm to assure both the farmer and his wife that he and his three Danish traveling companions would try to minimize the disruption to their daily routine. He convinced the farm owner that the spartan accommodations in the adjacent barn would be fine and the provision of food and water would be greatly appreciated. Leif insisted that he pay for their room and board and promptly gave the farmer a 2-inch stack of Danish Kroners, which would more than cover the expense and inconvenience created by the small resistance team's stay.

Given that the festive season was upon them, the local market owners would not be overly suspicious of the farmer's larger orders of food, wine and beer. Leif's companions spent 22 and 23 December 1944 resting and cleaning their weapons and recounting the activities of the past few weeks. While Leif paid close attention to the access road to the farm, he considered the probable route to their alternate safe house, which was approximately 6 miles east of their current location, towards the coastline. 'We should expect German patrols and must always be prepared with several options at our disposal.'

As the afternoon transitioned into evening, Leif's companions became noticeably bored and impatient. 'Exactly how long do we have to hide out here Bech?' asked one of his companions.

'A week, I suppose', he replied, 'I expect we can safely transition back to Aarhus amongst the crowds of post-holiday travelers.'

Clearly, this was not what his companions wanted to hear. Leif understood their frustration with the situation. After all, these men had families who lived less than a day's travel away from where they currently hid. Leif reassured them that he would be in communication with the regional commander that evening and would provide an update on the current situation. In the time being, he would go see their hosts – more specifically, the farmer's wife – about getting some food to quiet his hungry men.

The next morning, Leif accompanied the farmer into the town of Rønninge to place a telephone call to Bennike. During their drive into town, Leif noticed a newspaper on the floor of the truck. He leaned forward to pick it up and immediately noted that it was a copy of the *Reality*. It was an illegal publication, printed in defiance of the occupying Germans and given away for free.

Leif looked at the farmer as they drove and asked mildly, 'You know you could be arrested just for having this newspaper in your possession?'

The farmer retorted,

> I'm sure the authorities, especially the damn Gestapo, would be far more interested in you being in my truck than that anti-German propaganda newspaper.

The two men chuckled, and Leif threw the newspaper out of the window.

'True', Leif said, 'but no need bringing unwanted attention to us, is there?' Leif watched the newspaper in the side view mirror flutter and scatter in the breeze by the roadside behind them.

When they arrived in the village and before entering the post office to use the public telephone, Leif handed the farmer another substantial sum of Kroners and told him to purchase a goose for his family and one for his men. 'Buy some beer too, and if you can find a bottle of Akvavit, we would be most appreciative.' Christmas in a barn could be made a bit more comfortable with some good Danish beer and schnapps, he reckoned.

Leif reached Bennike by telephone and reported their situation, assuring him that he and his members of the team were secure and well cared for. Leif learned that the German supply train had been totally destroyed, making the mission a complete success. Disruption of railway lines had become a major issue for the Wehrmacht and rumors had been circulating that the commander of the German forces in that region of Jutland had been ordered back to Germany, probably to be reassigned to the dreaded Eastern Front as a result of his inability to quell the unrest in Jutland. As well, Leif learned that Bennike had received confirmation that Bjorn and his members of the team were also safe, having taken refuge at their designated safe house in the town of Ødsted. Leif and his team were to remain in their current location near Rønninge until 2 January 1945, at which time, if no further orders were received, they were to make their way back to Aarhus. There, Leif would return to work at the insurance office, where Bjorn would join him.

Relieved at the news, Leif was able to provide his colleagues with an update and his assurance that they would be heading home soon, probably on 2 January 1945. The question was, how would he keep them focused and content until then?

Leif met back up with his host and noticed that in the bed of the truck there were several large packages wrapped in brown paper and tied with twine, as well as a wooden crate full of Danish beer. Leif gave his companion a wry smile and said, 'You have been busy, my friend.'

'As have you', replied the farmer, 'I understand that there were some recent activities in Jutland, a couple of railway accidents and a prison break in Aalborg that you might be aware of?' he continued, with a knowing glance at his Leif, who was not sure if he should acknowledge his involvement in these recent missions, but chose to be truthful with his host, as he seemed about as honest and loyal a Dane as he had ever met. 'The supplies on that train we just destroyed will never get to the German troops fighting our Allies.' Leif explained,

> And those men we liberated from the hands of the Gestapo held in the Aalborg prison were either loyal Danish Resistance members defending our country from the German invaders or were just innocent Danish citizens who had been falsely accused by the Gestapo. Either way, they deserved our help.

The farmer nodded and said, 'Long live King Christian.' The farmer smiled and added, 'We had better be on our way.' Nothing more was said on the subject.

Upon arriving at the farm, both Leif and the farmer noticed activity at the side of the barn. They were cautious on their approach, fearing danger, but upon closer examination they realized that it was two of Leif's men working on the farmer's tractor, which, according to the farmer, had been running roughly and slipping gears recently. One of Leif's team was a mechanic and had spent the afternoon adjusting the carburetor and gear box and he now had the tractor running like new. Another of his men was in the farmhouse helping the hostess prepare for the Christmas Eve meal, washing and peeling potatoes, beets and turnips. Thrilled at the sight of two large geese for roasting instead of the chicken she was intending to slaughter from their own coop, the lady of the house, with her new helper, prepared the large birds and put them into the oven to roast. Within the hour, the drafty old farmhouse began to smell wonderful. Candles were lit, cold beer was offered, and it all felt a little bit like home.

The farmer's wife instructed their daughter to set the dining room table for eight people – the four family members and their four guests. Leif politely stepped forward to prevent the young girl from leaving the kitchen. 'We thank you kindly for the offer to dine with your family on this festive eve', he said,

> but I regret we cannot join you. We will gladly accept the food and drink you have prepared and will retire to the barn to allow your family to enjoy the pleasure of each other's company here at your dining table.

Not intended at an insult, Leif was uneasy about the level of German troop activity he had noticed while in town earlier that day and wanted to ensure that if the Gestapo were to pay a visit to their hosts' home, that they would not find a dinner table set for eight when only four people were reported living there. This was not the first time his uncanny ability to sense danger had served him well. Remarkably, less than two hours later, just as the farmer's wife was retrieving the roast geese from the oven, a young boy, a local resistance messenger rode his bicycle to the farmhouse and reported that a German patrol and possibly the Gestapo were searching several nearby homes and farms. Without a moment's delay – except for the time it took to bid farewell), the farmer's wife wrapped one of the roast geese in a burlap bag and put a couple of bottles of beer into each of their jacket pockets and with a sadness in her eyes wished them a merry Christmas. The four resistance members then gathered their weapons and made their way out the back door into the field towards the distant tree line.

Leif and his three companions trudged along the dark, wet and winding trails that crossed numerous fields and streams and small patches of forest, bypassing and avoiding all villages and houses along the way to their alternate safe house. At one point, as they approached the outskirts of the village of Nyborg, their destination, they observed a small convoy of German army trucks approaching from a distance. With quick and silent hand signals from Leif, the resistance members dispersed and took up positions on either side of the roadway, concealing themselves in the hedges with their weapons at the ready. Leif had no intention of engaging the enemy out here in unfamiliar terrain but had to be prepared to do so if the convoy were to stop and dismount troops near their present position. The three German trucks approached and, without incident, continued southward towards the town center at the port of Nyborg. Once the German convoy was out of sight, Leif retrieved the burlap sack, which contained their Christmas goose from behind the hedge and then gathered his small team together. 'Let's hope those trucks did not just drop off German troops anywhere nearby.'

It was almost 2100 hours and the light snow that had begun an hour earlier now began to fall more heavily. With their visibility reduced to just a few yards due to the developing snowstorm, the four resistance members approached their destination, a small, seaside inn on the southern outskirts of the village of Nyborg. As they neared their alternate safe house, their collective anxiety rose to an uncomfortable pitch. They knew that German troops were nearby and that they were all in unfamiliar territory with only the resistance network to assist them. Was this a trap? Were the Germans waiting for them?

Leif handed the burlap bag with their goose to one of his men, then passed his Bren gun over to another, telling them to look after both important items.

'I'm hungry', Leif whispered, with a grin and a wink, 'and we have a dinner date with that goose later tonight.' He instructed one of his colleagues to find a hidden and protected location to cover the front door of the inn and to be prepared to fire his weapon at anyone following Leif if he came running out. He sent the other two to cover the back entrance of the inn. They were all told to await Leif's all clear signal – a light flashing on and off three times. If after thirty minutes the signal was not sent, they were to assume that Leif had been apprehended and they should slip back into the darkness of the night and make their own way to an alternate place further down the coast for the night.

His team prepared, Leif turned towards the inn and took a moment to gather himself. Unsure of what awaited him in this 'safe house', his mind cycled through possible scenarios that he might face in the next few seconds. The snow had turned to sleet, and the weary resistance members were cold and damp as they crouched in the darkness watching their leader attempt to make contact with their new safe house host. Nerves were on edge. Leif collected his thoughts and moved out of the darkness towards the inn.

Leif reached the veranda of the inn, looked back towards the dark tree line where he knew his colleague was watching him, gave a nod and entered the inn. As he stepped into the foyer, he noticed that no one was behind the reception counter, but voices could be heard emanating from the adjacent room, which was the inn's restaurant and bar. Leif stood in the hallway considering his options, then he began to transform himself. He unbuttoned and then rebuttoned his jacket, purposely misaligning the buttons with the corresponding holes and loosened his tie. He then briskly rubbed his hands in his hair to complete the disheveled look as he adopted the air of a harmless drunk before entering the restaurant.

Leif stumbled into the room, nudging a table as he passed, which noisily rattled the place settings, while he inconspicuously scanned the room for threats. There was a man and a woman eating supper at a table. They were probably no threat. An old man at the bar, again, probably not a threat. But there, in the corner, two men in suits sitting at a table with drinks. 'They could be trouble', thought Leif. 'Gestapo?'

As he staggered up to the bar, he ordered a beer from the bartender who was also the inn's owner – and Leif's safe house contact. Continuing to feign drunkenness, Leif asked if there was a room available for the evening. Leif went onto explain that he was a maritime insurance employee and had missed the last ferry from Nyborg to Korsør and would need to find accommodations for the night before continuing to Copenhagen the next day.

This was the code scenario that the innkeeper was expecting – an insurance agent traveling to Copenhagen who had missed the night ferry. With a moment's hesitation, the innkeeper replied that regrettably he had no vacancies for the night. Surprised by the response, Leif looked closely at the innkeeper whose eyes were fixed past him on the two men sitting at the back of the bar. When the innkeeper looked back at Leif, the message was clear: it is not safe here.

In a voice just loud enough for the two Gestapo agents to hear, the innkeeper announced that he would call for a taxi that could take him back into town to a suitable hotel. Twenty minutes later, the three compatriots, who were diligently waiting outside the inn and who had begun to be concerned about their situation, were alerted when a taxi pulled up to the inn. Now pretending to be drunk, Leif was helped by the innkeeper towards the waiting taxi. 'Get in the taxi from the side facing the inn and slide out the other side and then hide in the ditch.' Leif staggered towards the vehicle with the assistance of the innkeeper. 'I expect the Gestapo will follow the taxi if they want to speak with you. I will come get you in a few minutes either way.' Leif slipped a few hundred Kroners into the innkeeper's hand as the innkeeper spoke to the taxi driver. 'Take this drunken fool to the Nyborg Arms Hotel. Make haste, he may be sick to his stomach at any time.' He handed the driver the wad of money that Leif had just given him and winked, before wishing Leif and the taxi driver a merry Christmas.

Just as the innkeeper slammed the passenger door shut, Leif slipped out the opposite passenger door, closed it quietly and dashed in a low, hunched run into the darkened ditch. There he waited motionless as he watched the taxi depart. Leif's colleagues cautiously cocked their weapons in preparation for a possible enemy engagement. No sooner had the taxi driven off when the two Gestapo agents appeared at the doorway and inquired as to the destination of the drunken traveler. The innkeeper apologized to his customers for disturbing their evening and acted annoyed at the drunk's conduct. He told the two German officials that he had recommended the Nyborg Arms Hotel as they had more availability than most inns at this busy time of year. With that, the two Germans got into their staff car and proceeded towards town in pursuit of the taxi.

Leif re-entered the inn and gave his worried colleagues the all clear signal with the back door porch light. Then he and the other three agents met with the innkeeper in the kitchen to discuss their situation. 'Clearly you cannot remain here.' said the innkeeper.

> Although my friend, the taxi driver, will give a good account and say that his sick, drunken passenger was left on a street corner in town, the Gestapo may come back here tonight to ask further questions.

'Let me make a telephone call.' The innkeeper motioned Leif to follow him. Within thirty minutes, arrangements were made for the small resistance team to hide out at a vacant cottage a few miles further down the coast from the inn. The innkeeper drove the four agents, their roast goose and their beers to the small cottage overlooking the ocean. It was an ideal location, as it had only one long, exposed driveway from which approaching vehicles could clearly be seen well in advance of their arrival.

As the four agents thanked the innkeeper for his assistance, he wished them all merry Christmas and pulled out a bottle of Alborg Akvavit from his coat pocket. With a look to Leif, he uncorked the bottle and offered him the first swig. Each man took a drink and shook hands with the innkeeper. The innkeeper left the bottle of Akvavit and drove away with the understanding that he would return with food as soon as he could – likely in a day or so.

Leif did not like the idea of hiding sheepishly from the enemy in this remote cottage. However, he knew that they must be prepared to slink away into the shadows for a time if they were going to continue their missions back in central Jutland. Strangely enough, it was not the fear of being killed or even of being captured that gave Leif the most concern, it was the fear of being taken out of the fight. He had recently heard of a fellow OSS agent named Jensen Schmidt (codenamed Birch) who had been operating in southern Denmark and had been forced to flee Denmark when his underground network was infiltrated by the Gestapo and his father imprisoned and ransomed for Birch's surrender. That scenario hit too close to home for Leif, so he turned his thoughts to getting a fire started and some food in their stomachs. Within the hour, the four weary men were sitting around the fireplace listening to the calming sound of the crackling fire. Leif enjoyed the soothing, almost hypnotic effect of the flickering firelight that created shadows that danced across the cabin's walls and ceiling. The beers were opened and consumed, and the delicious goose, though cold and somewhat battered by its six-hour trek across the Danish countryside, was devoured with great delight.

The remainder of that evening, 24 December 1944, was spent huddled around the warm hearth of a stone fireplace in the abandoned cottage by the sea, on the outskirts of Nyborg, Denmark. Melancholy to be so far from family on Christmas Eve, Leif enjoyed the opportunity to really get to know the brave men he had been working with these past few weeks. During his first two and a half months working with the Danish Resistance, Leif had had little time to get to know these men on a personal basis. These young men all had lives of their own. They were sons, brothers, fathers and uncles. Tonight, with food and drink beside a warm fire they would form a bond, not just as soldiers, but as men, men with families and loved ones celebrating this Christmas Eve without them.

That evening, each member of the team took turns on sentry duty at the window, watching the access road for any approaching danger, which thankfully never came. As the beer and Akvavit supplies were consumed, they relaxed more, and each took turns recounting their families' Christmas traditions and their favorite memories of Christmases past.

One of Leif's colleagues spoke of his family's traditional holiday menu, which included his companion's favorite meal: fishcakes. Though Leif enjoyed hearing about and respected his colleague's reminiscences, he could not help but be amused by the mention of this traditional culinary entre. Leif recalled that as a boy, fishcakes were too often a staple of the Bangsbøll family's dinner menu. Leif thought of the many times he had secretly removed the dreaded food item from his dinner plate and temporarily hidden it or wedged it under the table top in order to dispose of the evidence after dinner.

As the tenuous yet progressively tranquil evening passed into night and the night passed into the early morning hours, the conversations grew more subdued and introspective, more sentimental. Leif felt a sense of calm that his small part of this war was, at least for this night, at peace. This night was about the fellowship between comrades-in-arms remembering the peace, love and fellowship of Christmases past with their friends and family. Nonetheless, the stress of not knowing if they were truly safe or just on the verge of being captured by a merciless enemy remained ever present – especially an enemy who would not convey the courtesies of the Geneva Convention as a captured combatant soldier, but rather, treat one as a lawless spy, as an enemy of the state and, as such, have no limits to their cruel forms of retribution. But that night, far from friends and family they felt triumphant in their successes against their enemy and thankful for each other's company.

At the approach of dawn, Leif completed his second sentry duty of the night. He woke his replacement, who was asleep on the couch, with a gentle nudge of his shoe. Leif then found a comfortable corner of the cottage to get some rest. He leaned back into the over-stuffed armchair, looking upwards at the wooden rafters of the ceiling and thought to himself, 'Well this is quite an adventure.'

It had been just under three months since he parachuted into Denmark. He had established himself as an effective OSS agent and gained the confidence of the local and regional Resistance leadership, not to mention the respect of the Danish freedom fighters themselves. He and Bjorn had trained over sixty new recruits and had completed two successful sabotage missions without any direct casualties.

Yes, there had been no direct casualties that he knew of. However, there were those who suffered from the collateral damage of his actions. Leif was consumed by the thought that other resistance fighters, their family or friends had been caught up in the Gestapo's web of investigations and midnight searches of homes following the two sabotage missions that he had led. Their loss and suffering would weigh heavy on Leif's shoulders as he contemplated the magnitude of the Gestapo's response on the helpless local Danish population. It was a weight that he would have to bear if he were to complete his mission and a weight that would continue to increase until this work was done and every German soldier and secret police were killed, captured or retreated back to Germany.

* * *

Leif's final conscious thought before drifting off to sleep was a memory of a Christmas dinner as a child in Copenhagen, where he and his little sister Inge sat across the table from each other with their mother and father serving them delicious Christmas treats. He could picture his father carving the goose, his mother serving vegetables and freshly baked bread. The fireplace crackled and the candles flickered. Leif could almost smell the food. It was delightful. That evening so long ago, young Leif had brought a couple of his favorite painted lead toy soldiers to the dinner table and lined them up in front of his dinner plate. There they stood as if on parade. They had been a Christmas gift from his father, and he cherished them. Now, in the mind's fog between wakefulness and slumber, Leif hovered momentarily. The tired soldier began to drift off to sleep and somewhere from the depth of his subconscious he asked himself, 'My toy soldiers, where are my beautiful soldiers? Father, Father, are you safe?' Then the heavy, yet unimaginably soft veil of sleep enveloped the tired, young warrior and all was dark and quiet.

Chapter 23

The Reckoning

'Armies do not always suffice to save a nation,
while a country defended by its people is ever invincible.
And a nation fighting for its liberty, ought not to adhere
rigidly to the accepted rules of warfare.'

Napoléon Bonaparte, 1820

Autumn 1944 had been a period of uninterrupted advances for the Allies, as they broke out of the Normandy region preparing to push further across France, Belgium and the Netherlands. In conjunction, knowing that Denmark would be the next occupied country to be liberated, the OSS in London stepped up their resupply orders to the Danish Resistance, doubling their size and frequency, ensuring their shadow warriors were well equipped with weapons, ammunition, radio technology and Allied uniforms, concentrating their efforts heavily in Copenhagen, where the Wehrmacht and Gestapo housed their central quarters, which would be essential to retake for victory.

The orders to resistance cells through the region were clear and concise. Drive the spike into the Germans and make them bleed and watch over their shoulders every moment of every day and night.

Unfortunately, the increase in resistance activities in Jutland, thanks to the OSS's additional resupply missions to Leif and the other Danish Resistance cells had ramifications; namely a redoubled vigilance by German security forces, leading to a significant rise in Gestapo interception rates and casualties on both sides. Brutal firefights, casualties and the capture of resistance members became more common practice. The covert war, the intelligence war, fought far away from the battlefields was getting bloody ugly.

* * *

By mid-January 1945, it seemed as if all the hard work, the Allies heroic sacrifices, had not been in vain. Germany was weakening, militarily retreating, though not in disorder – the Wehrmacht was still a powerful and professional army – not prone to panic or disorder. However, the Wehrmacht was beginning to gasp for oxygen and relied more heavily on nationalistic dreams. Hitler was facing increased disillusionment, if not outright revolt from his generals, while many soldiers were deserting and surrendering to the Allies in growing numbers.

With the victory at Bastogne, thanks to the 101st Airborne Division and General George S. Paton's Third United States Army, the painful lessons of the Battle of the Bulge still fresh in their memory, the Allies regrouped to continue their push towards Berlin. In hindsight, they could have benefited from Clifford Henry's golden rule: 'in facing near ruin, Germans will always elect to leave all their blood on the ground rather than admit defeat.'

* * *

Leif had just hung up the telephone with Gold, the regional resistance leader, when the German staff car, with Major Manfred Schmidt, the commander of the central Jutland region sitting in the back seat, pulled up in front of the maritime insurance company in Aarhus just after 0900 hours on the 20 January 1945.

'Hello, Heir Bech', the uniformed officer said, while scanning the room. 'I'm Major Manfred Schmidt.' Major Schmidt was an imposing site. Large in stature – 6 foot 2 inches in height, dressed in a well pressed uniform with several rows of ribbons, including the prestigious Iron Cross, which adorned the throat of his starched collar.

'Jesus Christ', Leif thought, 'was the Wehrmacht listening in on his telephone line? And if so, their response time was impressive.'

'I'm the garrison commander in the Horsens Aarhus area.' Schmidt continued. 'Do you have a spare moment for a chat?'

Leif thought, 'I don't want to talk to this Kraut at any time.' But he got up from his desk and beckoned Schmidt to sit with him. He lit a cigarette and searched for an object to focus on, an OSS trick to help him organize his racing thoughts. 'Have the German's somehow connected me to the two train sabotage missions last month?' Leif realized that it could be any number of events or activities he had been involved with the resistance over the past three months that could have led to this encounter with this German major. The Germans may have connected the dots that with the arrival and opening of Leif's insurance brokerage firm from Copenhagen – the heart of the Danish struggle – that resistance activity had doubled, if not tripled here in Jutland, with far more success than before. 'It doesn't matter what brought him to my door', Leif thought, 'none of the explanations bode well for me.'

> Heir Bech, I understand that you were recently detained by my colleagues during a routine identity sweep, and that you had moved here to Aarhus from Copenhagen recently?

Schmidt continued,

> I make it my business to know everything that goes on within my little slice of Denmark. I frequent the restaurants, go to the quaint shops, befriend all the owners. And today, I'm on my regular perambulation and wanted to meet the new businessman in town. Welcome. Maritime insurance is it?

Leif dragged hard off a fresh cigarette trying to hold back the acid rising from his stomach and burning a trail up his throat. He was under no illusion this impromptu visit meant life or death. 'Yes, mostly maritime insurance and brokerage our office in Copenhagen wanted to expand into Jutland, so here I am.' Leif replied.

'The name Bech', Schmidt continued, sitting down, 'this is a Germanic name, is it not?'

Leif focused on the impressionist painting passed Schmidt's head, behind which, in a false wall, he and Bjorn hid their heavy weapons and short-wave radio. If at any point the conversation with Schmidt went off the rails, Leif would turn the conversation to art and offer to show him the piece up close, and then kill him. Such a drastic and overt action against a German commander would surely end Leif's clandestine status here in Denmark – if he survived, he'd probably be ordered back to Britain. Leif was mentally considering his options, having seen what the German method of interrogation entailed. Ironically, the notion of killing Schmidt allowed Leif to find the mental space he needed to play the major's little game. To volley back from his side of the net, he replied in note-perfect German, 'Yes, my family is originally from Hamburg. After the Furst World War my grandfather moved us to Copenhagen to start a new life.'

The major could not repress a smile upon hearing his native tongue spoken with such effortless fluency. It reminded him of home.

'My family roots are still firmly planted in Germany, Major Schmidt.' Leif said. 'I'm a proud German at heart. Although, I love this little Scandinavian nation of Denmark.'

'Heir Bech', Schmidt said, his heart warmed, 'I too have fallen for the simple charms of this jewel on the Baltic. I especially enjoyed my time in your capital.' Schmidt, enjoying this repertoire of an interrogation, decided to join Leif in smoking and extracted a cigar from his tunic breast pocket, 'You see Heir Bech', he continued, snipping off the end of the cigar with a steel cutter, then dropping the severed end in Leif's ashtray, where it whirled around like an acorn on a blustery day, 'I arrived as part of the initial invasion, excuse me, liberating forces back in 1940.' He lit a long match on the side of the desk, then ignited the cigar, letting the leaves inside burn and pop, puffing hard to build up a solid glowing top and filling the office with its sweet, pungent aroma.

> Initially, I was assigned to our headquarters in Copenhagen for almost a year, before being transferred to Jutland and given the responsibility of managing the region's affairs. Then I spent an appalling year on the Eastern Front and was fortunate enough to be reassigned here.

Leif responded, flattering Schmidt's sense of himself, 'Those were quite challenging responsibilities I'm sure.'

'Yes, this was a good promotion', Schmidt said through a smoke filled grin, 'and I like to believe I've earned my commander's faith in my abilities and loyalties.'

'Herr Major, from what I understand, you've done far more', Leif retorted, having found Schmidt's soft underbelly – 'God he's vain' –

> though I've only been in business here in Aarhus for two months, I'd heard a great deal about you from the local business community and understand that you are a fair and reasonable officer.

Schmidt was thrown back on his heels, shocked by Leif's brazenness.

> I care very little what the local rabble think of me, as long as they comply completely with my orders and the will of the Führer – without question or hesitation.

'Yes, I understand major.' Leif said softly, showing no hint of recalcitrance.

Schmidt smiled, noticing the submissive change in Leif's demeanor. Storing it up as a code to be deciphered later. 'I imagine you can. Yes, I do.' He slid his chair further from Leif's desk and crossed his legs, showcasing his tall, shiny leather boots. 'So, the head office of your agency is located in Copenhagen – yes?'

Leif nodded. 'Yes, it is.'

'And where exactly is that office?'

'There it is.' Leif thought.

> The subtle end to the pleasantries and the quick swing into direct questioning. I forced his hand, made him go here faster than he'd wanted. But there's a problem, I see it in his eyes: he wants to like me. He wants to test me harder and faster than most because he wants a friend, a Germany ally. He doesn't want to arrest me.

Leif replied, '242 Gothersgade Straße.'

'Yes. Oh yes.' Schmidt said, looking pensive for a moment. 'Then it is of course close to the Scandic hotel. Yes?' Then added, 'That is the very first place I stayed when I arrived in Copenhagen back in April 1940.'

'The Scandic is a glorious, historical hotel.' Leif said, preparing his second volley over the major's net.

* * *

But I believe, Heir Major, you may be misremembering. The Scandic Hotel is not near our offices on Gothersgade Straße. The King Christian IV Hotel is the closest and nicest hotel to my firm's head office.

The major's face was blank. 'You're quite sure about that, Heir Bech?'

'Quite positive.' Leif retorted, with an air of confidence while staring out the office front window to the street. 'Are there German soldiers waiting out there for the signal from Major Schmidt?' thought Leif.

'I'm not certain I agree.' Schmidt was doubling down, trying to shake Leif's confidence.

'Heir Major', Leif said, forcefully, 'it's the King Christian Hotel.'

A small stitch popped in the tight purse of Schmidt's mouth. 'The Scandic? What was I thinking, Heir Bech?' He slammed the flat of his open hand on the desk. 'What was I thinking? ... Of course, you are correct, it is the King Christian Hotel that I was thinking of.'

Leif smiled and relaxed as he crushed his cigarette in the ashtray. 'Men in our line of work... men rolling a Sisyphean rock up a hill every day, we cannot be expected to retain every little detail. Can we?' They both laughed. But the major laughed, feigning understanding of Leif's reference to the story of Sisyphus and its place in Greek mythology was clear to Leif. 'He's a braggard', thought Leif. 'He's unable to accept the fact that someone else knows more than he.'

Schmidt stared at Leif for an awkward moment, assessing the verbal exchange they just had. 'This Leif is sure of himself, is respectful but does not seem to fear me.' The German major's demeanor flipped like a switch and was suddenly upbeat and solicitous. Leif had passed his test. Schmidt had already done his research through his Gestapo contacts in Copenhagen, verifying Jørgen Bech's life, school records and work background in the capital – it all checked out thanks to the detailed cover story with falsified records, which the OSS, SOE and the resistance had created and planted in expected search locations in Copenhagen. Leif was a conscientious Dane and an ambitious, up and coming maritime insurance broker. But most importantly, he was German by birth and appeared to be loyal to the Fatherland.

Schmidt declared,

> Countrymen is what we are, Heir Bech. And as fellow devotees of the Fatherland, allow one German to take another to lunch this afternoon. We can talk further about this lovely, yet sometimes troubling country we both call our temporary home.

The major lowered his voice to a hoarse whisper,

> And perhaps, as a personal favor to a fellow German, you could lend me your assistance on some local matters, to help ensure peace for the fatherland in Denmark.

Leif rose from the desk, extended his hand to cement their budding relationship. 'It would be honor and pleasure major. And I insist you let me take you to lunch.'

Leif had found his opening, a way to gain intelligence from the local German commander and plant disinformation in return. In an instant, Leif knew that he was going to use Schmidt to set his trap to eliminate a traitor and collaborator, Ivar Nielson. It was a fraught move, like juggling knives, but worth the risk. He was flying blind now, improvising as he went – just like his instructors at Camp X had taught him. He would have to rely on his own skill set and intuition in this new, dangerous relationship with Schmidt. There was no time to report his plan up the chain of command to Gold or get OSS leadership in London to agree – Leif was going to engage and use a German commander in some complex skullduggery to achieve his mission objectives.

Leif's two-hour meal with Schmidt that afternoon, which included several beers each and two shots of Akvavit, plus half a pack of shared cigarettes, was illuminating on several levels. First, Schmidt was clearly a dedicated chain smoker, but to avoid a lecture on bourgeois vices from his elitist peers, he switched to cigars. Also, the major conveyed and underlying frustration by the impenetrable style of Nazi bureaucracy and clearly had misgivings about their ability to prosecute the war to a successful end, even if the tide seemed to be momentarily turning back in the Germans' favor. 'It's working', Leif thought, 'I've become his psychiatrist. He's bonded to me.'

But it took until dessert before Leif could began his disinformation campaign against Nielsen, when the major asked what he thought – as a business owner – of the local transportation infrastructure. Leif lit another cigarette and slowly pontificated, spinning the big lie.

Quite frankly, I'm terribly unimpressed with the local logistics capabilities. Several of my shipments have been delayed or fallen through completely by the incompetence of a local firm. One of which I'd note had come highly recommended.

Schmidt, sharing Leif's disdain, replied, 'Civilian amateurs.'

'And when I confronted the owner' Leif said, 'Ivar Nielsen, I believe his name is, and told him of my dissatisfaction with his services, he protested…'

'Nielsen?' Schmidt said, his mind suddenly reeling. 'That's surprising.'

'It gets worse…' Leif said, fattening up the major for the kill.

When I voiced my complaints to Nielsen, he called me, and I quote 'a German leech'. He said I was sucking Danish money from the tit of Denmark all for the good of Nazis invaders.

'What an insult.' Schmidt said. 'Heir Bech, you've been a Dane since birth. Who is this Nielson fellow to say such things?'

'My sentiments precisely – I presume he had been investigating me and was refering to my German heritage.' Leif said, squinting through the blue cigarette smoke. 'Then he told me it was at "his discretion when I would receive his transport services".'

'I find this troubling.'

Schmidt continued,

I work with this man Nielsen. He seems sincere in his greed and his unabashed fear of my authority. Let me talk to him. I will tell him to make it up you somehow…

'Now I've got you', Leif thought, 'now you're mine.' Now for the evidence.

Thank you for that offer major, but how can Mr Nielsen make up the night of October 31st to me? I had a major shipment scheduled to be delivered to Copenhagen, but it was delivered three days late – the delay cost me 500 Kroner. When I questioned him on the matter, Nielsen told me it was because all his trucks and drivers were busy with more imperative deliveries in the area around Kolding and Aalborg. Can you get him to explain that? To make up for that?

The major nearly dropped the fork about to pass his lips as he thought

That was the night of the attack on our supply train near Kolding and the assault on the prison in Aalborg. That train was destined to support Army Group B's failed offensive in Belgium. It makes sense now. The resistance had help coordinating these two attacks. They had Ivar Nielsen.

Leif watched the cogs turn across a suddenly silent Schmidt's face and knew the damage was irrevocable for Nielsen. The first step to his downfall had been planted: doubt.

After lunch, Schmidt immediately contacted the region's Gestapo chief and alerted him to his suspicions regarding Ivar Nielsen as a resistance operative. The allegations were dismissed outright. The Gestapo commander was adamant that his staff had worked closely with Nielsen since the occupation and he was above reproach. But Schmidt had totally fallen for Bech's OSS psychological training and now trusted him over the Gestapo. He had become like an animal who had caught the scent of its prey and would not rest until he'd run it down.

Leif knew he was committed to play this subtle, dangerous game with the German commander, knowing that not only would Nielsen be brought down, but he was building a valuable plant in Schmidt, one he could feed false intelligence to and possibly learn from the German commander, valuable information for the OSS for the remainder of the war.

Bech called Gold directly and outlined this new development with the German commander. Gold listened, and like a biblical judge, scrupulously weighed Leif's intentions. 'This was a risky and bold initiative and I'm glad you brought it to my attention.'

Holding the telephone to his face, Leif said, 'Mr Gold, I don't live under the illusion that anything happening in Denmark bypasses your attention.'

'Smart boy. Nothing does.' said Gold. 'Your plan to engage Major Schmidt is approved.' And then he added. 'Be careful'.

* * *

Leif's *coup-de-grace* against Nielsen occurred three days later. Bjorn had spent two days producing falsified, highly detailed and incriminating documents delineating Nielsen's deeds on behalf of the resistance, and his misdeeds against the German occupiers, including plundering and financial duplicity. Once completed, Bjorn gave Leif the falsified documents and Leif, along with two dozen of their resistance cell made their way to the west coast of Jutland, where Leif led an assault mission against a German coastal radar station near the village of Thyboron. An attack that would set the stage for Nielsen's downfall.

Bjorn and a handful of resistance soldiers remained with the two trucks, well concealed from the road. They would be held in reserve in case things went wrong during the assault. Leif and his fifteen resistance assault team members silently slipped into the dense tree line, 300 yards south of the radar station just after midnight. They waited in the cold damp air. 'No one smokes' reminded Leif, 'we're too close to the Germans. We'll let them sleep contently until just before dawn.' As daybreak approached, Leif looked north towards the German installation, whose outline was just discernible. With the coast and its wide, sandy beach and grass-toped dunes of Jutland on his left, the target was vulnerable. The night was overcast and the dark gray of the North Sea merged into the lightening gray of the horizon above. It was time. Pointing to his right, Leif gave the order, 'Spread-out and move forward.'

Leif slowly cocked his machine gun to minimize the metallic noise and patted the canvas satchel slung over his shoulder – the one that carried the falsified documents in the side pocket. The satchel also contained spare ammunition clips and six hand grenades. The assault on the quiet, secluded radar site was swift and violent. In less than two minutes, half a dozen German soldiers were killed and Leif's men had possession of the radar equipment and communications room. The remainder of the small German garrison, twelve in total, were making a defensive stand from the protection of their sleeping quarters – a large stone farmhouse in the center of the compound.

With the radar station temporarily in Danish hands, explosives were planted adjacent to the radar array antenna and detonated, destroying it and the communications room directly below it. Now, looking for a suitable place to discard the satchel with the false documents, Leif, was notified of two Danish casualties. Leif was led to one of his fallen comrades who lay in the tall grass adjacent to the beach. With sporadic gunfire within the radar station compound growing more aggressive each moment, a reminder that the German's were not out of this fight, Leif knelt beside the young Dane who had just sacrificed his all for his country. After a brief moment of silence, Leif gently placed the satchel partially under the young man's lifeless body, making the subterfuge of the scene even more believable. Leif then gave the order to his remaining men to withdraw, leaving two of his senior soldiers to provide coving fire for their retreat. Soon after, the German soldiers began to rally and counterattack, to retake their radar installation. The Danish raiding party had vanished into the misty gray dawn. During their reoccupation of the installation, the Germans discovered the remains of the two dead partisans, one in the dunes with the satchel containing the incriminating documents about Nielsen. Calls to the Gestapo headquarters were immediately made.

The OSS's handiwork would appear 'lost' in the fog of war, inadvertently left behind in the resistance force's chaotic escape during the German counterattack which retook the installation from the resistance. Like a soothsayer's foresight, this is exactly how Leif had envisioned how the encounter with the Germans would unfold.

That evening, following the disturbing report of an attack on the Thyboron radar station, Schmidt received the found satchel containing the documents. He poured himself a brandy and smoked a cigar as he gloated and reread the newly found evidence of resistance activity involving Nielsen. It was an excellent evening. The next morning Schmidt called call his Gestapo counterpart to gloat: 'You were wrong about Ivar Nielsen.' said Schmidt.

Later that morning, Schmidt telephoned the maritime insurance company in Aarhus. 'Heir Bech', he said, with a dollop of honey on his tongue,

> you have provided a great service to the Fatherland. You were correct about Nielsen. Not only have you saved us from internal treachery, I have bested my Gestapo counterpart and proven him wrong about Nielsen.

'Heir Schmidt', Bech said, granting Schmidt all the glory he craved, 'I'm happy to have done my part to assist the Fatherland.'

'The next time we have lunch Heir Bech', the major said, delighted, 'I will be buying the schnapps.' Lowering his voice, he said, 'I have to go now, the Gestapo will be going out to pay Mr Nielsen a visit shortly.' Leif smiled to himself knowingly. He and Bjorn had already been out to visit Nielsen earlier that morning.

When the Gestapo descended upon Nielsen's trucking company's office to arrest him, they found him dead. To the Gestapo officers' dismay, he found Nielsen sitting slumped over at his office desk, white foam could be seen oozing from his mouth, indicated that he had taken a cyanide capsule. Clearly, from the Gestapo's perspective, Nielsen had seen them arrive and had preferred death over Gestapo interrogation. What the Gestapo did not know was that the cyanide had been provided by Leif an hour earlier.

Though Nielsen did die of cyanide poisoning, the circumstances were not, in fact, how the Gestapo surmised. Earlier that morning, prior to the Gestapo's arrival, Leif and Bjorn sat in their Sedan watching and waiting for Nielsen to arrive at his trucking company's office. Shortly after 0700 hours, the two OSS agents watched Nielsen unlock and enter his office. Leif waited a minute and then followed him in. Nielsen's workers were not expected for at least another hour. The Gestapo, however, could arrive at any time, so Leif made arrangements for lookouts to be placed near the Gestapo headquarters and along the route from Aarhus to Horsens, with orders to phone Nielsen's office when they spotted the Gestapo on route in order to give Leif and Bjorn sufficient warning.

Earlier that morning, with his Walther PPK pistol in his hand, Leif had entered Ivar's office. Surprised at the unexpected arrival and even more so at the sight of the weapon pointed at him, Nielsen demanded to know, the meaning of all this intrusion. 'I keep no cash on hand here at the office, so you're wasting your time.' Nielsen said.

In a calm, deliberate voice, Leif announced that he was not there to rob him and went on to outline the facts of Nielsen's traitorous behavior, which would warrant his immediate execution at the hands of the Danish Resistance, for whom Leif was now representing both judge and executioner. Though defiant at first, Nielsen soon became frantic to redeem himself and admitted that his business had prospered under the rule of the occupying German forces, but that he, in turn, employed many local Danes who relied on him for work. His words were met with only silence. Nielsen pleaded for mercy when it came to his role in the deaths of the three Danes killed in the resupply mission near Vejle.

'I didn't mean for anyone to get hurt; you must believe me!' he pleaded. 'I was ordered, threatened by the Gestapo to report any unusual or suspicious activities. Surely you must understand, I didn't think anyone would get killed.'

Leif continued listening to Nielsen's desperate pleas without conveying any visible reaction. He knew that Nielsen was desperate, and that human nature would have him promise anything at this moment to assuage his captor. Leif would not be swayed and thought 'Guilty as charged.'

He could have disposed of the traitor then and there for the price of a bullet from his pistol, but he had planned a more efficient method of implementing Nielsen's sentence. Leif's scheme would not only implicate Nielsen as a double agent, working for the Allies through the Danish Resistance, it would mislead the Gestapo in their search for the true resistance members. Bjorn had created sufficient incriminating evidence in the form of letters, written orders and work invoices, all of which implicated Nielsen as a part of the local resistance network. This false evidence would seal Nielsen's fate with the Gestapo. It was now time for his reckoning.

Leif continued to stare at Ivar and then spoke softly. He detailed the planted evidence at the radar station attack the previous night and the Allied weapons and ammunition that were, at that very moment, being placed in his warehouse and that would soon be found by the Gestapo. Leif emphasised that with the planted evidence in the Gestapo's possession, no matter what Nielsen said, the end result would be a long series of gruesomely painful interrogation sessions that would lead to his slow and agonizing death at the hands of the cruel and sadistic Nazis, who would undoubtedly be motivated by their outrage at Nielsn's successful duplicity of their authority. Leif allowed that statement to linger for a moment and then added, 'Mr Nielsen, I will offer you a way out, which will be quick and painless.'

Placing his pistol into his jacket pocket, Leif, kept his eyes fixed on Nielsen and reached up to his lapel to retrieve the cyanide capsule hidden in the material. Meanwhile, Nielsen stared back in disbelief, his world was unravelling about him. Leif placed the cyanide capsule on Nielsen's desk and with two fingers slowly slid the L-tablet closer to Nielson, who looked up at Leif with wide, wild eyes of disbelief. 'You… you're not serious?' stammered Nielsen – more of a statement than a question.

Leif retrieved his pistol from his pocket and slowly leaned forward, placing both hands on the desk and said, while gesturing with a quick nod of his head towards the office door,

> The Gestapo are on their way. In one minute, I will be walking out that door and you will be dead, Ivar. Make no mistake, you are a treasonous Dane. However, despite your traitorous collaboration with the Nazis, I am prepared to offer you this way out.

Leif glanced down at the white powder-filled capsule on the desk.

> What I am offering you is an honorable, painless option, through which your family will be spared the indignation of having your reputation as a traitor dragged through the mud. You kill yourself, and with the corroborating evidence we have produced and planted, it will appear as if you were a heroic member of the resistance, not a vile traitor. I will be content because Denmark will have one less traitor and the Germans will be content, as they have one less Danish Resistance fighter to contend with.

This time, with the barrel of his pistol, Leif pushed the cyanide capsule a little bit closer to Nielsen and stated, 'Bite down hard and within five seconds it will all be over. Quick and painless.' Sweat was pouring from Nielsen's forehead, his eyes staring at the capsule. 'Time is running out, Ivar.' Leif stressed.

Just as Leif had prearranged, Bjorn drove their car into the compound at breakneck speed and jammed on the breaks, skidding to a stop in the gravel parking lot adjacent to Nielsen's office. Nielsen's head instinctively turned towards the noise of the unseen skidding vehicle.

'CHRIST, WE'RE DONE FOR! – THE GESTAPO ARE HERE!' exclaimed Leif as he turned towards the door with his gun in the firing position. A moment later, he heard a low, grotesque gurgling sound behind him. Leif turned back to look at Nielsen, the traitor who was now splayed back in his chair, his neck tilted unnaturally back, eyes wide open and white foam oozing from his mouth. Leif thought 'The L-tablet had performed exactly as expected.' The sound of the cyanide capsule being crushed between Nielsen's teeth was the last sensation that he ever felt or heard.

Seconds later, the telephone rang, and Leif picked up the receiver. 'Yes?' he said softly into the phone.

'The Gestapo are on their way…', the voice on the line said, 'they will be there in twenty minutes.' The telephone line went dead. Leif hung up and walked towards the door. As Leif emerged from Nielsen's office, he gave Bjorn a quick nod to confirm that Nielsen had been eliminated. The two OSS agents quickly completed the rest of their pre-arranged subterfuge: planting incriminating evidence, including falsified documents, a few Allied supplied weapons, a case of ammunition and one broken shortwave radio in the Nielsen warehouse.

Even though Nielsen was a traitor – a now dead traitor – he wasn't the one Gold was actively hunting. The traitor that the resistance was looking for was far bigger game. Soon enough, Leif would learn that Nielsen was just one small pawn in a bigger, more dangerous game being played.

Chapter 24

Do What Must Be Done

'Something is rotten in the state of Denmark.'
William Shakespeare, *Hamlet*

Vagn Benneke, now promoted to Gold's COS entered the maritime insurance office, quickly locked the door behind him and then proceeded to close all the window blinds facing the street, quickly plunging the room into near darkness, save for scatterd thin lines of sun light on the floor and walls, creeping through gaps in the slats.

Leif fixed Benneke with a curious stare and slowly reached into his righthand side desk drawer for his Walther PPK. 'What's happened, have you been followed?'

'No, I wasn't followed, I made sure of that.' Benneke said, running his hand through his hair. Benneke had something important on his mind – that was clear to Leif, who stood up from behind his desk. 'I thought we were meeting this evening, to discuss the next resupply drop. What's happened?'

'There will be no meeting this evening… for there will be no resupply drop in the foreseeable future.' He crossed the office and sat down before Leif's desk and put a pack of cigarettes on the desk. 'You'll want one of those.'

Leif pulled his own brand from his jacket. 'I'll stick with mine. So, what's this all about Vagn?' said Leif.

Benneke lit his cigarette, watched with fascination as the smoke interacted almost magically with the late afternoon rays of light seeping through the window and then agitated by the spinning fan blades above,

> That was some impressive work – the way you eliminated that traitor Ivar Nielsen. But we have a far bigger problem than Nielsen… a far bigger problem.

Leif lifted Benneke's lighter off his cigarette pack, which was on his desk, to light his own.

Benneke leaned in towards the desk.

Gold ordered me here this morning to tell you that we have identified a traitor within the Danish government. As far as we can tell, this traitor has been working with the Germans for almost two years. His treason was just uncovered as he tried to betray one of our senior agents within the resistance – a man known as 'The Shepherd'. This Shepherd fellow is a master manipulator and is very cunning – but cautious. He has survived two Gestapo interigations already, and after the last one, the Krauts even apologized for wasting his time.

Leif laughed and said, 'This is a man I want to meet.'

'And you probably never will – well, not until the war is over and won.' Benneke retorted.

'Does this Shepherd fellow have a real name?'

'I don't know it. Only Gold knows his true identity.'

'And this "Shepherd" claims what?'

That the traitor, who's divulging secrets to the Germans is someone inside the Danish government apparatus. The Ministry of Foreign Affairs to be precise.

Leif raised his index finger for emphasis. 'This is a grave charge to be making against the Danish government. I'm supposed to take this Shepherd at his word. On what authority?'

'That man – The Shepherd', Bennek said, 'has almost single-handedly orchestrated the secret relocation of 8,000 Danish Jews to neutral Sweden. His integrity is impeccable.'

* * *

Leif understood what Benneke was referring to. Since August 1943, the Nazi occupation of Denmark had taken a drastic turn for the worst, especially for the Jewish population. The occupying force having perfected several years of antisemitic pogroms in Poland and Germany ruthlessly transferred over and applied the same tactics in their small Scandinavian nation, ultimately leading to the systematic arrest and incarceration of more than 30,000 Danish Jews, many of whom had been forcibly shipped to concentration camps as slave labor.

As an outward show of defiance, Denmark's King Christian X, although not Jewish himself, began to wear the yellow arm band emblazoned with the Star of David, a Nazi stricture commanding all native Jews to self-identify. Although that gesture was strictly symbolic, King Christian also had more concrete rebellious plans in mind. He ordered the development of a secret evacuation plan that would offer free and safe passage to neutral Sweden for any Danish Jews who wished to flee.

In direct contravention of Nazi orders, the Royal Danish Navy – particularly the Royal Danish Naval Reserve Fleet – with the tacit authority of the King, authorized dozens of medium and small coastal patrol and logistics support vessels under Commodore Fredrik Bangsboll's command to secretly and methodically shepherd the Jews into Sweden right under the noses of their German occupiers.. The German troops in Denmark paid little attention to the activities of the Royal Danish Reserve Fleet which were mostly small, coastal patrol boats, focusing their attention on the real threat, the remnants of the Royal Danish Combat Fleet, which had not been scuttled, and suspended their operations in 1943, under heavy German guard at the two main naval ports of Copenhagen and Frederikshavn.

According to The Shepherd, the Copenhagen resistance – where he resided – had been noticing a distinct increase in Gestapo activities and obstruction of resupply missions from the Allies and intercepting of escaping Jews to Sweden. In response, they launched an internal investigation, the results of which singled out one individual, the assistant to the Minister of Foreign Affairs for the Danish government. This minister's assistant has compromised the office. He's a traitor passing on information to the Germans for reasons yet unknown. A decision came down from on high, this traitor's immediate removal is necessary before any further damage can be done.

* * *

'Alright', Leif said, convinced by the accusation, but still confused by Benneke's presence in his office, 'what do you want me to do about this?'

'Gold wants you to remove the problem – personally.'

Leif leaned-back in his chair to consider what Benneke had just said. 'Why me?'

'Because you're good at what you do and Gold trusts you.' Benneke said, matter of factly, and rested his folded hands on Leif's desk.

Leif waited for a moment and asked the obvious question, 'Does this traitor have a name?'

'Victor Larsen.' said Benneke.

All we know of him is that he is 28 years old, born and raised in Copenhagen and is a graduate of Solvegade School, class of '38. His father, a shoe salesman died several years ago. Larsen lives with his mother in a modest appartment not far from the ministry.

'Victor Larsen', Leif thought,

I know that name… a memory from his youth crept through the synapse of his brain. He's two years older than me. He was a year ahead of me.

We played on the soccer team and… we acted in Hamlet together in a school play.

Leif's expression did not change and he did not convey to Benneke his knowledge of or previous association with Victor Larsen.

Benneke continued,

Our agents within the government have verified The Shepherd's suspicions and we know that this Larson fellow, though only a clerk, is well connected within the Ministry of Foreign Affairs as an assistant to the minister, with access to much information about certain resistance operations. We have uncovered facts that he has acted with intent to harm Denmark and benefit for himself and has been doing so over the past year. On numerous occasions he has fed the Germans, and in particular the Gestapo with damaging intelligence about the Danish Resistance, and most recently, about our agent The Shepherd and his efforts to save Danish Jews from the German labor and concentration camps, frequently being referred to now as death camps.

Leif nodded slowly as the gravity of the situation began to sink in.

Benneke stubbed out his cigarette in the ashtray on Leif's desk and immediately placed a new cigarette between his lips and lit it. You are to kill the traitor, Larsen. Benneke then added, 'You'll need to interrogate him first and determine if there are others working with him.' Benneke paused and then concluded his instructions, 'I'm sure that killing a fellow Dane is not an act you welcome, and I'm sorry to be the bearer of such an unenviable errand', Benneke said, attempting to sound paternal, 'but it is necessary.'

It was. Leif knew that part was true. It seemed as if his entire time in Jutland had been leading to this – bestow death upon all Germans soldiers and to anyone who aids them. Death. Killing German soldiers guarding supply trains was one thing. But there was the incident with Sophie, whom he narrowly escaped executing because of Ragla's vigorous intervention and improvisation on his part. Next was the shell game he played with Ivar Nielsen ending in his death, although not technically by Leif's hand. Now there was Victor Larsen, his first victim, to be assassinated in cold blood. Killing in combat is one thing, but this… what a truly unsentimental education. Leif looked up at Benneke and quoting his hero Hamlet said, 'That which we should do – we should do.'

Benneke smiled and began to convey the details. We believe Larsen will be in motion soon. As a test and to prove their case against the Danish administrative clerk, the resistance arranged to feed the suspected traitor with false information regarding an upcoming shipment of Danish Jews from Copenhagen to Trelleborg, Sweden. When the Gestapo raided the suspected port warehouse on the night of the fictitious shipment of Jewish escapees, only a warehouse full of construction equipment was found. When confronted by his German contact, the traitorous clerk was surprised that the shipment of Jews had been a hoax set up by the resistance and Larsen quickly realized that he had been duped – and was now in grave danger. The traitor's fear of the Germans was one thing and up until now, he had been on good terms with the Gestapo, having provided them with useful information about some Danish Resistance activities that he was privy to and several internal Danish government plans that he thought the Germans would be interested in knowing. If he had been found out by his Danish colleagues, not only was he no longer useful to the Gestapo but he would be marked as a traitor in the eyes of his countrymen and particularly by the Danish Resistance.

Briefly, he thought that his German contacts might reward him for his previous efforts and make arrangements to send him to Germany to continue his work as a supporter of the Third Reich. Then reality set in and he faced the cold, hard facts that the Gestapo did not care about him or any other collaborator for that matter – collaborators were useful only until they were not. Up until now, Victor Larsen had been useful to the Gestapho, but the Gestapo would just as soon dispose of him to avoid any further complications. Victor Larsen, assistant administrative clerk to the Danish foreign minister knew he had to disappear… and quickly.

* * *

Larsen presented his identify card and travel authorization papers to the ticket agent at the Copenhagen central train station. As a member of the support staff of the minister of foreign affairs, Larsen had freedom to travel within Denmark as he deemed necessary. That benefit was about to be put into good use to get himself as far away from Copenhagen and his colleagues at the ministry as possible and, of course, to distance himself from the Danish Resistance who knew by now that he had been working with the Germans.

Benneke outlined what they knew of Larsen's escape plans:

> Larsen purchased a one-way, first-class ticket to Aalborg for this Friday afternoon and has emptied all his bank accounts. We expect he intends to hide in Aalborg with some degree of anonymity. Unbeknownst to Larsen, standing in line at the train station, several places behind him, was a Danish plain-clothed police detective who had been assigned to follow him. Upon showing the ticket clerk his police credentials, the detective

asked for the destination and itinerary of passenger Victor Larsen who had just purchased a train ticket.

'That gives you have less than two days to make whatever arrangements you need to make to complete your mission.' Benneke then slid a folded piece of paper across the desk to Leif. On it, it read: 'Train J-147 departs Copenhagen at 1615 hours this Friday.' The train makes serval stops, including one at Aarhus at 1810 hours, and finally arriving at Aalborg at 1925 hours. Leif had a little over twenty-four hours to prepare his plan to intercept, interrogate and eliminate this target – this threat.

Bjorn drove Leif to the Aarhus train station, fifteen minutes before the scheduled arrival of the J-147 train from Copenhagen. During the drive, the two agents did not speak much, but Bjorn sensed there was something deeply troubling Leif. Bjorn surmised that it was because Leif had just been given orders to kill a fellow Dane. Even though Larsen had been identified as a known traitor by the Danish government, he felt that Leif was uneasy about this assignment. Such an act was ethically challenging and Bjorn was relieved not to have to be a direct part of it.

When they arrived at the train station, Leif told Bjorn to expect him back the following afternoon and that he would make his own travel arrangements back to their Aarhus office by taxi. Without further discussion, Leif exited the car and proceeded into the train station where he purchased a first-class, round-trip ticket to Aalborg, train departing at 1810 hours.

The J-127 train arrived in Aarhus right on time. A dozen passengers stood on the platform waiting to board the train to Aalborg and about the same number of passengers disembarked at the train at Aarhus. Leif, carrying his leather valise and a small suitcase proceeded through the first two cars for the coach passengers and was greeted by the conductor as he entered the first-class seating area where he presented his ticket and surveyed the passengers already seated. The car was less than half full, mostly businessmen traveling for work he supposed. Leif wondered if he would recognize his former schoolmate – it had been more than ten years since he had seen Victor Larsen.

Proceeding forward along the aisle, scanning the car's occupants, Leif immediately ruled out eight of the ten passengers as not being his target. Then, to his left, four rows up, there was a man in his mid-twenties, reading a newspaper and wearing a dark suit, glasses and a fedora. The side profile looked familiar. Leif's heart sank. 'That's him.'

Leif had originally planned to remain behind his target, unseen and to follow Larsen upon their arrival at Aalborg and initiate his apprehension when the opportunity presented itself. But for some reason, unknown even to Leif, he spontaneously changed his plan. Leif continued along the aisle of the car, past Larsen and took a vacant seat one row ahead of and on the opposite side of the aisle. This would allow Larsen the opportunity to see and possibly recognize him. Still unsure of his sudden change of plan, Leif did not feel threatened by Larsen. After all, they were old friends and Larsen was a clerk, a treacherous bureaucrat clerk, not a combatant. Leif was now resolved in his assignment. From all accounts from the Danish Resistance, Larsen had repeatedly committed acts of treason. Larsen was a traitor to his nation in time of war and had harmed his country and jeopardized hundreds of Danish lives by passing sensitive information to the enemy. For these reasons, the Danish Resistance command had ordered his apprehension, interrogation and elimination. For Leif, the question now was, how to accomplish these three tasks most effectively and efficiently.

No sooner had Leif sat down and extracted his newspaper from his valise than he sensed he was being observed – Larsen's eyes were upon him. Leif would wait for Larsen to make the first move, which Leif expected would probably come most naturally upon arrival at Aalborg, their mutual destination, a brief forty-five minute trip. Leif read his newspaper and remained relaxed during the short journey. As expected, when the train pulled into the Aalborg station and as passengers began to gather their belongings to disembark, their eyes met with a flash of recognition. After a moment's hesitation, a broad smile came across Victor Larsen's face. 'Leif', he asked, 'is that you?'

Not wishing to undermine his feigned look of surprise, Leif hesitated a few seconds while looking at his old friend before returning the smile, extending his and saying, 'Victor, Victor Larsen, how are you, old friend?'

Judging by Larsen's genuinely pleased demeanor at their encounter, Leif could tell that Larsen did not suspect this to be anything other than a chance meeting of two old friends. 'How naïve you are Victor.' And as the two old friends became reacquainted, the thought crossed Leif's mind,

> Have I become so hardened and suspicious of others due to my OSS training and life's experiences as an agent that I can no longer truly trust anyone anymore?

Larsen told Leif that he was taking a break from his boring job with the government in Copenhagen and would be staying in Aalborg indefinitely. Leif told his old friend that he was working in the nearby town of Aarhus and was on business in Aalborg for the next day or so. Leif indicated that he was staying at the Phønix Hotel and that they should meet for dinner. Larsen expressed his delight at the idea and confessed that in his haste to get out of Copenhagen that he had not yet secured hotel accommodations. So, the two old friends walked the short distance together from the train station to the Phœnix Hotel where Leif, using his true name on his reservation obtained the key to his room since Larsen knew both Leif Bangsbøll and Jørgen Bech, Leif could not use his agent persona of Jørgen Bech. Larsen obtained a room for himself for a week and, their accommodations secured, Leif suggested a local bistro for dinner.

The two men casually strolled down the quiet streets of Aalborg. As they walked, Leif explained that after their time together in Sølvgades school, he had gone on to the Royal Danish Naval Academy, where and obtained a degree as a maritime engineering, and was now working for a maritime insurance and services company, originally founded in Copenhagen but now with an office in Aarhus. Hoping to get Larsen to convey his sentiments about the war, Leif casually mentioned that life under the Nazi occupation was 'not so bad for his business.' Larsen skimmed over his post-Sølvgades school employment activities, outlining that for the past three years he had been working as an assistant to the minister of foreign affairs and despite the obvious political friction between Germany and Denmark over Denmark's occupation, Larsen found that Germany had provided many benefits to those Danes who were willing to embrace the Third Reich's ambitious leadership role for Europe. Larsen described how he enjoyed the privileges and protection that his work in the minister's office gave him from the trials and tribulations that the average Dane experienced under the German occupation. Larsen's statements, though innocent enough so far, began to convey to Leif that his old friend had become a selfish fool who was now involved in things far above his capabilities to fully comprehend.

Upon arrival at the bistro, Leif called the waiter over and immediately ordered two Tuborg beers and two shots of Leif's favorite Danish schnapps – Aalborg Akvavit. Leif wished to appear to impress Larsen in a fitting manner to celebrate their fortunate reunion by ordering the more expensive, yet locally produced Akvavit. By the time the third round of drinks was consumed, Larsen was feeling quite relaxed and was enjoy telling his old friend how his foolish boss, the minister of foreign affairs and the Danish government, in general, were so misguided in their resistance to Germany's wartime, expansionist goals.

'Think how rich and powerful Denmark could be if we allied ourselves with the Third Reich?' declared Victor.

'Shhh, keep your voice down, Victor', cautioned Leif. 'Not all Danes feel the way we do.'

Leif, whose ability to resist the intoxicating effects of alcohol was remarkable, knocked back another shot of schnapps and immediately ordered another round. 'We need to make a toast to old friends crossing paths.' Leif announced. Happy to comply, as soon as the waiter brought their refills, Larsen raised his glass and with somewhat slurred speech toasted their good fortune at having met so unexpectedly. Feeling the effects of the alcohol on an empty stomach, Larsen's head was swimming. He suggested they order some food. After giving their meal orders to the waiter, Leif excused himself to go to the toilet. On his way past the bar, he told the waiter to hold off on placing their food order for another thirty minutes. Leif wanted the alcohol to have its full effect on Larsen's empty stomach and sense of judgment.

Upon returning to the table with another round of Akvavit, Leif looked down at Victor who obviously was not used to this level of imbibing. 'Perfect', thought Leif, 'the less awareness you have, the better for me, my friend.' 'Here Victor, one more round before dinner arrives.' The two old friends clinked their glasses together and enthusiastically and simultaneously said, '*Skål*! [Cheers!]'

The schnapps no longer burned his throat, but Larsen wished that the food would arrive soon. A few minutes later, their meals arrived, along with a bottle of wine that Leif had ordered. The food was delicious, and the wine was expensive. Leif thought to himself, 'It's the least I can do for his old friend who will not see another sunrise.' Though Larsen knew he did not need any more alcohol, Leif seemed to be filling their glasses as soon as they were only half empty. As the room began to oscillate slightly, Larsen thought, 'The food was delicious and the wine exceptional.'

Leif knew that Larsen was now in a state in which he could be easily manipulated and began to set the stage for drawing out what Larsen was hiding.

'You know Victor', he began,

> I'm so sick of this damn war. I hear that every day our king rides around on his horse, through the streets of Copenhagen wearing that blasphemous Jewish symbol. Does he not realize that he's just antagonizing the Germans?

Larsen slammed his fist onto the table, causing the wine glasses to jump and splash onto the white tablecloth. The sudden noise caused the other patrons in the restaurant to stop momentarily and stare in his direction.

With a slight slur to his speech and placing his extended index finger unsteadily over his lips in a gesture of silence as he looked around the room apologetically, he said, 'Pardon me.' And then added, as he emptied his wine glass, 'I could not agree with you more Leif!' Larsen looked at Leif as if he was contemplating his next statement carefully, and after a moment he said,

> You know Leif, I have tried my best to convince our government authorities within my ministry to embrace our German guests. After all, once this war is over and Germany is victorious, Denmark will have to account for its

obstinate behavior towards the Third Reich. And I, for one, plan to land on the side of the winners in this war.

After another moment's pause, Larsen went on,

> I think I should get a medal from the Germans for the important information I have provided them. In fact, I think I should get a medal from Denmark too, for trying to save our country from its ineffective government.

Glancing around the room to see if anyone was listening and then leaning forward towards Leif, Larsen whispered,

> For instance, sometimes I hear about Royal Danish Navy ships transporting Jews to neutral Sweden. I have been reporting this to the German authorities, but I get little thanks in return, except for a few Kroners thrown my way now and again.

Though Leif was unaware that his father had already been questioned by the Gestapo regarding his knowledge of Danish Jews being spirited away to neutral Sweden using Danish naval vessels, Leif grimaced inwardly at Larsen's words and at the thought that his father was the senior naval officer responsible for the use of any Royal Danish Navy Reserve vessel for such anti-German activity. It immediately dawned on him that Larsen's treasonous acts had directly endangered his father. Leif's face remained expressionless, but something inside him changed. It was as if something dark and ominous had been disturbed deep in the waters of a fjord, generating only the slightest ripple to the distant surface – anger was now lurking deep below the surface. 'Leif, are you alright?'

Leif, blinked and returned to the moment and with great restraint, nodded and feigned his approval of Larsen's explanation of how he had attempted to warn the Germans of the Danish Navy's anti-German activities. 'Now', Leif thought,

> for the most important question I have for this traitor... I need to know if there were other accomplishes – other traitors within the Danish Foreign Ministry working with Victor.

Leif leaned forward towards his dinner companion and confided,

> Victor, there must be other, like-minded patriots in the Danish government who could help you convince the minister or possibly even the king about the benefits of aligning themselves with the Third Reich... are there not?

Larsen seemed to deflate a little at this suggestion. 'No, I seem to be alone, at least within the ministry, as no one seems to appreciate my views on the war.' With despair and disappointment in his voice, he continued, 'Only the Germans seem to listen to what I have to say.'

With a few additional leading questions, Leif had heard enough. Larsen was guilty of treason, of that there was no doubt and it was clear that he had been working alone – all alone and for selfish, misguided reasons. Leif finished his meal in silence as Larsen rambled on about how unappreciated he was and how he had passed important information about the Danish government and the resistance movement to his German contact. Larsen believed that he had provided vital information for which he felt he still had not been properly rewarded. Leif was certain that Larsen would get exactly what he deserved later that evening.

With their dinner consumed and their wine bottle empty, Leif paid their bill and got up from the table, offering a supporting hand to Larsen who was unsteady on his feet at this point.

'Oh my, I believe I am drunk, Leif!' exclaimed Larsen as he bumped into a nearby vacant table, jarring the place settings and empty glasses and creating a clatter of shifting glasses and cutlery. 'You know, Victor', said Leif, 'I think we need to walk off some of this booze.'

Leif and Victor staggered out the restaurant onto the darkened streets of Aalborg. It was damp, and a fog hung in low-lying places. As the two men slowly made their way down the street, Leif surveyed their surroundings and guided them along his planned route as Victor rambled on with only partially coherent statements about his thankless efforts to save Denmark and the idiots he was forced to work with within the ministry.

Despite his deep disappointment in his former friend's traitorous conduct and his revulsion at his foolish boasting about his deeds to help the Third Reich, Leif did not relish his next actions. Leif was now moving in automatic motion with a slight dullness to his senses, thanks to the alcohol he had consumed – he could handle a great deal of alcohol, but he was not completely impervious to its effects. And this night, they had consumed much alcohol. Though still clear enough of mind and capable of responding appropriately, Leif loathed the thought of what he was about to do. He said to himself, 'Make it quick and painless, do not frighten him and it will all be over soon and the mission will be completed.'

The streets were deserted, but even if there happened to be anyone watching the scene, it would only appear that two drunken companions were stumbling home after a night on the town. The two men wobbled towards Leif's intended point of departure from the main street. Leif knew the area of Aalborg well and had chosen the secluded intersection where the railway line crossed the main road into the town. They were more than 25 yards onto the darkened railway lines with fog banks on both sides of them masking their movement when Larsen mumbled some recognition that they were walking on a railway track.

'Leif, is this a shortcut to the hotel?' he asked. 'You know, it's dangerous to be walking on railway tracks.' A smile slowly lit up his face. 'Hey Leif', he mused, 'this is just like when we were children out late and getting into mischief.'

'Yes, that is true Victor, but that was a long time ago. But have no fear, I will keep a lookout for any trains.' Leif assured him. The two men were now more than 100 yards from the road, deep into the darkness of the tree shrouded, fog blanketed railway line and completely invisible from the road from which they had come. Leif did not want to prolong this task any longer than he had to and did not intend to confront Larsen with his traitorous acts. Leif was not going to be his judge, jury and executioner. He had his orders; tonight, he would be just the executioner.

As they slowly moved along the railway tracks in the shrouded darkness, Leif momentarily loosened his grip on his friend's arm so he could reach into his jacket pocket for what was needed. Victor felt the supporting arm and shoulder of his companion momentarily disengage from his and for a moment felt off balance, as though he might fall onto the train tracks. But just as suddenly, Larsen felt the firm grip of a strong hand on the back of his jacket collar holding him up. Grateful of the support to keep himself upright, the last words Larsen ever spoke were 'Thank you, Leif.'

The sharp report of the Walther PPK pistol was crisp in the cool night air. As anticipated, the echo of the gunshot was muffled by the surrounding trees and fog. Larsen was dead before his body hit the gravel covered ground. Leif stood over the lifeless body of his former friend and traitor for a long moment, scanning their surroundings, particularly towards the road from which they had just come. There was no movement to be seen. The only sound that could be heard was the barking of a dog in the distance, startled by the noise of the gunshot. Leif looked down at Larsen's prone body and thought about how far his old friend had strayed from the path and how cruelly unfortunate it was that he was the one required to make the reckoning of accounts. Nonetheless, he soothed himself with the understanding that it is a warrior's duty to carry out his assigned orders… the war must be won and the sacrifice of the few for the needs of the many must remain the mantra.

With Larsen's body now hidden under the thick brush at the side of the railway track and all his personal effects confiscated, Leif turned and walked towards his hotel. Despite having consumed far more alcohol that evening than he was accustomed to, he thought to himself, 'I could really use a drink right now.'

Slightly hungover, Leif checked out of the Phøenix Hotel early the next morning to catch the first train back to Aarhus. With the room key he had taken from Larsen the previous evening, Leif secured Larsen's belongings from his unused room and departed the hotel. The owner of the hotel, a member of the local resistance assured Leif that there was no record of the check in or check out for either Leif Bangsbøll or Victor Larsen.

Upon his return to his office in Aarhus, he said nothing more to Bjorn about his mission other than,

> Send a message to Gold advising him that the assignment in Aalborg has been completed without incident. The target had been working alone and is no longer a threat.

Mentally exhausted from his ordeal in Aalborg the previous night, Leif spent the day in his office, with the door shut. There, he made telephone calls to clients of his fictitious Aarhus engineering and shipping company to keep up his façade of a conscientious local businessman. At the end of the day, he stepped out of his office, and waiting patiently at his desk in the outer office was his friend and partner, Bjorn. 'Leif, do you want to talk about it now?' asked Bjorn.

Leif hesitated and realized that Bjorn had called him by his real name for the first time since they were in London, preparing for this mission. That was over five months earlier.

'Yes Alfred', referring to him by his real name, 'but not here, let's go get some food and I'll tell you all about it.'

Chapter 25

The World is a Stage

'I am the good shepherd. The good shepherd
would lay down his life for his sheep.'

'John 10:11', *Bible*

Bjorn had maintained regular radio communications with their OSS operations officer and their handler back in London and filled Leif in on recent intelligence reports and the upcoming resupply schedule. Without having to ask the OSS for additional weapons and ammunition, the OSS/SOE headquarters had ordered the doubling of resupply missions to the resistance to correspond with the Allied offensive pushing across France and Belgium. The effectiveness of the sabotage attacks that Leif had led in Denmark along with similar resistance efforts across Denmark and in Belgium, the Netherlands and France had not gone unnoticed by General Eisenhower, Supreme Allied commander, and his headquarters staff. Both the OSS and SOE were realizing the impact they were having – distracting and disrupting German operations, as was most evident in the OSS's sabotage mission and the disruption of railway lines in Denmark, which had just recently prevented Wehrmacht supplies and reinforcements stationed in Denmark from reaching Belgium and participating in the Battle of the Bulge. Every German unit that could be held in these non-frontline areas meant one less unit facing the armies of the advancing Allies. American OSS and British SOE agents in Denmark, Norway, Belgium, France, Yugoslavia and Greece were doing their part to keep German combat forces and their reserve units pinned down by their irregular counterinsurgency warfare.

With the recent successes of the Danish/Jutland resistance missions, Gold assigned Leif an additional thirty volunteer fighters from other local teams. These freedom fighters were mostly men, but there were a few women volunteers as well. The female factor provided an added, but no less risky, capability, especially when gathering information about or infiltrating German organizations, as these women resistance members, often employed as administrative clerks, hosts, waitresses or escorts, could gain access to significant information that few men of the resistance could.

This infusion of additional fighters brought Leif's resistance cell up to fifty personnel. Despite being told that these thirty new fighters had been trained, Leif insisted that all of them undergo additional training and perform under his or Bjorn's personal supervision prior to being assigned any significant missions. The first three weeks of January 1945 were spent reviewing the resistance communication network and methods to furtively observe, assess and report on German military activities. Once confident in the new fighters' understanding and capabilities to operate within and between resistance cells – and what to do in the event of mission failure or Gestapo intervention – Leif and Bjorn conducted additional instructional classes in assembling explosive devices and various techniques of sabotage. Leif was impressed by the caliber and motivation of his new team members. Whether they could perform under mission conditions was something that only could be determined during the actual operations. But he was pleased with what he saw. Soon enough, Leif's team would be tested again.

* * *

On 26 January 1945, Agent Bech received notification that a major OSS resupply mission would be conducted on 29 January. Leif had already assessed several alternate drop zones and had selected a place known as Horsens Fjord. The drop zone was large and was located in a remote area outside of the village of Gylling, between the towns of Horsens and Odder. Arrangements were made to have three teams of four resistance personnel, many of whom were recent recruits, preposition themselves for the reception of sixteen air dropped resupply containers. The resupply delivery was executed precisely as planned, with all sixteen containers being received without incident. Within two hours of delivery, the weapons, ammunition and explosives were safely and secretly moved by trucks and even by horse-drawn wagons and hidden at three separate storage sites in and around the town of Horsens for future distribution and use. The new team members had performed admirably.

Recent reports from the OSS indicated that the Allied offensive into Germany was progressing well and that it was only a matter of weeks before Denmark could expect the British and Canadian armies to break through to southern Denmark. This would mark the beginning of the true rise of the Danish Resistance against their German oppressors. Leif knew that he needed to get as many of the Allied weapons, ammunition and radios he had in various secret storage sites into Copenhagen as soon as possible. Little did Leif know that very soon an opportunity would arise from a highly unlikely source that would offer a unique solution to this mission requirement.

Reflecting on the game of cat and mouse with the Germans over the Christmas holidays, Leif was content to be back in Aarhus and the routine of the insurance façade, while leading the local resistance in collecting intelligence on German troop activities and intentions. Likewise, in the aftermath of the radar station attack and the elimination of Ivar Nielsen, Major Schmidt, the German regional commander, was satisfied that he had been correct about his suspicions of Nielsen, and even more pleased that the local Gestapo director had been so very wrong. Schmidt also realized that Jørgen Bech had been instrumental in leading him towards Nielsen. During the first week of February 1945, just weeks following Nielsen's death, Schmidt came unannounced to Leif's office and invited him out for drinks. Drinks the German officer would offer to pay for but knew Leif would insist on covering the bill.

After they had finished their first round of drinks, Schmidt pronounced, 'You are a true and loyal German, Heir Bech. Thanks to your assistance we have rid ourselves of another Danish partisan vermin.' He spat the name, 'Ivar Nielsen.'

'My assistance?' asked Leif innocently, feigning any understanding. 'How did I help you with Mr Nielsen?'

> Ah, Bech, you don't even realize that your observations a few weeks ago about the limited trucking services in this region at the end of October and Ivar Nielsen's local activities gave me a clue to his involvement with the resistance. *Danke, vielen dank*! [Thank you very much!] Shall we have another drink, Bech?

'Thank you for your kind words, major', replied Leif, 'and thank you for your offer. However, I must decline your hospitality. I have so much to do this afternoon – I need a clear head!' he demurred, as he started to rise from his bar stool. 'Nonsense!' insisted Schmidt. 'Business can wait!'

Leif replied,

> I'm afraid that it cannot wait, major. You see, business has not been good lately. With all the disruption of the railway and road lines, much of the spare ship parts for my clients' vessels that need to get to the port of Copenhagen have been delayed or lost. I fear my customers will not be patient and I may lose my job and will have to close our office here in Aarhus if business does not improve. But these are not your concerns, major.

Leif, turning to walk away, lamented, 'So, I must get back to the office to make some calls to see if I can get an urgent shipment to Copenhagen by week's end.'

But then he stopped and added,

The World is a Stage   273

> You know, despite being a double crossing partisan, Ivar Nielsen did provide a decent transportation service to the average businessman too. And now with him gone, and all his assets confiscated by the Wehrmacht, it leaves us businessmen with even fewer resources to move our products to and from market.

Before Leif could reach the door of the restaurant, Schmidt caught up to him, gently grabbed Leif by the elbow and led him back to his barstool. 'Heir Bech', he said,

> to show you how grateful the Third Reich is for your assistance in eliminating this wanted Danish Resistance operative, and as a gesture from one loyal German to another, I am prepared to assist you with the shipment of the spare parts to Copenhagen that you just mentioned. As you have indicated, all of Nielsen's assets are now the property of the Wehrmacht, which means they are mine. And as such, I will authorize the use of one of these trucks to move your freight to the Fredericia railway station to get the shipment to the port of Copenhagen by the end of the week. If you can deliver the shipment to Fredericia by noon tomorrow, I will see to it that appropriate arrangements are made to get the shipment onto the afternoon train for Copenhagen.

Unsure if he had truly duped the German officer or if he was walking into a Nazi trap, Leif did what he was trained to do: improvise and act with confidence. Like a grateful and loyal ally of Germany, Leif accepted the generous offer, shook hands vigorously with the major and ordered another round of schnapps.

Before departing company that afternoon, Schmidt took out his notepad and wrote a brief order.

Notice to anyone concerned,

> *Mr Jorgen Bech, of the Maritime Insurance and Services Brokerage of Aarhus, Denmark, and bearer of this letter is authorized shipment of six crates of commercial ship parts from Horsens to Fredericia and from Fredericia to Copenhagen on 18 February 1945. Use of the former transportation assets of the Nielsen Trucking Company of Horsens is also authorized.*
>
> *M. Schmidt, Major*
> *12th Grenadiers, Central Jutland Command*
> *17 February 1945*

In order to make this complex transaction work in such a short period of time, and to reduce the risk of being compromised, Leif knew he would have to count on only those he trusted the most. He knew that the transfer of the six large crates of equipment (five containers of Allied weapons, ammunition, radios and uniforms, along with one container of actual ship parts) had to pass through German inspection at the railway yards at the beginning and end of the shipment's journey, which would be a challenge to complete successfully – so many things could go wrong. Leif returned to his office, explained to Bjorn the opportunity that developed and made several telephone calls.

The next morning, with the assistance of Bjorn as his driver, Leif picked up a truck from Nielsen's garage, drove to the warehose where the crates of weapons were stored and loaded the six large wooden crates loaded the six large wooden crates onto the truck, and drove to the Fredericia railway yard. The five crates containing the Allied military equipment had been modified overnight. The standard 2-inch nails sealing the crate lids had been replaced by 6-inch wooden screws. Only the crate with the actual ship parts was left with the standard 2-inch nails securing its lid. If the crates were to be inspected, they had to minimize the chances of the crates with Allied equipment being opened. Leif and Bjorn also arrived as late as possible to minimize the time available for load inspection. Upon presentation of the six crates and the accompanying note from Schmidt, the sergeant in charge of the rail loading dock said, 'You are late, the train is scheduled to depart in twenty minutes.'

Without waiting for a reply from Leif and Bjorn, the sergeant ordered one of his civilian railway yard employees to inspect the containers. With a crow bar and hammer in his hands, the middle-aged Danish railway worker approached the six containers. Bjorn was sitting on one container, smoking a cigarette and politely got up and offered the crate for inspection. The lid pried off easily and the civilian inspector shouted, 'Looks like a drive shaft and valve assembly here, sergeant.' The sergeant noted the contents onto the train's cargo manifest.

As the civilian inspector moved to the next container Leif approached the sergeant, while Bjorn offered the civilian inspector a cigarette. 'Sergeant, as you can see by the orders, personally written by Major Schmidt, these ship spares must be in Copenhagen by the end of the day.' Then pointing at the open crate, and speaking in his best, formal, polite German, he continued, 'You see, ship spare parts. Shall we move this along? I hope I do not need to ask for Major Schmidt to intervene on my behalf – yes?'

The sergeant looked at Leif and over to where his inspector was having a cigarette, while chatting happily with Bjorn. Exasperated, the sergeant glanced back at Leif, turned towards his office and shouted towards the loading dock, 'Quit wasting time, old man, and get those crates onto the train – *Schnell*! [Quickly!]'

Leif and Bjorn parked outside the railway yard, waited and watched the train depart. 'Right on time', commented Bjorn, 'you have to admire the efficiency of the Germans when it comes to transportation schedules.'

Leif smiled and said, 'Let's hope the Germans manning the railway yard in Copenhagen are equally as inept.'

The two OSS agents drove back to Horsens to drop off the truck, then continued back to Aarhus where they would wait for news from the Danish Resistance in Copenhagen. As the hours passed, Leif checked the time frequently and was visibly preoccupied – and for good reason. Knowing that the reception of the shipment in Copenhagen would also take a great deal of guile, Leif had called upon the one person he trusted more than anyone: his father.

* * *

Commodore Frederik Bangsbøll, who had assumed command of the Royal Danish Reserve Fleet in Copenhagen shortly after the German occupation of Denmark, was most willing to assist his son and the resistance. As the commander of the Danish Naval Reserves, Frederik's role was to ensure neutral sovereignty of Danish waters and de-conflict naval activities with the German Kriegsmarine (navy) – a task that had become increasingly difficult, as the relationship with the Danish government and its military became strained under the oppressive jackboot of the Nazi occupation.

However, on this day, Frederik would play a far different role with the German occupiers. For this assignment, Frederik was disguised as an old Danish truck driver and delivery man, working for the Maritime Insurance and Services Company of Copenhagen. His assignment: to pick up six crates of spare ship parts sent from Horsens/Fredericia on behalf of their regional office and under the orders of the German garrison commander of the Jutland region.

Leif had made a telephone call to his father the previous day and after some long overdue father-son talk, Leif explained the rapidly evolving situation. His father was eager to help. At the time, Leif had recently learned that his father, who was still in a senior navy command position, had joined the resistance. However, Frederik's ability to be actively engaged in resistance-related operations was limited do to his relatively high-profile position within the Danish Admiralty. Though he had been able to pass important intelligence reports to the resistance on German naval activities, the opportunity to be directly involved in a daring, clandestine mission as well as overseeing the clandestine escape of hundreds of Danish Jews to Sweeden using his Naval Reserve fleet, directly under the nose of the Germans, was exactly what Frederik wanted to do and was perfectly suited for. Frederik's self-confidence and commanding presence could be intimidating and he expected that he might have to give a grand performance at the Copenhagen railway station if this mission was to succeed. Though he would not be working directly with his son, the fact that he knew that Leif was orchestrating the task and would be subjected to similar circumstances at the Horsens railway station inspired Frederik and gave him a deep sense of pride that he was in fact 'working with his son' on this mission.

For both of their safety and due to security protocols arising from his wartime role as an OSS agent, Leif had had limited communications with his father in recent years. He had only sent his father three letters over the previous three years to let his father know that he was still alive. Leif knew that he had to be careful of what he wrote so as not to compromise his work with the OSS nor endanger his father with any possible connection to Leif's true activities if the Gestapo intercepted the letters.

Other than the previous day's telephone call to his father to ask him to help in the reception of the Allied equipment being shipped to Copenhagen care of the German supply train, Leif's most recent correspondence with his father had been four months earlier. He had sent a letter soon after his parachute jump back into Denmark at the commencement of his current mission. The letter, written on 22 October 1944, was written in a code-like manner, and read as follows:

Dearest Father,

I hope this letter finds you safe and in good health. Since my last correspondence to you much as changed for me. I completed my work program with our Norwegian cousins in 'Little Norway'. (I have completed the Norwegian pilot training with the British Commonwealth Air Training Plan at the Norwegian airfield known as Little Norway in Toronto, Canada.) *However, I have since received and accepted a job offer from an important businessman, the one in a wheelchair, who lives in the big, white house south of Little Norway. I'm sure you know the one.* (I have accepted an assignment with the United States government.) *I have taken on an interesting job and am living close to where old Harald Bluetooth grew up.* (I'm living near Aarhus, Denmark, where our family ancestor, King Harald Bluetooth was born and lived.)

Thank you for all that you did for me growing up; your many lessons have proven to be most valuable in my current endeavors.

I hope to see you soon as I expect that our visitors may be moving home soon enough. (The German occupation of Denmark will soon be over.)

With loving regards, your son,
Leif (Jocom)
22/10/44

While the content of the letter was vague, the message embedded in the letter had been clear enough to Frederik, who understood that his son had somehow been recruited into the United States military. The reference to the old, crippled man in the 'white house' was surely President Franklin D. Roosevelt. Frederik presumed that Leif was working with the equivalent to the British SOE, the Americans' special operations force, the OSS, which Frederik knew was actively supporting the Danish Resistance and was now operating within Denmark. And now Frederik would be directly helping his son too.

* * *

The following afternoon, Frederik, dressed as a common laborer, backed his cargo truck – which the local resistance team leader had provided – up to the loading dock at the Copenhagen railway station. With the typed written cable in his hand from Leif's maritime insurance and services company office of Aarhus, Jutland, outlining the delivery of the spare parts under the authority of Major Manfred Schmidt, 12th Grenadiers and garrison commander of the Horsens-Aarhus region, Frederik knocked on the frame of the open door to the shipping and receiving office. There, a haggard looking corporal was holding the telephone to his ear; clearly, someone of higher authority was on the other end of the line and was shouting some rather unpleasant things at the young German soldier.

'Yes, sir! Yes, yes, sir, that will be done, right away! Yes, sir – Heil Hitler!' The young, exacerbated corporal slowly placed the telephone back in its cradle and seemed to deflate like a balloon into his wooden swivel chair. After a moment's pause, he noticed a bearded man standing at his doorway. Noting that the figure was not a German officer or non-commissioned officer, the young corporal remained seated and slumped comfortably in his chair, and asked, without looking directly at Frederik, 'What do you want, old man?'

Normally Frederik would have dealt with such insolence with swift, dynamic and enthusiastic disciplinary measures. However, Frederik knew he had a role to play in this mission and had to remain in character to see the important transaction through to its successful completion. Using his most formal German dialect, and his recently acquired resistance codename of Shepard, Frederik addressed the German soldier: 'I beg your pardon, captain', said Frederik apologetically in German, 'I am Frederik Shepard, the delivery driver.'

'Captain? You fool, I am a corporal!' retorted the warehouse delivery supervisor.

'Forgive me, corporal, I am old and do not see as well as I once did and thought that whoever was running this busy train station must be an important officer – a captain at least.'

'Well, thank you for that', said the corporal, 'at least you demonstrate some understanding of the importance of my job.'

The corporal held out his hand and snapped his fingers, gesturing impatiently to Frederik to pass him the paperwork. 'I expect you are here to pick up or drop off some "important" freight that you must have attended to straightaway?' asked the corporal sarcastically.

Frederik handed the corporal the cable with his instructions,

> Well, in fact, corporal, I am here to take delivery of an important shipment of spare parts for my company's merchant ship that has been stuck here in Copenhagen for the past week.

Frederik had been advised that one crate containing the 'real' spare parts was sealed only with short nails and could be easily identified from the other five well secured containers by an identifier below the black stenciled shipping address: the letters FCSB… his initials, Frederik Christian Sørensen Bangsbøll. Frederik followed the German corporal as he walked across the warehouse loading docks towards the recently arrived railcars and drew open the sliding door to the train car with a rumbling shudder of steel and heavy wood. The corporal running the shipping and receiving section clearly considered this 'miscellaneous cargo' from Horsens to be unimportant. However, the freight still needed to be processed in accordance with German military regulations. Realizing that he had to take the initiative in this situation, Frederik said as the railcar door clanged open,

> Corporal, I must insist that we inspect the contents of this shipment before I sign for it, as the previous delivery had the incorrect parts and my supervisor has threatened to fire me if I return with the wrong load again.

Without missing a step, the young corporal patted the crowbar that hung on his utility belt as he climbed aboard the railcar and replied, 'Not to worry, old man. Nothing comes through my warehouse without me verifying its authenticity.'

As planned, the decoy container had been the last to be loaded onto the railcar and was thus the closest and most accessible for inspection. Unfortunately for Frederik, however, the corporal maneuvered himself past that crate and began to attempt to pry open the lid of the second crate. Standing on the platform, Frederik could hear the young man struggling. Clearly the 6-inch screws securing the lid were doing their job.

'Perhaps, corporal, you should try more leverage to open the crate', suggested Frederik helpfully. Both men were breaking into a sweat simultaneously – for completely different reasons. The corporal continued his efforts while Frederik watched on.

'Listen to me, old man...' The corporal broke off mid-sentence. Interrupted either by fate or, more likely thought Frederik, by the 'Viking God Loki, Nordic God of Good Fortune and Trickery', the telephone in the corporal's office began to ring.

Frustrated with his inability to wedge the crowbar under the crate's lid, and now infuriated by the incessant ringing of his office telephone, the young corporal cried out, '*Scheiße*! [Shit!]' threw the crowbar down onto the floor of the railcar, making a thondorous noise in the canvanass compartment, jumped over the crates and ran towards his office to answer the telephone.

Several minutes later when he returned, he found Frederik hunched over the first crate, with the lid pried open, inspecting the contents of the crate.

'Ah wonderful, an engine drive shaft connector and a steam valve, just as ordered!' exclaimed Frederik to himself, but just loud enough to ensure the corporal could hear. Still bent over the crate, he turned and looked at the corporal who was watching him.

'Leverage, corporal, leverage.' Frederik said with a wry smile on his face. The corporal did not appreciate the insinuated jibe but had other things to worry about. The next train was due in twenty minutes and he needed to clear the loading dock. Plus, he had had just about enough of this arrogant old Dane, and replied sarcastically,

> Well, old man, why don't you try to use some leverage to pry the lazy arse of your fellow Danes I have working for me and get those damn crates out of my sight!

The corporal signed the transit receipt document and abruptly handed it to Frederik. With a polite node, Frederik said in perfect German, '*Danke corporal, vielen danke.* [Thank you, corporal, thank you very much.]'

* * *

Within the hour, the Copenhagen resistance cell had the Allies' shipment of weapons, ammunition, radios and Allied uniforms secured in one of their safe warehouses and Bjorn, back in Jutland, had received radio confirmation that the delivery had been completed without incident. The Allied weapons of war had been sent by Danish Resistance in Jutland and delivered to the resistance in Copenhagen all thanks to Schmidt and the efficiency of the German Wehrmacht's transportation and supply system.

When Bjorn came into Leif's office with the news of the mission's successful completion, the relief that Leif felt was enormous. He trusted his father and had all the confidence in the world in him, but the thought that he could have been captured by the Germans and interrogated and tortured by the Gestapo, all for helping Leif complete his mission, had weighed heavily on his mind. At that moment, he wanted more than anything to see his father again. Bjorn could see the emotion on his friend's face.

'Bech', he said, 'that was a dangerous thing your father just did for us. It must have taken a great deal of courage for you to ask to ask him to help.'

Leif smiled and replied,

> I owe all my successes in life to the lessons taught me by that old sea dog. I knew that if anyone could pull off such a brazenly bold bluff, it would be him. I knew he would come through for us – for Denmark.

Bjorn then said, 'Gold wants you to call him directly – immediately.' Leif smiled and assumed it would be to congratulate him on the successfully delivery of Allied weapons to Copenhagen right under the German's noses. Leif was wrong.

Gold's tone was not congratulator, rather, the conversation was more of an interrogation than a discussion about the mission's success. Gold's first and only question was,

> How did you select and recruit the truck driver who picked up the crates of weapons from the German loading docks at the Copenhagen train station?

Pausing a moment to formulate his answer Leif replied, 'He is a trusted old friend.' Though not completely truthful, Leif considered it a reasonable response, as he did not want to compromise his father's position within the Admiralty or as a member of the resistance.

'Old friend?' replied Gold.

> This 'old friend' of yours happens to be one of our most valued resistance operatives we have in Copenhagen… he goes by the name 'The Shepherd'. By having him involved in your clandestine capper as a delivery truck driver, you put one of our most valuable assets in harm's way Bech.'

Leif was dumbfounded. It appeared that his father, Commodore Frederik Bangsbøll, was the infamous Danish Resistance agent known only as The Shepherd, who was responsible for the freedom and safe passage of several thousand Danish Jews to Sweden curtesy of the Royal Danish Naval Reserve

Fleet. Leif, almost giddy at this news suddenly realized that despite Gold's almost omnipresent knowledge of the workings of the Danish Resistance network, the layers of OSS and Danish Resistance cover stories were working very effectively, as Gold was clearly not privy to the fact of either Jørgen Bech's true identity as Second Lieutenant Leif Bangsbøll of the United States Army and OSS agent nor that Leif's father, Commodore Frederik Bangsbøll of the Royal Danish Navy, was, in fact, The Shepherd. This cloak and dagger stuff is really working thought Leif.

Leif did not want to prolong this discussion with Gold any further and concluded,

> Sir, time was of the essence, I needed someone I could trust on very short notice. I called a trusted old friend, he agreed and he did exactly what was needed and did it exceedingly well. As a result, you have the Allied weapons, radios and uniforms you requested and the German's are none the wiser.

Chapter 26

The Road Ends

> 'Next to a battle lost, the greatest
> misery is a battle gained.'
>
> Duke of Wellington, Waterloo, 1815

The day after the safe delivery of Leif's 'spare marine parts' for the Danish Resistance cell in Copenhagen, Leif called Major Schmidt to advise him that the shipment had arrived safely in Copenhagen and to thank him for his assistance in this business matter. Schmidt agreed to meet Leif for dinner that evening, but when he arrived, Leif noted that the German officer appeared to be preoccupied. After a few drinks and some strained conversation about how disconcerting the war effort was from a German perspective, it became apparent to Leif that Schmidt had finally come to the realization that

The Ryvangen Assault Map, May 1945, used by Agen Bech / Scecond Lieutenant Bangsboll, with Bangsboll's Danish Resistance arm band, and pistol. (recreation 2020). (*Courtesy of the Bangsboll family photo collection*)

the end of the war was near. The Third Reich was about to fall. Leif also knew that extracting from Schmidt whatever details he could about the Germans' defense and withdrawal plans would aid the Allied victory, and particularly the offensive actions that the Danish Resistance planned to execute along with the Allied liberation forces.

The two men drank and spoke for hours. Leif did most of the listening and learned that although the leadership of the Wehrmacht knew the inevitability of their defeat, there was no mention of a peaceful, orderly surrender. It was apparent that the Germans planned to fight to the bitter end. Though Leif knew this would lead to more death and destruction within his beloved country, he was also content in a way, as this would give him and his Danish freedom fighters the opportunity to directly confront their Nazi occupiers in combat, rather than continuing to snipe at them from the shadows with clandestine, sabotage missions as they had been forced to do for the past three years. It was, in fact, almost a relief to learn that he would get the chance to fight, in open combat, the vile occupying force that infested his country and had wrecked death, destruction and, as yet, untold atrocities across Europe, Scandinavia, the Balkans, throughout the Mediterranean and North Africa. There he sat drinking and speaking amicably with a willing cog of the German war machine. Leif and Schmidt knew the end was near. But only one of them knew they would be on the side of a righteous victory.

Leif's coded report to London the next day outlined his assessment of Schmidt's views on their intent to fight to the end. 'So be it', thought Leif, 'we'll just kill more of you.' He also thought, with a smirk on his face, of a quote from one of his favorite Shakespeare's plays, *Julius Caesar*, 'Beware the ides of March.' On 15 March 1944, just three weeks after his brazen shipment of Allied weapons using a German supply train, Leif led a bold daylight sabotage mission against Jutland's major railway hub at Skanderborg. Leif had been very pleased with the previous three sabotage missions against Germain supply trains transiting through Jutland destine for, but never to reach, frontline German troops in Germany, France and Belgium. However, the cunning young leader now thought that it was time to change their targeting objectives for the resistance's next sabotage mission. Leif knew that blowing up railway lines in isolated locations in the dark of night was one thing, but to hit the Germans in broad daylight at one of its transit vital points was brazenly daring – the Germans would not expect it. With the explosives smuggled into the Skanderborg railway yard the previous day, Leif, disguised as a railway worker with falsified papers, reported for duty at the railway yard facilities under the very eyes of the German sentries and Danish security guards, and succeeded in planting several explosive devices in critical areas within the facility. The explosives were detonated by delay action fuses, allowing Leif a timely escape and resulted in the destruction of a German supply train, including two locomotives, as well as inflicting major damage to the switching station and telegraph office. The facility was out of action for over a week and the loss of valuable German supplies incalculable. As a result, additional German troops were assigned to the Skanderborg railway yard and at other important rail links and vital points throughout Denmark. This disruption of German resupply activities and the reallocation and reinforcement of troops to non-combat sentry duties was one of the key objectives the OSS had given to the resistance forces – Jutland's Danish Resistance network was operating with calculated efficiency.

Two weeks later, at the end of March 1945, as the Allied forces were converging on Berlin and the defeat of Germany seemed imminent, Leif placed a coded radio request to his OSS leadership in London that he be brought back to Britain in anticipation of an Allied seaborne and airborne invasion of Denmark. 'I want to come in fighting!' he explained to his OSS commander.

Leif was told, not to expect a seaborne or airborne Allied invasion of Denmark, but instead to support the British and Canadian armies, which, as part of Operation Eclipse, was pushing aggressively northward towards southern Denmark from the Netherlands through northern Germany. As a result, Leif and Bjorn were ordered to relocate to the capital and establish themselves with the Danish Resistance network in Copenhagen. There, they were to prepare to initiate resistance activities within Copenhagen and the surrounding area in the coming weeks in direct support of the Anglo-Canadian offensive driving northward towards the capital.

Travel from Aarhus to Copenhagen for Leif and Bjorn was far easier than they had expected. The German troop presence at checkpoints and railway transit points had recently diminished, as many of the occupying forces were being redistributed and concentrated at the most likely Allied points of attack, notably in southern Denmark and along the western coast of Denmark/Jutland. Relying on brazen guile and his excellent spoken German, Leif, posing, as a maritime insurance agent from Aarhus with falsified travel papers to their head office in Copenhagen, slipped through the German security web and arrived in Copenhagen on 31 March 1945.

With his OSS orders verified by the resistance leadership, and with the strong support of Gold, the regional commander, Leif was brought in to meet with the resistance team leaders in Copenhagen. Together they would organize and prepare themselves to increase sabotage missions and direct attacks against the occupying German forces in and around the capital. The Danish Resistance would go on the offensive once notification had been received that the British and Canadian armies had crossed the border from Germany into southern Denmark.

During the month of April 1945, Leif led small daily and nightly harassing attacks on various German installations and headquarters facilities, as well as on German checkpoints and convoys in and around the capital city. Some attacks were planned for specific targets, such as the German army and Gestapo headquarters in Copenhagen; others were targets of opportunity, such as ambushes on German troop and supply convoys coming into or departing the capital.

On the evening of 3 May 1945, Leif was summoned to meet with Gold and several other senior Danish Resistance leaders to discuss plans to liberate Copenhagen. The meeting took place in a dimly lit basement apartment below a popular restaurant near the port, on Nyham Street, located where the Nyhavnsbroen bridge crosses the Havnebussen canal. As the senior man present, Gold commenced the meeting by giving them the news they had all been waiting to hear: the British and Canadian armies had crossed into Denmark through the southern border towns of Saed and Padborg and were smashing through German defenses, moving rapidly north towards Copenhagen. 'This is our opportunity time to attack on all fronts', said Gold.

Once the cheers of excitement had died down, the resistance leaders got to work; a map of the city was laid out on the table and the small band of freedom fighters spent the next two hours discussing plans for simultaneous assaults on various German positions within the capital.

* * *

Leif was assigned the assault on the German garrison at Ryvangen, located in the northeastern district of Copenhagen. Ryvangen garrison was strategically situated at a transport hub, where a main railway line and major roadway entered the city and was the largest, most well defended installations the Germans had within the city. Accordingly, Leif was allocated the largest number of troops for his mission – 100 Resistance members, of which 25 were current or former soldiers from the Royal Danish Army. Leif was pleased. He felt that he had been given sufficient resistance fighters, a quarter of whom were trained Danish soldiers, a warehouse full of weapons and munitions at his disposal and an important German target to attack. The Allied weapons, ammunition, radios and uniforms that Leif had recently smuggled into Copenhagen for the resisitance would soon be in use by the Danish Resistance fighters as they fought to take back their capital.

With the meeting concluded, Gold signaled to Benneke, his COS, who went upstairs to the restaurant and came back moments later with a bottle of "Aalborg" Akvavit and a tray with eight glasses. The alcohol was poured and the assembled resistance leaders raised their glasses. 'To victory and the end of Nazi occupation!' declared Gold. Their glasses clinked and the smooth, clear liquid was consumed in one quick tilt.

The following day, Leif and Bjorn met with the five senior ranking soldiers of the assigned contingent. In turn, each sergeant was allocated twenty resistance members, including an equal share of the remaining trained soldiers, creating five twenty-man platoons. Leif knew this construct would be easier to organize and control during the mission and indicated that each platoon leader would be issued a radio, weapons and ammunition to outfit their platoons at the assembly point the morning of the attack. His final instruction to the five sergeants was that no military uniforms would be worn; everyone in the assault force would be wearing civilian clothing.

'If we are going to catch the German garrison by surprise, we can't be strolling around the streets of Copenhagen in "Allied or" Royal Danish Army uniforms', said Leif. He also understood that the design and color of the Royal Danish Army uniform looked all too similar to the German Wehrmacht uniform. During this assault and those still to come during the liberation of Denmark with the Allies assistance, he did not want Danish soldiers or resistance members being mistaken for German soldiers. Grudgingly, Danish sergeants accepted the orders from this 'civilian' and dispersed to prepare for the following morning's mission.

The next morning, Saturday, 5 May 1945, the 100 members of Leif's assault force, all wearing civilian clothing, moved amongst the thousands of other Danes who were going about their business, commuting to and from work, shopping or just out enjoying the Danish spring morning. Using various forms of public and private transportation, Leif's assault force began to assemble. At 1000 hours the last of the resistance force members arrived at Saint Theresa's Church in the suburb of Østerbro in the north-west area of Copenhagen. Leif had selected Saint Theresa's as the assembly point because he knew that groups of people entering the large church would not look suspicious and the church was ideally located just a few blocks north of their objective – the German garrison at Ryvangen.

Leif, Bjorn and a dozen of their most trusted team members had arrived at the church earlier that morning in two trucks carrying the weapons, ammunition and radios to be distributed prior to the attack. Also loaded into the trucks were a half a dozen wheelbarrows, buckets and dozens of shovels and picks. Leif had also requested of Gold that he advise the director at the nearby Bispebjerg Hospital to be prepared to receive casualties. Bispebjerg Hospital was located just a few streets south-east of Ryvangen garrison. With his plan in his head and his 100 soldiers now fully armed and seated in the pews before him, Leif stood at the front of the church to address his brave, yet motley looking crew of freedom fighters. The first thing he did was to clarify who he was.

> You may know me as Jørgen Bech, and you may be aware that I've spent the last seven months, along with my colleague, Bjorn Toller, in Jutland leading your brothers and sisters there in the fight against the Nazis.

After a moment's pause, he continued, 'I am, in fact, Second Lieutenant Leif Bangsbøll and this is Sergeant Alfred Keller of the United States Army.'
Murmurs of surprise spread through those gathered.

> I have orders from your resistance Commander Gold to take the nearby German garrison at Ryvangen and, with your help, that is exactly what we are going to do.

Second Lieutenant Bangsboll went on to explain the attack plan and gave out his orders to each of the Royal Danish Army sergeants. These non-commissioned officers were now much more receptive to taking orders from an army officer rather than the civilian named Jørgen Bech. Leif went on to explain how their forces would be divided into two assault teams of forty fighters, with the third group of twenty held in reserve. The reserve force were to remain at the church until they received further orders. Using the wheelbarrows to carry and hide most of their weapons, the two assault teams would carry shovels and picks looking, at first glance, like a crew of construction workers on their way to a work site. One team, led by Leif, would approach the German garrison's main entrance from the west on Tuborgvej Road via the Ryvangs alley. This route was ideal as it was bordered by trees and thick hedges and would provide good cover as they approached their objective. The other assault team, led by Bjorn along with the senior Danish sergeant, would lead their men to the eastern side of the garrison, which ran along Rymarkvej Road. It was furthest from the garrison's main gate and was less well guarded.

At precisely 1145 hours, while many of the German soldiers in the garrison were in the mess hall eating their lunch, Leif, with a shovel balanced over his shoulder and a Tommy gun hidden and slung over his back, approached the front gate of the German garrison. The row of men walking just behind Leif were similarly outfitted with shovels or picks, each with a concealed weapon slung over their shoulder or hidden under their coats. Walking beside them were several men pushing wheelbarrows, now empty of weapons and full of construction tools. Behind them, obscured from view, were the rest of the force who had their weapons at the ready. From the German guardhouse vantage point at the main gate, it appeared that a group of construction workers were crossing Tuborgvej Road, on their way to a worksite – exactly as Leif had planned. To the surprise of the two armed German guards at the gate, the group of Danish construction workers crossed the street and just kept walking right towards the garrison entrance.

When one of the German guards yelled, 'HALT!' Leif just kept walking. The guard yelled 'HALT!' again. After taking two more steps, Leif dropped his shovel, which made a clanging sound as it hit the cobblestone roadway, and in one smooth continuous motion brought the Tommy gun up, pointing directly at the German guard. '*HANDEN HOCH!*' [HANDS UP!]' Leif ordered. The German soldier was young and inexperienced. He hesitated. '*HANDEN HOCH!* [HANDS UP!]' shouted Leif again.

Staring at the Tommy gun pointed at him, the surprised and frightened German soldier complied with the order. As the young guard capitulated, Leif saw the second guard un-shouldering his weapon and raising it to aim. Without hesitation, Leif opened fire and the second German soldier was immediately thrown back against the guardhouse wall by the impact of three rounds to the chest. The first German guard, now terrified, dropped his rifle – it too clattered as it struck the brick roadway. The frightened German sentry stretched both hands high in the air. From behind, Leif suddenly heard the discharge of a dozen rounds from several rifles, which were firing into the second floor window of the guardhouse that held a German machine gun position, killing or wounding the other German guards and eliminating that threat.

Leif called to his team, 'Forward now, to the mess hall and headquarters buildings!'

As planned, half of his team ran forward into the garrison towards the mess hall, where they knew many of the garrison's troops would be eating their midday meal. Some of the German soldiers had brought their weapons with them, but many, lulled into complacency over the years in a relatively peaceful city under occupation had left their weapons behind in their lock-up or at their place of duty. As a result, the resistance force quickly overwhelmed the German soldiers, killing a dozen and capturing a dozen more.

Meanwhile, Leif led the rest of his team into the garrison headquarters building, securing the surroundings after a brief but intense firefight. Just as Leif and his team were rounding up the German radio operator and the garrison commander, he heard the heavy exchange of gunfire across the open field towards the eastern side of the garrison compound where Bjorn was launching his team's attack. Leif recognized that different types of weapons make distinctly different sounds when they are fired. To his dismay, much of what he now heard were German weapons in use. He had a reserve force back at the church and needed them to immediately move out to reinforce the team assaulting the eastern side of the garrison.

Looking at his radio man, Leif instructed him,

> Contact the reserve force and tell them to move towards the fight on the eastern side of the garrison as quickly as possible. Then, let Sergeant Keller know that help is on the way.

Taking twenty of his forty-man team, Leif moved out at a run towards the sound of the battle and thought 'Hopefully, we can catch the Germans between our two attacking forces.'

Leif and his team did not get more than 50 yards when a German machine gun position at the far eastern side of the compound, about 200 yards away, opened up. Immediately three of his team were cut down in a hail of bullets. Leif shouted for the rest to take cover, but there was little to be found – a couple of trees and a small drainage ditch were all they had for concealment and protection from the withering fire of the Germans' 42-millimeter machine gun. From his position in the ditch, Leif could see that the German machine gun emplacement had an unobstructed enfilade field of fire over the wide compound that he and his team needed to cross to aid their companions and finish the fight.

After a quick assessment of their situation, Leif ordered his team to remain in place and provide covering fire for him. A moment later, the seventeen remaining resistance fighters began firing at the German machine gun position. This was his chance: Leif got to his feet and began running forward. Two, three, four, five seconds passed and no return fire from the German machine gun emplacement.

Then suddenly, from another position, 100 yards further south from the original machine gun threat, came a rapid burst of automatic gunfire from a second German machine gun position. A dozen 42-millimeter Mauser heavy machine gun rounds impacted the ground five feet in front of Leif. The explosion of dirt and stones churned up by the high velocity rounds struck him like a brick wall and he went down. From the perspective of both his Danish colleagues behind him and from the German gun position in front of him, Leif had been killed.

The sergeant that Leif had left in charge was a professional soldier and immediately ordered half of the remaining team to engage the second German machine gun impalement. Just as he was preparing to launch himself forward toward Leif's now prone, motionless body, the sergeant was stunned to see Leif jump to his feet and continue his dash across the open field towards the garrison building. Through the smoke and noise of the battle, the two German machine gun positions did not immediately notice the lone soldier advancing until he was almost to the safety of the garrison building. Leif's sergeant saw it all; Leif was running as fast as he could with his Tommy gun firing from the waist in the general direction of the Germans. One of the German machine gunners had spotted the running man and bursts of exploding earth began to strafe the ground, chasing the moving figure and getting closer and closer to him. Then, just as Leif seemed to have reached the protection of the building that he ran towards, the side of the building exploded in a hail of machine gun rounds. A dust cloud enveloped and obscured the small building for several seconds. Again, Leif's sergeant thought that this was surely the end of him. 'No one can be that lucky to have come that close to death twice in just a matter of a few seconds and survive.'

The sergeant shouted at his men to conserve their ammunition, but to keep enough firing at the two machine gun nests to keep them busy, while he quickly figured out what they were to do now. They were in the middle of a killing zone, with their leader 'dead' and the reserve force committed to another, totally separate part of the battle.

Then, out of the corner of his eye, the sergeant saw movement. He could not believe his eyes – Leif was standing, leaning against the wall of the building waving his arm over his head. He was alive and signaling his intentions. Leif then turned and went behind the building towards the other besieged resistance team. The sergeant knew that their only hope of survival now lay in Leif's hands and thought,

> I must get Keller and his resistance team to breach the eastern sector of the garrison to eliminate these two German machine gun positions or we're all dead!

Soaked in sweat, his face covered in dirt, Leif breathed heavily with his heart pounding from the exertion of running across the 200 yards of open field, leaned against the building and gathered his thoughts. As the dust settled around him, he waved to his men in the field.

'Look, I've made it!' he thought as he signaled to get their attention. Assuming that one of his men had seen him, he turned and moved behind the building, towards the other firefight going on with his second assault team.

Leif thought,

> Things went so smoothly at first, I was sure we had caught the Krauts flat footed but those two 42-millimeter emplacements were an extremely unwelcome surprise… and why were those German guns facing into the garrison yard, not outwards towards an external threat?

That puzzled him greatly, but he had other, more pressing, concerns at the moment. As he moved forward, the sound of the second firefight grew louder and his attention was drawn away from the previous fight to the here and the now of the second battle confronting him.

Leif moved behind the second building. Running in a crouched position, he passed under an open window and heard shouting in Danish. Leif stopped abruptly and yelled back in Danish. He called out for one person to come out of the building with their hands up. A minute later, an older man wearing a gray prisoner's uniform emerged, barefoot and afraid, with his hands in the air. The old man cautiously walked towards him. 'Who are you? Why are you here?' demanded Leif.

'I'm Doctor Arne Jensen. I'm a prisoner.' Glancing back over his shoulder, he continued, 'We are all prisoners.'

'How many of you are there?' asked Leif.

'About twenty-five', he replied, then added matter-of-factly, 'there were more, but they're gone now.'

Suddenly Leif understood why the machine guns in this part of the garrison were pointed inward. It was a prison camp, as well as a German garrison.

'Tell your friends to stay in the building away from the windows. Tell them the Danish Resistance is here to free them.' Leif looked at the older man closely and said, 'The fight is not over, but I will come back for you when it is.'

He then pulled his Walther PPK pistol from its holster from under his jacket and handed it to the old man. 'If the door of your building opens without a Danish voice asking to come in first, you start shooting every German you see.'

With trembling hands, the old man took the weapon, nodded and said was, 'I will try.'

Leif continued towards the sounds of the gunfire. On the way, he passed what was clearly a pistol firing range, with five lanes and a dirt abutment for targets and for the rounds to safely sink into. After crossing it and climbing through a thick hedge on the far side, he entered an adjacent field that he thought was another firing range, but then stopped in his tracks. He saw four wooden posts mounted in the ground about 10 feet apart with a dirt abutment behind them. This was not a firing range – it was an execution site!

The crack of a bullet breaking the sound barrier near his head immediately brought his attention back to his task and the threat of danger around him. Ahead, he saw several men in civilian clothing with weapons huddled behind a building not more than 30 yards away. The noise of the battle prevented them from hearing his shouts. Leif waved and got their attention. They waved for him to come to them. They were clearly frightened and did not want to move from their position of relative safety.

Carefully timing his approach to the building across the road, Leif unloaded the rest of his Tommy gun's clip towards the German position and then took off at a dead run. Crossing the open space in just a few seconds, he found himself back in the presence of his Danish comrades from Sergeant Keller's assault team. Though relieved at seeing the dozen resistance fighters looking back at him, all anxiously expecting direction or at least reassurance that all was not lost, Leif realized that many of these men were merely teenaged boys. 'Where is your sergeant?' he asked.

Immediately one of the youngest said, 'Killed. Killed, outside the gate.' Another, older man then interjected, 'He was wounded. I saw him go down, but only wounded. He is outside the back gate where most of our people are.'

Leif looked around to assess their situation and asked if anyone had a radio. 'Yes, sir, right here.' said one of the boys. The radio was passed along to Leif, who tried to contact Bjorn but was unsuccessful. Moments later, the radio crackled to life and he was talking to Sergeant Olson who was leading the reserve force. Olson indicated they were also pinned down outside the eastern gate, approximately 100 yards east from Leif's position.

> Yes, my reserve force is here supporting Sergeant Teller and about twenty other Danes who led the initial assault. But we can't approach the gate. The Germans have strong firing positions directly in front of us in the two story, red brick building I think it might be their barracks. I counted at least six weapons firing from the second floor windows and two from ground floor windows. It is impossible for us to advance.

Olson continued,

> There are two burning vehicles in front of the barracks – a troop truck and an armored car. We put both out of action at the start of the attack. The surviving German soldiers retreated into the barracks and have now established a strong defensive position – over.

Leif was impressed with the soldier's calm demeanor and his clear, concise assessment of the tactical situation and replied, 'Well done, sergeant.'

> I need you and your team to keep those Germans pinned down in their barracks. I have a dozen men with me and we are located about 50 yards north of the barracks, facing the side of the building. There are only two windows facing us, so we will assault the building from this flank – over.

'Affirmative. We will continue to engage the barracks and cover your movement – over.'

Leif said to his men, 'Okay, boys, prepare to earn your pay.'

One of the younger resistance fighters looked at his friend and whispered, 'We're getting paid for this?'

'Don't be stupid, it's just an American saying!' replied the friend.

'Does everyone have a weapon and ammunition?' Leif asked as he scanned their nervous, sweaty faces. They all nodded. One of the men indicated that he had two hand grenades and three others indicated that they too had at least one hand grenade each.

The oldest man in the group, who looked to be well into his sixties, pulled from his satchel a glass bottle petrol bomb and grinned and said, 'This is very effective as well.'

Leif replied, 'Very good.'

> Once we get across this clearing, over to the barracks, I'll need you men with grenades to clear the lower floor of the building. Understood? You with the Molotov cocktail, that gets used last, once we have shocked the Germans with the grenades.

They nodded.

> I need all of you to spread out as we move across the open ground and have your weapons pointed at the barrack's windows and roof top. At the first sign of enemy fire or even movement open up quickly, as we will be exposed and will only have the element of surprise for a few seconds.

Looking at the boy with the radio, Leif added, 'Tell the reserve force we are moving out in one minute.'

As expected, thirty seconds later, the level of friendly fire from the reserve force of resistance fighters outside the eastern gate increased substantially. The face of the German barracks was being ravaged by rifle fire, which kept the German defenders hunkered down, away from the windows.

'NOW!' shouted Leif and he took off running towards the German position; his dozen fighters fanning out as instructed behind and beside him. As the small resistance force was midway across the field, several flashes of weapons being fired came from the second floor window of the barracks and, as instructed, Leif's mobile assault team returned heavy fire as they ran. When they reached the building Leif shouted, 'GRENADES NOW! INTO THE GROUND FLOOR WINDOWS!'

Moments later, the bottom floor of the barracks erupted with five explosions. Smoke poured from the windows and doorway. Flames then erupted as the petrol bomb was lit and exploded in the interior of the ravaged building's first floor.

'Spread out men, and keep your weapons trained on the doorway and upper windows!' Bangsbøll directed.

A minute later, with the lower floor of the barracks now engulfed in flames, the first German soldiers appeared at the doorway and were immediately riddled with gunfire from Leif's team. Desperate German shouts from inside the barracks could be heard and several German weapons were thrown out of the doorway onto the steps of the building. Leif yelled in German, '*KOMM MIT ERHOBENEN HOCH!* [COME OUT WITH YOUR HANDS UP!]'

More weapons were thrown onto the steps and cautiously the first German soldier emerged, as instructed, with his hands in the air. More followed, looking shocked and frightened. Some were coughing and all their faces were black with soot from the smoke pouring out of their barracks. Six more Germans exited the building and were rounded up by Leif's men. Some sporadic firing from the front of the barracks could still be heard, but it was lessening in intensity.

Leif called for the radio, but the boy with the radio was no longer amongst them. All of them looked back at the open field they had just crossed. The lifeless body of the young man lay on the grass. The boy had been hit by the burst of German gunfire from the upper window as they assaulted the barracks. Leif, knowing that the fight still hung in the balance, said, 'I need that radio.'

Without hesitating, one of the older men in the group turned and ran to retrieve it. Leif's first radio call was to his initial assault force, which was still pinned down in the field adjacent to the PoW compound by the two German machine gun emplacements. He instructed them to keep the German machine gunners busy while he flanked them and put them out of action. Then, once Leif had advised Olson at the eastern, back gate to advance and secure the rest of the German barracks, he told him that he was leaving two of his men to guard their German PoWs at the back of the barracks. He and the rest of the team were going to move on the two machine gun positions that were still threatening the other assault force.

Leif and his seven remaining fighters cautiously approached the first German machine gun emplacement from its left flank. The Danes could see only the muzzle of the German weapon protruding from the bunker, spitting fire and lead onto the compound where Leif's first assault team remained pinned down. The German soldiers manning the gun emplacement could not see the Danes approaching. The Danes encircled three sides of the German gun position and simultaneously opened fire and threw the last grenade into the gun emplacement. The first German machine gun position went silent. Similarly, the second machine gun emplacement was put out of action. Half a dozen stunned German soldiers who had survived the sudden onslaught were taken as a PoWs.

Suddenly it was quiet – the fighting had ceased across the entire garrison. The German garrison was back in Danish hands. The battle had taken less than an hour. Across the city there were similar acts of defiance by armed Danes who were taking back their capital. All the attacks were strategically important but none were as large and so fiercely contested as the Ryvangen engagement.

The eighty German soldiers taken as PoWs at Ryvangen were kept under guard and assembled within the confines of the garrison's pistol range. The two officers taken prisoner, the commander, a major and one captain were taken by Leif and a Royal Danish Army sergeant and were tied to the execution posts. Leif had no intentions of executing anyone, but he wanted to frighten the Germans to ensure they complied and fully capitulated. The German soldiers, assembled in the adjacent pistol firing range could hear the feeble cries for mercy from their two officers. Witnessing the humiliation of the two German officers was distinctly dissatisfying for Leif. However, after five years of subjugation under the Nazis, the rest of the Danish Resistance fighters seemed quite content to witness the German officers beg for mercy.

As the Danish Resistance fighters gathered in front of the garrison headquarters building to care for their wounded, Leif was reunited with his OSS partner and friend, Alfred Keller. They hugged each other in a long embrace. Bjorn explained that his radio had been destroyed by a bullet that had injured his hand at the outset of their assault. A moment later, the old man, the doctor and former PoW of the Germans who Leif had encountered during the assault, meekly approached Bangsboll and Keller and carefully handed the pistol back to the resistance force leader. 'Sir, I believe this is yours.'

'Did you have to use it doctor?' asked Leif.

'No, but I was prepared to!' stated Dr Jensen proudly.

Leif replied with a grin, 'I'm sure you were. You and the rest of your brave friends are free. Would you like to be taken to the hospital?'

'No thank you', the doctor replied, 'I will stay here and assist with the wounded, but if you don't mind, my fellow inmates would like to go over to the kitchen for some food.'

'Of course, doctor.' Leif gestured to one of his sergeants to escort the former Danish PoWs over to the mess hall for a meal.

'Sergeant', said Leif, 'send someone to find a bottle or two of Akvavit. These men look like they could use a stiff drink.'

Chapter 27

Just One More Mission…

'The great love the Danish people
bear him – who despite his faults,
their affections convert his sins to graces.'

William Shakespeare, *Hamlet*

On 7 May 1945, after six long years under brutal Nazi occupation, Denmark was liberated. Inspired by the British and Canadian troops under the command of Field Marshal Bernard 'Monty' Montgomery who were advancing from the south, the Danish Resistance had risen-up in force in hundreds of locations – killing, capturing or chasing out German troops. Leif successfully led a heroic attack on the German garrison at Ryvangen was one of the most significant and decisive Resistance-led actions against the Germans. Leif did not land on the beaches, weapons firing like he had hoped, however, the assault on Ryvangen garrison, well planned and audaciously executed, provided some degree of solus to the young Dane. Leif spent the rest of May and part of June in Copenhagen, working with the British and Canadian armies. Major General Colin Gibbons, the director of the SOE, accompanied by Lieutenant Colonel Winklehorn, the American COS of the OSS's London office, joined Leif in Copenhagen on the 10 May 1945. Under the direction of Gibbons, Winklehorn and his British SOE counterpart assigned to Montgomery's staff began to take charge of the situation. One of their primary assignments was to oversee and facilitate the handling of German PoWs within Denmark and Norway, and to identify and segregate any high value officers within the Wehrmacht leadership or Gestapo and search for any scientific specialists, such as engineers and technicians from the V-1 rocket program. Leif was also tasked with ensuring that the search for Danish citizens who had collaborated with the Germans was done in an orderly, controlled and legal manner. The tendency for vigilantism and vengeance was real and needed to be quelled.

* * *

Lieutenant Leif Bangsboll, OSS Agent with Sergeant Alfred Keller (Agent Bjorn Toller) in background, following the defeat of Nazi Germany. Photo taken in Copenhagen Denmark, mid-May 1945. Note both American soldiers are wearing the Danish Resistance arm band on their left sleeves. (*Photo courtesy of the author's family collection*)

On 11 May 1945, at the Danish Admiralty building in Copenhagen, Leif was reunited with his father after five years and one month of war, separation and Nazi occupation. When Leif saw his father, he thought he had aged twenty years. Frederik, meanwhile, thought his son looked fit and strappingly fine in his United States Army combat fatigues and wearing the blue and red arm band, denoting his affiliation with the Danish Resistance. That afternoon, Leif made a point to locate and introduce Gold, the regional resistance leader, to his father. To Leif's surprise, Frederik and Gold knew each other well, as they had communicated regularly and collaborated on several operations during the occupation, including Frederik's final and most exciting assignment, which his son had recruited him for: the receipt of the shipment of Allied weapons and equipment at the Copenhagen railway yard, care of Hitler and his Wehrmacht's reliable transportation system. It was during this meeting that Leif and Gold learned that the Danish Resistance agent known as The Shepherd was none other than Commodore Frederik Bangsbøll, Leif's father. 'It appears', Frederik said, that my efforts to secret the Danish Jews to Sweden, right under the Nazi's noses had earned me this moniker – I was only doing my duty and happened to be in the right position within the Admiralty to get it done.

At the end the day, Leif and Frederik drove home to Naerum, passing through the Osterbro district of Copenhagen, within two blocks of the Ryvangen garrison. The garrison was once more manned with Danish soldiers, where less than a week earlier, Leif had led the Resistance in a life-and-death struggle with its German occupiers. Now Denmark was liberated, and he and his father were once again free to move about their beloved Copenhagen as they wished – as free men.

The two spoke for hours, recounting the challenges of the war and some of the remarkable feats achieved. Frederik was fascinated and proud to hear of his son's involvement in the capture of the Ryvangen garrison from the Germans.

Commodore Frederik Bangsboll, Royal Danish Navy and son, Leif Bangsboll, First Lieutenant United States Army, reunion after the liberation of Denmark from five years of Nazi occupation, Copenhagen Denmark, May 1945. (*Photo courtesy of the author's family collection*)

In turn, Leif was elated to hear his father recount of his performance at the Copenhagen rail yard, when he retrieved the OSS weapons that Leif had sent on the German supply train.

After a few beers and a half-dozen cigarettes, the two leisurely prepared a simple supper together. It was a beautiful, warm evening, so they sat in the back yard, watching the sunset, overlooking the Kattegatt Straight, the entrance to Copenhagen harbor, and enjoyed the simple pleasure of each other's company. After dinner, just as the Scandinavian sky's violet horizon began to reveal a universe of stars, Fredrik brought out two fresh glasses and a bottle of Aquavit. They toasted the end of the war and the coming of peace. They toasted their fallen comrades. They toasted family and friends. Then Frederik made a final toast: "Jocom" said Frederik, "To our parents' children."

The two men raised their glasses, smiled at each other and repeated in unison: "To our parents' children." This was a toast his father had taught Leif as a child, which he said was made especially for Leif. Secretly it was Leif's

Just One More Mission... 299

SOE (Special Operations Executive) / American OSS (Office of Strategic Services) Victory Dinner, Wivex Hotel in Copenhagen, July, 1945. OSS Commander, Major-General Gubbins (Center), Lieutenant Bangsboll (Second row, tenth from the left). (*Photo courtesy of the United States Army*)

favorite toast. Following a long, reflective silence, Leif said, "I plan to take the ferry tomorrow and spend the weekend on Bornholm; would you come with me, Father? "Frederik's demeanor suddenly changed.

"Leif, you have obviously not heard the latest intelligence reports. After heavy bombing from Russian naval and air forces, yesterday, the Russian's have

Lieutenant Bangsboll (center) with colleagues at SOE (Special Operations Executive) / American OSS (Office of Strategic Services) Victory Dinner at the Wivex Hotel, Copenhagen, July, 1945. (*Photo courtesy of the United States Army*)

landed on Bornholm. They've rounded up the German garrison of 400 soldiers who had been occupying the island during the war. The Russians are staking a claim to the island." This disturbing news brought an otherwise wonderful evening to an abrupt end.

Later that night, lying in his boyhood bedroom, Leif could not fall asleep. He was relieved that the war was won and over and seeing his father alive and well was of great importance to him; but the thought that his little island in the Baltic was now occupied by the Russians ate at his soul. Leif had planned to travel out to Bornholm, hopefully with his father, to stay at their family's summer home in Sveneke and to pay his respects at the gravesite of his mother and two sisters. It had been 15 years since he last stood over the family plot hand-in-hand with his father. So much had happened since then and so much had changed. Leif needed to return to Bornholm, but that visit would have to wait.

As a result of the news of the Russian occupation of Bornholm, Leif chose to remain with his father in Copenhagen for a few more days. The next morning, Frederik went back to the Admiralty to begin making arrangements to bring back the many Danish naval ships that had been dispersed to the safety of neutral Sweden at the beginning of the war. His son continued with his interrogations of German PoWs and commenced the search for known Danish collaborators and traitors. Justice must be served.

Lieutenant Leif Bangsboll, receiving United States Distinguished Service Cross medal from Commander SOE / OSS, Major-General Gubbins, July 1945. (*Photo courtesy of the United States Army*)

Lieutenant Bangsboll adorned with U.S. Distinguished Service Cross medal, London England, July 1945. (*Photo courtesy of the United States Army*)

Leif's plan to stay only a few days with his father stretched into two weeks. Father and son reveled in this new, calm atmosphere of the city. During the last week of May 1945, after spending a rejuvenating stay at his boyhood home with his father, Leif, knowing he would receive new orders from the OSS, took the opportunity to travel back to Jutland and the towns of Aarhus and Horsens to visit and bid farewell to his former resistance team members. While in Jutland, Leif also made two special detours – to visit the Hans Fletcher, his Horsens' region resistance team leader, and secondly, to go to the village of Skive, to pay a visit to Olaf and Ragla Gustovson, the farmer and resistance member whose farm Leif had landed in during his initial insertion mission in the early morning of 6 October 1944. Olaf and his wife – who had also assisted Leif with the Sophie Halverson situation – were immensely glad to see Leif again and spent an evening getting news of how Copenhagen had been liberated and together recalling the adventures of the past few years.

* * *

By early June 1945, Leif and the OSS and their SOE colleagues were wrapping up their investigations and post-war reports in Copenhagen. On 17 June 1945, OSS and SOE agents and staff in Denmark held a victory dinner to celebrate the Danish Resistance and the accomplishments of the OSS and SOE in defeating the Nazi occupiers. Approximately 200 fellow agents and support staff assembled in the grand ballroom of the Wivex Hotel, Tivoli Park, Copenhagen. The Danish hosts put on a spectacular meal – a true Danish smorgasbord. The beer and Akvavit flowed freely and the victorious comrades-in-arms celebrated late into the night.

A week after the victory dinner, Leif received orders from the OSS headquarters in London, calling him back to Britain. There, his assignment was to complete detailed reports on his activities as an OSS/SOE agent while in occupied Denmark and to contribute to the collection of lessons learned from other OSS and SOE agents. Those documented lessons would later be used to educate and train new agents.

Returning to London was bittersweet. London was scared, but remarkable in its resilience, observed Leif. The collective pride at enduring five years of German onslaught and the elation that Britain had been victorious were palpable on every street corner and in every setting. Leif enjoyed reuniting with his fellow OSS and SOE colleagues and made an effort to frequent many of the sites of London, including his favorite clubs and pubs. One evening he stopped by the Café de Paris, which was owned by his wartime Danish friend, Martin Poulsen. Upon arrival, Leif was disappointed to find that the building was boarded up.

Dorothy Henry, standing outside her home at 231 King Street East, in Oshawa, Ontario Canada beside Leif's new car, purchased with his WWII backpay, August 1945. (*Photo courtesy of the author's family collection*)

Apparently, the subsequent damage done during the blitz had weakened the building's foundation and major repairs, or possibly even demolition, were in its future. Poulsen was nowhere to be found. Leif stood in front of the now boarded up restaurant and recalled his friend and colleague Nicole, the SOE agent who was killed by the Nazis just days after their one and only date here at the now defunct Café de Paris. Leif thought to himself, 'So many good things are gone…'

Then, in early July 1945, Leif received new orders to return to OSS headquarters in Washington DC, where he was to prepare for a deployment into the Pacific theater of war against the Japanese. Once back in Washington DC, knowing he would be shipped out again in the near future, Leif felt that he needed to take some leave. On 1 August 1945, Leif was granted six weeks leave by his OSS director.

* * *

The first thing Leif did with the bundle of backpay that he had earned for his time in Denmark over the past year, was to buy a car. With the intent of impressing a young Canadian lady, Leif selected a Ford Super Deluxe Coupe, two door, canary yellow convertible. With a brand new car at his disposal and plenty of cash in his pocket, Leif drove north up Interstate Highway 95 towards

Canada. His destination was 231 King Street East, Oshawa, Ontario. True to his word when he had bid farewell to Margaret and Clifford Henry in November 1942, Leif returned for a long awaited visit. There, Leif reacquainted himself with the Henry family, and particularly with Dorothy-Jean Henry, now 18 years old. The sweet young girl he had met three years earlier was now a beautiful young woman. Dorothy had enrolled at Branksome Hall College, an all-girls school in Toronto, and was spending the summer with her family in Oshawa when her secret love returned from the war – just as he had promised.

On 15 August 1945, while still on leave in Canada, to the great fortune of Leif and so many other Allied soldiers, news of the unconditional surrender of Japan was announced. The Second World War was over. Now, with the prospect of being assigned to fight the Japanese lifted from his shoulders, Leif was able to rest and actually relax for the remainder of his leave with the Henry family. Or so he thought.

On 20 August 1945, less than a week after the end of the Second World War, a cablegram addressed to, newly promoted, First Lieutenant Bangsbøll, United States Army was delivered, care of the Henry residence on King Street in Oshawa. Leif was ordered to report for duty to OSS headquarters in Washington DC immediately.

For Leif, and the piece of his soul that was Prince Hamlet, revenge and been wrought – Denmark had been liberated. To America and the Western Allies – they had prevailed – Captain Ahab was no more and the great white whale was free to roam the oceans as he pleased.

But now, a new sinister threat loomed just over the horizon… the great Soviet bear and the Cold War it would bring. Unknown to Leif at that moment, conditions in the Soviet Zone of occupied Germany were developing for which the United States Department of War and the OSS believed Lieutenant Leif Bangsboll was ideally suited. Agent Alexander Hudson, using his secret identity as Jørgen Bech was being resurrected again.

Epilogue

Here ends *An O.S.S. Secret Agent Behind Enemy Lines*, the first of two books chronicling the incredible life and remarkable military career of Leif Bangsbøll.

The second book, entitled *U.S. Special Forces Commando*, continues Leif's epic story of duty, honor, loyalty and clandestine adventures with his face to face encounter with KGB agents deep within Soviet occupied Berlin in autumn 1945.

Appendix

Introduction to *U.S. Special Forces Commando*

'Commando: a combatant, or operative of an elite light infantry or special operations force, specially trained for carrying out raids and operating in small teams behind enemy lines.'

Oxford Dictionary

Standing before the gates of the fortified city of London, Sweyn Haraldsson, known as Forkbeard, the reigning king of Denmark and Norway and now the leader of the Viking invasion of England, surveyed his army's final objective. Before the month's end, on Christmas Day AD 1013, King Sweyn 'Forkbeard' Haraldsson of Denmark and Norway would become the first Viking king of England.

Nine-hundred and thirty-two years later, on 5 May 1945, with the Battle of Ryvangen, over and won, Second Lieutenant Leif Bangsbøll, United States Army, alias Jørgen Bech, Danish Resistance operative, codenamed Alexander Hudson, and a descendant of King Forkbeard, stood on the field of the Battle at Ryvangen. There, on his beloved homeland of Denmark, Leif felt the eyes of his Viking ancestors gazing down upon him from Valhalla, and hoped they would be proud. A victorious warrior and liberator from the Nazi scourge, Leif had fulfilled his destiny – or so he thought.

Then, on 10 September 1945, four months after the Allies had declared victory in Europe and only four weeks after the fall of Japan and the end of the Second World War, recently promoted First Lieutenant Leif Bangsbøll, stood once again in front of the Brandenburg Gate. Berlin, now looked very, very different. His one previous visit to Berlin had been in April 1939. Leif was 20 years old then and a spectator and invited guest accompanying his father, Commodore Frederik Bangsbøll, as the Danish representatives for Adolf Hitler's grand fiftieth birthday celebrations. Now scared by five years of relentless American and British aerial bombardment and weeks of Russian tank shells and bullet, the massive Brandenburg Gate still stood in defiance, battered and looming ominously above him. Surrounded by massive piles of rubble, where once stood fashionable German homes and apartments and a multitude of government buildings, which had supported Hitler's Third Reich. Gone were the 50,000 German troops marching on parade with methodic rhythm in jackboots along the Tiergarten Straße. The parade route, once lined with hundreds of thousands of adoring German citizens and a modest delegation of foreign leaders and government representatives occupying the dignitary stands in Pariser Platz was now empty, save for those meager Berliners scavenging through the carnage for sustenance. Leif reflected upon his situation: 'The world is no longer recognizable.' Berlin, now an Allied war prize, despite its devastation, had been divided into four sectors: British, American, French and Russian. The capital city itself, situated deep within the Soviet Zone. Leif, once again in his covert disguise as Jørgen Bech is now a Danish engineer working for the International Red Cross. Post-war peace had been only a fleeting moment for Leif; he had been assigned another new dangerous mission: to infiltrate Soviet occupied Germany and spy on the Russians – work with the Soviet Zone of occupied Germany under the watchful eyes of the Soviet Army of occupation and its relentless KGB (secret police) and be the eyes and ears of the American government – as an OSS operative.

U.S. Special Forces Commando, continues the epic tale of *An O.S.S. Secret Agent Behind Enemy Lines*, following the incredible life and military career of Leif Bangsbøll, now as one of the first Cold War warriors to see action against his Soviet counterparts. Post-Second World War Russia, an emerging superpower and former ally, was a growing adversary of the West, suspicious of all outsiders, especially Westerners – including the International Red Cross workers. The Soviet military and KGB were everywhere – administering their authority over the defeated Germans and the Western sponsored Red Cross workers with an iron fist. The Soviets watched the West's humanitarian efforts to relieve the suffering of the defeated, subservient German people with disdain. The Soviets had no compassion or concern for the well-being of the German 'fascist' survivors of the war. 'They were all Hitlerites who had invaded Mother Russia and reaped death, destruction and deprivation upon its people for four long years.' However, the Soviets' views concerning the West's reconstruction plans were quite another story. The West's money and reconstruction efforts were welcomed, albeit reluctantly. Russia's economy was in tatters and they needed the influx of Western finances and engineering support to rebuild Russia's portion of new Germany: East Germany, which the Kremlin intended would become a key buffer between their Russian homeland and Allied-controlled western Europe.

Leif had slipped into Soviet occupied Germany with OSS supplied, falsified documents and credentials. Yes, the Soviets were suspicious to the point of paranoia, and in this case, the Soviets were justified in their suspicion…

Bibliography

Books
Fitzgerald, F. Scott, *The Great Gatsby*
Melville, Herman, *Moby Dick*
Nordhoff, Charles and Hall, James Norman, *Mutiny on the Bounty*
Shakespeare, William, *Hamlet*
Shakespeare, William, *Julius Caesar*
Shakespeare, William, *Macbeth*
Shakespeare, William, *Othello*, 1603
Bible, 'John 10:11'
Bible, 'Matthew 28:16–20'
Bible, 'Psalm CVII'
Handbook of Irregular Warfare
Queensbury Rules

Diaries and Journals
Shackleton, Edward

Newspapers
Anglo-Saxon Chronicle
Reality
The New York Times
The Times

Magazines
National Geographic

Mottos
492 Bombardment Group, United States Army
Danish Royal Life Guards
Unofficial motto of the Office of Strategic Services

Photographs
Bangsboll family collection
United States Army, United States

Poems
Henley, William Ernest, *Invictus*, 1888

Quotes
Aristotle
Binyon, Laurence, 1914
Bonaparte, Napoléon
Campbell, Joseph
Churchill, Sir Winston
Clausewitz, Carl von
Darwin, Charles
Devereux, Robert
Disraeli, Benjamin
Donovan, Colonel William
Fairbairn, Major William
McCain, Senator John
Nelson, Lord Horatio
Santayana, George
Seneca, Lucius
Shakespeare, William
Tolkien, J.R.R.
Tzu, Sun
Vegetius, Flavius
Wellington, Duke of

Radio
BBC News Archieves

Research
British Army, United Kingdom
British Army, United Kingdom
Canadian Army, Canada
Danish Embassy
Danish Archives
Danish Royal Military Museum, Denmark
National Geographic Society, United States
Norwegian Air Force, Norway
Norwegian Embassy
Royal Air Force, United Kingdom
Royal Canadian Air Force, Canada
Royal Canadian Military Institute, Toronto, Canada
Royal Canadian Mounted Police, Canada
Royal Canadian Navy, Canada
Royal Danish Army, Denmark
Royal Danish Naval Academy, Denmark
Royal Danish Navy, Denmark
Royal Navy, United Kingdom
Sølvgades School, Copenhagen, Denmark
University of Cambridge, Cambridge, United Kingdom
University of Oxford, Oxford, United Kingdom
United States Air Force, United States
United States Army, United States
United States Army Air Corps, United States
United States Government, United States
United States Navy, United States

Dear Reader,

We hope you have enjoyed this book, but why not share your views on social media? You can also follow our pages to see more about our other products: facebook.com/penandswordbooks or follow us on X @penswordbooks

You can also view our products at www.pen-and-sword.co.uk (UK and ROW) or www.penandswordbooks.com (North America).

To keep up to date with our latest releases and online catalogues, please sign up to our newsletter at: www.pen-and-sword.co.uk/newsletter

If you would like a printed catalogue with our latest books, then please email: enquiries@pen-and-sword.co.uk or telephone: 01226 734555 (UK and ROW) or email: uspen-and-sword@casematepublishers.com or telephone: (610) 853-9131 (North America).

We respect your privacy and we will only use personal information to send you information about our products.

Thank you!